Advanced Methods in Computer Graphics

Ramakrishnan Mukundan

Advanced Methods in Computer Graphics

With examples in OpenGL

Springer

R. Mukundan
Department of Computer Science and Software Engineering
University of Canterbury
Christchurch, New Zealand

ISBN 978-1-4471-6070-0 ISBN 978-1-4471-2340-8 (eBook)
DOI 10.1007/978-1-4471-2340-8
Springer London Dordrecht Heidelberg New York

British Library Cataloguing in Publication Data
A catalogue record for this book is available from the British Library

Printed on acid-free paper

Springer is part of Springer Science+Business Media (www.springer.com)

To my daughter
Lalitha

Preface

The field of Computer Graphics has evolved rapidly over the past decade following the development of a large collection of algorithms and techniques for various applications in modelling, animation, visualisation, real-time rendering and game engine design. Advances in graphics hardware capabilities and processor technology have continuously fuelled this growth. As a result, this field continues to have enormous potential for further research and development. Computer graphics has also been one of the popular subjects in the computer science and computer engineering disciplines for several years. It is a field where one could always find new and interesting ideas, elegant algorithms and robust implementations.

I have been teaching both introductory and advanced courses on computer graphics for the past 12 years, and have constantly observed the enthusiasm of students in learning as well as mastering various techniques used for three-dimensional modelling, rendering and animation. The visual effects some of these methods produce captivate their interest, and motivate them to further study and research more advanced techniques. This book evolved from a compilation of my lecture notes and reference material for a graduate course in advanced computer graphics taught in the Department of Computer Science and Software Engineering at the University of Canterbury. The primary aim of this book project has been to develop a reference text suitable for both students and researchers, providing an in-depth and comprehensive coverage of important methods that are useful in the field of character animation. Working towards this goal, I soon realised that a book covering a large number of subfields ranging from physically based simulation to non-photorealistic rendering would be a highly ambitious project. This book includes a selection of topics which I consider as fundamental to the area of animation and rendering, and I hope that it will contribute to a deeper and broader understanding of key algorithms used in advanced computer graphics.

I am very much indebted to the graduate students and staff in the Department of Computer Science and Software Engineering, University of Canterbury, for their support, valuable feedback, and encouragement. My sincere thanks go to Dr. Richard Lobb (Adjunct Senior Fellow, Department of Computer Science and Software Engineering, University of Canterbury) for devoting so much of his valuable time and expertise for reviewing the manuscript. I am thankful to Dr. Christian Long (Department of English, University of Canterbury), for copy-editing the manuscript. His thorough and meticulous checking of spelling, punctuation and grammar has helped improve the clarity of the material presented.

I would like to thank the editorial team members for their help throughout this book project. While the manuscript was being prepared, a series of unfortunate events, including the passing away of my mother, and two major earth quakes in Christchurch, brought the progress to a standstill for several months. Special thanks to Helen Desmond and Beverley Ford for their continuous encouragement. They showed a tremendous amount of patience, and always so kindly agreed to extend the manuscript submission deadline a number of times.

I am very grateful to my family for their endless support. I greatly appreciate their patience and understanding throughout the time when I was obsessed with writing this book.

Department of Computer Science
and Software Engineering
University of Canterbury
Christchurch, New Zealand

R. Mukundan

Contents

Chapter 1
Introduction

1.1 Advanced Computer Graphics

Computer graphics algorithms are being increasingly used in many scientific and technological areas, with an explosive growth in applications requiring three-dimensional rendering and animation. The expansion of computer graphics into diverse and interdisciplinary areas is the result of many factors such as the ever increasing power and capability of the graphics hardware, decreasing hardware costs, availability of a wide range of software tools, research advancements in the field, and significant improvements in graphics application programming interface (API). Additionally, vast amounts of resources including images, 3D models, and libraries are now easily available to developers and researchers for their work. With the emergence of programmable graphics hardware, the power of graphics APIs to render complex models and scenes has greatly increased, and it has become easier to create faster and robust implementations of several advanced algorithms. Following these developments, there is also an increasing need for reference books that give an in-depth coverage of advanced methods that are fundamental to many application domains.

Advanced computer graphics is a field that encompasses a vast range of topics and a large number of subfields such as game engine development, real-time rendering, global illumination methods and non-photorealistic rendering. Indeed, this field includes a large body of concepts and algorithms not generally covered in introductory graphics texts that deal primarily with basic transformations, projections, lighting, three-dimensional modelling techniques, texturing and rasterization algorithms.

This book aims to provide a comprehensive treatment of the theoretical concepts and associated methods related to four core areas: articulated character animation, curve and surface design, mesh processing, and collision detection. The area of character animation is further subdivided into scene graphs, skeletal animation, quaternion rotations and kinematics. A principal objective of this book is to serve as a reference text for both students and researchers. It is designed for courses that build

R. Mukundan, *Advanced Methods in Computer Graphics: With examples in OpenGL*,
DOI 10.1007/978-1-4471-2340-8_1, © Springer-Verlag London Limited 2012

upon introductory computer graphics concepts. The topics discussed in the book are commonly covered in graduate or advanced undergraduate graphics courses. These include the theoretical as well as the implementation aspects of several algorithms. To help students understand the concepts clearly, a set of demonstration programs is included with each chapter. Necessary class libraries giving the implementations of important methods of each class are also provided. Some of the concepts that have recently found a great deal of importance in research such as dual quaternion transformations, and bounding interval hierarchies are also presented.

1.2 Supplementary Material

Each chapter is accompanied by a collection of software modules and demonstration programs that show the details and working of key algorithms. All programs are written in C++. The reader is assumed to be familiar with the basic OpenGL library, which is a easy-to-program, widely accepted cross platform API for developing graphics applications. To keep the implementations simple, shader language functions or any other OpenGL extensions are not used. The source codes including relevant class definitions and input files can be downloaded from Springer's website, http://extras.springer.com/978-1-4471-2339-2.

The programs are written entirely by the author, with the primary aim of motivating students to explore further each technique, and to implement their own creative ideas. They are just tools which developers and researchers could use to build larger frameworks or to try better solutions. A simple programming approach is used so that students with minimal knowledge of C/C++ language and OpenGL will be able to start using the code and work towards more complex or useful applications. None of the software is optimized in terms of algorithm performance or speed. Similarly, object oriented programming concepts are not heavily used, leaving room for a lot of further development.

1.3 Notations

In order to have a clear distinction between points, vectors and other mathematical entities, the following notation is normally used in this book. Note that in exceptional cases, a different notation may be used in each of the following categories to avoid ambiguity. For example, a tangent vector to a curve may be denoted by $\boldsymbol{T}(t)$ instead of $\boldsymbol{t}(t)$.

Point: A point is generally denoted by an uppercase letter in italics as P. The three-dimensional coordinates of P will be written as (x_p, y_p, z_p). The vector representation of P having the same components as above will be denoted as $\boldsymbol{p}$. The coordinates of the point P_1 will be written as either (x_{p1}, y_{p1}, z_{p1}) or, if there is no ambiguity, as simply (x_1, y_1, z_1).

Vector: A vector will be denoted by a lowercase letter in italics and bold font as $\boldsymbol{v}$. Its vector components will be noted as (x_v, y_v, z_v).

Complex number: Complex numbers are treated as two-dimensional vectors and denoted using a lowercase letter in italics and bold font as $\boldsymbol{z}$.

Quaternions: Uppercase letters in italic font (such as Q) will be used to denote quaternions. Dual-quaternions will be denoted using uppercase letters in bold and italic font as $\boldsymbol{Q}$.

Line segment: A line segment will be noted using its end points as AB.

Triangle: A triangle will be denoted using its vertices as ABC and its area as ΔABC. A triangle may also be named using an uppercase letter in italics as T.

Plane: Uppercase Greek symbols such as Γ, Π, will be used for denoting planes and general polygonal surface elements.

Matrices: Matrices will be denoted using uppercase letters in bold font as $\mathbf{M}$.

1.4 Contents Overview

This section gives an outline of subsequent chapters of the book. Chapter 2 should be treated as revision material on analytical properties of geometrical primitives and may be skipped if you have a good mathematical background. Chapters 3, 4, 5, 6 are closely related to the area of character animation. Chapters 7, 8, 9 deal with mutually independent topics, and can be read separately in any order.

Chapter 2 – Mathematical Preliminaries: This chapter outlines important mathematical concepts related to points, vectors, transformations, lines and planes that are fundamental to several methods in computer graphics. Subsequent chapters in the book make use of the results presented here.

Chapter 3 – Scene Graphs: This chapter introduces scene graphs and gives examples to show their importance in representing transformation hierarchies in articulated models. A sample implementation of the basic scene graph structure is provided.

Chapter 4 – Skeletal Animation: This chapter discusses the animation of two different types of articulated character models. The processes of vertex blending, vertex skinning and keyframing are introduced. The chapter also gives a sample implementation of a skeleton animation module.

Chapter 5 – Quaternions: Quaternions are extensively used in animations to represent three-dimensional rotations. This chapter gives a comprehensive coverage of quaternion algebra, transformations and quaternion based methods for rotation interpolation. A recently introduced concept of dual quaternions is also presented.

Chapter 6 – Kinematics: This chapter presents forward and inverse kinematics solutions for animating a joint chain. Iterative algorithms suitable for graphics applications are also presented.

Chapter 7 – Curves and Surfaces: This chapter gives an in-depth treatment of parametric curves, splines and polynomial interpolants. Fundamental techniques in curve and surface design using Hermite splines, cardinal splines and B-splines are presented in detail.

Chapter 8 – Mesh Processing: This chapter discusses mesh data structures and algorithms. Important edge-based data structures useful for processing adjacency queries are introduced. Algorithms for mesh simplification, subdivision and parameterization are presented. The chapter also outlines methods for polygon triangulation, which is generally a key component of mesh processing algorithms.

Chapter 9 – Collision Detection: This chapter details commonly used bounding volume representations of objects in collision detection algorithms, and presents the computation of bounding volume overlap tests. Bounding volume hierarchies and spatial partitioning trees are also discussed in detail.

Chapter 2
Mathematical Preliminaries

Overview

Mathematical operations on points, vectors and matrices are needed for processing information related to geometrical objects. Even in the modelling of a simple three-dimensional scene, vectors and matrices play an important role in specifying an object's position, orientation and transformations. Methods for lighting, intersection testing, projections, etc., use a series of vector operations. This chapter gives an overview of computations using geometrical primitives and shapes that form the basis for several algorithms presented in subsequent chapters of the book.

Parametric representations are often used in methods involving geometrical primitives. This chapter deals with analytical equations of lines, planes and curves, and their applications in geometrical computations. Properties of three-dimensional transformations are discussed using their matrix representations. The chapter also introduces concepts such as signed area and distance, affine combinations of points and barycentric coordinates.

2.1 Points and Vectors

A point is the most fundamental graphics primitive, and is represented in a three-dimensional Cartesian coordinate system by the 3-tuple (x, y, z), where x, y, z denote the distances of the point from the origin of the system along the respective axes directions. In graphics, we commonly use an extended coordinate system, where the same point is denoted by the 4-tuple $(x, y, z, 1)$. This representation is called the homogeneous coordinate system. Homogeneous coordinates provide a unified and elegant framework for representing different types of transformations and projections that are commonly applied to both points and vectors (Box 2.1).

R. Mukundan, *Advanced Methods in Computer Graphics: With examples in OpenGL*,
DOI 10.1007/978-1-4471-2340-8_2, © Springer-Verlag London Limited 2012

Box 2.1 Homogeneous Coordinate System

A 3D point given by homogeneous coordinates (a, b, c, d) where d is non-zero, has an equivalent representation in Cartesian coordinates given by $(a/d, b/d, c/d)$.

The 4-tuple $(a, b, c, 0)$ denotes a point at infinity that has associated with it a directional vector (a, b, c).

The many-one mapping from homogeneous to Cartesian space is shown below:

$(hx, hy, hz, h) \Rightarrow$ 3D Point (x, y, z) for all non-zero values of h.
$(x, y, z, w) \Rightarrow$ 3D Point $(x/w, y/w, z/w)$ if $w \neq 0$.
$(x, y, z, 0) \Rightarrow$ 3D Vector (x, y, z).

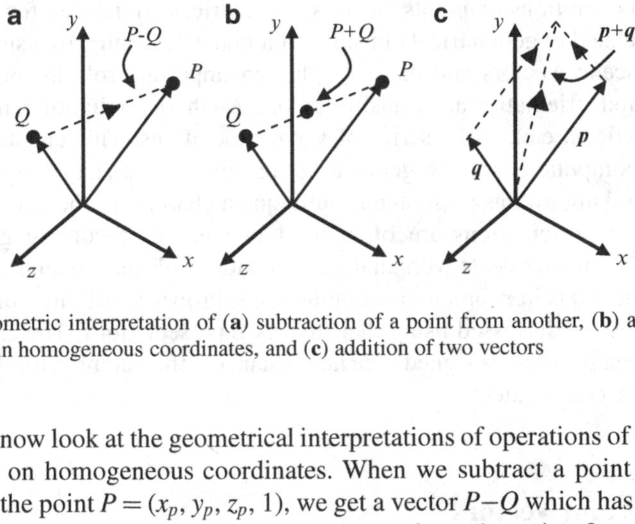

Fig. 2.1 Geometric interpretation of (**a**) subtraction of a point from another, (**b**) addition of two points given in homogeneous coordinates, and (**c**) addition of two vectors

We will now look at the geometrical interpretations of operations of addition and subtraction on homogeneous coordinates. When we subtract a point $Q = (x_q, y_q, z_q, 1)$ from the point $P = (x_p, y_p, z_p, 1)$, we get a vector $P - Q$ which has components $(x_p - x_q, y_p - y_q, z_p - z_q, 0)$. This vector originates from the point Q and is directed towards the point P, and is denoted as $\overrightarrow{QP}$. The direct addition of two points P and Q is not a geometrically valid operation, as it can produce different results depending on the coordinate reference frame used. If we use the homogeneous coordinate representation of P and Q as given above, the operation of addition yields $(x_p + x_q, y_p + y_q, z_p + z_q, 2)$, which is actually the midpoint of the line segment PQ (Fig. 2.1b). Points can, however, be added in a special way called the affine combination (see Sect. 2.7) that gives a well-defined point. The addition of two vectors $\boldsymbol{p} = (x_p, y_p, z_p, 0)$ and $\boldsymbol{q} = (x_q, y_q, z_q, 0)$ is always a valid operation that produces another vector $\boldsymbol{p} + \boldsymbol{q} = (x_p + x_q, y_p + y_q, z_p + z_q, 0)$. This vector is along the diagonal of the parallelogram formed by $\boldsymbol{p}$ and $\boldsymbol{q}$.

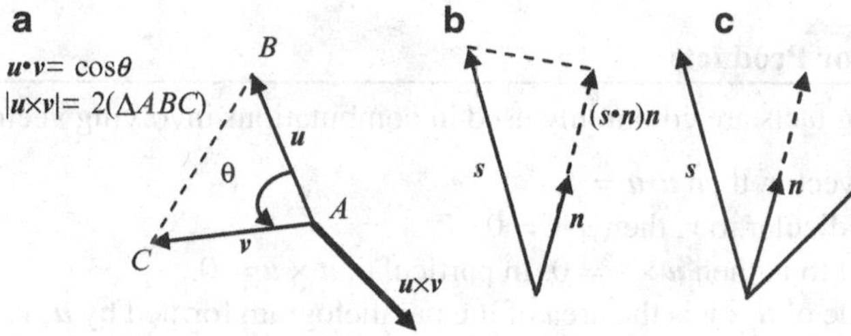

Fig. 2.2 (a) Dot-product and cross-product of two vectors *u*,*v*. (b) Projection of a vector *s* on a unit vector *u*. (c) Reflection of a vector *s* with respect to a unit vector *n*

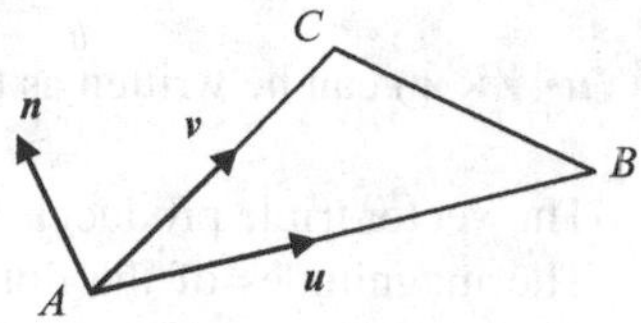

Fig. 2.3 The normal vector and area of a triangle specified using vertex coordinates can be computed with the help of two vectors defined along the edges

Like addition, the operations of negation and scalar multiplication should also be carefully performed on points represented in homogeneous coordinates. It can be seen that the operation of negation given by $-P = (-x_p, -y_p, -z_p, -1)$ in effect yields the same point P. In general, the operation of scalar multiplication defined as $sP = (sx_p, sy_p, sz_p, s)$ for any non-zero value of s, gives the same point P.

We will often require the computation of angles between two vectors. This and other operations, such as projection, require vectors to be normalized first. The normalization of a vector is the process of converting it to a unit vector that has a magnitude 1. In order to normalize a vector $\boldsymbol{p} = (x_p, y_p, z_p, 0)$, we simply divide each element by the vector magnitude d given by

$$d = |\boldsymbol{p}| = \sqrt{x_p^2 + y_p^2 + z_p^2} \tag{2.1}$$

If $\boldsymbol{v}$ is a two-dimensional vector (x_v, y_v), then the vector $\boldsymbol{v}^{\perp} = (-y_v, x_v)$ is perpendicular to and on the left side of $\boldsymbol{v}$. The vector $\boldsymbol{v}^{\perp}$ is sometimes called the perp-vector. It may be noted that $\boldsymbol{v}^{\perp\perp} = (-x_v, -y_v) = -\boldsymbol{v}$.

Two important vector operations used in graphics are the dot-product and the cross-product. Given two unit vectors $\boldsymbol{u} = (x_u, y_u, z_u, 0)$ and $\boldsymbol{v} = (x_v, y_v, z_v, 0)$, their dot-product $\boldsymbol{u} \bullet \boldsymbol{v} = x_u x_v + y_u y_v + z_u z_v$ is equal to the cosine of the angle between the vectors. The cross-product $\boldsymbol{u} \times \boldsymbol{v} = (y_u z_v - y_v z_u,\ z_u x_v - z_v x_u,\ x_u y_v - x_v y_u,\ 0)$ is a vector perpendicular to both $\boldsymbol{u}$ and $\boldsymbol{v}$, so that $\boldsymbol{u}$, $\boldsymbol{v}$, $\boldsymbol{u} \times \boldsymbol{v}$ form a right-handed system (Fig. 2.2). Obviously, this operation is useful for computing the surface normal vector of a planar element defined by two vectors $\boldsymbol{u}$ and $\boldsymbol{v}$. The magnitude of $\boldsymbol{u} \times \boldsymbol{v}$ (denoted by $|\boldsymbol{u} \times \boldsymbol{v}|$) gives twice the area of the triangle formed by the two vectors (Figs. 2.2a and 2.3). For unit vectors, $|\boldsymbol{u} \times \boldsymbol{v}|$ is also equal to the sine of the angle between the two vectors (Box 2.2).

Box 2.2 Vector Products

The following facts are commonly used in computations involving vectors:

If $\boldsymbol{u}$ is a unit vector, then $\boldsymbol{u} \bullet \boldsymbol{u} = 1$.
If $\boldsymbol{u}$ is perpendicular to $\boldsymbol{v}$, then $\boldsymbol{u} \bullet \boldsymbol{v} = 0$.
If $\boldsymbol{u}$ is parallel to $\boldsymbol{v}$, then $\boldsymbol{u} \times \boldsymbol{v} = 0$. In particular, $\boldsymbol{u} \times \boldsymbol{u} = 0$.
The magnitude of $\boldsymbol{u} \times \boldsymbol{v}$ is the area of the parallelogram formed by $\boldsymbol{u}$, $\boldsymbol{v}$.
The scalar triple product $\boldsymbol{u} \bullet (\boldsymbol{v} \times \boldsymbol{w})$ gives the volume of the parallelepiped formed by the vectors $\boldsymbol{u}$,$\boldsymbol{v}$ and $\boldsymbol{w}$. The value does not change with a cyclic permutation of the vectors: $\boldsymbol{u} \bullet (\boldsymbol{v} \times \boldsymbol{w}) = \boldsymbol{v} \bullet (\boldsymbol{w} \times \boldsymbol{u}) = \boldsymbol{w} \bullet (\boldsymbol{u} \times \boldsymbol{v})$.

$\boldsymbol{u} \bullet (\boldsymbol{v} \times \boldsymbol{w})$ can be written as the determinant $\begin{vmatrix} x_u & y_u & z_u \\ x_v & y_v & z_v \\ x_w & y_w & z_w \end{vmatrix}$

The vector triple product $\boldsymbol{u} \times (\boldsymbol{v} \times \boldsymbol{w})$ is the same as $(\boldsymbol{u} \bullet \boldsymbol{w})\boldsymbol{v} - (\boldsymbol{u} \bullet \boldsymbol{v})\boldsymbol{w}$.
The magnitudes of the dot and cross products of two vectors $\boldsymbol{u}$ and $\boldsymbol{v}$ are related by the equation: $|\boldsymbol{u} \times \boldsymbol{v}|^2 = |\boldsymbol{u}|^2 |\boldsymbol{v}|^2 - (\boldsymbol{u} \bullet \boldsymbol{v})^2$.

We saw in the previous paragraph that both the dot and the cross products of two unit vectors can give us the information about the angle between them in the form of trigonometric functions `cos()` and `sin()` respectively. Note that the function `acos`($\boldsymbol{u} \bullet \boldsymbol{v}$) returns the angle in the range $[0, \pi]$ only. Neither can we use `asin`($|\boldsymbol{u} \times \boldsymbol{v}|$) to determine the angle correctly because the resulting value will always be in the restricted range $[0, \pi/2]$ (even though `asin()` returns a value in the range $[-\pi/2, \pi/2]$, since $|\boldsymbol{u} \times \boldsymbol{v}|$ is always positive, so would be the result). We will explore ways to compute the true angle in the range $[-\pi, \pi]$ in Sect. 2.2.

If we represent the vertices of a triangle by points $A = (x_a, y_a, z_a)$, $B = (x_b, y_b, z_b)$, $C = (x_c, y_c, z_c)$, the surface normal vector and the area of the triangle can be obtained from the cross product of two vectors $\boldsymbol{u}$, $\boldsymbol{v}$ constructed as shown in Fig. 2.3.

The normal vector $\boldsymbol{n}$ of the triangle in Fig. 2.3 has components (x_n, y_n, z_n) given by

$$\begin{aligned} x_n &= y_a(z_b - z_c) + y_b(z_c - z_a) + y_c(z_a - z_b) \\ y_n &= z_a(x_b - x_c) + z_b(x_c - x_a) + z_c(x_a - x_b) \\ z_n &= x_a(y_b - y_c) + x_b(y_c - y_a) + x_c(y_a - y_b) \end{aligned} \tag{2.2}$$

The above vector is the same as $\boldsymbol{u} \times \boldsymbol{v}$. The area of the triangle ABC can be computed from the above components of the normal vector as follows:

$$\Delta ABC = \frac{1}{2}\sqrt{x_n^2 + y_n^2 + z_n^2} = \frac{1}{2}|\boldsymbol{u} \times \boldsymbol{v}| \tag{2.3}$$

Let us turn our attention to another important vector operation called projection. A vector s can be projected onto a unit vector n, with the projected vector given by $(s \bullet n)n$ (see Fig. 2.2b). This also implies that the length of the projection of s on a unit vector n is $s \bullet n$. We can use this fact to express any vector s in terms of its projections along three mutually orthogonal unit vectors u, v, and w as

$$s = (s \bullet u)u + (s \bullet v)v + (s \bullet w)w \tag{2.4}$$

If s is also a unit vector, then the terms $s \bullet u$, $s \bullet v$, $s \bullet w$ are called the direction cosines of the vector in the coordinate space spanned by the unit vectors u, v, and w. In a new coordinate space defined by u, v, and w, the components of any vector s are therefore given by ($s \bullet u$, $s \bullet v$, $s \bullet w$).

The reflection of the vector s with respect to a unit vector n is the vector r that lies on the plane containing s and n as shown in Fig. 2.2c, such that the angle between r and n is the same as the angle between s and n. The reflection vector is commonly used in lighting calculations and ray tracing, where s stands for the vector towards a light source, and n is the surface normal vector. The vector components of r can be computed using the formula

$$r = 2(s \bullet n)n - s \tag{2.5}$$

2.2 Signed Angle and Area

In the previous section, we noted that the computation of the angle between two vectors using `acos()` or `asin()` functions always yielded only positive values in the range [0, π]. One may suggest using the function `atan2`($|u \times v|$, $u \bullet v$). This form of computation of angle has the advantage that neither u nor v needs to be normalized. However, this function also returns values in the positive range [0, π] only, because the numerator $|u \times v|$ is always positive. The difference between the positive and negative sense of angle is completely view dependent. For vectors residing on the two-dimensional xy-plane, the direction to the viewer is always implied to be the $+z$ direction. In a general three-dimensional case, we need to specify this view direction in order to determine the signed angle in the range $[-\pi, \pi]$ between two given vectors.

If we denote the view direction by w (Fig. 2.4), the angle measured from u to v is positive if the sense of rotation from u to v is anticlockwise when viewed from w. In other words, if w is in the same direction as $u \times v$, then the angle is positive, otherwise negative. We can now define the signed angle between u and v with respect to the view vector w as

$$\theta = \text{sign}((u \times v) \bullet w).\cos^{-1}\left(\frac{u \bullet v}{|u||v|}\right) \tag{2.6}$$

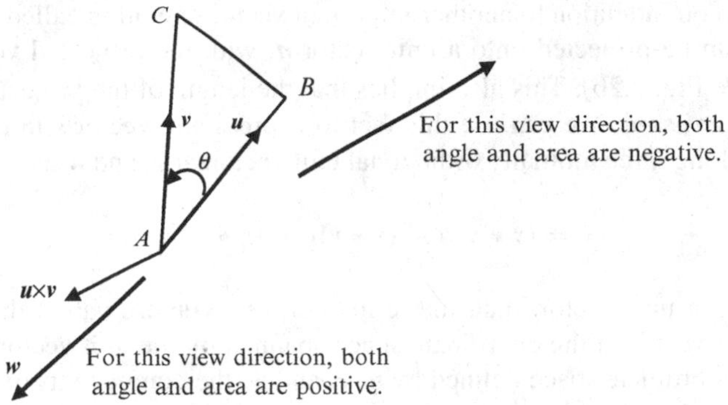

Fig. 2.4 The angle between two vectors and the area of the triangle formed by the vectors can have either a positive or a negative sign depending on the orientation of the vertices with respect to a given direction

If $\boldsymbol{u}$ and $\boldsymbol{v}$ are two-dimensional vectors on the xy-plane, we can have the following simplified form for the signed angle:

$$\theta = \texttt{atan2}(x_u y_v - x_v y_u, x_u y_u + x_v y_v) \tag{2.7}$$

We can also define a view-dependent sign for the area of a triangle based on the above concept. If the view vector $\boldsymbol{w}$ has components $(x_w, y_w, z_w, 0)$, Eq. 2.3 now gets modified as follows:

$$\begin{aligned}\Delta ABC &= \{\text{sign}(x_n x_w + y_n y_w + z_n z_w)\}\left(\frac{1}{2}\sqrt{x_n^2 + y_n^2 + z_n^2}\right)\\ &= \text{sign}(\boldsymbol{n} \bullet \boldsymbol{w})\left(\frac{1}{2}\,|\boldsymbol{u} \times \boldsymbol{v}|\right)\end{aligned} \tag{2.8}$$

where x_n, y_n, z_n are computed from the vertex coordinates using Eq. 2.2.

For a triangle on the xy-plane, the right-hand side of the above equation reduces to $z_n/2$. Thus the signed area of a triangle with vertices $A = (x_a, y_a)$, $B = (x_b, y_b)$, $C = (x_c, y_c)$ is

$$\Delta ABC = \frac{1}{2}\left(x_a\left(y_b - y_c\right) + x_b\left(y_c - y_a\right) + x_c\left(y_a - y_b\right)\right) \tag{2.9}$$

The signed area is positive only if the vertices A, B, C are oriented in an anticlockwise sense with respect to the view direction. The signed area of a triangle is useful in determining if a point is inside the triangle or not. This method is discussed in detail in Sect. 2.8. The concepts presented above are also used for defining the orientation of three points. Three points A, B, C are said to be oriented in the anticlockwise sense with respect a direction $\boldsymbol{w}$ if

$$((B - A) \times (C - A)) \bullet \boldsymbol{w} > 0. \tag{2.10}$$

If the above condition is satisfied, the three points are said to make a left turn when viewed from the direction $\boldsymbol{w}$. With reference to Fig. 2.4, the equivalent condition in vector notation is $(\boldsymbol{u} \times \boldsymbol{v}) \bullet \boldsymbol{w} > 0$. On the xy-plane, the three points make a left turn if

$$x_a(y_b - y_c) + x_b(y_c - y_a) + x_c(y_a - y_b) > 0. \tag{2.11}$$

The reversal of the inequality implies a right turn. The points are collinear if the above expression yields 0. In the next section we will use vector notations and related operations to get concise forms of line and plane equations.

2.3 Lines and Planes

Lines and planes form integral parts of three-dimensional models and virtual worlds. A good understanding of line and plane equations and their analytical properties is essential for the development of many applications. For example, even a simple ray tracing application requires the computation of several line-plane intersections.

A straight line segment can be defined using two points, say $P = (x_p, y_p, z_p, 1)$ and $Q = (x_q, y_q, z_q, 1)$. The equation of this line in terms of a single parameter t can be expressed as

$$x = x_p + t(x_q - x_p);\ y = y_p + t(y_q - y_p);\ z = z_p + t(z_q - z_p) \tag{2.12}$$

For any value of t between 0 and 1, the above set of equations gives the coordinates of a point on the straight line that lies between P and Q. We can also write the equation of this line segment using vector notation as follows:

$$\boldsymbol{r} = \boldsymbol{p} + t\boldsymbol{m}, \quad 0 \le t \le 1. \tag{2.13}$$

where $\boldsymbol{r} = (x, y, z, 1)$, $\boldsymbol{p} = (x_p, y_p, z_p, 1)$ and $\boldsymbol{m} = Q-P$. The above equation can also be used to represent a ray starting from the point $\boldsymbol{p}$ and having a direction given by the vector $\boldsymbol{m}$. In this representation, $\boldsymbol{m}$ is generally a unit vector and t can have any positive value. The line given in Eq. 2.12 can be rewritten in the standard form by eliminating t:

$$\frac{x - x_p}{x_q - x_p} = \frac{y - y_p}{y_q - y_p} = \frac{z - z_p}{z_q - z_p} \tag{2.14}$$

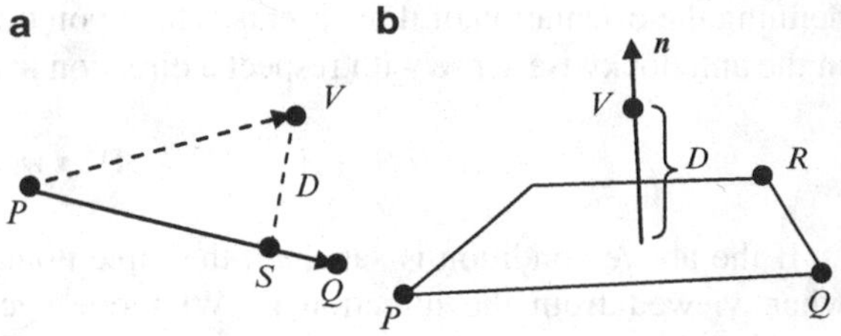

Fig. 2.5 Computation of shortest distances of a point V from (**a**) a line PQ and (**b**) a plane PQR

From the above equation, we immediately get the condition for the collinearity of three points $P = (x_p, y_p, z_p, 1)$, $Q = (x_q, y_q, z_q, 1)$ and $R = (x_r, y_r, z_r, 1)$:

$$\frac{x_r - x_p}{x_q - x_p} = \frac{y_r - y_p}{y_q - y_p} = \frac{z_r - z_p}{z_q - z_p} \tag{2.15}$$

Using Eq. 2.12, we can determine the point S on the line PQ that lies closest to a general three-dimensional point $V = (x_v, y_v, z_v, 1)$. The shortest distance of the point V from the line is given by VS (Fig. 2.5), where S is the projection of the point V on PQ. The point S satisfies the condition that the line segments PQ and VS are orthogonal to each other. Using this condition, the parametric value t of the point S can be obtained as follows:

$$t = \frac{(x_v - x_p)(x_q - x_p) + (y_v - y_p)(y_q - y_p) + (z_v - z_p)(z_q - z_p)}{(x_q - x_p)^2 + (y_q - y_p)^2 + (z_q - z_p)^2} \tag{2.16}$$

Substitution of the above value in Eq. 2.12 gives the coordinates of the point S. The shortest (or the perpendicular) distance D of the point V from the line PS is obtained as the distance $|V{-}S|$.

A plane in three-dimensional space is uniquely defined by three non-collinear points, or equivalently, by a point P that lies on the plane and its surface normal vector $\boldsymbol{n}$. The equation of the plane in terms of the coordinates of the three points $P = (x_p, y_p, z_p, 1)$, $Q = (x_q, y_q, z_q, 1)$, $R = (x_r, y_r, z_r, 1)$, is given by the determinant

$$\begin{vmatrix} x & y & z & 1 \\ x_p & y_p & z_p & 1 \\ x_q & y_q & z_q & 1 \\ x_r & y_r & z_r & 1 \end{vmatrix} = 0. \tag{2.17}$$

From this equation of the plane, we get the condition for the coplanarity of four points P, Q, R, S:

$$\begin{vmatrix} x_p & y_p & z_p & 1 \\ x_q & y_q & z_q & 1 \\ x_r & y_r & z_r & 1 \\ x_s & y_s & z_s & 1 \end{vmatrix} = 0. \tag{2.18}$$

The determinant is equivalent to $(P-Q)\bullet(\boldsymbol{r}\times\boldsymbol{s})+(R-S)\bullet(\boldsymbol{p}\times\boldsymbol{q})$. The condition in Eq. 2.18 also points to the fact that the vectors $(Q-P)$ and $(R-S)$ are coplanar. Thus we can rewrite the above equation using the following scalar triple product:

$$(R-P)\bullet\{(Q-P)\times(S-R)\}=0. \tag{2.19}$$

The surface normal vector $\boldsymbol{n}$ for the above plane can be obtained (similar to Eq. 2.2), by taking the cross-product of vectors $Q-P$ and $R-P$. The components of $\boldsymbol{n}$ written as a column vector are given below:

$$\begin{bmatrix} x_n \\ y_n \\ z_n \\ 0 \end{bmatrix} = \begin{bmatrix} (y_q-y_p)(z_r-z_p)-(y_r-y_p)(z_q-z_p) \\ (z_q-z_p)(x_r-x_p)-(z_r-z_p)(x_q-x_p) \\ (x_q-x_p)(y_r-y_p)-(x_r-x_p)(y_q-y_p) \\ 0 \end{bmatrix} \tag{2.20}$$

The plane equation can be written in point-normal form as

$$(x-x_p)x_n+(y-y_p)y_n+(z-z_p)z_n=0 \tag{2.21}$$

which can always be simplified into a linear equation $ax+by+cz+d=0$, or expressed using vector notation as

$$(\boldsymbol{r}-\boldsymbol{p})\bullet\boldsymbol{n}=0, \quad \text{or equivalently,} \ \boldsymbol{r}\bullet\boldsymbol{n}=-d, \tag{2.22}$$

where $d=-\boldsymbol{p}\bullet\boldsymbol{n}$. The point of intersection of this plane and a ray can be obtained by substituting the equation of the ray, $\boldsymbol{r}=\boldsymbol{q}+t\,\boldsymbol{m}$, in the above equation and solving for t.

$$t=\frac{-(\boldsymbol{q}\bullet\boldsymbol{n})-d}{\boldsymbol{m}\bullet\boldsymbol{n}} \tag{2.23}$$

The denominator in the above equation becomes zero when the line is orthogonal to $\boldsymbol{n}$, i.e., parallel to the plane. The shortest distance D of the point $\boldsymbol{v}$ from the plane (see Fig. 2.5b) is given by the equation

$$D=\frac{(x_v-x_p)x_n+(y_v-y_p)y_n+(z_v-z_p)z_n}{\sqrt{x_n^2+y_n^2+z_n^2}}=\frac{(\boldsymbol{v}\cdot\boldsymbol{n})+d}{|\boldsymbol{n}|} \tag{2.24}$$

The above term is also called the signed distance of the point $\boldsymbol{v}$ from the plane, as it assumes a positive value if $\boldsymbol{v}$ is on the same side as $\boldsymbol{n}$, and a negative value otherwise. In general, if the plane's equation is given in the normal form $ax+by+cz+d=0$, where $a^2+b^2+c^2=1$, the signed distance of the point $\boldsymbol{v}=(x_v, y_v, z_v)$ is given by

$$D=ax_v+by_v+cz_v+d \tag{2.25}$$

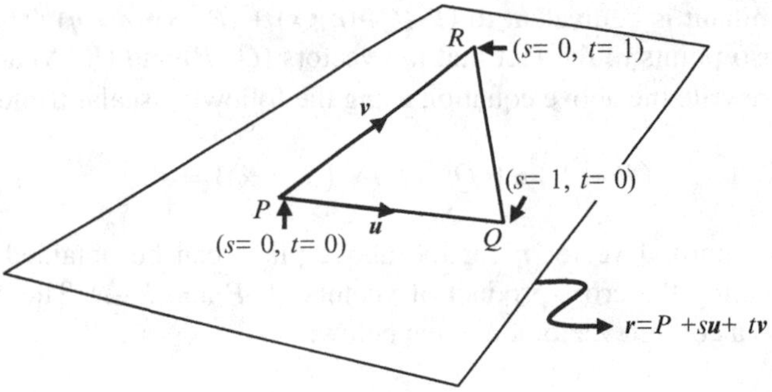

Fig. 2.6 Two-parameter representation of a plane

The above expression can be thought of as the dot product between the vector (a, b, c, d) and $(x_v, y_v, z_v, 1)$, which is the homogeneous representation of $\boldsymbol{v}$. Note that the unit normal vector to the plane is given by (a, b, c). Signed distances are extensively used in collision detection and point inclusion tests using bounding volumes.

Given three non-collinear points P, Q, R, we can have a parametric representation of the plane through the points as

$$\boldsymbol{r} = P + s(Q - P) + t(R - P) = P + s\,\boldsymbol{u} + t\boldsymbol{v} \tag{2.26}$$

where $\boldsymbol{u}$ and $\boldsymbol{v}$ are vectors along two sides of the triangle PQR (Fig. 2.6). An alternate form for the above equation that expresses any point on the plane as a linear combination of the vertices of the triangle is

$$\boldsymbol{r} = P(1 - s - t) + s\ Q + tR \tag{2.27}$$

For every point $\boldsymbol{r}(s, t)$ inside the triangle, the following properties hold:

$$0 \le s \le 1, \quad 0 \le t \le 1, \quad 0 \le s + t \le 1. \tag{2.28}$$

In addition to the above conditions, points along the edge PQ satisfy the parametric equation $t = 0$. Similarly, the edge PR is characterized by the equation $s = 0$, and RQ by the property $s + t = 1$.

2.4 Intersection of 3 Planes

An interesting problem commonly encountered while working with planes is the computation of the point of intersection (if it exists) where three planes meet. Even if it is guaranteed that no two planes are parallel, there can be three different configurations in which three planes can meet (Fig. 2.7).

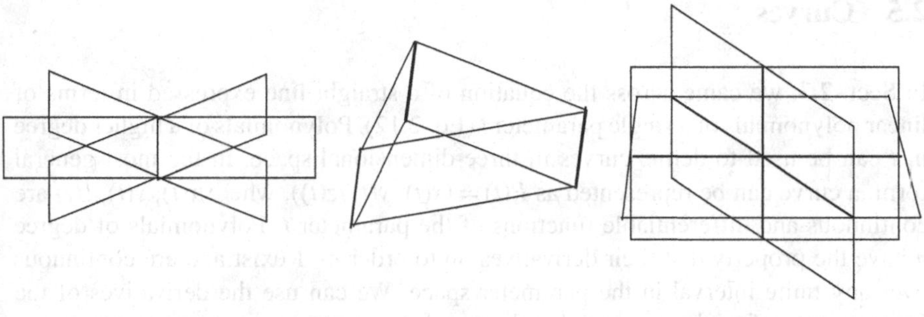

Fig. 2.7 Three different configurations in which three non-parallel planes can meet

In the first configuration in Fig. 2.7, the lines of intersection formed by taking two planes at a time coincide with the result that we get a single line of intersection. In the second configuration, the lines of intersections are parallel even though the planes are not. It can be easily proven that if two lines of intersection are parallel, then the third is also parallel to the other two. This situation arises when the three surface normal vectors of the planes are all coplanar. In the third configuration, the non-parallel lines of intersection meet at a single point.

Let the three planes be given by the equations (see Eq. 2.22) $\boldsymbol{r}\bullet\boldsymbol{n}_i = -d_i$, $(i = 1, 2, 3)$ where $\boldsymbol{n}_i$s are unit normal vectors. The directions of the three lines of intersection are then specified by the cross products $\boldsymbol{n}_1 \times \boldsymbol{n}_2$, $\boldsymbol{n}_2 \times \boldsymbol{n}_3$, and $\boldsymbol{n}_3 \times \boldsymbol{n}_1$. The point of intersection, if it exists, can be expressed as a linear combination of these three vectors (Goldman 1990):

$$\boldsymbol{p} = a(\boldsymbol{n}_1 \times \boldsymbol{n}_2) + b(\boldsymbol{n}_2 \times \boldsymbol{n}_3) + c(\boldsymbol{n}_3 \times \boldsymbol{n}_1) \tag{2.29}$$

The above point lies on all three planes. Substitution in the plane equations gives

$$\begin{aligned} b\{\boldsymbol{n}_1 \bullet (\boldsymbol{n}_2 \times \boldsymbol{n}_3)\} &= -d_1 \\ c\{\boldsymbol{n}_2 \bullet (\boldsymbol{n}_3 \times \boldsymbol{n}_1)\} &= -d_2 \\ a\{\boldsymbol{n}_3 \bullet (\boldsymbol{n}_1 \times \boldsymbol{n}_2)\} &= -d_3 \end{aligned} \tag{2.30}$$

The scalar triple products on the left side of the above equations are all equal (see Box 2.2). Equation 2.29 can now be written as

$$\boldsymbol{p} = \frac{-d_1(\boldsymbol{n}_1 \times \boldsymbol{n}_2) - d_2(\boldsymbol{n}_2 \times \boldsymbol{n}_3) - d_3(\boldsymbol{n}_3 \times \boldsymbol{n}_1)}{\boldsymbol{n}_1 \bullet (\boldsymbol{n}_2 \times \boldsymbol{n}_3)} \tag{2.31}$$

For the first two configurations shown in Fig. 2.7, the vectors $\boldsymbol{n}_1$, $\boldsymbol{n}_2$, $\boldsymbol{n}_3$ are coplanar, and the denominator of the above equation becomes zero. For the third configuration, the equation returns a valid point.

2.5 Curves

In Sect. 2.3, we came across the equation of a straight line expressed in terms of linear polynomials of a single parameter t (Eq. 2.12). Polynomials of a higher degree in t can be used to define curves in three-dimensional space. In the most general form, a curve can be represented as $P(t) = (x(t), y(t), z(t))$, where $x(t)$, $y(t)$, $z(t)$ are continuous and differentiable functions of the parameter t. Polynomials of degree n have the property that their derivatives up to order $n-1$ exist and are continuous over any finite interval in the parameter space. We can use the derivatives of the functions to define the tangential and normal directions to the curve at any point, and also to construct an orthonormal basis at any point on the curve.

The tangent vector at $P(t)$ is given by the first derivative with respect to t, i.e., $P'(t) = (x'(t), y'(t), z'(t))$. The unit tangent vector is denoted as

$$\boldsymbol{T}(t) = \frac{P'(t)}{|P'(t)|} \tag{2.32}$$

The tangent vector represents the local orientation of the curve at a point. If the parameter t denotes time, then $P'(t)$ represents the instantaneous velocity of the moving point $P(t)$. The distance travelled from a starting point $A = P(t_0)$ to the current point, or in other words the arc length measured from A, is given by

$$s(t) = \int_{t_0}^{t} |P'(u)|\, du = \int_{t_0}^{t} \sqrt{(x'(u))^2 + (y'(u))^2 + (z'(u))^2}\, du \tag{2.33}$$

Using the above equation we can express t as a function of arc length s, and re-parameterize the curve as $P(s) = (x(s), y(s), z(s))$. The chain rule for differentiation gives

$$P'(t) = P'(s)s'(t) = P'(s)|P'(t)| \tag{2.34}$$

from which we find that $P'(s)$ is equivalent to the unit tangent vector $\boldsymbol{T}(t)$. For convenience, we denote $P'(s)$ by $\boldsymbol{T}(s)$. Since $\boldsymbol{T}(s)\bullet\boldsymbol{T}(s) = 1$, it immediately follows that $\boldsymbol{T}(s)\bullet\boldsymbol{T}'(s) = 0$. Thus the instantaneous rate of change of the tangent direction is parallel to the normal vector at that point. If the unit normal direction at $P(s)$ is denoted as $\boldsymbol{N}(s)$, we have

$$\boldsymbol{T}'(s) = \frac{d\,(\boldsymbol{T}(s))}{ds} = \kappa(s)\boldsymbol{N}(s) \tag{2.35}$$

The proportionality factor $\kappa(s)$ is called the curvature of the curve at $P(s)$. The curvature is a measure of the deviation of the curve from a straight line. For a straight line, $\kappa(s) = 0$ at all points. The magnitude of the curvature is easily obtained as $|\kappa(s)| = |\boldsymbol{T}'(s)|$, and the unit normal direction at $P(s)$ is given by

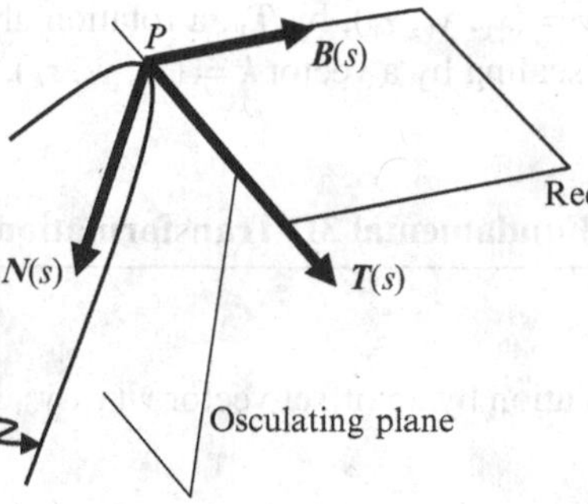

Fig. 2.8 Frenet frame attached to a curve at the point P

$$N(s) = \frac{P''(s)}{|P''(s)|} = \frac{P'(t) \times (P''(t) \times P'(t))}{|P'(t)|\,|P''(t) \times P'(t)|} \tag{2.36}$$

The plane containing the tangent vector and the normal vector is known as the osculating plane. The cross-product of the two unit vectors $\boldsymbol{T}(s)$ and $\boldsymbol{N}(s)$ gives the direction of the unit bi-normal vector denoted by $\boldsymbol{B}(s)$:

$$\boldsymbol{B}(s) = \boldsymbol{T}(s) \times \boldsymbol{N}(s) = \frac{P'(s) \times P''(s)}{|P'(s) \times P''(s)|} = \frac{P'(t) \times P''(t)}{|P'(t) \times P''(t)|} \tag{2.37}$$

The three unit vectors $\boldsymbol{T}, \boldsymbol{N}, \boldsymbol{B}$ form an orthonormal basis as shown in Fig. 2.8. This local reference system is called the Frenet frame. The derivative of the bi-normal vector $\boldsymbol{B}'(s)$ is perpendicular to both $\boldsymbol{B}(s)$ and $\boldsymbol{T}(s)$, and hence parallel to $\boldsymbol{N}(s)$:

$$\boldsymbol{B}'(s) = \frac{d\,(B(s))}{ds} = -\tau(s)\boldsymbol{N}(s) \tag{2.38}$$

The term $\tau(s)$ is called the torsion of the curve at s. Torsion is a measure of how much the curve deviates from the osculating plane.

The plane containing the tangent and binormal vectors is called the rectifying plane (Fig. 2.8). The plane formed by the normal and binormal vectors is called the normal plane.

The Frenet frame is useful for defining the local orientation of objects that move along a curved path. It can also be used for defining the eye-coordinate system for a camera that undergoes a curvilinear motion.

2.6 Affine Transformations

In this section, we consider linear transformations of three-dimensional points and vectors. The homogeneous coordinate system (Sect. 2.1) allows all transformations including translations to be represented using 4×4 matrices. We denote a translation by a vector $\boldsymbol{v} = (x_v, y_v, z_v)$, by $\mathbf{T}_v$, a rotation about the x-axis by an angle by θ, by $\mathbf{R}_\theta(x)$, and a scaling by a vector $\boldsymbol{k} = (x_k, y_k, z_k)$, by $\mathbf{S}_k$ (Box 2.3).

Box 2.3 Fundamental 3D Transformations (Fig. 2.9)

$$\mathbf{T}_v\text{: Translation by an offset vector } v\ (x_v, y_v, z_v) = \begin{bmatrix} 1 & 0 & 0 & x_v \\ 0 & 1 & 0 & y_v \\ 0 & 0 & 1 & z_v \\ 0 & 0 & 0 & 1 \end{bmatrix}$$

$$\mathbf{R}_\theta(x)\text{: Rotation by an angle } \theta \text{ about the } x\text{-axis} = \begin{bmatrix} 1 & 0 & 0 & 0 \\ 0 & \cos\theta & -\sin\theta & 0 \\ 0 & \sin\theta & \cos\theta & 0 \\ 0 & 0 & 0 & 1 \end{bmatrix}$$

$$\mathbf{R}_\theta(y)\text{: Rotation by an angle } \theta \text{ about the } y\text{-axis} = \begin{bmatrix} \cos\theta & 0 & \sin\theta & 0 \\ 0 & 1 & 0 & 0 \\ -\sin\theta & 0 & \cos\theta & 0 \\ 0 & 0 & 0 & 1 \end{bmatrix}$$

$$\mathbf{R}_\theta(z)\text{: Rotation by an angle } \theta \text{ about the } z\text{-axis} = \begin{bmatrix} \cos\theta & -\sin\theta & 0 & 0 \\ \sin\theta & \cos\theta & 0 & 0 \\ 0 & 0 & 1 & 0 \\ 0 & 0 & 0 & 1 \end{bmatrix}$$

$$\mathbf{S}_k\text{: Scaling by factors } k_x, k_y, k_z = \begin{bmatrix} x_k & 0 & 0 & 0 \\ 0 & y_k & 0 & 0 \\ 0 & 0 & z_k & 0 \\ 0 & 0 & 0 & 1 \end{bmatrix}$$

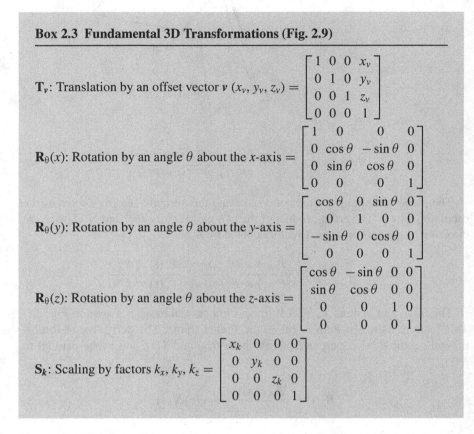

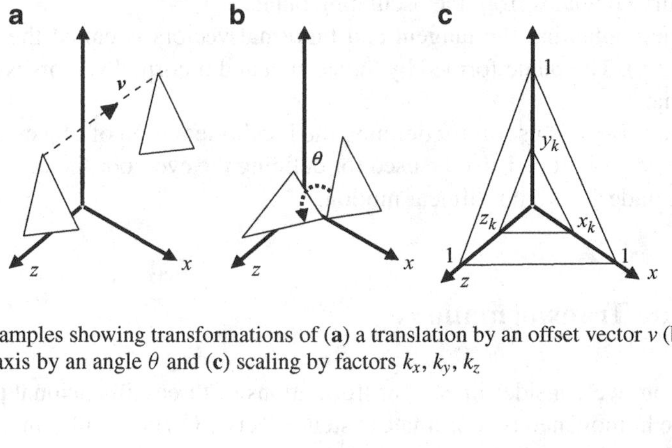

Fig. 2.9 Examples showing transformations of (**a**) a translation by an offset vector v (**b**) a rotation about the x-axis by an angle θ and (**c**) scaling by factors k_x, k_y, k_z

A linear transformation followed by a translation is called an affine transform. A general transformation can be given in matrix form as follows:

$$\begin{bmatrix} x'_p \\ y'_p \\ z'_p \\ 1 \end{bmatrix} = \begin{bmatrix} a_{00} & a_{01} & a_{02} & a_{03} \\ a_{10} & a_{11} & a_{12} & a_{13} \\ a_{20} & a_{21} & a_{22} & a_{23} \\ 0 & 0 & 0 & 1 \end{bmatrix} \begin{bmatrix} x_p \\ y_p \\ z_p \\ 1 \end{bmatrix} \quad (2.39)$$

In the above equation, the matrix elements a_{ij}'s are all constants. (a_{03}, a_{13}, a_{23}) denote the translation components, and (x_p, y_p, z_p, 1) the point on which the transformation is applied. The translation parameters do not have any effect on a vector (x_v, y_v, z_v, 0). Under an affine transformation, line segments transform into line segments, and parallel lines transform into parallel lines. A fixed point of a transformation is a point that remains invariant under that transformation. For example, every point along the x-axis is a fixed point for the transformation $\mathbf{R}_\theta(x)$. Similarly, the origin is a fixed point for the scale transformation. The most general rotation of an object with the origin as a fixed point, is the rotation by an angle θ about an arbitrary vector $\boldsymbol{v} = (x_v, y_v, z_v, 0)$ passing through the origin. The matrix for this transformation is given below.

$$\mathbf{R}_\theta(\boldsymbol{v}) = \begin{bmatrix} x_v^2 A + C & x_v y_v A - z_v B & x_v z_v A + y_v B & 0 \\ x_v y_v A + z_v B & y_v^2 A + C & y_v z_v A - x_v B & 0 \\ x_v z_v A - y_v B & y_v z_v A + x_v B & z_v^2 A + C & 0 \\ 0 & 0 & 0 & 1 \end{bmatrix} \quad (2.40)$$

where $A = (1-\cos\theta)$, $B = \sin\theta$, and $C = \cos\theta$. A rotation about an axis parallel to the x-axis, with an arbitrary fixed point P, can be obtained by first applying a translation $\mathbf{T}_{-p}$ from P to the origin, a rotation $\mathbf{R}_\theta(x)$ with origin as the fixed point, and finally a translation $\mathbf{T}_p$ back to the original position P. In matrix form, we write the composite transformation as $\mathbf{T}_p\mathbf{R}_\theta(x)\mathbf{T}_p{}^{-1}$. Here $\mathbf{T}^{-1}$ denotes the inverse of the transformation $\mathbf{T}$. For a translation, the inverse of $\mathbf{T}_p$ is $\mathbf{T}_{-p}$; and for a rotation, the inverse of $\mathbf{R}_\theta(\boldsymbol{v})$ is $\mathbf{R}_{-\theta}(\boldsymbol{v})$. A transformation of the form $\mathbf{TRT}^{-1}$ is called the conjugate of $\mathbf{R}$.

We have just seen a few examples of affine transformations that are commonly used for generating new points by transforming existing ones. We could also combine the coordinates of a set of points using a linear equation to obtain a new point. Such interpolation methods are discussed in the next section.

2.7 Affine Combinations

A linear combination of a set of points P_i ($i = 1,2,\ldots n$) produces a new point Q as shown below:

$$Q = \sum_{i=1}^{n} w_i \; P_i \quad (2.41)$$

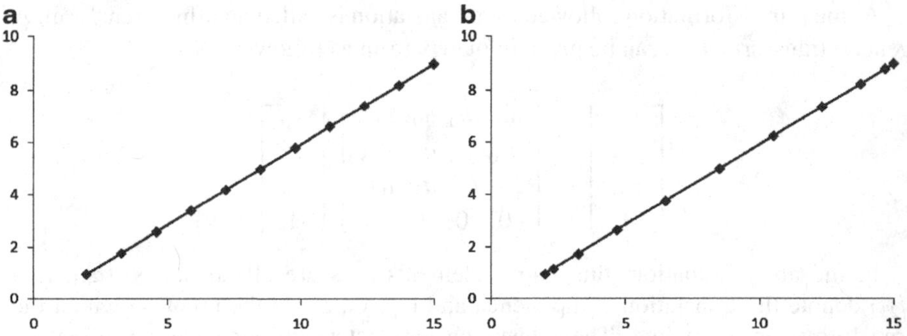

Fig. 2.10 (**a**) Linear interpolation and (**b**) trigonometric interpolation between two points

where the coefficients (weights) w_i are constants. If the weights satisfy the condition

$$\sum_{i=1}^{n} w_i = 1., \tag{2.42}$$

then Eq. 2.41 gives an affine combination of points. Additionally, if $w_i \geq 0$, for all i, then w_i's form a partition of unity, and Eq. 2.41 is said to give a convex combination of points. As a special case, when $n = 2$, we get the formula for linear interpolation between two points P_1 and P_2:

$$Q = (1 - t)P_1 + t\ P_2, \quad 0 \leq t \leq 1. \tag{2.43}$$

An interesting variation of the above equation can be derived by expressing the parameter t as a function of an angle α, given by $t = \cos^2\alpha$. Then the coefficient $(1-\ t)$ becomes $\sin^2\alpha$, and Eq. 2.43 takes the form $Q = \sin^2\alpha\ P_1 + \cos^2\alpha\ P_2$. However, this trigonometric interpolation formula gives a non-uniform distribution of points on the line when α is varied from 0° to 90° in equal steps. A comparison of linear and trigonometric interpolations is given in Fig. 2.10. In Fig. 2.10a, the parameter t is varied uniformly in the range [0–1] in steps of 0.1, and in Fig. 2.10b, the angle α is varied uniformly in the range [0–90] in steps of 9°. Higher order interpolation between points is discussed in Chap. 7 (Box 2.4).

Box 2.4 Bernstein Polynomials

Given a positive integer value n, we can construct $n + 1$ polynomials of degree n of a parameter t as follows:

$$\beta_{i,n}(t) = \binom{n}{i}(1 - t)^{n-i}t^i, \quad i = 0, 1, 2, \ldots, n.$$

These polynomials form a partition of unity, *i.e.*, $\sum_{i=0}^{n} \beta_{i,n}(t) = 1$.

Therefore, they can be used to generate convex combinations of points. Given $n+1$ points P_i, $i=0,\ldots,n$, we define a point $Q(t)$ as

$$Q(t) = \sum_{i=0}^{n} \beta_{i,n}(t)\, P_i$$

As the parameter t is varied from 0 to 1, we get a continuous parametric curve called the Bezier curve. The equations for $n = 1, 2, 3$ are given below.
First degree (linear): $Q(t) = (1-t)\,P_0 + t\,P_1$
Second degree (quadratic) : $Q(t) = (1-t)^2 P_0 + 2(1-t)t\,P_1 + t^2 P_2$
Third degree (cubic) : $Q(t) = (1-t)^3 P_0 + 3(1-t)^2\,t\,P_1 + 3(1-t)t^2 P_2 + t^3 P_3$

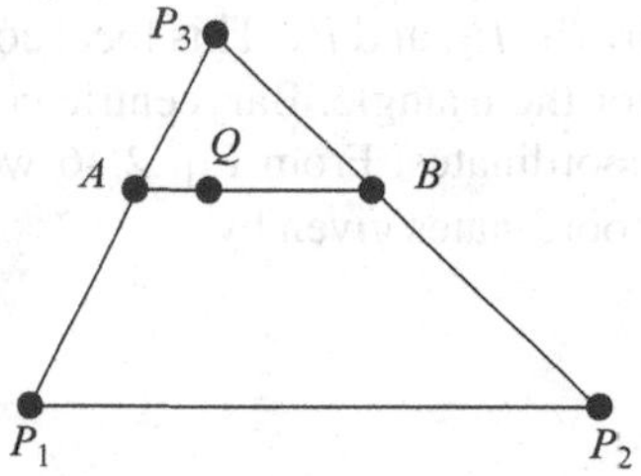

Fig. 2.11 A bilinear interpolation scheme first interpolates along the edges to get the values at A and B, and then uses another linear interpolation along the line AB to get the value at Q

Given a triangle with vertices P_1, P_2 and P_3, we can perform a bilinear interpolation between the values defined at the vertices to get the interpolated value at an interior point Q (Fig. 2.11). Using this scheme, we can compute the colour value at any point inside a triangle, given the colour values at the vertices. A scan-line parallel to the base of the triangle sweeps the plane and generates the values of A and B using the linear interpolation equation in Eq. 2.43 with the same parameter t. Another linear interpolation between of A and B with a parameter s gives the value of Q. Thus we get

$$Q = (1-s)\,\{(1-t)P_1 + t\,P_3\} + s\,\{(1-t)\,P_2 + t\,P_3\}, \quad 0 \le s,t \le 1. \tag{2.44}$$

The above equation could be simplified into a simple convex combination of vertex points as

$$Q = (1-k_1-k_2)P_1 + k_1 P_2 + k_2 P_3, \quad 0 \le k_1, k_2, k_1+k_2 \le 1, \tag{2.45}$$

where $k_1 = s(1-t)$ and $k_2 = t$. The bilinear interpolation of vertex coordinates shown above can be generalized to interpolate any quantity or attribute inside a triangle, given its values at the vertices. Examples of such vertex attributes are colour, texture coordinates and normal vectors. In the next section, we will consider another closely related interpolation method for triangles.

2.8 Barycentric Coordinates

The barycentre of a rigid body is its centre of mass. For a triangle, the barycentre is its centroid. Given vertices P_1, P_2, P_3 of a triangle, the centroid C can be easily computed as the average of the vertex coordinates $(P_1 + P_2 + P_3)/3$. Thus C can be represented as a convex combination of the vertex points. Indeed, Eq. 2.45 has just shown that any point Q inside the triangle could be expressed as a convex combination of vertices. If we re-write Eq. 2.45 as

$$Q = \lambda_1 P_1 + \lambda_2 P_2 + \lambda_3 P_3, \quad 0 \leq \lambda_1, \lambda_2, \lambda_3 \leq 1, \quad \lambda_1 + \lambda_2 + \lambda_3 = 1, \tag{2.46}$$

then the point Q is uniquely specified by a new set of coordinates $(\lambda_1, \lambda_2, \lambda_3)$ defined by P_1, P_2, and P_3. This local coordinate system is called the barycentric coordinates for the triangle. Barycentric coordinates are also sometimes referred to as trilinear coordinates. From Eq. 2.46 we see that the vertices themselves have barycentric coordinates given by

$$\begin{aligned} P_1 &= (1, 0, 0) \\ P_2 &= (0, 1, 0) \\ P_3 &= (0, 0, 1) \end{aligned} \tag{2.47}$$

As seen earlier, the centroid C has barycentric coordinates (1/3, 1/3, 1/3). The barycentric coordinates of a point Q with respect to P_1, P_2, P_3 have a geometrical interpretation as the ratios of the areas of triangles QP_2P_3, QP_3P_1, QP_1P_2 to the area of the triangle $P_1P_2P_3$. In the following equations, the symbol Δ denotes the signed area of a triangle:

$$\lambda_1 = \frac{\Delta Q P_2 P_3}{\Delta P_1 P_2 P_3}, \quad \lambda_2 = \frac{\Delta Q P_3 P_1}{\Delta P_1 P_2 P_3}, \quad \lambda_3 = \frac{\Delta Q P_1 P_2}{\Delta P_1 P_2 P_3} \tag{2.48}$$

The barycentric coordinates given in Eq. 2.48 are unique for every point on the plane of the triangle. They can be directly used to get the interpolated value of any quantity defined at the vertices of the triangle. If f_{P1}, f_{P2}, f_{P3} denote the values of some attribute associated with the vertices, then the interpolated value at Q is given by

$$f_Q = \lambda_1 f_{P1} + \lambda_2 f_{P2} + \lambda_3 f_{P3}. \tag{2.49}$$

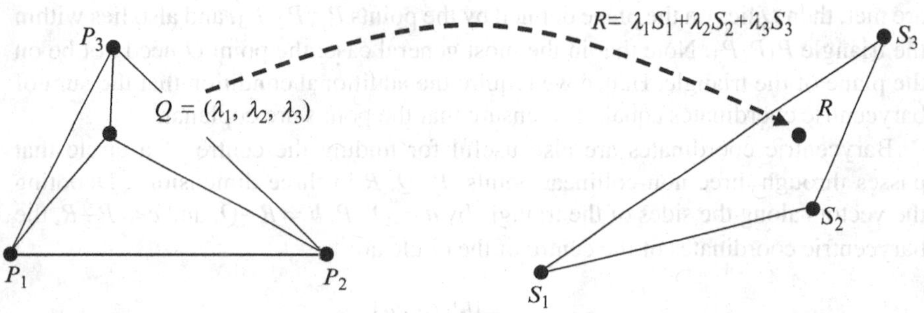

Fig. 2.12 A one-to-one mapping of points from one triangle to another can be obtained using barycentric coordinates

Using barycentric coordinates we can establish a one-to-one mapping of points from within one triangle to another. For any given interior point Q of the first triangle, we compute the barycentric coordinates. The linear combination of the vertices of the second triangle with the barycentric coordinates of Q gives the coordinates of the corresponding point R inside the second triangle (Fig. 2.12). We can use this mapping to transfer values from the interior of the first triangle to the second. As an immediate application of this transfer, we can map an image (or texture) from one triangle to another.

In a simplified two-dimensional case where $P_1 = (x_1, y_1)$, $P_2 = (x_2, y_2)$, $P_3 = (x_3, y_3)$, $Q = (x_q, y_q)$, the expressions for the barycentric coordinates of Q given in Eq. 2.48 assume the following form:

$$\lambda_1 = \frac{x_q(y_2 - y_3) + x_2(y_3 - y_q) + x_3(y_q - y_2)}{x_1(y_2 - y_3) + x_2(y_3 - y_1) + x_3(y_1 - y_2)}$$

$$\lambda_2 = \frac{x_q(y_3 - y_1) + x_3(y_1 - y_q) + x_1(y_q - y_3)}{x_1(y_2 - y_3) + x_2(y_3 - y_1) + x_3(y_1 - y_2)}$$

$$\lambda_3 = \frac{x_q(y_1 - y_2) + x_1(y_2 - y_q) + x_2(y_q - y_1)}{x_1(y_2 - y_3) + x_2(y_3 - y_1) + x_3(y_1 - y_2)} \tag{2.50}$$

If any of the above quantities is negative, then the point Q lies outside the triangle $P_1P_2P_3$. Thus barycentric coordinates find applications in point inclusion tests. In a general three-dimensional case, however, the area of a triangle computed using Eq. 2.3 would always be positive, and correspondingly the area ratios in Eq. 2.48 would also be positive. As previously discussed in Sect. 2.2, the computation of signed areas of triangles requires a view vector $\boldsymbol{w}$. Since we need this vector to be fixed with respect to every triangle in Eq. 2.48, we can conveniently choose $\boldsymbol{w} = (P_2 - P_1) \times (P_3 - P_1)$. Now the barycentric coordinates λ_1, λ_2 and λ_3 in Eq. 2.48 can be computed by applying the formula in Eq. 2.8 to each of the triangles QP_2P_3, QP_3P_1, QP_1P_2 and $P_1P_2P_3$. If the conditions $\lambda_1 + \lambda_2 + \lambda_3 = 1$, $0 \leq \lambda_1, \lambda_2, \lambda_3 \leq 1$

are met, then Q lies on the plane defined by the points P_1, P_2, P_3, and also lies within the triangle $P_1P_2P_3$. Note that in the most general case, the point Q need not be on the plane of the triangle. Hence we require the additional condition that the sum of barycentric coordinates equals 1 to ensure that the points are coplanar.

Barycentric coordinates are also useful for finding the centre of a circle that passes through three non-collinear points, P, Q, R in three dimensions. Denoting the vectors along the sides of the triangle by $\boldsymbol{a} = Q-P$, $\boldsymbol{b} = R-Q$, and $\boldsymbol{c} = P-R$, the barycentric coordinates of the centre of the circle are

$$\lambda_1 = \frac{-|\boldsymbol{b}|^2(\boldsymbol{c}\cdot\boldsymbol{a})}{2|\boldsymbol{a}\times\boldsymbol{b}|^2}$$
$$\lambda_2 = \frac{-|\boldsymbol{c}|^2(\boldsymbol{a}\cdot\boldsymbol{b})}{2|\boldsymbol{a}\times\boldsymbol{b}|^2}$$
$$\lambda_3 = \frac{-|\boldsymbol{a}|^2(\boldsymbol{b}\cdot\boldsymbol{c})}{2|\boldsymbol{a}\times\boldsymbol{b}|^2} \tag{2.51}$$

The centre of the circle is then given by the following linear combination of the three points:

$$C = \lambda_1 P + \lambda_2 Q + \lambda_3 R. \tag{2.52}$$

In the following section, we will look at the application of vectors in the Phong-Blinn illumination model used for lighting calculations in the OpenGL pipeline.

2.9 Basic Lighting

The hardware accelerated lighting model that is traditionally used in Computer Graphics applications is based on Phong-Blinn approximation for an omni-directional point-light source. A local illumination model that does not account for complex effects such as reflections, refractions, shadows and indirect illumination is found to be generally adequate for a majority of graphics applications. In this model, light-material interaction is simply modelled using a component-wise multiplication of material colour and light colour. We can represent colour by a vector comprising of red, green and blue components as $\boldsymbol{c} = (r, g, b, 0)$. This vector model can be further generalized by replacing the fourth component by k that represents the transparency (or opacity) term which can take non-zero values. In the discussion that follows, $\boldsymbol{m_a}$, $\boldsymbol{m_d}$, $\boldsymbol{m_s}$ denote respectively the ambient, diffuse and specular components of material colour, and $\boldsymbol{I_a}$, $\boldsymbol{I_d}$, $\boldsymbol{I_s}$ the corresponding components of the light source. Each of these colour components is typically a 3-tuple consisting of red, green and blue values. For notational convenience, we represent $\boldsymbol{m_a}$ by

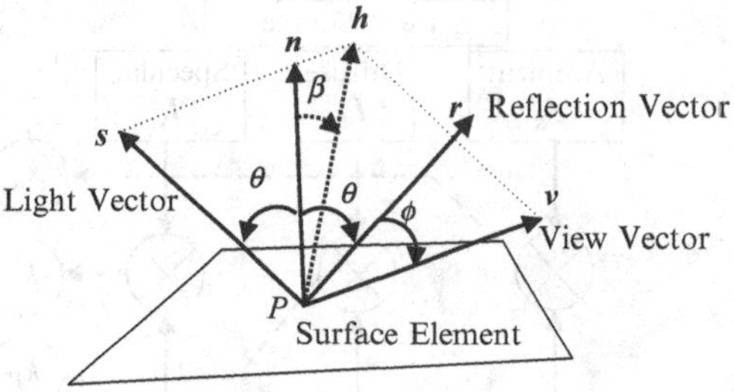

Fig. 2.13 Important vectors and angles between them, used in lighting calculations

the vector (r_{ma}, g_{ma}, b_{ma}), $\boldsymbol{I_a}$ by the vector (r_{ia}, g_{ia}, b_{ia}), and so on. The ambient light-material interaction is then modelled by the component-wise vector product

$$\boldsymbol{m_a} \otimes \boldsymbol{I_a} = (r_{ma}r_{ia}, g_{ma}g_{ia}, b_{ma}b_{ia}) \tag{2.53}$$

Figure 2.13 shows the geometry of unit vectors used for computing diffuse and specular reflections from a surface. From a point P on a surface, $\boldsymbol{s}$ denotes the unit vector towards the light source, $\boldsymbol{n}$ the unit surface normal vector, and $\boldsymbol{v}$ the unit vector towards the viewer. The perceived intensity of reflection at the viewer's position varies with changes in the angles between these vectors. The variations in diffuse and specular reflections are represented by multiplicative factors k_d and k_s respectively. According to the Lambertian reflectance model, the intensity of diffuse reflection from a surface is uniform in all directions, and varies as the cosine of the angle θ between the light source vector $\boldsymbol{s}$ and the surface normal vector $\boldsymbol{n}$, and is therefore proportional to $\boldsymbol{s}\bullet\boldsymbol{n}$. If the angle between the two vectors is greater than 90°, the normal vector faces away from the light source vector, and the surface is in shadow. In such a situation, the value of k_d must be set to 0. We therefore have the following view-independent factor for the diffuse term:

$$k_d = \max(\boldsymbol{s} \bullet \boldsymbol{n}, 0) \tag{2.54}$$

The specular reflection factor k_s is computed as a function of the cosine of the angle ϕ between the direction of unit specular reflection $\boldsymbol{r}$ given by Eq. 2.5 and the unit view vector $\boldsymbol{v}$, with an exponent f known as the shininess term or the Phong's constant. The exponent is useful in controlling the overall brightness and the concentration of the specular highlight.

$$k_s = \max(\cos^f \phi, 0) = \max((\boldsymbol{r} \bullet \boldsymbol{v})^f, 0) \tag{2.55}$$

The Blinn's approximation eliminates the need for computing the specular reflection vector using Eq. 2.5 by defining a unit vector $\boldsymbol{h}$ along the direction $\boldsymbol{s} + \boldsymbol{v}$. This vector is called the half-way vector. If $\boldsymbol{n}\bullet\boldsymbol{h} = \cos\beta$, then equating the angles on either side of $\boldsymbol{h}$ gives

$$\theta + \beta = \theta - \beta + \phi \tag{2.56}$$

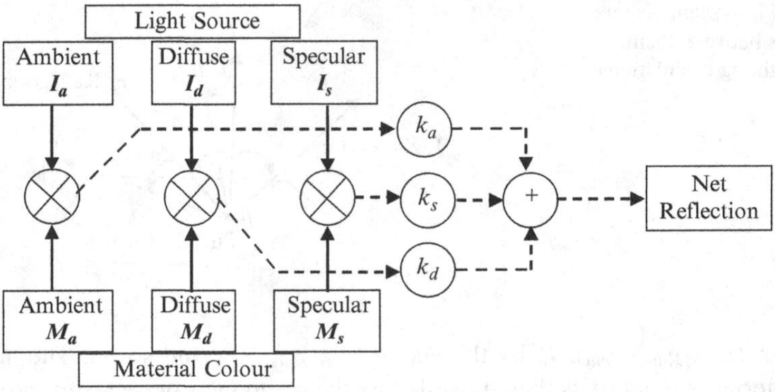

Fig. 2.14 Schematic of the calculations performed in a basic lighting model

From the above equation we find that $\phi = 2\beta$. The term $\boldsymbol{r}\bullet\boldsymbol{v}$ in Eq. 2.55 can therefore be replaced with $\boldsymbol{n}\bullet\boldsymbol{h}$ by absorbing the factor 2 in k_s. This gives the Blinn's approximation for k_s:

$$k_s = \max((\boldsymbol{n} \bullet \boldsymbol{h})^f, 0). \tag{2.57}$$

A schematic of the lighting computation using the Phong-Blinn illumination model outlined above is given in Fig. 2.14.

2.10 Summary

This chapter reviewed some of the geometrical computations involving points, lines, planes, triangles and curves, that are fundamental to many algorithms in computer graphics. Important concepts such as homogeneous coordinate representation of points, signed angles, signed areas of triangles, and barycentric coordinates were outlined. Equations relating to affine transformations and affine combinations of points were discussed. This chapter also gave the equations for a basic lighting model consisting of ambient, diffuse and specular components of reflection.

The concepts presented in this chapter will form the foundation for several methods that will be discussed in subsequent chapters. The next chapter introduces a hierarchical structure that is useful for modelling transformations applied to articulated models and other similar objects containing interconnected parts.

2.11 Supplementary Material for Chap. 2

The section `Chapter2/Code` on this book's companion website contains code examples demonstrating the application of concepts discussed in this chapter. A brief description of these programs is given below.

1. **Point3.cpp**

Additional files:
`Point3.h`
`Point3Test.cpp`

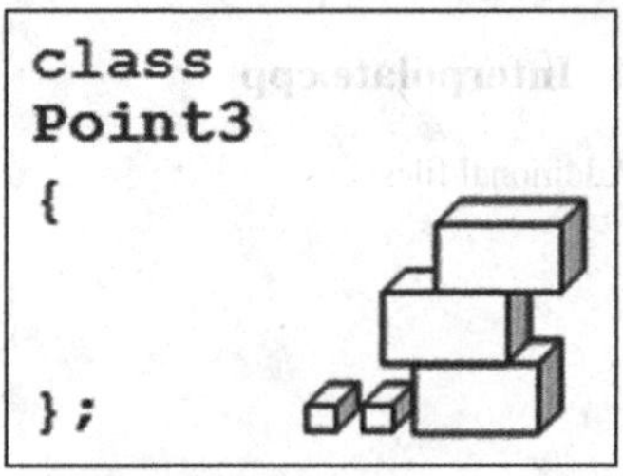

The `Point3` class supports most commonly used operations on points represented using 4-dimensional homogeneous coordinates. The class has the subclass `Vec3` that supports vector operations such as dot and cross products, vector magnitude calculation and normalization. The documentation of these classes can be found in Appendix A.

2. **Triangle.cpp**

Additional files:
`Triangle.h`

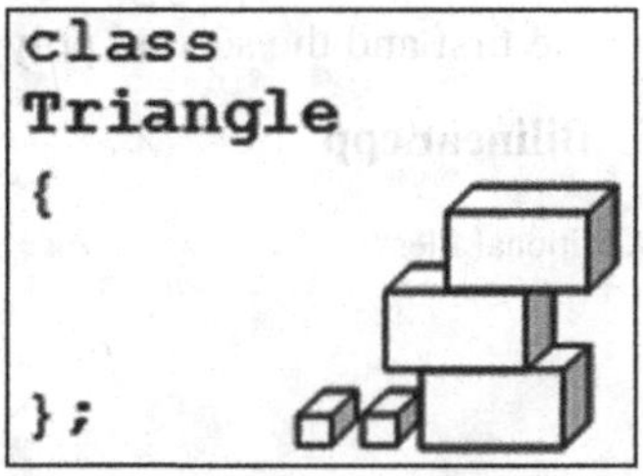

The `Triangle` class provides methods for computing area, surface normal vector, and the barycentric coordinates of a point with respect to a triangle. It also has functions for performing the point inclusion test and bilinear interpolation. The documentation of this class can be found in Appendix A.

3. **Matrix.cpp**

Additional files:
`Matrix.h`

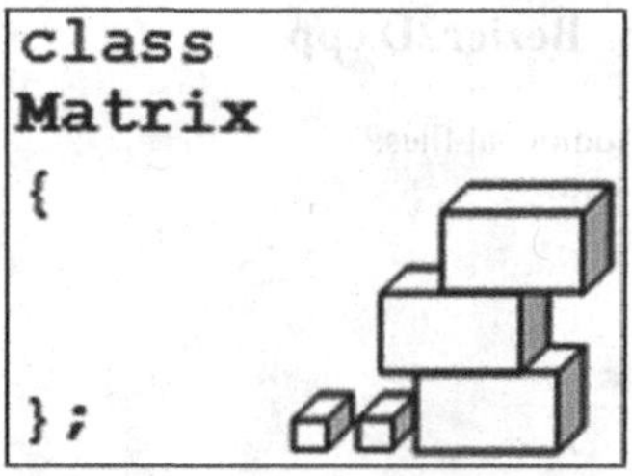

The `Matrix` class contains methods for matrix operations (using 4×4 matrices) such as addition, multiplication, computation of transpose and inverse matrices, and transformation of points. The documentation of this class can be found in Appendix A.

4. **Interpolate.cpp**

Additional files:
`None`

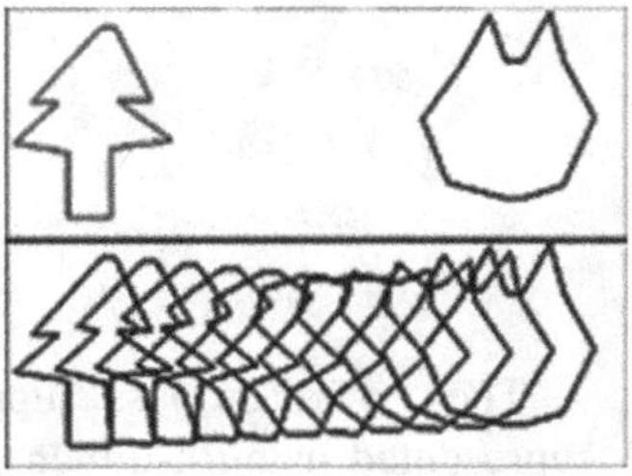

The program creates a shape-tween between two user-defined polygonal shapes using simple linear interpolation between corresponding vertices. Use left mouse clicks on the upper left side of the screen to define the first polygonal shape. Similarly, use right mouse clicks on the upper right side of the screen to draw the second polygon. Pressing the space bar creates the shape-tween between the first and the second polygons in the bottom half of the window.

5. **Bilinear.cpp**

Additional files:
`None`

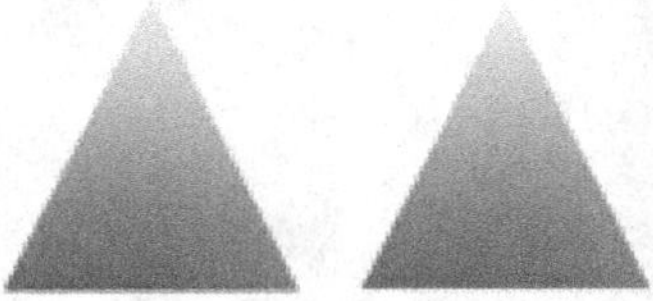

The program uses Eq. 2.45 to obtain a bilinear interpolation of color values at the vertices to fill the interior of a triangle. For comparison, a second similar triangle is rendered using the OpenGL pipeline that uses the Gouraud shading algorithm. The vertex colours are randomly generated every time the space bar is pressed.

6. **Bezier2D.cpp**

Additional files:
`None`

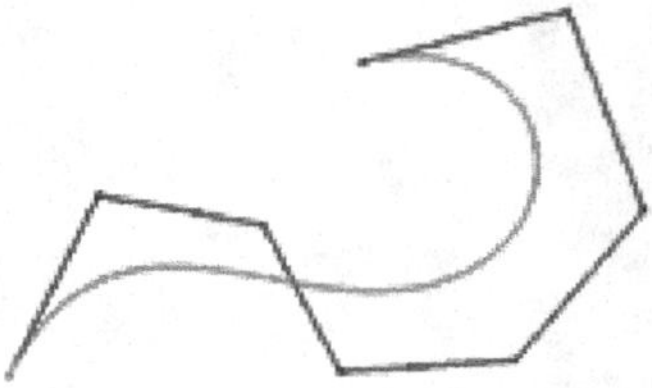

The program uses Bernstein polynomials (Box 2.4) to generate a two-dimensional Bezier curve for a set of user-defined control points. Use left mouse clicks on the screen to define a set of control points. The control polygonal line is shown in red colour. The Bezier curve for the input points is simultaneously drawn in blue colour.

7. **Barycentric.cpp**

Additional files:
```
Point3.h
Triangle.h
Point3.cpp
Triangle.cpp
```

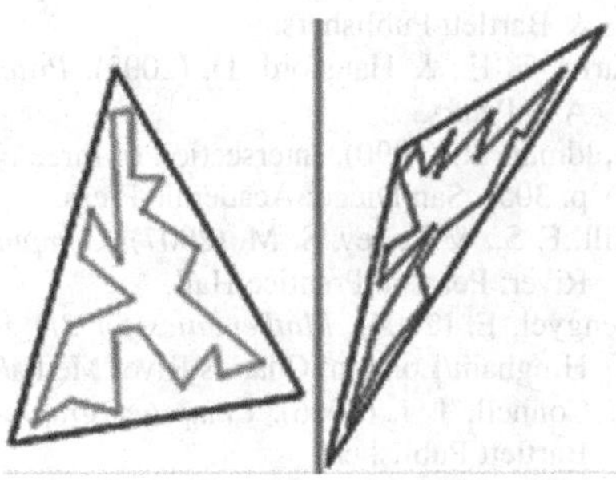

The program uses barycentric mapping (Fig. 2.12) to map points from one triangle to another. Two triangles are displayed when the program is initiated. Use left mouse clicks inside the left triangle to specify a few points. The points are connected using a polygonal line drawn in magenta colour. The map of these points and the polygonal line connecting them inside the triangle on the right hand side are simultaneously drawn in blue colour.

2.12 Bibliographical Notes

Several books on introductory computer graphics provide an outline of concepts discussed in this chapter. Some recent publications that can serve as excellent references are Angel (2008), Hill and Kelley (2007), and McConnell (2006). A number of books give emphasis to the mathematical tools used in computer graphics. Notable in this area are Vince and Vince (2006), Lengyel (2004), Buss (2003), Schneider and Eberly (2003), and Dunn and Parberry (2002).

Comninos (2006) gives a comprehensive coverage of topics on vector and matrix algebra, transformations, lighting and shading models. A concise description of homogeneous coordinates and their applications in computer graphics can be found in Vince (2001). Topics in linear algebra and topology that are used in many algorithms in computer graphics are discussed at length in Agoston (2005) and Farin and Hansford (2005).

References

Agoston, M. K. (2005). *Computer graphics and geometric modeling*. London: Springer.
Angel, E. (2008). *Interactive computer graphics: A top-down approach using OpenGL* (5th ed.). Boston/London: Pearson Addison-Wesley.

Buss, S. R. (2003). *3-D computer graphics: A mathematical introduction with OpenGL*. New York: Cambridge University Press.
Comninos, P. (2006). *Mathematical and computer programming techniques for computer graphics*. London: Springer.
Dunn, F., & Parberry, I. (2002). *3D math primer for graphics and game development*. Plano: Jones & Bartlett Publishers.
Farin, G. E., & Hansford, D. (2005). *Practical linear algebra: A geometry toolbox*. Wellesley: A K Peters.
Goldman, R. (1990). Intersection of three planes. In A. S. Glassner (Ed.), *Graphics gems* (Vol. I, p. 305). San Diego: Academic Press.
Hill, F. S., & Kelley, S. M. (2007). *Computer graphics: Using OpenGL* (3rd ed.). Upper Saddle River: Pearson Prentice Hall.
Lengyel, E. (2004). *Mathematics for 3D game programming and computer graphics* (2nd ed.). Hingham/London: Charles River Media/Transatlantic.
McConnell, J. J. (2006). *Computer graphics: Theory into practice*. Boston/London: Jones and Bartlett Publishers.
Schneider, P. J., & Eberly, D. H. (2003). *Geometric tools for computer graphics*. Amsterdam/ London: Morgan Kaufmann.
Vince, J. (2001). *Essential mathematics for computer graphics fast*. London: Springer.
Vince, J., & Vince, J. E. (2006). *Mathematics for computer graphics* (2nd ed.). London: Springer.

Chapter 3
Scene Graphs

Overview

A scene graph is a data structure commonly used to represent hierarchical relationships between transformations applied to a set of objects in a three-dimensional scene. It finds applications in a variety of acceleration and rendering algorithms. A scene graph could also be used to organize visual attributes, bounding volumes, and animations as a hierarchy in a collection of objects. In the most general form, any scene related information that can be organized in a hierarchical fashion can be stored in a scene graph. It also provides a convenient way of representing logical groups of objects formed using their spatial positions or attributes. In this chapter, we will outline the fundamental properties of scene graphs, look at some of the implementation aspects and consider a few applications.

3.1 The Basic Structure of a Scene Graph

The structure and contents of a scene graph will obviously depend on the type of information it stores, or equivalently, the set of operations it is used for. Let us consider a simple tree structure that contains three types of nodes:

1. The root node of the tree represents the whole collection of objects in a three-dimensional scene. We call this node *World* or *Virtual Universe*. The root node is a special type of a group node.
2. A group node is an internal node of the tree. It can contain any number of children, and represents a logical grouping of objects. A group node does not store geometrical data, but it can contain some semantic information such as transformations or visibility attributes applied to a group.
3. Every leaf node represents either an object or a part of an object, and maintains the necessary geometrical information in addition to some semantic information. Camera and light sources may also be represented by leaf nodes.

R. Mukundan, *Advanced Methods in Computer Graphics: With examples in OpenGL*, DOI 10.1007/978-1-4471-2340-8_3, © Springer-Verlag London Limited 2012

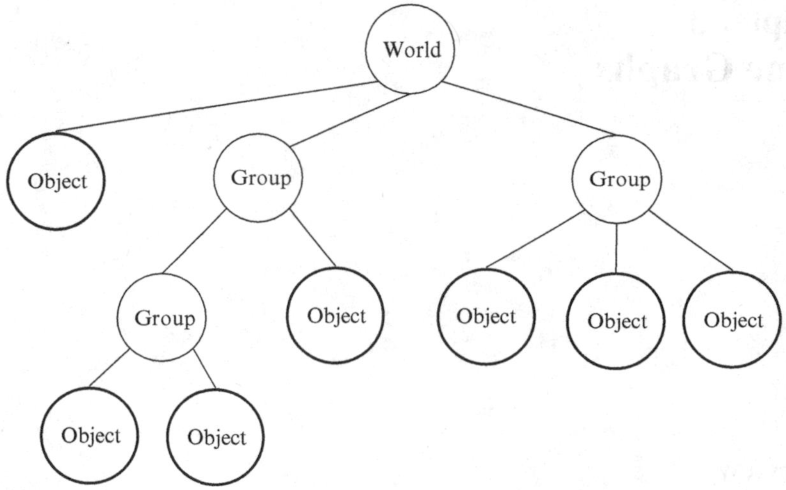

Fig. 3.1 An example of a scene graph, where every internal node is a group node and every leaf node is an object node

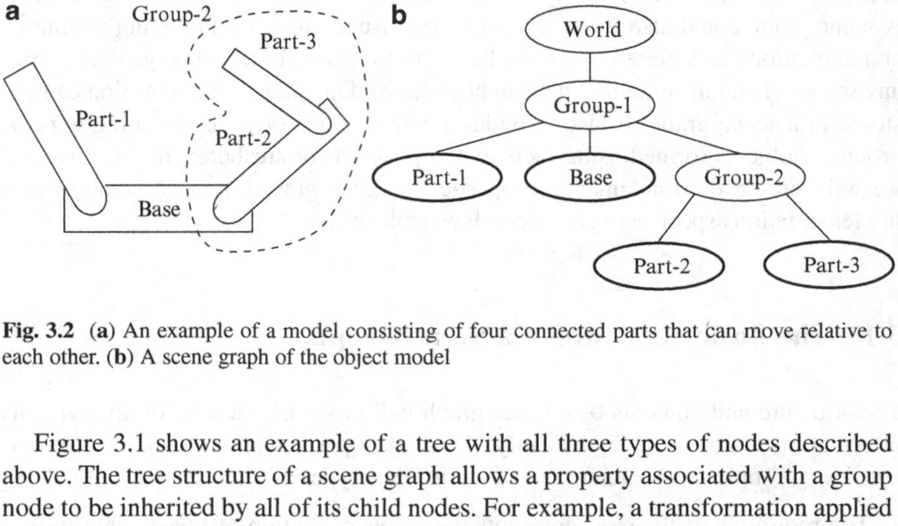

Fig. 3.2 (**a**) An example of a model consisting of four connected parts that can move relative to each other. (**b**) A scene graph of the object model

Figure 3.1 shows an example of a tree with all three types of nodes described above. The tree structure of a scene graph allows a property associated with a group node to be inherited by all of its child nodes. For example, a transformation applied to a group node can be considered as also applied to all its children. Similarly, a bounding volume, if attached to a group node, also represents the overall bounding volume for the whole collection of its child nodes.

A scene graph is particularly useful for animating a composite object that has several parts which should move as if the parts are all physically connected to each other. A typical example of such an object is an articulated character model. We illustrate the formation of a scene graph using a simple model consisting of four interconnected parts: *Base*, *Part-1*, *Part-2*, and *Part-3*, as shown in Fig. 3.2.

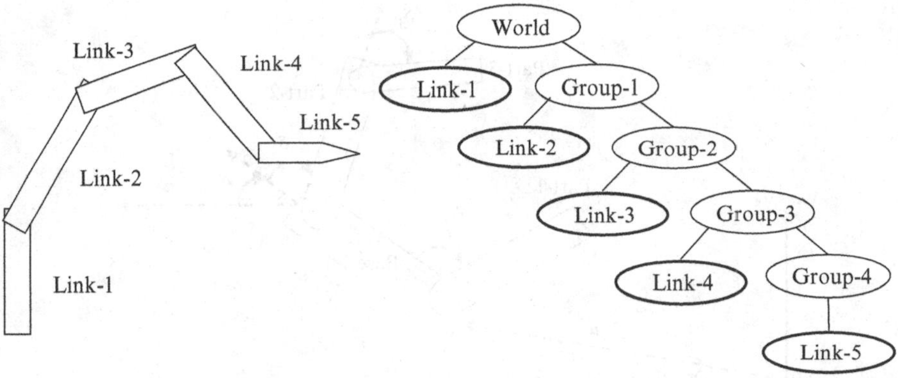

Fig. 3.3 A 5-link joint chain and its scene graph

As can be seen from the diagram of the scene graph, the whole model is first subdivided into three logical groups *Part-1*, *Base* and a subgroup *Group-2* to which *Part-2* and *Part-3* belong. Shortly we will see how we can assign transformation parameters to the individual nodes of the scene graph in such a way that the parts can rotate relative to each other while at the same time remaining connected as a single animatable object. We now consider a closely related object model, a joint chain consisting of five links as shown in Fig. 3.3.

Joint chains similar to the one shown above are commonly found in robotics and articulated models in computer graphics. The scene graph represents a hierarchical subdivision of the model, where at the first level, the whole object belongs to a single group *World*. At the next level of subdivision we have *Link-1* and a subgroup *Group-1* that contains the remaining links. Any rotational transformation applied to *Group-1* affects all members of that group. It may appear that the group node *Group-4* is redundant as it has only one child. However, the node is useful to provide a clear separation between the initial transformations applied to the object in *Link-5* in its own coordinate system and the transformations applied relative to *Link-4*'s frame. We will also later add a camera as an object belonging to *Group-4*. The transformation hierarchy represented by scene graphs is explored in more detail in the next section.

3.2 Transformation Hierarchy

A transformation applied to one part of an object often cascades with the transformations applied to the adjacent interconnected parts. For example, a change in the orientation of *Part-2* of the model in Fig. 3.2a also affects *Part-3*. Such dependencies can be easily converted into hierarchical representations that are suitable for scene graphs. We consider below three examples involving hierarchical transformations: (i) the model of a mechanical part shown in Fig. 3.2, (ii) an articulated character model, and (iii) a small planetary system.

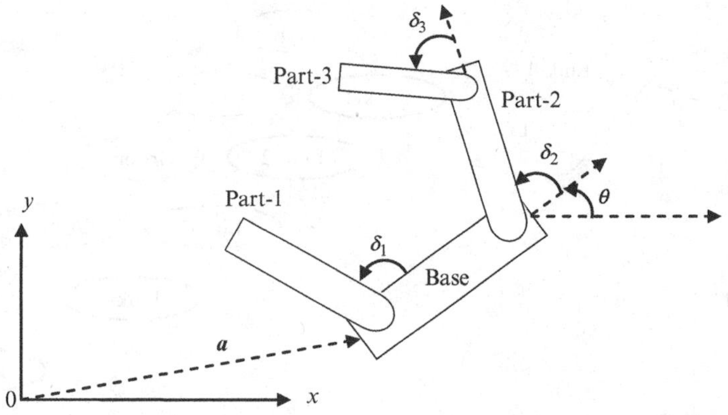

Fig. 3.4 A general transformation of the model in Fig. 3.2, showing translational and rotational parameters associated with links. The x and y axes denote the reference frame for the world coordinate system

3.2.1 A Mechanical Part

A general two-dimensional transformation of the model in Fig. 3.2a along with the translational and rotational parameters of each link is shown in Fig. 3.4. We will use $\mathbf{T}(\boldsymbol{a})$ to denote a translation by a vector $\boldsymbol{a}$, and $\mathbf{R}(\theta)$ to denote an anticlockwise rotation through an angle θ. Note that the joint angles $\delta_1, \delta_2, \delta_3$ define relative angles of rotations of one part with respect to another. In order to build the transformation hierarchy, we have to consider first the transformation of each link from its own local coordinate frame to the coordinate frame of its group. The sequence in which the transformations are applied is shown in Fig. 3.5.

As shown in Fig. 3.5, transformations are applied from the leaf nodes upward to the root of the scene graph. *Part-3* is first rotated by an angle δ_3, and then translated along the length of *Part-2* by a vector $\boldsymbol{d_3}$. This composite transformation has a matrix given by $\mathbf{T}(\boldsymbol{d_3})\mathbf{R}(\delta_3)$. *Group-2* now contains *Part-2* and the transformed version of *Part-3*. In other words, both *Part-2* and *Part-3* have been transformed into the coordinate space of *Group-2*. It should be noted here that any rotational transformation of *Part-2* is always applied to *Group-2*. The transformation matrix $\mathbf{T}(\boldsymbol{d_2})\mathbf{R}(\delta_2)$, effectively converts the points from the coordinate system of *Group-2* to that of its parent group, *Group-1*. Figure 3.6 shows the scene graph with the transformation matrices added to the tree nodes.

From the above discussion, we note that every node transformation is defined relative to the node's parent. At a leaf node, a transformation converts vertices from the local coordinate space of an object to its parent's coordinate space. If an object node has an identity transformation $\mathbf{I}$, it only shows that its parent's node has the same coordinate reference frame as the object node. This also means that any transformation applied to that node is actually applied to its parent group node. In the above example, transformations applied to the *Base* are actually applied to *Group-1*, and they indirectly affect the transformations of each of *Group-1*'s child nodes.

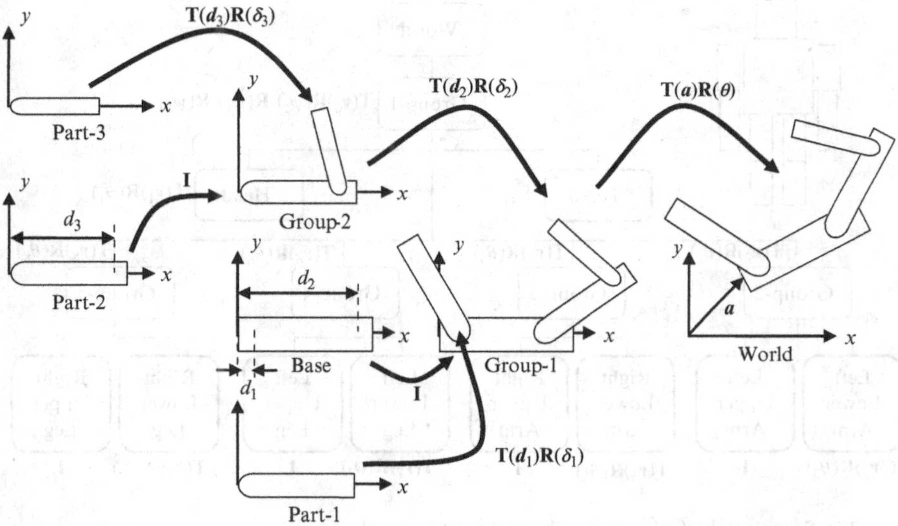

Fig. 3.5 Each moveable component of an object model is transformed from its local coordinate space to its group's space, and subsequently to the coordinate space of the group's parent

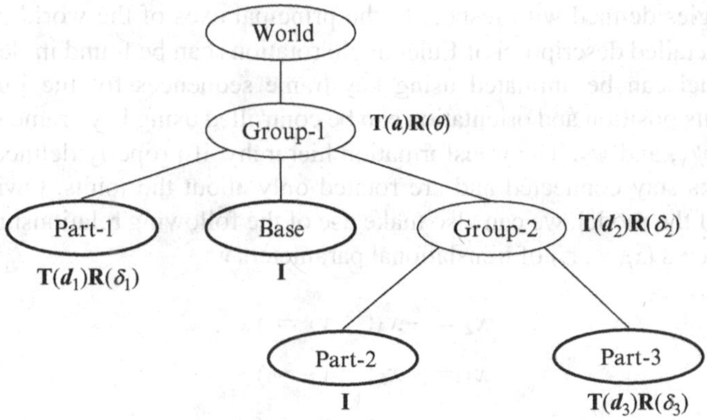

Fig. 3.6 Scene graph with transformation matrices attached to nodes

3.2.2 A Simple Character Model

We now consider an articulated character model and its scene graph shown in Fig. 3.7. As in the previous example, we can define the translational and rotational transformations for each node, based on the joint position and angle of each link relative to its parent. Vectors $v_1 \ldots v_9$ denote the offsets of the origin of the links relative to their parent's local coordinate system in the initial configuration. The vector v_0 denotes the position of the base link (Torso) in the world coordinate frame.

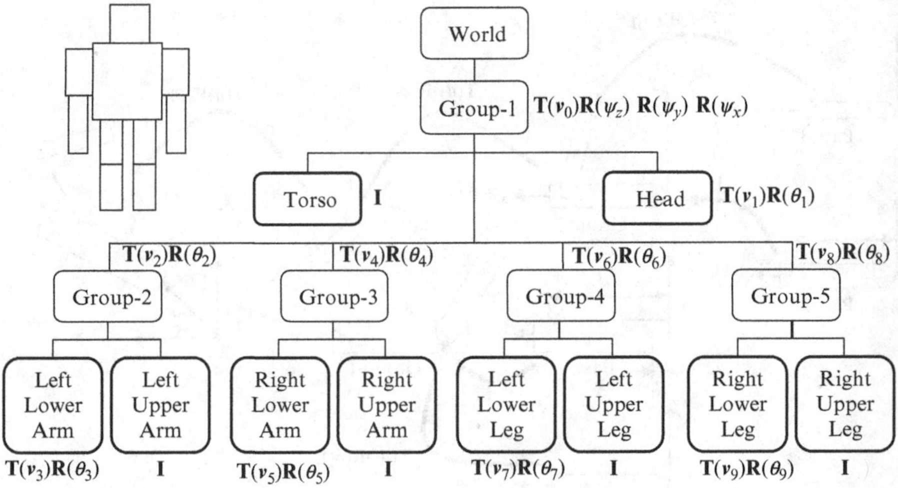

Fig. 3.7 Scene graph of a basic articulated character model

The angles ψ_x, ψ_y, ψ_z represent a generalized rotation of the whole model in terms of Euler angles defined with respect to the principal axes of the world coordinate system. A detailed description of Euler angle rotations can be found in Sect. 5.4.1.

The model can be animated using key-frame sequences for the joint angles $\theta_1..\theta_9$, and its position and orientation can be controlled using key-frame sequences for $\boldsymbol{v}_0$, ψ_x, ψ_y, and ψ_z. The transformation hierarchy, if properly defined, ensures that the links stay connected and are rotated only about the joints. Owing to the symmetry of the model, we can also make use of the following relationships among the components (x_i, y_i, z_i) of translational parameters $\boldsymbol{v}_i$:

$$\begin{aligned} x_2 &= -x_4; \quad y_2 = y_4 \\ x_3 &= -x_5; \quad y_3 = y_5 \\ x_6 &= -x_8; \quad y_6 = y_8 \\ x_7 &= -x_9; \quad y_7 = y_9 \end{aligned} \tag{3.1}$$

3.2.3 A Planetary System

As the third example, we consider a simple planetary system consisting of the Sun, the Earth and the Moon. The translational and rotational parameters used in modelling the system are shown in Fig. 3.8.

The rotation angles θ_E, θ_M represent the spin of the Earth and the Moon respectively about vertical axes, ϕ_E denotes the revolution of the Earth-Moon

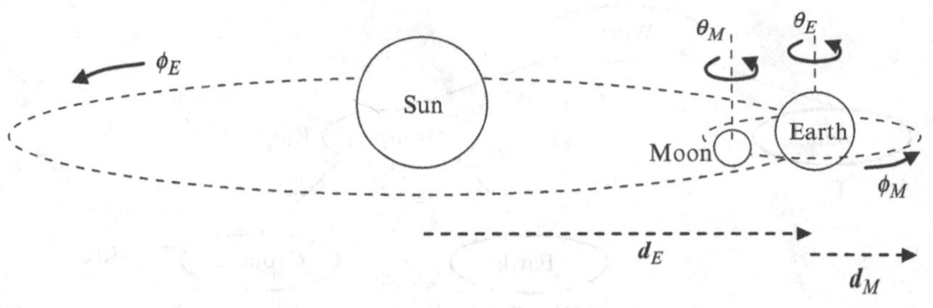

Fig. 3.8 A simple planetary system showing the translational and rotational parameters used for the construction of its scene graph

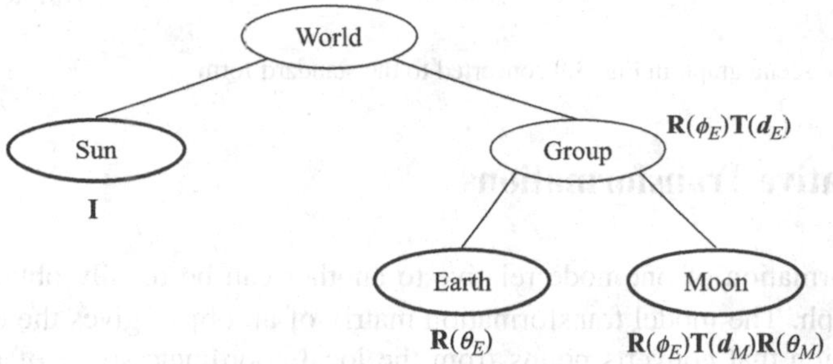

Fig. 3.9 Scene graph of the planetary system

system around the Sun, and ϕ_M the revolution of the Moon around the Earth. The scene graph for this system is shown in Fig. 3.9.

One notable difference between the planetary system example and the previous ones is the form of transformation matrices applied to nodes. Most of the transformations applied in a hierarchical fashion have a general form $\mathbf{T}(v)\mathbf{R}(\theta)$, which is a rotation followed by a translation. In simple implementations, the structure of nodes is often designed to accept only transformations of the form $\mathbf{T}(v)\mathbf{R}(\theta)$ or $\mathbf{I}$. Scene graphs where transformations at internal nodes have one of the forms $\mathbf{I}$, $\mathbf{T}(v)$, $\mathbf{R}(\theta)$, or $\mathbf{T}(v)\mathbf{R}(\theta)$ are said to be in the standard form. The example given in Fig. 3.9 is an exception to this rule. However, this scene graph can be easily converted to the standard form with the addition of a group node as shown in Fig. 3.10.

The equivalence of the scene graphs in Figs. 3.9 and 3.10 can be verified by obtaining the combined final transformation matrices applied to the leaf nodes. In a scene graph, transformations are combined using a recursive procedure starting at the root node, accumulating transformations at internal nodes and ending at object nodes. This process will be explained in detail in the next section.

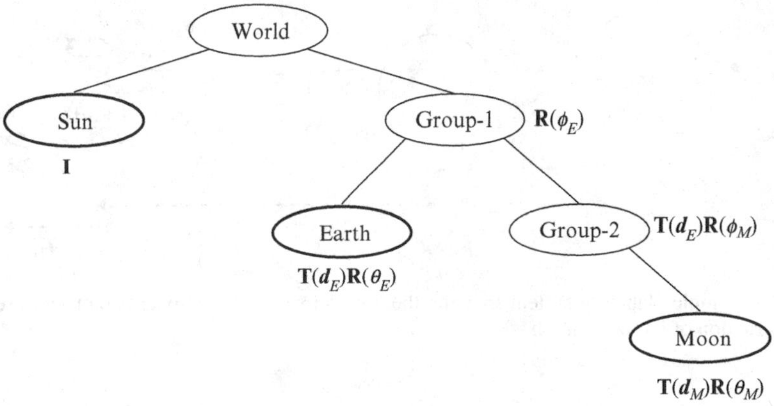

Fig. 3.10 The scene graph in Fig. 3.9 converted to the standard form

3.3 Relative Transformations

The transformation of one node relative to another can be readily obtained from a scene graph. The model transformation matrix of an object gives the composite transformation that converts points from the local coordinate space of the object to the world coordinate space. In a scene graph, this is the transformation of the object node relative to the root (the world node). The composite matrix can be obtained by collecting all matrices along the path from the root node to the leaf node representing the object. At each node, the matrix is post-multiplied by the transformation matrix of that node. The process is illustrated in Fig. 3.11, where node transformation matrices are denoted by letters **A**..**G**. The model transformation matrix of the object node in the figure is **ABCDE**.

Leaf nodes can also be used to represent fictitious objects such as light sources and camera. In Fig 3.11, the transformation from the coordinate system of the camera to world coordinates is given by **AFG**. The inverse of this matrix, $(\mathbf{AFG})^{-1}$, transforms a point from world space to camera space. This matrix is called the view matrix. The combined model-view matrix that transforms the object's local coordinates to camera space is therefore given by $(\mathbf{AFG})^{-1}\mathbf{ABCDE}$, or equivalently, $\mathbf{G}^{-1}\,\mathbf{F}^{-1}\mathbf{BCDE}$. An upward tree traversal from a leaf node to root can be quickly performed if every node has a pointer to its parent. On the other hand, a downward traversal would typically require a recursive algorithm similar to the depth-first search method.

The above example can be generalized to a procedure for finding the transformation from one object's local coordinate frame to another's. If we require the transformation from *Object-1* (source) to *Object-2* (target) in a scene graph, we have to first find the Lowest Common Ancestor (LCA) of both the object nodes. Let the transformation matrix of this common ancestor be denoted by **M** (Fig. 3.12). Let $\mathbf{S_1} \ldots \mathbf{S_m}$ denote the transformations of nodes starting from the child of LCA

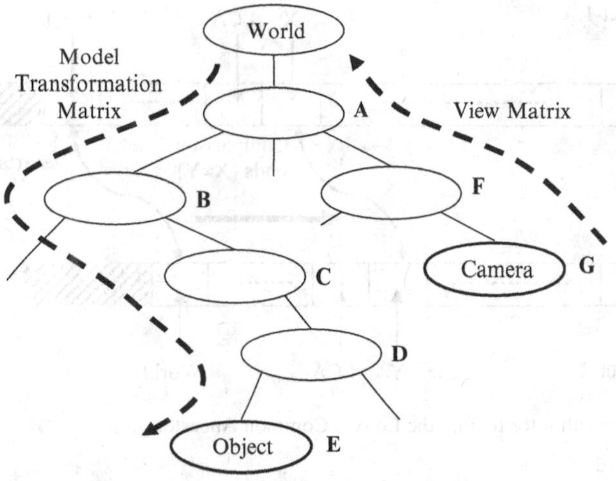

Fig. 3.11 Computation of the model transformation matrix of an object represented by a leaf node in a scene graph

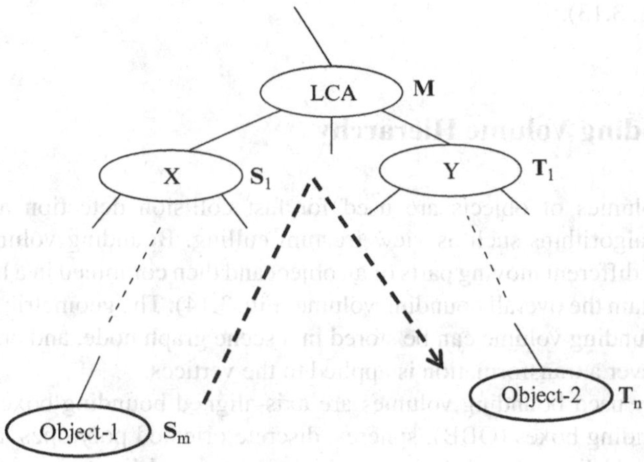

Fig. 3.12 Representing Object-1's coordinates relative to Object-2's local reference frame requires the computation of the Lowest Common Ancestor (LCA) of both the nodes

towards *Object-1*, and $\mathbf{T_1}..\mathbf{T_n}$ the transformations towards *Object-2* as shown in Fig. 3.12. The composite transformation from the source's frame to the target's frame is given by the matrix $\mathbf{T_n}^{-1}..\mathbf{T_1}^{-1}\mathbf{S_1}..\mathbf{S_m}$. Note that this matrix product does not involve the transformation **M** of the LCA or any of its ancestors.

There are several well-known algorithms to compute the Lowest Common Ancestor of two nodes in a tree. A simple method uses two lists of nodes visited in sequential upward traversals of the tree from the two nodes towards the root. The last item of both lists would be the world node. Corresponding entries in the

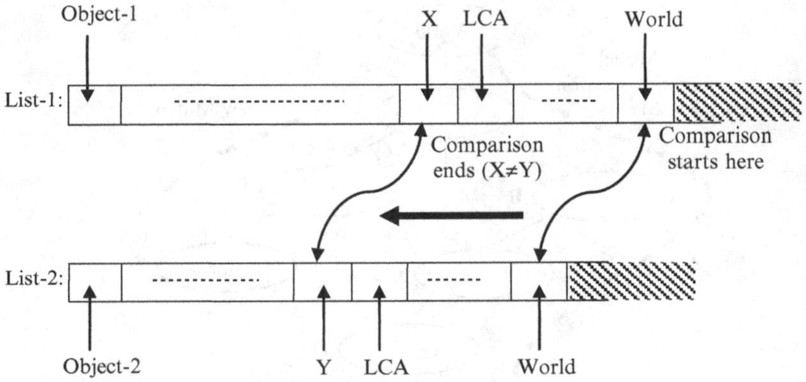

Fig. 3.13 An algorithm for finding the Lowest Common Ancestor

lists are compared for equality, starting from the last item towards the beginning of each list. The process of comparison stops when the list entries are different. The previous matched entry in the lists gives the reference to the Lowest Common Ancestor (Fig. 3.13).

3.4 Bounding Volume Hierarchy

Bounding volumes of objects are used for fast collision detection and also in acceleration algorithms such as view frustum culling. Bounding volumes can be computed for different moving parts of an object and then combined in a hierarchical manner to obtain the overall bounding volume (Fig. 3.14). The geometric parameters defining a bounding volume can be stored in a scene graph node, and computed on the fly whenever a transformation is applied to the vertices.

Commonly used bounding volumes are axis-aligned bounding boxes (AABB), oriented bounding boxes (OBB), spheres, discrete oriented polytopes, and convex hulls. Each bounding volume has certain advantages and limitations over others, and is suitable for a specific set of applications. An AABB can be computed and represented using six parameters that define the minimum and maximum values of x, y, and z coordinates of points it encloses. However, these parameters will have to be recomputed every time an object is rotated. On the other hand, OBBs and spheres are rotation invariant. In this chapter, examples are provided using AABBs and spheres only. Other types of bounding volumes and their computational aspects are discussed in detail in Chap. 9.

Since the bounding volume parameters depend on the transformed object coordinates, bounding volume updates can be performed only after applying the transformations. Unlike transformations, this process starts at the nodes containing object primitives, and the bounding volume parameters of group nodes are updated

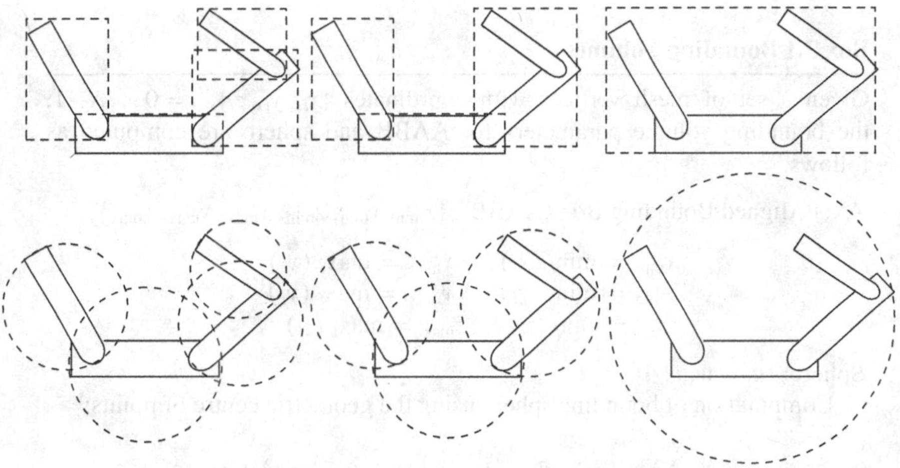

Fig. 3.14 Two-dimensional bounding volume hierarchies for the model in Fig. 3.2, using axis-aligned rectangles (*top row*) and circles (*bottom row*)

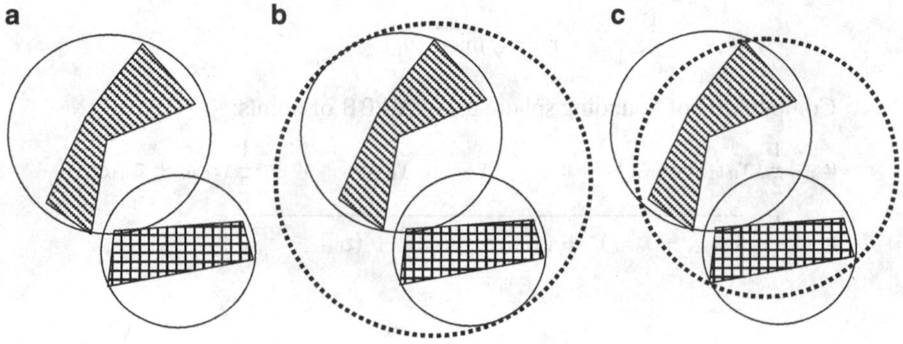

Fig. 3.15 (**a**) Bounding circles of two objects. (**b**) Combined bounding circle formed using the parameters of the two component bounding circles. (**c**) The minimal bounding circle

based on the computed values at the child nodes. It is therefore often desirable that the parameters defining a bounding volume stored at a group node can be computed based on the bounding volume parameters of its child nodes. It should also be noted here that such a computation may not always yield a minimal bounding volume. For example, the bounding sphere computed as the union of two bounding spheres may not necessarily be the minimal bounding sphere for the union of points within those spheres. A two-dimensional equivalent of this case is shown in Fig. 3.15, using bounding circles of two objects.

We discuss below the process of updating the bounding volume parameters (using AABBs and spheres as examples) at a group node based on the updated parameters of its child nodes. If there are n child nodes, we combine the volumes of

Box 3.1 Bounding Volumes

Given a set of mesh vertices with coordinates $\{x_i, y_i, z_i\}$, $i=0\ldots N-1$, the bounding volume parameters for AABB and sphere are computed as follows:

Axis Aligned Bounding Box (AABB): $\{x_{\min}, y_{\min}, z_{\min}, x_{\max}, y_{\max}, z_{\max}\}$

$$\begin{aligned} x_{\min} &= \min_i (x_i), & x_{\max} &= \max_i (x_i) \\ y_{\min} &= \min_i (y_i), & y_{\max} &= \max_i (y_i) \\ z_{\min} &= \min_i (z_i), & z_{\max} &= \max_i (z_i) \end{aligned}$$

Sphere: $\{u, v, w, r\}$
Computation of bounding sphere using the geometric centre of points:

$$u =, \tfrac{1}{N}\sum_{i=0}^{N-1} x_i, \qquad d_i = (x_i - u)^2 + (y_i - v)^2 + (z_i - w)^2,$$
$$i = 0 \ldots N-1.$$
$$v = \tfrac{1}{N}\sum_{i=0}^{N-1} y_i,$$
$$w = \tfrac{1}{N}\sum_{i=0}^{N-1} z_i, \qquad r = \sqrt{\max_i (d_i)}$$

Computation of bounding sphere using AABB of points:

$$u = \frac{1}{2}(x_{\min} + x_{\max}), \quad v = \frac{1}{2}(y_{\min} + y_{\max}), \quad w = \frac{1}{2}(z_{\min} + z_{\max})$$

$$r = \frac{1}{2}\sqrt{(x_{\max} - x_{\min})^2 + (y_{\max} - y_{\min})^2 + (z_{\max} - z_{\min})^2}$$

two children at a time and obtain the final bounding volume of the parent, in $n-1$ steps. Given two AABBs with parameters $\{x_{\min 1}, y_{\min 1}, z_{\min 1}, x_{\max 1}, y_{\max 1}, z_{\max 1}\}$ and $\{x_{\min 2}, y_{\min 2}, z_{\min 2}, x_{\max 2}, y_{\max 2}, z_{\max 2}\}$, the combined volume has parameters $\{\min(x_{\min 1}, x_{\min 2}), \min(y_{\min 1}, y_{\min 2}), \min(z_{\min 1}, z_{\min 2}), \max(x_{\max 1}, x_{\max 2}), \max(y_{\max 1}, y_{\max 2}), \max(z_{\max 1}, z_{\max 2})\}$ (Box 3.1).

In the case of spheres, let the parameters of the two volumes be given by $\{u_1, v_1, w_1, r_1\}$ and $\{u_2, v_2, w_2, r_2\}$. The required parameters of the combined sphere are denoted as $\{u_c, v_c, w_c, r_c\}$. First we compute the distance between the centres:

$$d = \sqrt{(u_2 - u_1)^2 + (v_2 - v_1)^2 + (w_2 - w_1)^2} \tag{3.2}$$

If $d \le |r_1 - r_2|$, then one of the spheres is inside the other. The combined sphere in this case is the same as the larger among the two spheres. If $d > |r_1 - r_2|$, the spheres either overlap or are disjoint. For this configuration, we compute the radius and the centre of the combined sphere as follows:

$$
\begin{aligned}
r_c &= \frac{1}{2}(d + r_1 + r_2) \\
u_c &= u_1 + \frac{1}{2d}(d - r_1 + r_2)(u_2 - u_1) \\
v_c &= v_1 + \frac{1}{2d}(d - r_1 + r_2)(v_2 - v_1) \\
w_c &= w_1 + \frac{1}{2d}(d - r_1 + r_2)(w_2 - w_1)
\end{aligned}
\tag{3.3}
$$

A detailed description of different types of bounding volumes, their computation and intersection tests is given later in Sect. 9.1.

3.5 Sample Implementation

In this section, we will discuss the design of a set of classes that implement the functionality of a scene graph with transformation matrices attached to its nodes. Internal nodes that can store a list of children, and also a transformation matrix, are represented by the class `GroupNode`. All transformation matrices are assumed to have the general form given by $\mathbf{T}(\mathbf{v})\mathbf{R}(\theta)$. The properties of leaf nodes are specified by three classes: `ObjectNode` that can represent a three-dimensional object, `CameraNode` that represents the camera, and `LightNode` that represents a light source. These three classes are derived from `GroupNode` so that we can store all child nodes (including group nodes and object nodes) with the same type, and also use polymorphic functions to implement tree traversal algorithms.

3.5.1 Group Node

The declarations of attributes and functions of `GroupNode` can be found in Listing 3.1 below. The primary functions associated with a group node include adding and removing children, and setting the transformation parameters. We use the `List` container of the Standard Template Library (STL) for storing references to the child nodes. The data members `_angleX`, `_angleY`, `_angleZ` specify the Euler angles of rotation about the principal axes of the group's coordinate frame. Similarly `_tx`, `_ty`, `_tz` denote the components of the translation vector along the principal axes directions. Together, these attributes define the composite transformation for the group node in the form $\mathbf{T}(\mathbf{v})\ \mathbf{R}_z(\psi_z)\ \mathbf{R}_y(\psi_y)\mathbf{R}_x(\psi_x)$, where $\mathbf{v}$ is the translation vector, and ψs denote Euler angles. The function `render()` is called on the root node to render the scene.

Listing 3.1 Class definition for a group node

```
#include <list>
using namespace std;

class GroupNode
{
private:
    list<GroupNode*> _children;
protected:
    GroupNode* _parent;
    float _tx, _ty, _tz, _angleX, _angleY, _angleZ;
    virtual void draw();
public:
    GroupNode()
        : _parent(NULL),
          _tx(0.0), _ty(0.0), _tz(0.0),
          _angleX(0.0), _angleY(0.0), _angleZ(0.0) {}
    virtual ~GroupNode() {}
    void addChild(GroupNode* node);
    void removeChild(GroupNode* node);
    void translate(float tx, float ty, float tz);
    void rotateX(float angle);
    void rotateY(float angle);
    void rotateZ(float angle);
    void inverseTransform()const;
    void render();
    GroupNode* getParent() const;
    int getChildCount() const;
};
```

3.5.2 Object Node

The class definition for an object node must cater to the requirements of defining and storing three-dimensional object models. Listing 3.2 gives the declarations of important attributes and functions of the class. To simplify the implementation, we use only the built-in objects provided by the GL Utility Toolkit (GLUT) of the OpenGL API. These objects are assigned numbers using the enumerated type `ObjType`. When an object is initially defined using the `setObject()` function, it may also be optionally scaled using parameters `_scaleX`, `_scaleY` and `_scaleZ`. These parameters are used to set the values of the corresponding data members of the class. An object may also be given a material colour using the function `setColor()`. A scene is rendered by calling the function `render()` of the `GroupNode` class on an instance that represents the scene graph's root. This function in turn calls the polymorphic function `draw()` which is declared as `virtual` in `GroupNode`. The implementation of the function in `ObjectNode` will call the necessary OpenGL functions to apply the transformations and to draw the object.

Listing 3.2 Class definition for an object node

```
class ObjectNode : public GroupNode
{
public:
    enum ObjType
        { CUBE, SPHERE, TORUS, TEAPOT, CONE, TETRAHEDRON };
    ObjectNode()
        : GroupNode(),
          _object(CUBE),
          _scaleX(1.0f), _scaleY(1.0f), _scaleZ(1.0f),
          _colorR(1.0f), _colorG(1.0f), _colorB(1.0f)
        {}
    ~ObjectNode() {}
    void setObject (ObjType object,
              float scaleX, float scaleY, float scaleZ);
    void setColor(float colorR, float colorG, float colorB);
private:
    ObjType _object;
    float _scaleX, _scaleY, _scaleZ;
    float _colorR, _colorG, _colorB;
    void draw();
};
```

3.5.3 Camera Node

Any three-dimensional scene is assumed to have an active camera that contains information about the projective transformation used while rendering the scene. The camera also provides the view matrix needed for the transformation of vertices to the eye coordinate space. A camera can be added to a scene graph as a special type of object node. Listing 3.3 gives the class definition for the camera node. Since only one instance of the camera is used in a scene at any point in time, the class `cameraNode` is defined as a singleton class. It has a private constructor, and the static instance is made available to a program using the function `getInstance()`. The frustum parameters are specified by an application by calling the function `perspective()`. The function `projection()` uses these parameters to set up the projection matrix, and is called by `render()` of the GroupNode class. The view transformation matrix is constructed by the function `viewTransform()` by traversing the tree along the path from the camera node to the root node (Fig. 3.11). The class does not store any drawable object, and therefore `draw()` has an empty function body.

3.5.4 Light Node

The `LightNode` class as defined in Listing 3.4 has a simple structure containing no public functions other than the constructor. The constructor accepts a single integer between 0 and 7 as the argument which directly represents one of the OpenGL light

Listing 3.3 Class definition for a camera node

```
class CameraNode : public GroupNode
{
private:
     float _fov, _aspect, _near, _far;
     static bool flag;
     void draw() {};
     CameraNode()
          : GroupNode(),
            _fov(60.0f), _aspect(1.0f),
            _near(1.0f), _far(1000.0f)
           {}
    CameraNode(const CameraNode&);
    CameraNode& operator = (const CameraNode&);
    static CameraNode* camera;
public:
    static CameraNode* getInstance();
     void perspective
          (float fov, float aspect, float near, float far);
     void projection()const;
     void viewTransform()const;
     ~CameraNode() { flag = false; }
};
```

Listing 3.4 Class definition for a light node

```
class LightNode : public GroupNode
{
private:
     int _glLight;
     void draw();
public:
     LightNode(int glLight)
          : GroupNode(),
           _glLight(glLight)
          {}
     ~LightNode() {}
};
```

sources GL_LIGHT0, ..., GL_LIGHT7. In OpenGL, light sources are transformed like any other point. The function draw() defines the initial position of the light source at (0,0,0), and transforms it exactly like its counterpart in ObjectNode. The class does not store or set any other light or material properties. They can be set by the application by directly calling the appropriate OpenGL functions. The same applies to setting OpenGL states such as enabling lighting, selecting two sided lighting, enabling colour material, and so on.

The sample implementation of a scene graph discussed above concatenates only transformation matrices along different paths from the root node to the leaf nodes. The hierarchical structure of a scene graph allows several other attributes to be propagated from an internal node to object nodes through various branches. One such attribute is the visibility of a node. If a node's visibility attribute is set to false, then the visibility attribute of every node in that sub-tree can also be implicitly set to false by using a logical AND operation with the values from the parent nodes. Thus an object node will not be rendered if any of its ancestors has a visibility attribute set to false. A similar attribute that can be attached to the nodes is transparency. The transparency values can be multiplied together along every path from the root node, to determine the net transparency of objects stored in the leaf nodes.

3.6 First-Person View

The design of the camera node as outlined in the previous section permits a highly flexible implementation of a scene graph, since the only static instance of the class can be obtained anywhere by calling the `getInstance()` function. The camera node need not even be a part of the scene graph, if the camera is meant to be in a fixed location with respect to the scene. In this case, the transformations defined for the camera node specify the position and the orientation of the camera with respect to the origin of the world coordinate frame. These transformations will be directly used to obtain the view matrix for the whole scene.

Often you will require the first-person view of a scene with the camera placed on a moving object. For the articulated character model in Fig. 3.7, the first-person view is provided when the camera is attached to the head. This is done by first applying transformations to the camera node so that it points to the right direction in the coordinate frame of the object node to which it should be attached. In the scene graph, the object node is replaced by a new group node. Both the camera node and the object node are attached to the new group node as its children. Figure 3.16 shows the reference frame (x_e, y_e, z_e) of the camera and the coordinate frame (x, y, z) of the head of the character model. The camera initially points towards $-z_e$ direction. It is rotated about the y-axis by 180° to point towards the head direction. This transformation is represented by the matrix $\mathbf{R}(\phi)$. Figure 3.16 also shows the modified portion of the scene graph in Fig. 3.7 with the addition of a new group node and the camera node.

Now consider the 5-link joint chain shown in Fig. 3.3. Robotic arms such as this can be found in autonomous systems for inspection, welding and painting. The arm is driven by feeding joint angles to the controllers. Some constraints may be applied to the joint angles based on the application requirements. For example, a robotic arm for welding or painting may require the end effector (denoted by Link-5 in Fig. 3.3) to be kept in a horizontal position. It may also be required to have a camera attached to the end effector to obtain a clear perspective of the surrounding scene from its viewpoint. The graphical rendering of the scene as viewed from the position of Link-5 can be obtained by adding the camera node to the group node *Group-4* as shown in Fig. 3.17.

From the previous examples, we have seen that the first step in the process of attaching a camera to an object node is to determine the transformation $\mathbf{R}(\phi)$ necessary to appropriately orient the camera in the local coordinate frame of the object. In the example in Fig. 3.17, this composite transformation comprises of two

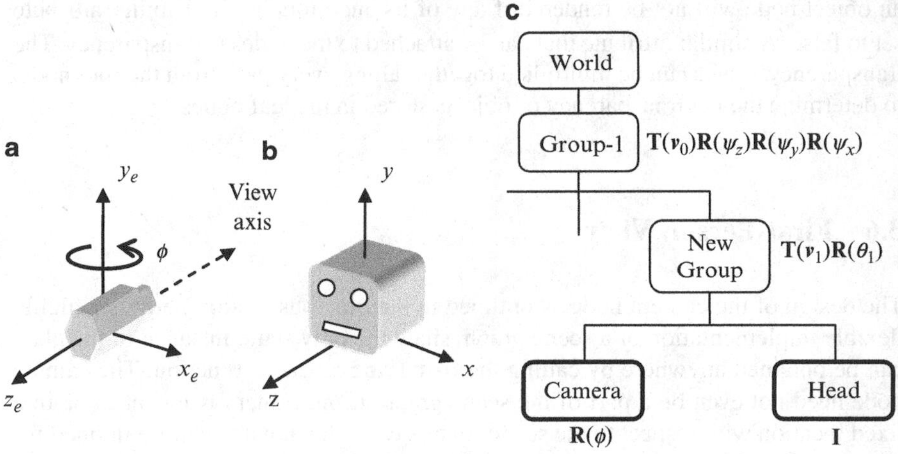

Fig. 3.16 **(a)** Camera coordinate system. **(b)** A 3D object "Head" in its local coordinate frame. **(c)** The modified portion of the scene graph in Fig. 3.7, with the camera node attached

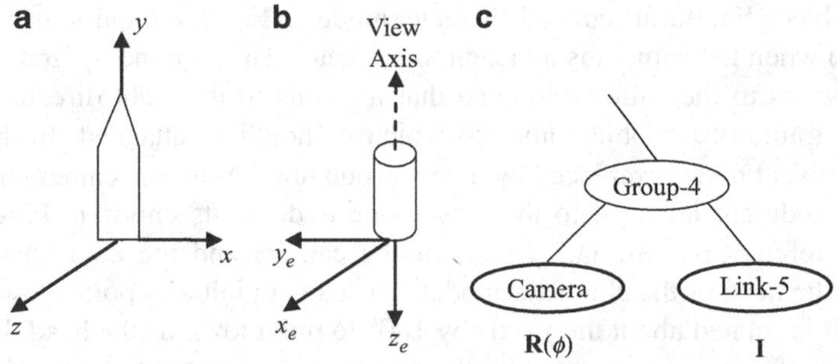

Fig. 3.17 **(a)** Local coordinate frame of a link of the joint chain in Fig. 3.3. **(b)** The desired orientation of the camera frame relative to the frame of the link. **(c)** Addition of the camera node to the scene graph in Fig. 3.3

rotations: a rotation of 90° about the x-axis followed by another rotation of −90° about the y-axis. The transformation functions given in Listing 3.1 allow us to define such rotations. It is also important to note that when a new group node is formed with the camera node and the object node as its children, transformations that were previously applied to the object node should now be applied to the camera as well. Therefore, the transformation matrix that was attached to the object node must now be transferred to the common group node. This would often leave the object node with the identity matrix as shown in Fig. 3.17.

3.7 Summary

Scene graphs are powerful data structures that can be used for hierarchical representations of transformations, bounding volumes and other visual attributes of groups of objects in a scene. This chapter showed the application of scene graphs in defining the transformations of interconnected systems. Robotic manipulator arms and articulated character models are examples of such systems containing one or more joint chains. Using a scene graph, the relative transformation of one object with respect to another can be easily computed. Relative transformations are useful for displaying billboards and first person views. This chapter also introduced the definition of a scene graph in the standard form. An object oriented framework for a scene graph was presented and some of the key implementation aspects were discussed.

The next chapter will show that scene graphs play an important role in skeletal animation. Skeletal structures and the associated hierarchical transformations used in vertex skinning algorithms fit perfectly well with the scene graph model.

3.8 Supplementary Material for Chap. 3

The folder `Chapter3/Code` on the companion website contains code examples demonstrating the application of the scene graph class in the modelling and rendering of simple three-dimensional scenes. A brief description of these programs is given below.

1. **GroupNode.cpp**

Additional files:
`GroupNode.h`

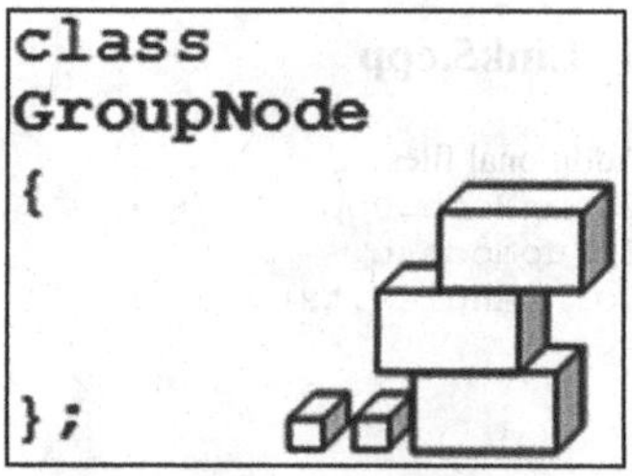

These are the header and implementation files for a scene graph class as discussed in Sect. 3.5. The documentation of methods in this class can be found in Appendix B.

2. **Scene3D.cpp**

Additional files:
`GroupNode.cpp`
`GroupNode.h`

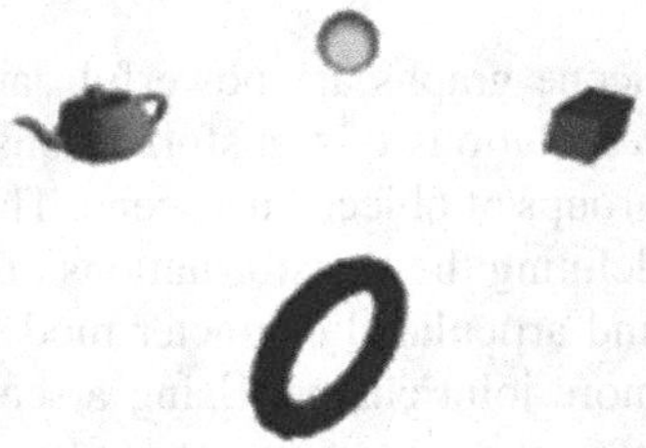

This program uses a scene graph to model a scene consisting of four different stationary objects and demonstrates the use of the classes discussed in Sect. 3.5. The scene graph has a simple structure consisting of the *World* node and four object nodes. The camera node is not attached to the scene graph and is independently transformed to simulate camera motion along a circular path around the group of objects. The light source is kept fixed in the middle of the scene, at its default position (0, 0, 0).

3. **Planet.cpp**

Additional files:
`GroupNode.cpp`
`GroupNode.h`

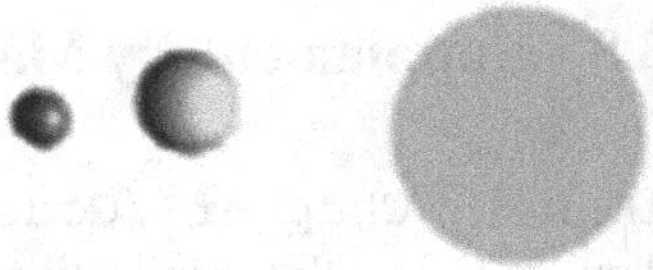

This program uses the scene graph in Fig. 3.10, to model the planetary system in Fig. 3.8. The angles of revolution of the Moon around the Earth, and the joint Earth-Moon system around the Sun are continuously updated to generate an animation sequence. The light source is kept fixed at the location of the Sun.

4. **Link5.cpp**

Additional files:
`GroupNode.cpp`
`GroupNode.h`
`JointAngles.txt`

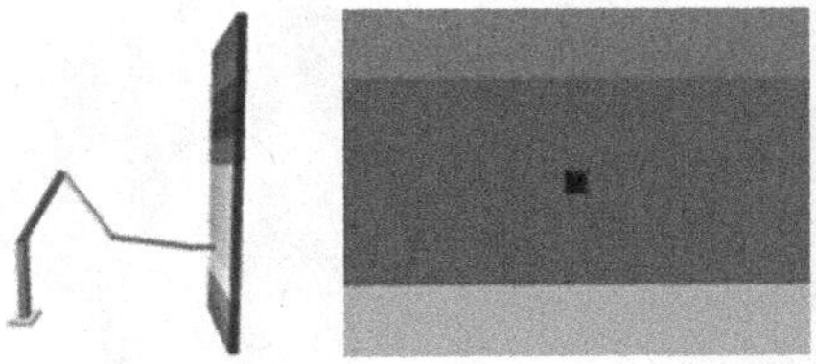

This program uses the scene graph model given in Fig. 3.3, to construct an animated 5-link robotic arm. The joint angles are read in from the file `JointAngles.txt`. The arm moves continuously up and down in front of a vertical coloured wall. The joint angles are defined such that the end effector of the arm is always horizontal. Pressing 'c' on the keyboard causes the scene graph to be modified as in Fig. 3.17 to produce the effect of the camera being placed on the end effector. This gives a close-up view of the coloured wall from the perspective of the continuously moving end effector.

5. **GlutMan.cpp**

Additional files:
GroupNode.cpp
GroupNode.h
WalkCycle.txt

The program GlutMan demonstrates the use of a scene graph in modelling and animating an articulated character model. A scene graph similar to the one given in Fig. 3.7 is used. The values of eight joint angles defining a simple walk sequence are read from the input file WalkCycle.txt and interpolated to generate a continuous animation sequence.

3.9 Bibliographical Notes

An excellent introduction to scene graphs and other tools for scene management can be found in Sherrod (2007). The book also deals with the design of data structures and algorithms for similar applications. Angel (2008), McConnell (2006) and McReynolds and Blythe (2005) give an overview of hierarchical modelling techniques and applications using scene graphs. Eberly (2007) contains a chapter on hierarchical scene representations, and provides a detailed description of scene graph operations designed for merging a set of bounding volumes.

Support for scene graphs including sophisticated high-level functionalities can be found in graphics APIs. Java-3D provides powerful classes for constructing the nodes of a scene graph that can be used for rendering scenes. Many examples of applications in Java can be found in Davison (2005). The M3G API of Java Micro Edition also contains a versatile collection of methods useful for retained-mode rendering based on scene graphs. These methods incorporate high-level functions for generating key-frame animations on mobile devices. Pulli (2008) provides an excellent coverage of the M3G API and shows the importance of scene graphs in the design of animation sequences.

OpenSceneGraph is a versatile high-level 3D graphics toolkit useful for the development of high-end graphics applications based on a full-fledged and powerful scene graph implementation. More information can be found on the website, http://www.openscenegraph.org.

References

Angel, E. (2008). *Interactive computer graphics: A top-down approach using OpenGL* (5th ed.). Boston/London: Pearson Addison-Wesley.

Davison, A. (2005). *Killer game programming in Java*. Beijing/Farnham: O'Reilly.

Eberly, D. H. (2007). *3D game engine design: A practical approach to real-time computer graphics* (2nd ed.). Amsterdam/London: Morgan Kaufmann.

McConnell, J. J. (2006). *Computer graphics: Theory into practice*. Boston/London: Jones and Bartlett Publishers.

McReynolds, T., & Blythe, D. (2005). *Advanced graphics programming using OpenGL*. Amsterdam/London: Morgan Kaufmann Publishers.

Pulli, K. (2008). *Mobile 3D graphics: With OpenGL ES and M3G*. Amsterdam/London: Elsevier/Morgan Kaufmann Publishers.

Sherrod, A. (2007). *Data structures and algorithms for game developers* (1st ed.). Hingham/Charles River Media/London: Thomson Learning [distributor].

Chapter 4
Skeletal Animation

Overview

This chapter discusses concepts such as vertex blending, vertex skinning and keyframing that are fundamental to the animation of articulated character models. Vertex blending is the process of constructing blending surfaces between two different parts that move relative to each other, in order to create the appearance of a single deformable object. Vertex blending is useful in the animation of character models constructed by joining together several individual components.

Mesh models of animatable characters are often subdivided into groups of vertices that represent moveable body parts. A skeleton is an abstract representation of this form of partitioning of a mesh. Skeletal animation refers to the process of computing the transformations of each segment in the skeleton using joint angles, and mapping them on to mesh vertices. The chapter discusses various stages in skeletal animation, describes the transformations applied to a mesh, and also outlines a scene graph based implementation.

4.1 Articulated Character Models

Animated character models can be found in numerous applications of computer graphics, ranging from simple computer games to virtual agents and computer generated feature films. Depending on the application requirements, the character mesh and the animation sequence can have varying levels of complexity. Sophisticated virtual character agents incorporate several forms of articulation including facial expression animation. In this chapter we will look at the basics of human character animation with simple polygonal models and a small number of joint angles.

We broadly classify character models into two groups: (i) character models constructed using several objects or "parts" where each object is independently transformed and moved into its respective position within the model, and (ii) single mesh models that are animated by attaching vertices to different transformation

R. Mukundan, *Advanced Methods in Computer Graphics: With examples in OpenGL*, DOI 10.1007/978-1-4471-2340-8_4, © Springer-Verlag London Limited 2012

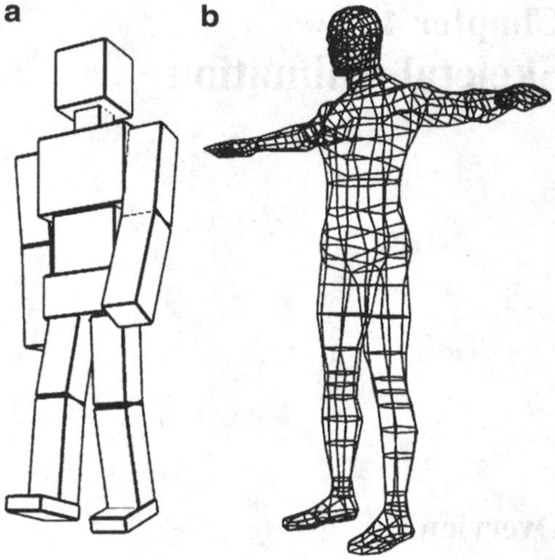

Fig. 4.1 Character models constructed using (**a**) several component objects, and (**b**) a single mesh

groups. An example of each type is shown in Fig. 4.1. The first model, the "Glut Man", is constructed entirely using scaled and transformed versions of cubes generated using `glutSolidCube()` or `glutWireCube()`, hence the name. The second belongs to the more commonly found class of mesh models.

In the case of the model constructed using individual parts, each component is first created in its own local coordinate space. A series of transformations is then applied to it based on where in a joint chain that component appears. This process, which is very similar to what we saw in the previous chapter (Fig. 3.5), is repeated for every part of the model to reshape the character in a required pose. The transformations often have a well-defined hierarchical structure as discussed in the context of scene graphs. Figure 3.7 shows how the main body parts of a simple humanoid model are transformed.

A character model defined using a single mesh surface as in Fig. 4.1b requires a completely different set of coordinate transformations, as all mesh vertices are specified in a common reference system. However, we should be able to use the same set of joint angles to animate this model also, producing a similar effect such as a walk cycle. We can indeed construct a "virtual" skeleton consisting of joints and links that has a structure similar to our previous model in Fig. 4.1a. We can then associate the skeleton with the continuous mesh. This association is done by attaching a set of vertices belonging to each body part (e.g., forearm) to the corresponding link of the skeleton. The scene graph based transformations computed using joint angles can now be directly applied to the skeleton. The mesh vertices are transformed using a simple method introduced in Sect. 4.4.2.

If a model is made up of several parts as in Fig. 4.1a, where parts move or rotate relative to their neighbours, gaps can appear at joints when the model is animated. The next section addresses this problem, and introduces the method of vertex blending for creating deformable surface patches between parts that move relative to each other.

4.2 Vertex Blending

When two different mesh objects attached to a common pivot rotate by different angles, certain parts of the surfaces can interpenetrate, and gaps can appear on the opposite side (Fig. 4.2a). Repairing or "re-meshing" an area where two surfaces interpenetrate is a difficult task. Moveable surfaces are therefore often separated by a small distance from each other, so that they do not touch for the allowable range of movement or rotation angles (Fig. 4.2b). A sphere is sometimes placed at rotary joints, as in Fig. 4.2c, to fill the gap. While this approach is suitable for robot-like models, interpolation methods could be used for obtaining a better approximation of blending surfaces between moving parts. The process of creating such in-between surfaces is called vertex blending.

Corresponding pairs of points on two moving parts can be joined together to form a triangular or quadrilateral element belonging to the intermediate surface. These elements could be further subdivided using a simple linear interpolation formula (Eq. 2.43) to get a tessellated surface (Fig. 4.3a). We discuss below higher order interpolation methods for generating blending surfaces (Fig. 4.3b).

In Chap. 2 (Sect. 2.7) we saw examples of second and higher degree interpolation functions with Bernstein polynomials as basis. We can use cubic Bezier polynomials to generate interpolating curves between moving parts with tangential continuity at end points. In Fig. 4.4a, P_0 and P_3 denote a pair of corresponding points on two moving parts of a character model. Q_0 and Q_3 are two points on the surfaces that are selected to define the local tangent directions P_0-Q_0 and P_3-Q_3 respectively. Using these tangent directions, we can specify two more points, P_1 and P_2, as

$$
\begin{aligned}
P_1 &= P_0 + \alpha(P_0 - Q_0) \\
P_2 &= P_3 + \alpha(P_3 - Q_3)
\end{aligned} \tag{4.1}
$$

where α is a positive quantity used to increase or decrease the length of the tangent vectors $P_1 - P_0$ and $P_2 - P_3$. Points on the interpolating Bezier curve are generated

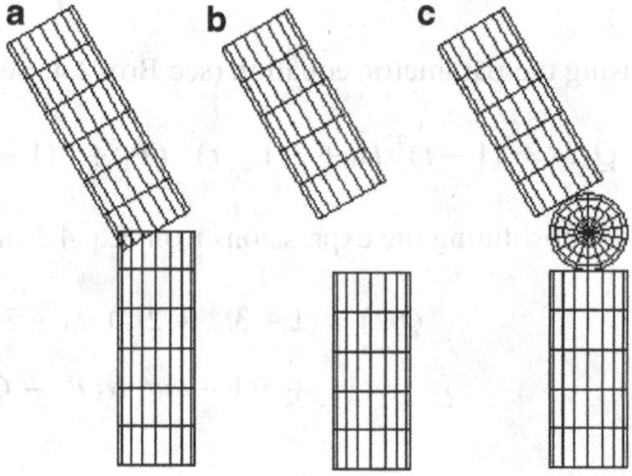

Fig. 4.2 (**a**) Moving parts of an animated model can interpenetrate and form gaps at joints. (**b**) Links can be separated by a short distance to avoid surface intersections. (**c**) A sphere is sometimes attached to a rotary joint to fill the gap between two moving parts

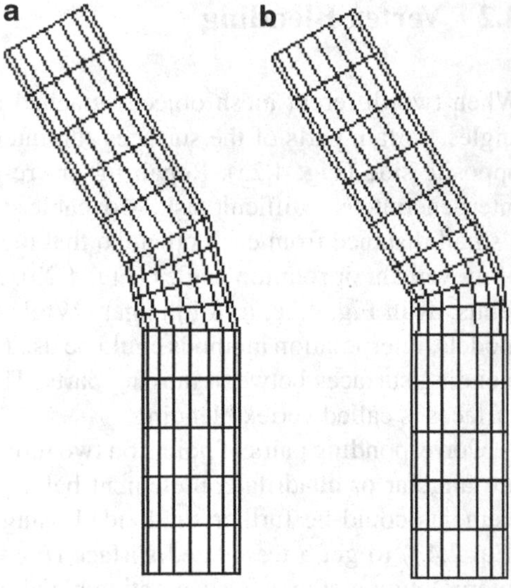

Fig. 4.3 Generation of blending surfaces using (**a**) linear interpolation and (**b**) Hermite interpolation

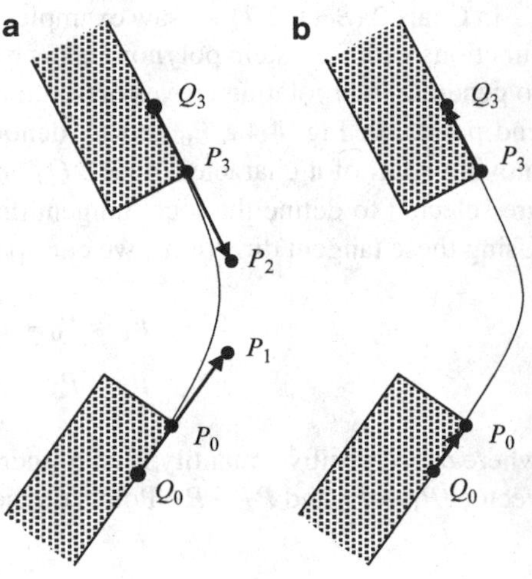

Fig. 4.4 Generation of a blending surface using (**a**) Bezier interpolation and (**b**) Hermite interpolation

using the parametric equation (see Box 2.4, Sect. 2.7)

$$Q(t) = (1-t)^3 P_0 + 3(1-t)^2\, t P_1 + 3(1-t)t^2 P_2 + t^3 P_3, \quad 0 \le t \le 1. \tag{4.2}$$

Substituting the expressions from Eq. 4.1 in the above equation gives

$$\begin{aligned} Q(t) =&(1-3t^2+2t^3)\, P_0 + 3(1-t)^2 t\, \alpha(P_0 - Q_0) \\ &+ 3(1-t)t^2\, \alpha(P_3 - Q_3) + (3t^2 - 2t^3)\, P_3 \end{aligned} \tag{4.3}$$

When α is increased, the weight of the tangent vectors on the interpolating curve is increased, and the curve gets closer to the tangents at the end points P_0, P_3. Care should be taken to ensure that the points P_0, P_1 both lie on the same side of the tangent $P_2 - P_3$, and similarly points P_2, P_3 lie on the same side of the tangent $P_1 - P_0$. Setting a large value of α violates this condition, resulting in a distorted Bezier curve.

A second interpolation method that is suitable for vertex blending is Hermite interpolation. Here, the tangent directions are defined using vectors $P_0 - Q_0$ and $Q_3 - P_3$ (Fig. 4.4b), and the interpolating curve is given by

$$\begin{aligned} H(t) =& (1 - 3t^2 + 2t^3) P_0 + (t - 2t^2 + t^3)\, \alpha (P_0 - Q_0) \\ &+ (-t^2 + t^3) \alpha (Q_3 - P_3) + (3t^2 - 2t^3) P_3 \end{aligned} \tag{4.4}$$

The coefficients of P_0, P_3 are exactly same as that of Bezier interpolation. Since tangents are defined along the direction of the curve from P_0 to P_3, Hermite interpolation does not have problems associated with large α values. Hermite and other types of approximating splines are discussed in more detail in Chap. 7.

4.3 Skeleton and Skin

Animating a three-dimensional character model (Fig. 4.1b) containing hundreds of vertices and polygons can be a challenging task. This task can be simplified to a great extent by grouping together a number of mesh vertices as forming body parts that move as a single unit, connected together by a set of joints. A human model may be modelled as a collection of body parts with joints at neck, shoulders, elbows, wrists, hips, knees, and ankles. The grouping of mesh primitives into body parts and the definition of joints depend on the complexity of the animation. In a simple walk sequence, for instance, the arms and legs could be considered as the only parts that move relative to the main body. For a more complex animation, one might require movement of the head, hands, fingers, facial muscle regions, and so on. Figure 4.5a shows how points in a mesh could be grouped into ten body parts: head (HEA), torso (TOR), left upper arm (LUA), left lower arm (LLA), right upper arm (RUA), right lower arm (RLA), left upper leg (LUL), lower left leg (LLL), right upper leg (RUL), and right lower leg (RLL). Every group can then have an abstract representation called a bone. The complete set of bones, along with their connectivity information, is called a skeleton (Fig. 4.5b).

The notion of a skeleton consisting of a set of joint chains comprised of bones is central to articulated character animation. A skeleton can be easily animated; i.e., the transformations for the bones can be easily determined given the angles at each joint. The skeleton has the hierarchical structure similar to that of the model in Fig. 4.1a, the main difference being that in a skeleton, each component or bone is just an

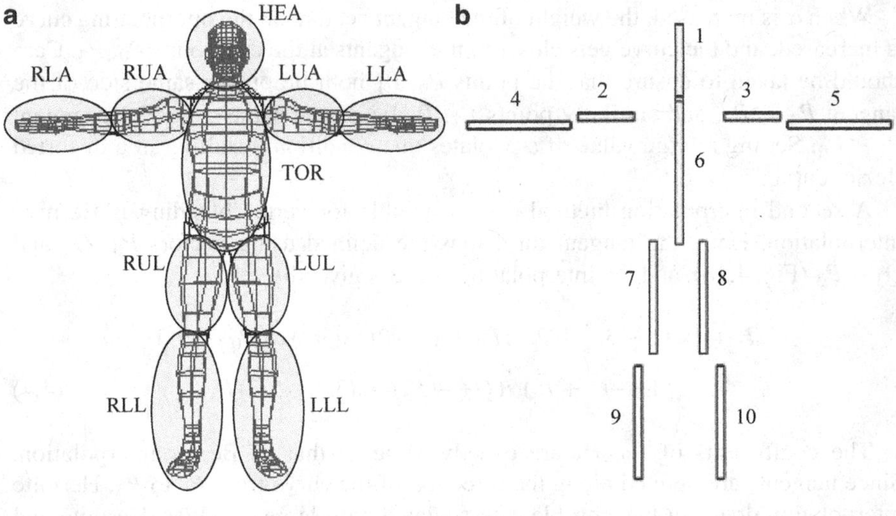

Fig. 4.5 (**a**) Vertices in a mesh model are grouped together into parts that move relative to each other. (**b**) A skeleton definition formed based on a vertex grouping

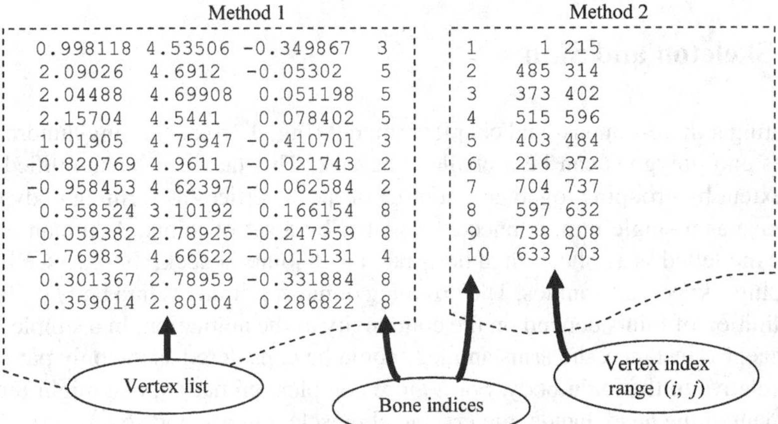

Fig. 4.6 Two simple ways of associating vertices with bones of a skeleton

abstract structure, not a graphics primitive. A bone essentially stores information about its position and orientation relative to its parent in the skeleton.

Every bone is given a unique index as shown in Fig. 4.5b. Vertices belonging to a group are associated with a bone using the bone's index. The part of a mesh represented by a bone is called its skin. In the example given in Fig. 4.5, the skin of bone "8" is the mesh segment that belongs to the set LUL. Two simple ways of associating groups of vertices with bones are shown in Fig. 4.6. In the first method, every entry in the vertex list is appended with a bone index. This method is suitable when vertices need to be associated with more than one bone (we will discuss this process later in Sect. 4.6). If several consecutive entries in the vertex list have the same bone index, then the second method is preferred where the minimum and maximum indices of a range of vertices are stored against a bone index.

4.4 Vertex Skinning

In order to define the hierarchical nature of a skeleton, the parent–child relationship between every two connected bones must be shown. We could represent a bone using a point with arrow(s) pointing to its child node(s), as in Figs. 4.7a, c. Another common representation of a bone uses triangles. Fig. 4.7b shows the mesh model of a human arm, and the associated skeleton consisting of a set of bones. Each bone stores the index of its parent and the bone's position relative to its parent. Using this information, a complete hierarchical structure can be built, as shown in Fig. 4.7c. There are two special nodes in this skeleton tree. The root node always represents the origin of the world coordinate system, and has an index 0. The base node is that bone in the skeleton which has root as its parent. The position and the orientation of the base define the pose of the skeleton in the world coordinate space.

Bones are not physical structures present in a polygonal mesh, but are only animation tools or controlling mechanisms used to transform the mesh in a realistic manner. A bone also loosely represents the region of influence of a transformation.

4.4.1 The Bind Pose

The hierarchical organization of bones in a skeleton allows the geometric transformation for each bone to be defined with respect to its parent. The transformations

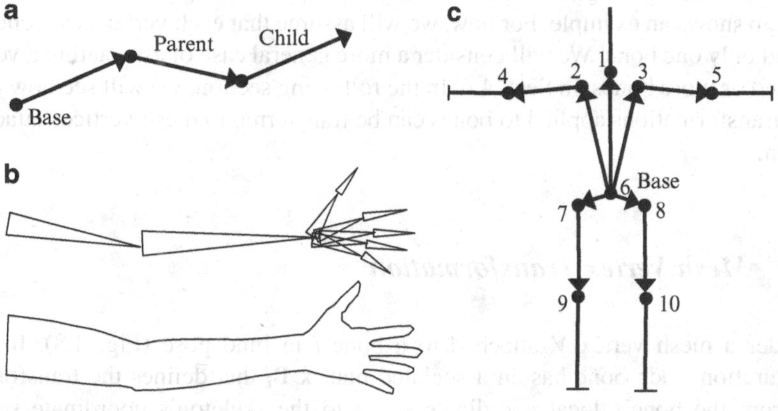

Fig. 4.7 **(a)** A simple joint chain. **(b)** A skeletal structure for the arm, hand and fingers. **(c)** Modified version of the skeleton in Fig. 4.5b

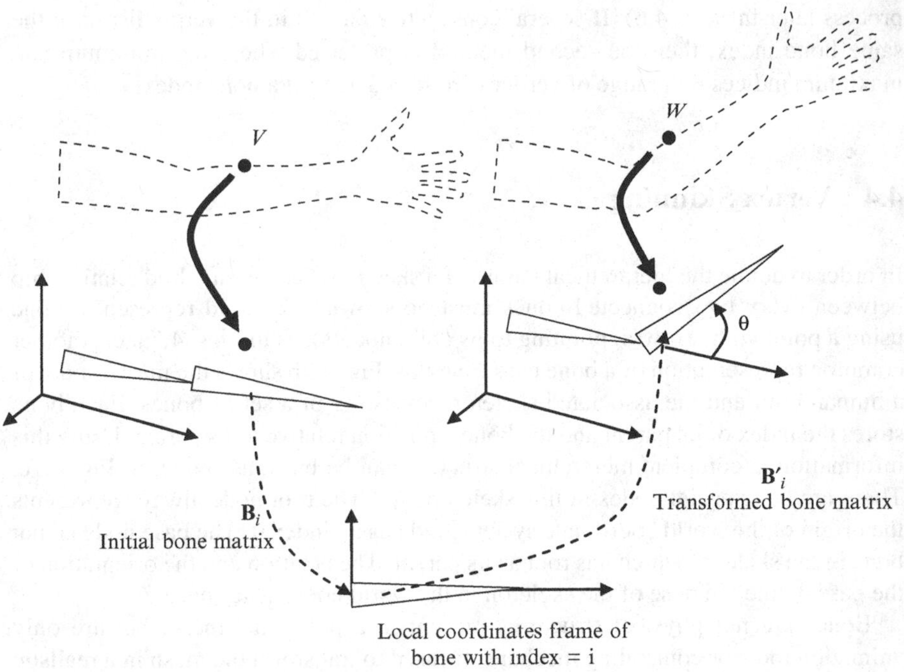

Fig. 4.8 Transformation of a mesh vertex V using the transformations of its bone

that are associated with a bone are normally a joint angle rotation followed by a translation from its parent bone. The translations of the bones, each relative to its parent, together define the initial configuration of a skeleton. For this configuration, the joint angles are set to 0. The corresponding mesh is said to be in the bind pose (Fig. 4.5a). The placement of bones in the skeleton can be obtained by first computing the axis-aligned bounding boxes (see Box 3.1 of Chap. 3) of vertex groups (defined as in Fig. 4.6), and then determining the joint positions for each box. Fig. 4.5b shows an example. For now, we will assume that each vertex is attached to one and only one bone. We will consider a more general case of associating a vertex with two or more bones, in Sect. 4.6. In the following section, we will see how joint angle transformations applied to bones can be transferred to mesh vertices attached to them.

4.4.2 *Mesh Vertex Transformation*

Consider a mesh vertex V attached to a bone i in bind pose (Fig. 4.8). In this configuration, each bone has an associated matrix $\mathbf{B}_i$ that defines the transformation from the bone's local coordinate space to the skeleton's coordinate space.

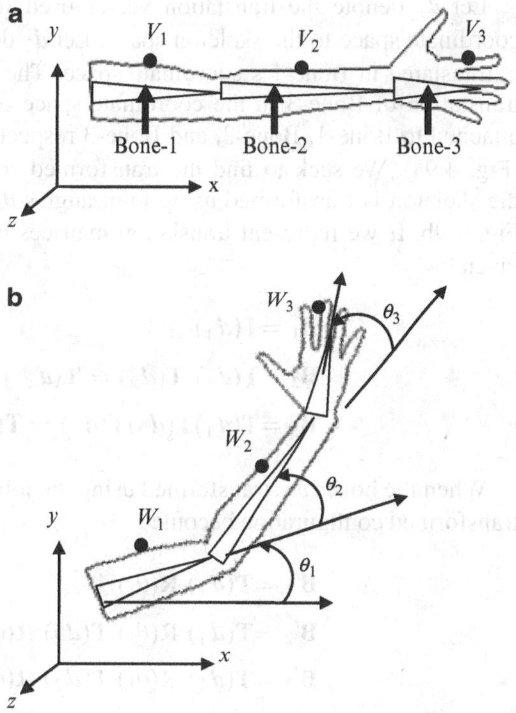

Fig. 4.9 An example showing transformations using three bones. (**a**) Bind pose and (**b**) transformed pose

This transformation depends only on the translations of bones in the hierarchy relative to their parents. The process of obtaining this transformation matrix will be discussed below. For a given joint rotation by an angle θ, the transformed configuration of the bone in the skeleton's coordinate space is represented by another bone matrix $\mathbf{B}'_i$. To get the transformed vertex W, we transfer the original point V from the coordinate space of the mesh (which is the same as the skeleton space) back to its bone's local coordinate space, and then apply the joint angle transformation to return to the skeleton space. In other words, the vertex V is first transformed using the inverse of the matrix $\mathbf{B}_i$, then by $\mathbf{B}'_i$. The first transformation gives the point $\mathbf{B}_i{}^{-1}V$. Applying the matrix $\mathbf{B}'_i$ to this point yields coordinates of the transformed point W. Thus

$$W = (\mathbf{B}'_i \mathbf{B}_i{}^{-1})V \tag{4.5}$$

The above equation is fundamental to skeletal animation, as it describes how transformations applied to a bone i can be propagated to an attached mesh vertex V. The matrix $\mathbf{B}_i$ depends only on the initial configuration of the skeleton, and therefore the points $\mathbf{B}_i{}^{-1}V$ can be pre-computed and used for the entire animation sequence. As an example, we consider the model in Fig. 4.9, and show how it can be transformed using a skeleton comprising of three bones.

Let $\boldsymbol{d}_1$ denote the translation vector used for moving Bone-1 from its local coordinate space to the skeleton space. Let $\boldsymbol{d}_2$ denote the vector by which Bone-2 is translated in Bone-1's coordinate space. The vector $\boldsymbol{d}_3$ similarly represents the translation of Bone-3 in the coordinate space of Bone-2. Vertices V_1, V_2, V_3 are attached to Bone-1, Bone-2, and Bone-3 respectively on the mesh in its bind pose (Fig. 4.9a). We seek to find the transformed coordinates of these vertices, when the skeleton is transformed using joint angles θ_1, θ_2, θ_3 respectively as shown in Fig. 4.9b. If we represent translation matrices by **T**, the initial bone matrices are given by

$$\begin{aligned}\mathbf{B}_1 &= \mathbf{T}(\boldsymbol{d}_1)\\ \mathbf{B}_2 &= \mathbf{T}(\boldsymbol{d}_1)\ \mathbf{T}(\boldsymbol{d}_2) = \mathbf{T}(\boldsymbol{d}_1 + \boldsymbol{d}_2)\\ \mathbf{B}_3 &= \mathbf{T}(\boldsymbol{d}_1)\mathbf{T}(\boldsymbol{d}_2)\mathbf{T}(\boldsymbol{d}_3) = \mathbf{T}(\boldsymbol{d}_1 + \boldsymbol{d}_2 + \boldsymbol{d}_3)\end{aligned} \tag{4.6}$$

When the bones are transformed using the joint angles, the bone matrices for the transformed configuration become

$$\begin{aligned}\mathbf{B'}_1 &= \mathbf{T}(\boldsymbol{d}_1)\ \mathbf{R}(\theta_1)\\ \mathbf{B'}_2 &= \mathbf{T}(\boldsymbol{d}_1)\ \mathbf{R}(\theta_1)\ \mathbf{T}(\boldsymbol{d}_2)\ \mathbf{R}(\theta_2)\\ \mathbf{B'}_3 &= \mathbf{T}(\boldsymbol{d}_1)\ \mathbf{R}(\theta_1)\ \mathbf{T}(\boldsymbol{d}_2)\ \mathbf{R}(\theta_2)\ \mathbf{T}(\boldsymbol{d}_3)\ \mathbf{R}(\theta_3)\end{aligned} \tag{4.7}$$

where **R** denotes a rotational transformation matrix. Now applying Eq. 4.5, we can write the expressions for the transformed vertex coordinates as

$$\begin{aligned}W_1 &= \mathbf{T}(\boldsymbol{d}_1)\ \mathbf{R}(\theta_1)\ \mathbf{T}(-\boldsymbol{d}_1)\ V_1\\ W_2 &= \mathbf{T}(\boldsymbol{d}_1)\ \mathbf{R}(\theta_1)\ \mathbf{T}(\boldsymbol{d}_2)\ \mathbf{R}(\theta_2)\ \mathbf{T}(-\boldsymbol{d}_1 - \boldsymbol{d}_2)\ V_2\\ W_3 &= \mathbf{T}(\boldsymbol{d}_1)\ \mathbf{R}(\theta_1)\ \mathbf{T}(\boldsymbol{d}_2)\ \mathbf{R}(\theta_2)\ \mathbf{T}(\boldsymbol{d}_3)\ \mathbf{R}(\theta_3)\ \mathbf{T}(-\boldsymbol{d}_1 - \boldsymbol{d}_2 - \boldsymbol{d}_3)\ V_3\end{aligned} \tag{4.8}$$

So far we have assumed that each vertex is associated with only a single bone. Section 4.6 discusses a more general case.

4.5 Vertex Skinning Using Scene Graphs

The vertex transformations (Eqs. 4.6, 4.7, 4.8) given in the previous section can be implemented using a scene graph for the skeleton. The scene graph is slightly different to the one we saw earlier in Chap. 3 (Fig. 3.3), in that each group node represents a bone with a matrix of the form $\mathbf{M} = \mathbf{TR}$ defining the relative transformation of the bone with respect to its parent. Each bone has a child node representing the set of mesh vertices associated with that bone. In Fig. 4.10, Bone-1, Bone-2, and Bone-3 form a joint chain in a skeleton, and S_2 denotes a

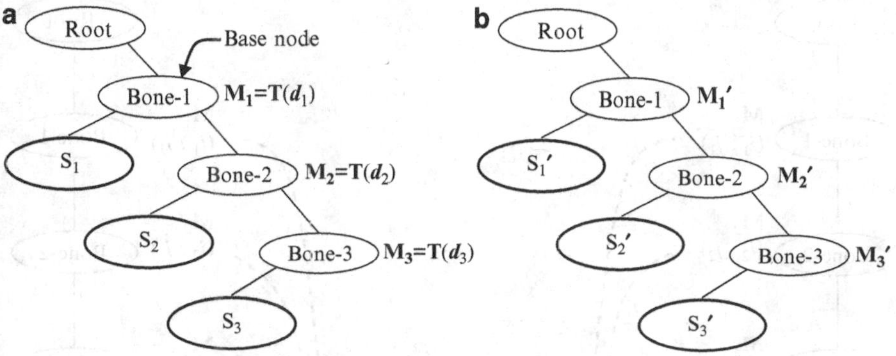

Fig. 4.10 (**a**) Scene graph of a joint chain used for the pre-processing phase. (**b**) The updated mesh vertices in the animation phase

set of mesh vertices associated with Bone-2. The initial bone matrix for Bone-3 is $\mathbf{B}_3 = \mathbf{M}_1\mathbf{M}_2\mathbf{M}_3$. The vectors $\mathbf{B}_i^{-1}V$ in Eq. 4.5 are obtained in a pre-processing phase, where each vertex set is transformed using the inverses of the matrices attached to nodes. As shown in Eq. 4.6, these matrices involve only translation components, and their inverses (as well as the product of inverses) can be easily computed. In the example given in Fig. 4.10a, a vertex V belonging to the set S_3 would be transformed into

$$V' = \mathbf{M}_3^{-1}\,\mathbf{M}_2^{-1}\,\mathbf{M}_1^{-1}V = V - \boldsymbol{d}_1 - \boldsymbol{d}_2 - \boldsymbol{d}_3 \tag{4.9}$$

As the tree is traversed from the root, matrices are combined by pre-multiplying the current product by the inverse of the matrix at the node, until a leaf node is reached. The vertices in a leaf node are transformed using the product of matrix inverses gathered up to that point. Thus the set S_3 becomes a new set $S_3{}'$ after the transformation in Eq. 4.9. The transformed set of vertices replaces the original set for the animation phase (Fig. 4.10b).

In the animation phase, matrices at scene graph nodes are updated using the joint angles of the bones. The updated matrices are represented by $\mathbf{M}'$ in Fig. 4.10b. The scene graph is again traversed from the root; matrices are combined, this time using post-multiplication, and applied to the vertices at leaf nodes to get the transformed mesh vertices. The vertices in the set $S_3{}'$ would transform according to the following equation:

$$W = \mathbf{M}_1{}'\,\mathbf{M}_2{}'\mathbf{M}_3{}'\;V' \tag{4.10}$$

If the set of vertices attached to each bone can be specified as a range of indices (i, j) where i is the start index and j the end index of the set as in Fig. 4.6, then the structure of the scene graph can be simplified to a great extent as shown in Fig. 4.11. The vertex indices in the pre-processing phase point to the initial vertex list $\{V\}$

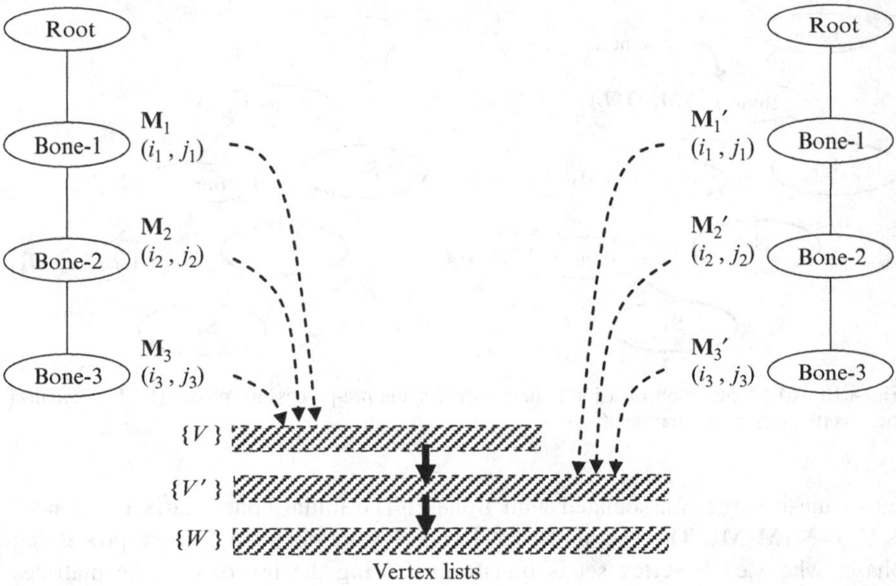

Fig. 4.11 Simplified scene graph for a joint chain using a vertex index range for each bone

of the mesh. After the pre-processing phase, they point to the list of intermediate vertices $\{V'\}$ that are used as inputs in the animation phase. The transformed list of vertices $\{W\}$ is used for rendering the mesh after applying joint angle rotations to the bones (Fig. 4.11).

4.6 Transformation Blending

If every vertex is attached to only a single bone, then transformations applied to the bones may cause mesh surfaces to interpenetrate at a joint (Fig. 4.12a, b).

Figure 4.12b also shows how large flat surface patches can appear at a joint when two adjacent vertices move away from each other because of a rotational transformation. It is intuitive to transform vertices in the neighbourhood of a joint using a combination of bone matrices which influence that joint. If i and j are two bones that influence a joint, then a vertex V in the vicinity of the joint may be transformed using a weighted combination of the bone's matrices $\mathbf{B}_i$ and $\mathbf{B}_j$. The weights w_i and w_j are usually selected based on the relative distances of the vertex from the bones (Fig. 4.13). The final transformed point W (Fig. 4.12c) is obtained as

$$W = \left\{w_i \left(\mathbf{B'}_i \mathbf{B}_i^{-1}\right) + w_j \left(\mathbf{B'}_j \mathbf{B}_j^{-1}\right)\right\} V \tag{4.11}$$

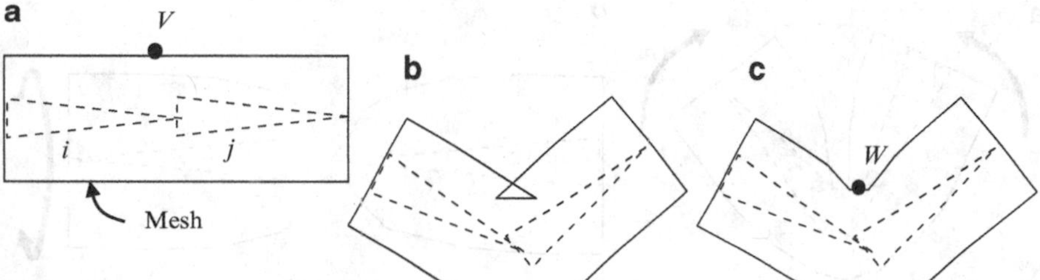

Fig. 4.12 (**a**) A joint formed by two bones, and the attached mesh. (**b**) Interpenetration of mesh surfaces at a joint. (**c**) Mesh transformation using a combination of two bone matrices

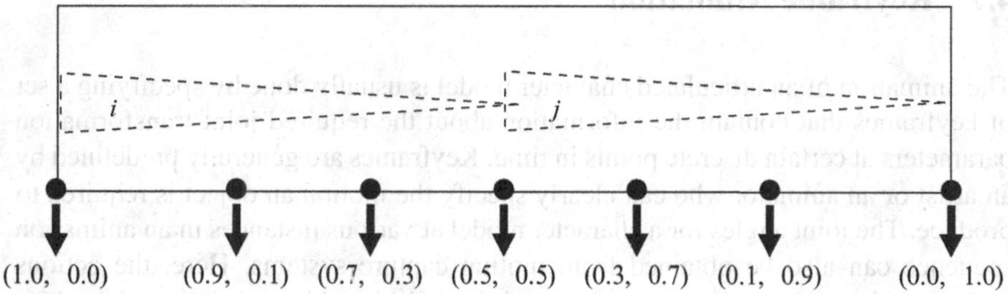

Fig. 4.13 Multiple weights associated with vertices for combining bone matrices

We also require the weights to satisfy the condition $w_i + w_j = 1$. A sample distribution of weights for mesh vertices of the joint in Fig. 4.12a is shown above (Fig. 4.13).

In general, if n bones with indices 1, 2, ..., n meet at a joint, the vertices surrounding the joint may be transformed using a matrix

$$\mathbf{M} = \sum_{i=1}^{n} w_i \, \mathbf{B}'\mathbf{B}_i^{-1} \qquad \text{where,} \quad \sum_{i=1}^{n} w_i = 1. \tag{4.12}$$

The method outlined above is called transformation blending, and it usually produces smooth mesh deformations near joints. However when the angle of rotation of a bone is very large compared to its parent, the averaging scheme in Eq. 4.11 can produce two types of undesirable artefacts shown in Fig. 4.14. The first one is called a collapsing elbow effect, which appears when the angle between the axes of two adjacent bones becomes small. In this situation, vertex points on the inner edge of the mesh that are located near the joint move towards the centre. The second type of artefact is called the candy-wrapper effect, where one of the bones is twisted by 180° about its axis. In this case, vertices with nearly equal weights get transformed to closely located points near the joint.

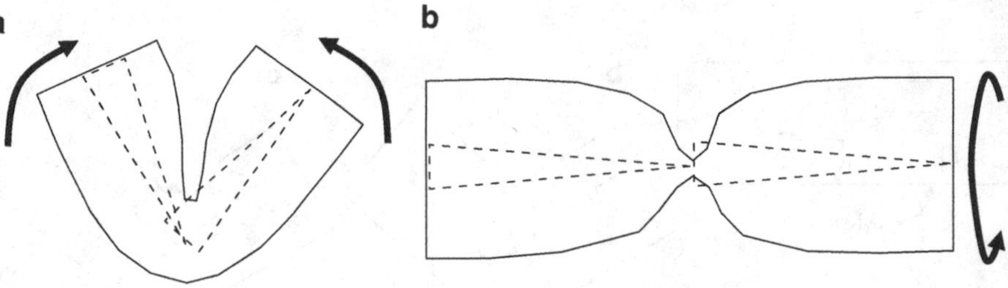

Fig. 4.14 (**a**) Collapsing elbow effect. (**b**) Candy-wrapper effect

4.7 Keyframe Animation

The animation of an articulated character model is usually done by specifying a set of keyframes that contain the information about the required joint transformation parameters at certain discrete points in time. Keyframes are generally predefined by an artist or an animator who can clearly specify the motion an object is required to produce. The joint angles for a character model at various instances in an animation sequence can also be obtained from motion capture systems. Here, the actions performed by a human actor are captured through the placement of markers near each joint of the body, and their recorded positions used to compute joint angles.

A keyframe is essentially a time stamp of important transformation parameters and, optionally, other attributes such as colour, transparency etc. that are needed to render one frame of an animation sequence. As an example, consider a keyframe

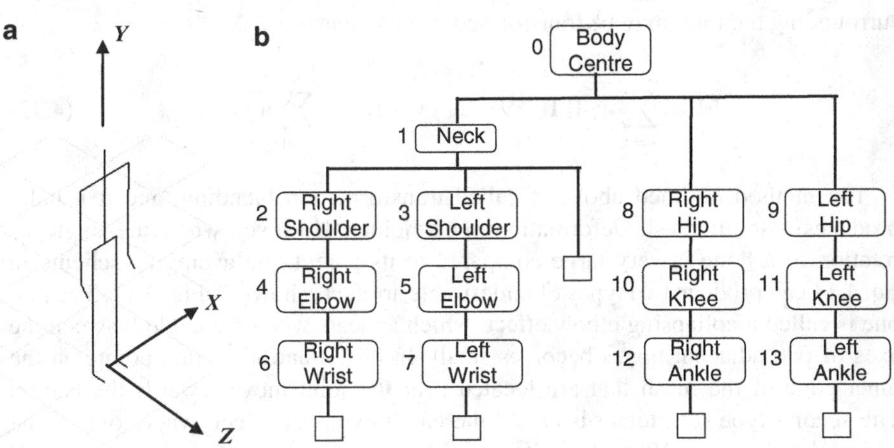

Fig. 4.15 (**a**) Model of a stick figure and (**b**) the joint chains used for its animation. The hierarchical structure of links consists of five branches (chains), and 14 internal nodes. A leaf node is indicated by a *blank square*

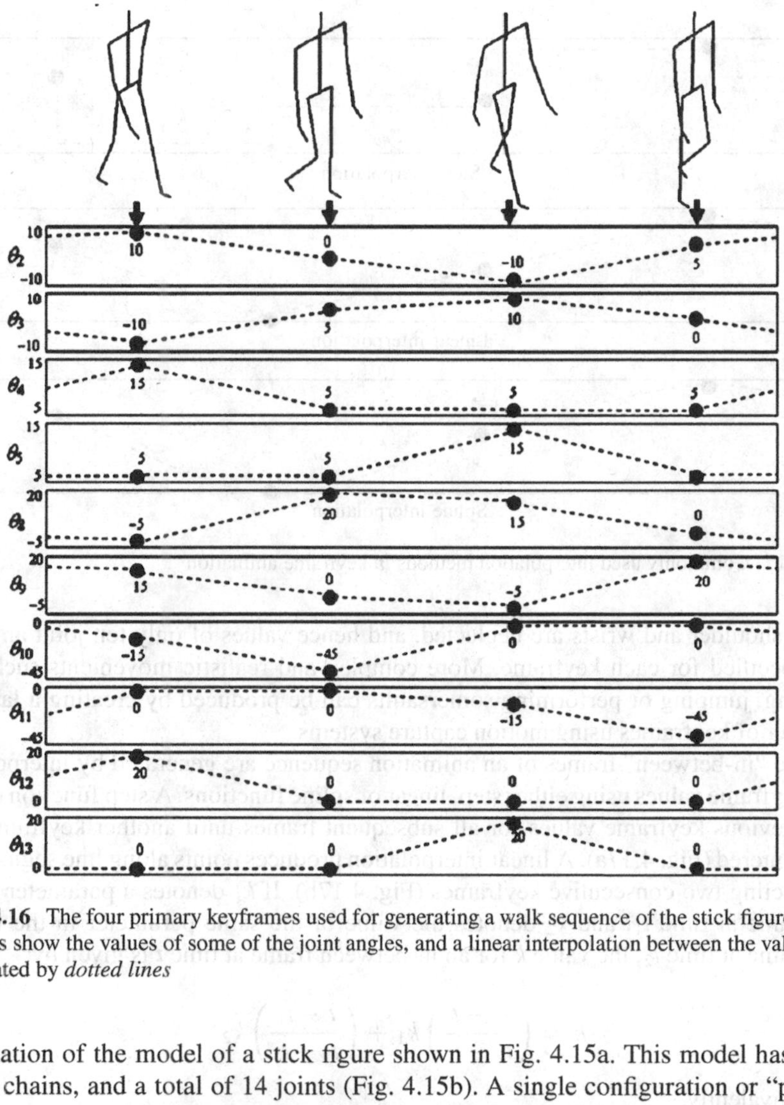

Fig. 4.16 The four primary keyframes used for generating a walk sequence of the stick figure. The graphs show the values of some of the joint angles, and a linear interpolation between the values is indicated by *dotted lines*

animation of the model of a stick figure shown in Fig. 4.15a. This model has five joint chains, and a total of 14 joints (Fig. 4.15b). A single configuration or "pose" of the model is therefore given by 14 joint angles $\theta_0, \theta_1, \ldots, \theta_{13}$, and the position (x_0, y_0, z_0) of the root joint. A joint rotation that moves a link forward (towards $+z$) is considered as positive. For example, the elbow joints are constrained to rotate the arm only forward, by assigning only positive values for θ_4 and θ_5. Similarly the knee joint angles $(\theta_{10}, \theta_{11})$ are always assigned a negative value. An alternative definition for these joint angles can be obtained by viewing them as rotations about the x-axis. In this case, the angles at shoulders and elbows will have negative values, and the angles at the knees will have positive values.

For a simple walk sequence for the stick figure, four key-frames are defined as shown in Fig. 4.16. These are the primary postures from which the intermediate motion can be generated by linear interpolation. In our example, movements of the

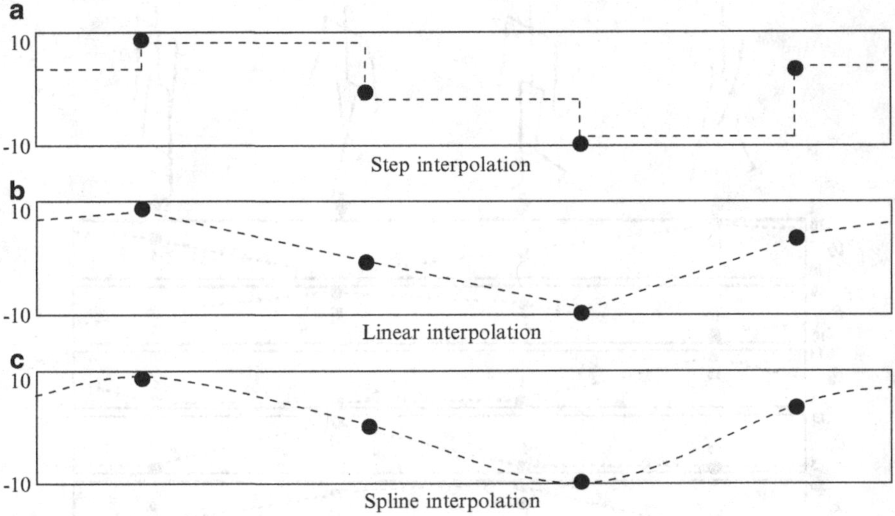

Fig. 4.17 Commonly used interpolation methods in keyframe animation

neck, shoulder and wrists are neglected, and hence values of only ten joint angles are specified for each keyframe. More complex and realistic movements such as running, jumping or performing somersaults can be produced by creating a larger number of keyframes using motion capture systems.

The "in-between" frames of an animation sequence are generated by interpolating keyframe values using either step, linear or spline functions. A step function uses the previous keyframe values for all subsequent frames until another keyframe is encountered (Fig. 4.17a). A linear interpolation produces points along line segments connecting two consecutive keyframes (Fig. 4.17b). If k_1 denotes a parameter in a keyframe at time t_1, and k_2 denotes the value of the same parameter in the next keyframe at time t_2, the value k for an in-between frame at time t is given by

$$k = \left(\frac{t_2 - t}{t_2 - t_1}\right) k_1 + \left(\frac{t - t_1}{t_2 - t_1}\right) k_2 \tag{4.13}$$

or equivalently,

$$k = (1 - \lambda)k_1 + \lambda k_2, \qquad 0 \leq \lambda \leq 1. \tag{4.14}$$

where

$$\lambda = \frac{t - t_1}{t_2 - t_1}, \tag{4.15}$$

For smoother motion interpolation, keyframe values are connected using piecewise cubic splines (Fig. 4.17c). Catmull-Rom splines are commonly used for this purpose, as they have properties of both C^0 and C^1 continuity between consecutive spline segments. Please refer to Chap. 7 (Sects. 7.2 and 7.5) for more information on Catmull-Rom and other types of splines that are useful for generating approximating curves and surfaces.

4.8 Sample Implementation of Vertex Skinning

In Sect. 3.5 we discussed the implementation of a scene graph class. For vertex skinning, we will use a highly simplified model where the information attached to each node is appended with a vertex index range given by the first and the last indices of the range. In this model, there is no need for an object node, and the vertices are processed at group nodes only. Listing 4.1 gives the class definition for a skeleton node. A documentation of the methods in this class can be found in Appendix C. Just like a scene graph node, a skeleton node also stores transformation parameters and a list of pointers to its child nodes.

4.8.1 Skeleton Node

The primary function of the `SkeletonNode` is to provide a convenient framework for representing the bone hierarchy and also to transform the vertex list of a mesh model using joint angles specified for each bone. The two functions `preprocessPhase()` and `animationPhase()` both initiate a recursive traversal of the tree to transform entries in the vertex lists as shown in Fig. 4.11.

It is useful to have a `Skeleton` class with functions to load a skeleton definition and to define joint angles for bones during animation (Listing 4.2). These two functions provide the main interface between the classes and the user application. A Skeleton object represents the whole skeleton of a mesh model consisting of several bones (skeleton nodes).

The contents of the skeleton definition file are organized as shown in Fig. 4.18. The `loadSkeleton()` function reads in the parameters and builds the hierarchical structure. The reference to the root node is available to the application via the function `getRoot()`.

4.8.2 Skinned Mesh Node

The `SkinnedMesh` class encapsulates data and related functions for loading a mesh file consisting of vertex and polygon lists, attaching a skeleton, and transforming the vertices using the joint angles associated with the bones of the skeleton (Listing 4.3).

As shown in Fig. 4.11, the `SkinnedMesh` class uses three vertex lists in the form of vectors to store the initial vertices of the mesh in bind pose, the intermediate set of vertices after the pre-processing phase, and the final set of vertices after

Listing 4.1 Class definition for a single node of a skeleton

```
#include "Matrix.h"
#include "Point3.h"
#include <list>
#include <vector>
using namespace std;

class SkeletonNode
{
private:
     list<SkeletonNode*> _children;
     int _firstIndex, _lastIndex, _parentIndex;
     SkeletonNode* _parent;
     float _tx, _ty, _tz, _angleX, _angleY, _angleZ;
     Matrix *_matrix, *_invMatrix;
public:
     SkeletonNode(int parentIndx, float tx, float ty,
                  float tz, int firstIndx, int lastIndx)
         : _parent(NULL),
         _tx(tx), _ty(ty), _tz(tz),
         _angleX(0.0), _angleY(0.0), _angleZ(0.0),
         _firstIndex(firstIndx), _lastIndex(lastIndx),
         _parentIndex(parentIndx)
           { _matrix = new Matrix();
             _invMatrix = new Matrix();
              updateMatrices();    }
     ~SkeletonNode() {}
     void addChild(SkeletonNode* node);
     void removeChild(SkeletonNode* node);
     void rotateX(float angle);
     void rotateY(float angle);
     void rotateZ(float angle);
     void attachVertices(int firstIndex, int lastIndex);
     void setParentIndex(int parentindex);
     int getParentIndex() const;
     int getFirstIndex() const;
     int getLastIndex() const;
     void initialize();
     Matrix* getMatrix() const;
     void updateMatrices();
     Matrix* getInverseMatrix() const;
   vector<Point3*> preprocessPhase(vector<Point3*> vertices);
   vector<Point3*> animationPhase(vector<Point3*> vertices);
     void transform1(vector<Point3*> vertices,
                        float tx, float ty, float tz);
     void transform2(vector<Point3*> vertices, Matrix matrix);
};
```

applying joint angle transformations. The mesh definition file has a simple structure consisting of the list of vertices and polygons. Polygons are specified using vertex indices (three indices for triangles and four for quads). The vertex index starts from 1. Figure 4.19 gives the mesh definition for a rectangular prism.

The framework described above also uses the `Point3` and `Matrix` classes for various vertex and transformation related functions (see Appendix A). This book's

Listing 4.2 Class definition for a skeleton

```
#include "SkeletonNode.h"
#include <vector>
using namespace std;

class Skeleton
{
private:
     SkeletonNode* _root;
     vector<SkeletonNode*> _bones;
     void attachBones();
public:
     Skeleton()
          : _root( new SkeletonNode() )
            {}
     ~Skeleton() {delete _root; }
     SkeletonNode* getRoot() const;
     void loadSkeleton(const string& filename);
     void rotate(int i, float angleX,
                    float angleY, float angleZ);
     void translateBase(float tx, float ty, float tz);
};
```

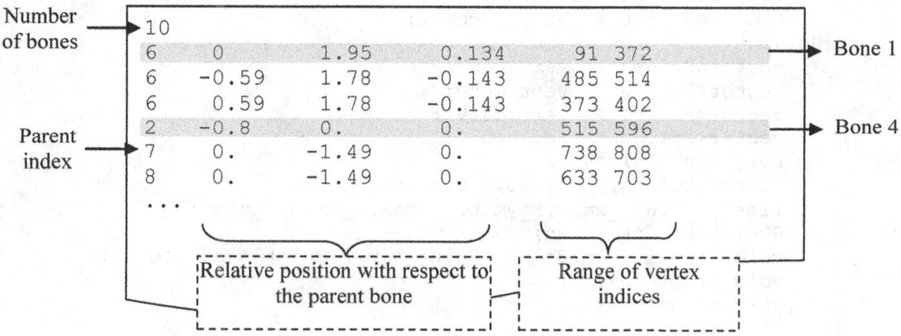

Fig. 4.18 Sample skeleton definition file

companion website contains the header and implementation files of all the above classes.

An example of a simple application using the skeleton animation framework is shown in Listing 4.4. At the initialization stage, both mesh and skeleton objects are created, corresponding data loaded from input files, the skeleton is attached to the mesh, and the `preprocess()` function is called on the mesh object. This function in turn passes the vertex data to the root node of the skeleton via the `preprocessPhase()` function and gets back the intermediate vertices. The `display()` function performs the animation of the mesh by defining joint angles for the bones. In the example, the function call `skeleton->rotate(3,30,0,-75)` is used to rotate the bone with index 3 by 30° about the x-axis and $-75°$ about the z-axis. The sequence of rotations is

Listing 4.3 Class definition for a mesh

```
#include <vector>
#include <string>
#include "Skeleton.h"
#include "Point3.h"
using namespace std;

struct Polygon
{
      int vert1, vert2, vert3, vert4;
};

class SkinnedMesh
{
public:
     enum PolyType {TRIANGLE, QUAD};
      SkinnedMesh(PolyType polytype)
           : _polytype(polytype),
             _skeleton(NULL)
            {}
      ~SkinnedMesh() {}
      void loadMesh(const string& filename);
      void render();
      void setColor(float colorR, float colorG, float colorB);
      void attachSkeleton(Skeleton* skeleton);
      Skeleton* getSkeleton() const;
private:
      vector<Point3*> _verticesV;
      vector<Point3*> _verticesW;
      vector<Point3*> _verticesVT;
      vector<Polygon*> _polygons;
      PolyType _polytype;
      float _colorR, _colorG, _colorB;
      float _xmin, _xmax, _ymin, _ymax, _zmin, _zmax;
      Skeleton* _skeleton;
      void normal(Point3* p1, Point3* p2, Point3* p3) const;
      void preprocess();
      void transform();
};
```

pre-defined. The function call `mesh->render()` is used inside the display loop to render the mesh with the transformed vertex coordinates.

4.9 Summary

This chapter addressed the problem of animating articulated character models. Character models are divided into two main categories: those constructed using individual component objects, and those modelled as a single mesh surface. The first category of objects requires blending of surfaces at the joints to avoid interpenetration of component objects and the appearance of gaps during animation.

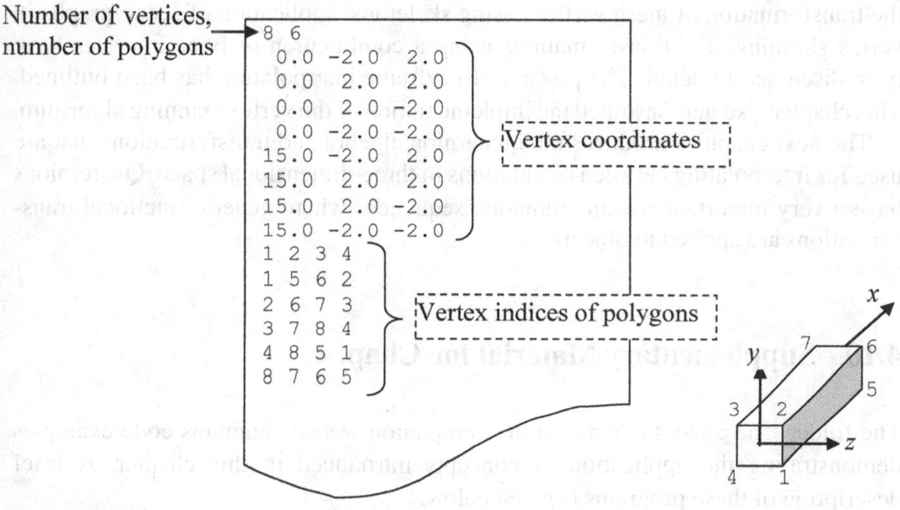

Fig. 4.19 A sample mesh definition file

Listing 4.4 Example of an application using the vertex skinning algorithm

```
SkinnedMesh* mesh;
Skeleton* skeleton;
   ...
void initialise()
{
      mesh = new SkinnedMesh(SkinnedMesh::QUAD);
      mesh->loadMesh("HumanModel.txt");
      mesh->setColor(1.0, 0.5, 0.0);

      skeleton = new Skeleton();
      skeleton->loadSkeleton("Skeleton.txt");
      mesh->attachSkeleton(skeleton);

      glClearColor(1.0f, 1.0f, 1.0f, 1.0f);
      glClearDepth(1.0f);
        ...
}
void display()
{
    ...
      skeleton->rotate(3, 30, 0, -75);
      mesh->render();
    ...
}
```

It was shown that Hermite polynomials and cubic Bezier polynomials could be effectively used for vertex blending.

This chapter also presented the vertex skinning algorithm which is a well-known method used in skeletal animation. Various aspects of vertex skinning including the transformation of mesh vertices using skeletons, application of scene graphs in vertex skinning, and transformations using a combination of bone matrices have been discussed in detail. The process of keyframe interpolation has been outlined. This chapter also demonstrated the implementation of the vertex skinning algorithm.

The next chapter introduces the quaternion algebra and transformations that are used for interpolating between orientations in three-dimensional space. Quaternions have a very important role in animation sequences where generic rotational transformations are applied to objects.

4.10 Supplementary Material for Chap. 4

The folder `Chapter4/Code` on the companion website contains code examples demonstrating the application of concepts introduced in this chapter. A brief description of these programs is given below.

1. **SkeletonNode.cpp**

Additional files:
`SkeletonNode.h`
`Point3.h`
`Matrix.h`
`Point3.cpp`
`Matrix.cpp`

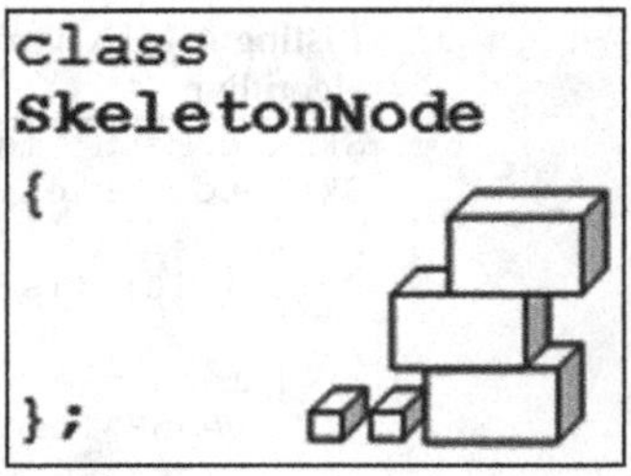

This class implements the basic functionalities of a scene graph for skeleton animation as detailed in Sect. 4.8. The class documentation can be found in Appendix C.

2. **SkinnedMesh.cpp**

Additional files:
`SkinnedMesh.h`
`Skeleton.h`
`SkeletonNode.h`
`Skeleton.cpp`
`SkeletonNode.cpp`

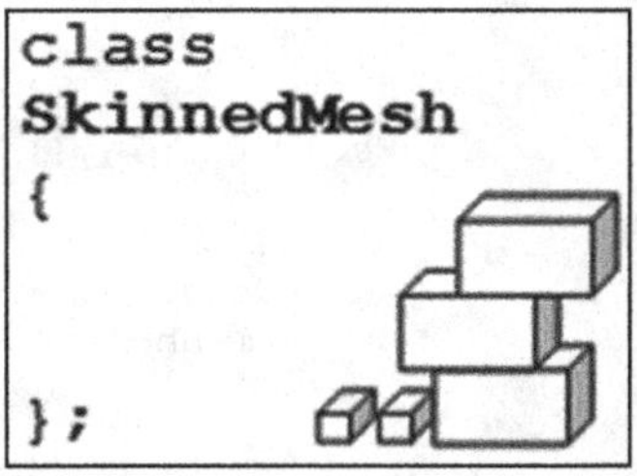

This class supports several functions for loading and rendering a skinned mesh file. A brief description of the class can be found in Sect. 4.8.2, and the class documentation in Appendix C.

3. **VertexBlending.cpp**

Additional files:
`None`

This program generates a blending surface between two cylinders using Hermite interpolation. Clicking the left mouse button starts the rotation of one of the cylinders. Use up or down arrow keys to increase or reduce the weight α of the tangent vectors. Press left or right arrow keys to change the view direction.

4. **TwoBoneTransform.cpp**

Additional files:
`None`

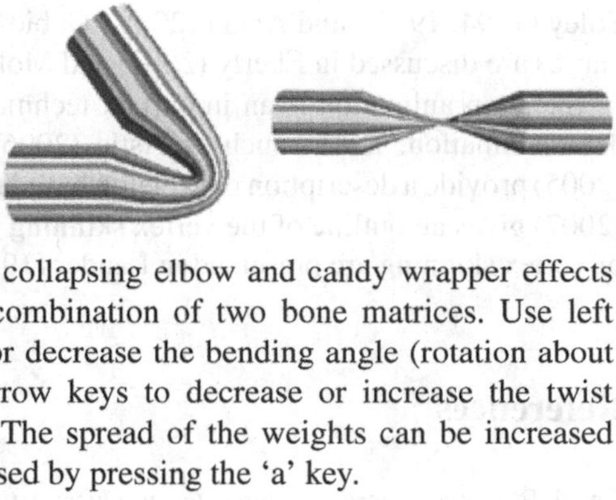

The program demonstrates the collapsing elbow and candy wrapper effects seen in transformations using a combination of two bone matrices. Use left and right arrow keys to increase or decrease the bending angle (rotation about the z-axis). Use up and down arrow keys to decrease or increase the twist angle (rotation about the x-axis). The spread of the weights can be increased by pressing the 's' key, and decreased by pressing the 'a' key.

5. **HumanModel.cpp**

Additional classes:
`Mesh`
`Skeleton`
`SkeletonNode`
`Point3`
`Matrix`

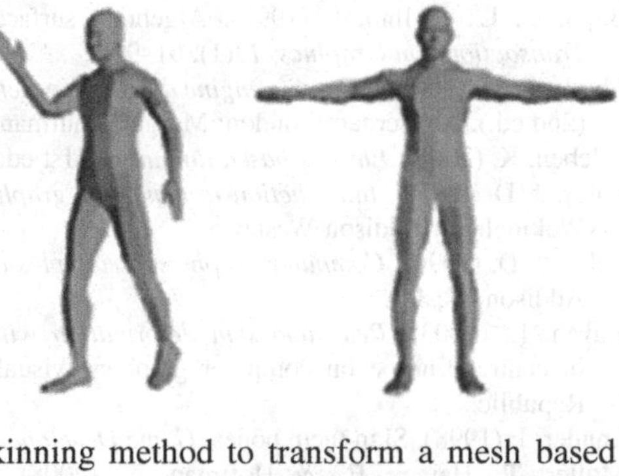

This program uses the vertex skinning method to transform a mesh based on transformations applied to a skeleton. It requires two input files, "Human-Model.txt" (mesh definition) and "Skeleton.txt" (skeleton definition). The bone indices are defined as given in Fig. 4.5. The bone transformations are defined inside the `display()` function of the program. Use left and right arrow keys to change the view direction.

4.11 Bibliographical Notes

Both vertex blending and vertex skinning are often used synonymously in computer graphics literature. In this book, vertex blending refers to an interpolation method between polyhedral surfaces, while vertex skinning refers to a completely different method of animating a mesh using a skeleton. The process of constructing blending surfaces between polyhedral objects is often referred to as polyhedral vertex blending. Such methods were originally introduced for Computer Aided Design (CAD) applications. Bajaj and Ihm (1992) gives the fundamental concepts for designing blending surfaces with Hermite polynomials. A description of parametric cubic curves and surfaces generated using Hermite polynomials can be found in Foley (1994, 1996), and Angel (2008). Cubic interpolation methods using Hermite curves are discussed in Eberly (2007) and Moller et al. (2008).

Skeleton animation is an important technique in game programming and character animation. Books such as Astle (2006), Moller et al. (2008) and Erleben (2005) provide a description of skeleton based mesh transformation methods. Eberly (2007) gives an outline of the vertex skinning method. The implementation aspects of vertex skinning are presented in Lander (1998) and Kavan (2003).

References

Angel, E. (2008). *Interactive computer graphics: A top-down approach using OpenGL* (5th ed.). Boston/London: Pearson Addison-Wesley.

Astle, D. (2006). *More OpenGL game programming*. Boston: Thomson/Course Technology.

Bajaj, C. L., & Ihm, I. (1992). Algebraic surface design with Hermite interpolation. *ACM Transactions on Graphics, 11*(1), 61–91.

Eberly, D. H. (2007). *3D game engine design: A practical approach to real-time computer graphics* (2nd ed.). Amsterdam/London: Morgan Kaufmann.

Erleben, K. (2005). *Physics-based animation* (1st ed.). Hingham: Charles River Media.

Foley, J. D. (1994). *Introduction to computer graphics* (Abridged and modified edn.). Reading/Wokingham: Addison-Wesley.

Foley, J. D. (1996). *Computer graphics: Principles and practice* (2nd ed.). Reading/Wokingham: Addison-Wesley.

Kavan, L. (2003). *Real-time skin deformation with bones blending*. International conference in central Europe on computer graphics, visualization and computer vision. Plzen, Czech Republic.

Lander, J. (1998). Skin them bones. *Game Developer, 5*, 11–16.

Moller, T., Haines, E., & Hoffman, N. (2008). *Real-time rendering* (3rd ed.). Wellesley: A.K. Peters.

Chapter 5
Quaternions

Overview

In computer graphics applications, quaternions are used to represent three-dimensional rotations. They provide some key advantages over the traditional way of defining generic rotational transformations using Euler angles. Quaternions are also extremely useful for interpolating between two orientations in three-dimensional space. Keyframe animations requiring orientation interpolation therefore find a very convenient mathematical tool in quaternions.

This chapter gives an overview of the algebra of quaternions, the geometrical interpretation of quaternion transformations, and quaternion based linear and spherical interpolation functions. A comparison of rotation interpolation methods using Euler angles, angle-axis representations, and quaternions is presented. The extension of quaternions to eight-dimensional dual quaternions and their usefulness in representing general rigid-body transformations are also discussed.

5.1 Review of Complex Numbers

Quaternions are hyper-complex numbers of rank 4, and therefore it is useful to review some of the basic concepts related to complex number algebra to gain a better insight into quaternion operations. Even though a complex number z is commonly represented in the form $a + i\,b$ where $i = \sqrt{-1}$, and a, b are respectively the real and imaginary parts of z, we will use the two-tuple notation (a, b) for z. With this notation, we can write $1 = (1, 0)$, and $i = (0, 1)$. These two-dimensional vectors $(1, 0)$ and $(0, 1)$ form an orthogonal basis for the complex space, where any number $z = (a, b)$ can be expressed as their linear combination $a\,(1, 0) + b\,(0, 1)$. The operations of addition, subtraction and multiplication in the field of complex numbers are defined as follows:

$$(a_1, b_1) \pm (a_2, b_2) = (a_1 \pm a_2, b_1 \pm b_2) \tag{5.1}$$

R. Mukundan, *Advanced Methods in Computer Graphics: With examples in OpenGL*,
DOI 10.1007/978-1-4471-2340-8_5, © Springer-Verlag London Limited 2012

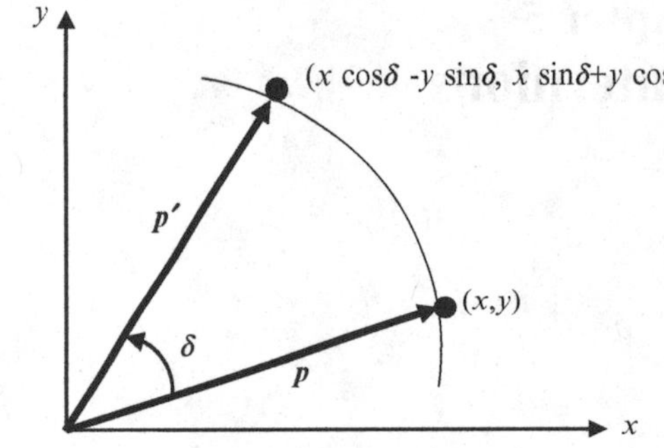

Fig. 5.1 Multiplication by a unit complex number has the effect of rotation of vectors and points about the origin on a two-dimensional plane

$$(a_1,\ b_1)(a_2,\ b_2) = (a_1a_2 - b_1b_2,\ a_1b_2 + a_2b_1) \tag{5.2}$$

$$c(a,b) = (ca, cb), \tag{5.3}$$

where c is a real number. The multiplication rule given in Eq. 5.2 establishes the fact that $i^2 = (0,1)\,(0,1) = (-1,\,0)$. The complex conjugate of $z = (a,\,b)$ is given by $z^* = (a,\,-b)$. The magnitude of z is a positive real number defined as

$$|z| = \sqrt{a^2 + b^2} \tag{5.4}$$

Using the multiplication rule, we find that

$$zz^* = |z|^2 = a^2 + b^2 \tag{5.5}$$

If a complex number z has a unit magnitude, then $zz^* = 1$. This implies that for a unit complex number, z^* is the multiplicative inverse of z. All unit complex numbers can be expressed in the general form

$$z = (\cos\delta, \sin\delta) \tag{5.6}$$

Consider any vector (or point) $\boldsymbol{p} = (x,\,y)$ in a two-dimensional coordinate system. If we treat $\boldsymbol{p}$ as a complex number, and multiply it by the unit complex number z given above, the product $z\boldsymbol{p}$ can be evaluated using Eq. 5.2 as follows:

$$\begin{aligned} \boldsymbol{p}' &= (\cos\delta, \sin\delta)(x,\,y) \\ &= (x\cos\delta - y\sin\delta, x\sin\delta + y\cos\delta) \end{aligned} \tag{5.7}$$

The transformed vector (or point) $\boldsymbol{p}'$ has the same magnitude as $\boldsymbol{p}$, and can be obtained by rotating $\boldsymbol{p}$ about the origin by an angle δ (Fig. 5.1). The unit complex vector therefore represents a rotation in two-dimensional space.

The geometrical interpretation of unit complex numbers as rotation operators forms the basis for the framework for an extended set of hyper-complex numbers called quaternions. We will see shortly that unit quaternions represent three-dimensional rotations. In the following section, we introduce the algebra of quaternion numbers.

5.2 Quaternion Algebra

We have seen above that the field of complex numbers have $1 = (1, 0)$, $i = (0, 1)$ as the orthogonal basis. The quaternion set has an extended orthogonal basis consisting of four elements $1 = (1, 0, 0, 0)$, $i = (0, 1, 0, 0)$, $j = (0, 0, 1, 0)$, $k = (0, 0, 0, 1)$. Thus a quaternion $Q = (q_0, q_1, q_2, q_3)$ has an equivalent representation $q_0 + q_1 i + q_2 j + q_3 k$, where the quaternion components q_i are all real values. The term q_0 is called the scalar part of Q, and the 3-tuple (q_1, q_2, q_3) the vector part. The operations of addition, subtraction and scalar multiplication are defined as follows:

$$(p_0, p_1, p_2, p_3) \pm (q_0, q_1, q_2, q_3) = (p_0 \pm q_0, p_1 \pm q_1, p_2 \pm q_2, p_3 \pm q_3) \quad (5.8)$$

$$c(q_0, q_1, q_2, q_3) = (cq_0, cq_1, cq_2, cq_3), \quad (5.9)$$

where c is any real number. Analogous to Eq. 5.2, the quaternion product is given by

$$\begin{aligned} &(p_0, p_1, p_2, p_3)(q_0, q_1, q_2, q_3) \\ &= (p_0q_0 - p_1q_1 - p_2q_2 - p_3q_3,\ p_0q_1 + p_1q_0 + p_2q_3 - p_3q_2, \\ &\quad p_0q_2 - p_1q_3 + p_2q_0 + p_3q_1,\ p_0q_3 + p_1q_2 - p_2q_1 + p_3q_0) \end{aligned} \quad (5.10)$$

From the above definition of a quaternion product, it is obvious that quaternion multiplication is not commutative. That is, for any two quaternions $P = (p_0, p_1, p_2, p_3)$, $Q = (q_0, q_1, q_2, q_3)$, the product PQ need not necessarily be the same as QP. If we denote the vector part of P by $\mathbf{v} = (p_1, p_2, p_3)$ and the vector part of Q by $\mathbf{w} = (q_1, q_2, q_3)$, then Eq. 5.10 becomes

$$(p_0, \mathbf{v})(q_0, \mathbf{w}) = (p_0q_0 - \mathbf{v} \bullet \mathbf{w},\ p_0\mathbf{w} + q_0\mathbf{v} + \mathbf{v} \times \mathbf{w}) \quad (5.11)$$

where $\mathbf{v}\bullet\mathbf{w}$ denotes the dot product and $\mathbf{v}\times\mathbf{w}$ the cross product of the two vectors. The right-hand side of Eq. 5.10 when treated as a column vector, can be conveniently expressed as a product of a matrix of elements of P and a vector containing elements of Q as given below.

$$PQ = \begin{bmatrix} p_0 & -p_1 & -p_2 & -p_3 \\ p_1 & p_0 & -p_3 & p_2 \\ p_2 & p_3 & p_0 & -p_1 \\ p_3 & -p_2 & p_1 & p_0 \end{bmatrix} \begin{bmatrix} q_0 \\ q_1 \\ q_2 \\ q_3 \end{bmatrix}, \quad (5.12)$$

or, equivalently as

$$PQ = \begin{bmatrix} q_0 & -q_1 & -q_2 & -q_3 \\ q_1 & q_0 & q_3 & -q_2 \\ q_2 & -q_3 & q_0 & q_1 \\ q_3 & q_2 & -q_1 & q_0 \end{bmatrix} \begin{bmatrix} p_0 \\ p_1 \\ p_2 \\ p_3 \end{bmatrix} \tag{5.13}$$

From Eq. 5.10, we can derive the following properties satisfied by the quaternion basis:

$$\begin{aligned} i^2 = j^2 = k^2 = ijk &= -1 \\ ij &= -ji = k \\ jk &= -kj = i \\ ki &= -ik = j \end{aligned} \tag{5.14}$$

Quaternions also form a commutative group under addition, where (0,0,0,0) is the identity element. Quaternion multiplication is associative, and distributes over addition. If P, Q, R are any three quaternions,

$$\begin{aligned} (PQ)R &= P(QR) \\ (P+Q)R &= PR + QR \\ P(Q+R) &= PQ + PR \end{aligned} \tag{5.15}$$

The conjugate Q^* of the quaternion $Q = (q_0, q_1, q_2, q_3)$ is defined as

$$Q^* = (q_0, -q_1, -q_2, -q_3) \tag{5.16}$$

Thus, if $Q = (q_0, \mathbf{w})$, then $Q^* = (q_0, -\mathbf{w})$. Also, $Q + Q^* = 2q_0$. The magnitude (also called the length, or norm) of Q denoted by $|Q|$, is

$$|Q| = \sqrt{q_0^2 + q_1^2 + q_2^2 + q_3^2} \tag{5.17}$$

By taking the magnitude of the quaternion product in Eq. 5.10 we get

$$|PQ| = |P||Q| \tag{5.18}$$

Using Eq. 5.11, it is easy to find that

$$QQ^* = Q^*Q = |Q|^2. \tag{5.19}$$

By dividing the above equation by $|Q|^2$, we get the equation for the quaternion inverse. If we denote the quaternion inverse of Q by Q^{-1}, then

$$Q^{-1} = \frac{Q^*}{|Q|^2} \tag{5.20}$$

A quaternion Q can be normalized to a unit quaternion by dividing each of its components by the length $|Q|$ given in Eq. 5.17. A unit quaternion satisfies the following equations:

$$\begin{aligned} |Q| &= 1. \\ {q_0}^2 + {q_1}^2 + {q_2}^2 + {q_3}^2 &= 1. \\ Q^{-1} &= Q^* \end{aligned} \tag{5.21}$$

If the real part q_0 of a quaternion is zero, it represents a vector (q_1, q_2, q_3) in three-dimensional space. Such a quaternion that has the form $(0, q_1, q_2, q_3) = (0, \boldsymbol{q})$ is called a pure quaternion. Similarly, quaternions of the type $(a, 0, 0, 0)$ with the vector component zero are called real quaternions. The algebra of real quaternions is the same as that of real numbers. Similarly, quaternions of the type $(a, b, 0, 0)$ behave exactly like complex numbers (a, b).

5.3 Quaternion Transformation

A special type of quaternion product in the form QPQ^* plays an important role in three-dimensional transformations. We have just seen that a vector $\boldsymbol{p}$ in the three-dimensional space corresponds to a pure quaternion $P = (0, \boldsymbol{p})$. An interesting fact that leads to the notion of a quaternion transformation is that given any quaternion Q and a pure quaternion P, the product $P' = QPQ^*$ is also a pure quaternion. Thus QPQ^* can be viewed as the transformation of a pure quaternion $P = (0, p_1, p_2, p_3)$ using another quaternion Q. We can derive the matrix form of this transformation by using Eq. 5.13 for obtaining the matrix expression for PQ^* and then using Eq. 5.12 for getting the final product $Q(PQ^*)$.

$$QPQ^* = \begin{bmatrix} q_0 & -q_1 & -q_2 & -q_3 \\ q_1 & q_0 & -q_3 & q_2 \\ q_2 & q_3 & q_0 & -q_1 \\ q_3 & -q_2 & q_1 & q_0 \end{bmatrix} \begin{bmatrix} q_0 & q_1 & q_2 & q_3 \\ -q_1 & q_0 & -q_3 & q_2 \\ -q_2 & q_3 & q_0 & -q_1 \\ -q_3 & -q_2 & q_1 & q_0 \end{bmatrix} \begin{bmatrix} p_0 \\ p_1 \\ p_2 \\ p_3 \end{bmatrix} \tag{5.22}$$

The following matrix equation immediately follows by multiplying the two matrices together, and setting $p_0 = 0$:

$$\begin{bmatrix} 0 \\ p'_1 \\ p'_2 \\ p'_3 \end{bmatrix} = \begin{bmatrix} 1 & 0 & 0 & 0 \\ 0 & q_0^2 + q_1^2 - q_2^2 - q_3^2 & 2\,(-q_0q_3 + q_1q_2) & 2\,(q_0q_2 + q_1q_3) \\ 0 & 2\,(q_0q_3 + q_1q_2) & q_0^2 - q_1^2 + q_2^2 - q_3^2 & 2\,(-q_0q_1 + q_2q_3) \\ 0 & 2\,(-q_0q_2 + q_1q_3) & 2\,(q_0q_1 + q_2q_3) & q_0^2 - q_1^2 - q_2^2 + q_3^2 \end{bmatrix} \begin{bmatrix} 0 \\ p_1 \\ p_2 \\ p_3 \end{bmatrix} \tag{5.23}$$

This equation defines the quaternion transformation of a three-dimensional point (or vector) $\boldsymbol{p} = (p_1, p_2, p_3)$ to another three-dimensional point (or vector) $\boldsymbol{p}' = (p_1', p_2', p_3')$. An alternative form of the equation can be derived as follows:

$$QPQ^* = (q_0,\ \boldsymbol{w})(0, \boldsymbol{p})(q_0, -\boldsymbol{w}), \tag{5.24}$$

where $\boldsymbol{w} = (q_1, q_2, q_3)$. Using Eq. 5.11 to expand the product term, we get

$$QPQ^* = (0, {q_0}^2\boldsymbol{p} + \boldsymbol{w}(\boldsymbol{p} \bullet \boldsymbol{w}) + 2q_0(\boldsymbol{w} \times \boldsymbol{p}) + \boldsymbol{w} \times (\boldsymbol{w} \times \boldsymbol{p})) \tag{5.25}$$

The above equation proves that the transformation of P is also a pure quaternion. We can therefore write

$$\boldsymbol{p}' = {q_0}^2\boldsymbol{p} + \boldsymbol{w}(\boldsymbol{p} \bullet \boldsymbol{w}) + 2q_0(\boldsymbol{w} \times \boldsymbol{p}) + \boldsymbol{w} \times\ (\boldsymbol{w} \times \boldsymbol{p}) \tag{5.26}$$

Further simplification of the right-hand side using vector algebra gives

$$\boldsymbol{p}' = ({q_0}^2 - w^2)\ \boldsymbol{p} + 2\boldsymbol{w}(\boldsymbol{p} \bullet \boldsymbol{w}) + 2q_0(\boldsymbol{w} \times \boldsymbol{p}) \tag{5.27}$$

where, $w^2 = |\boldsymbol{w}|^2 = {q_1}^2 + {q_2}^2 + {q_3}^2$.

It should be noted that QPQ^* generally is not a scale-preserving transformation because

$$|P'| = |Q|^2|P| \tag{5.28}$$

If we impose the constraint that Q is a unit quaternion (*i.e.*, $|Q| = 1$), we get a scale-invariant (or length-preserving) transform. With this additional criterion, we can also write the inverse quaternion transform in a concise form as

$$P = Q^* P' Q \tag{5.29}$$

We also note that when P is the zero-quaternion (0, 0, 0, 0), so is P'. Therefore the origin is a fixed point of the transformation. A length-preserving transformation with a fixed point is a rotation. In the following sections we will attempt to find a geometric interpretation of the quaternion transformation as a pure rotation in three-dimensional space, and express the components of a unit quaternion in terms of the angle and the axis of rotation.

5.4 Generalized Rotations

Before we further analyze the transform properties of quaternions, it would be worthwhile to review some of the key concepts relating to general three-dimensional rotations.

Any composite transformation that preserves length, angle and area is called a rigid-body transformation. If a rigid body transformation has also a fixed point (pivot), then it is a rotation. A rotation can be measured in terms of the angular deviation of an orthogonal right-handed system fixed on the rotating body, with the origin of the system at the fixed point of rotation. In Fig. 5.2a, *Ox, Oy, Oz* are the axes of an orthogonal triad before rotation, and Ox_t, Oy_t, Oz_t denote the transformed axes directions after a rotation about *O*. The coordinate reference frame is inertially fixed and is represented by *X, Y, Z* axes.

A general rigid body transformation of an object without a fixed point can be treated as a rotation followed by a translation. Such a transformation can be equivalently performed by first carrying out a rotation that aligns the axes parallel to the final directions, followed by a translation that moves the fixed point *O* to its final position O_t (Fig. 5.2b). While any translation can be unambiguously represented by a three component vector, a general rotation may be specified in several ways. In the following, we consider the Euler angle and angle-axis representations of three-dimensional rotations.

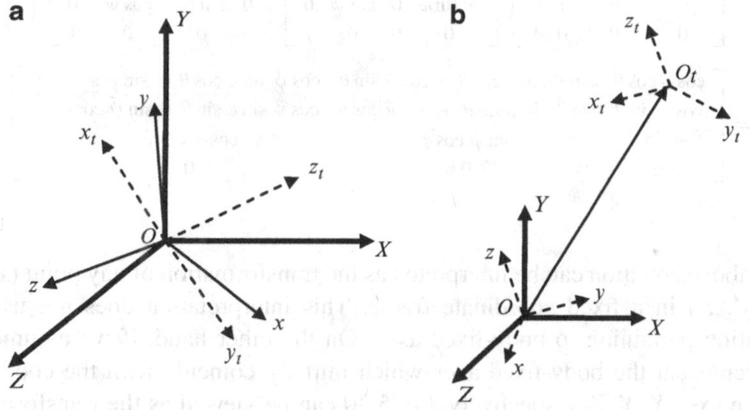

Fig. 5.2 **(a)** A generalized rotation with a fixed point *O* that transforms the directions of body-fixed axes from $O(x, y, z)$ to $O(x_t, y_t, z_t)$. **(b)** A general transformation without a fixed point

5.4.1 Euler Angles

The Euler's theorem on rotations states that any general rotation can be performed using a sequence of elementary rotations about the coordinate axes passing through the fixed point. The theorem further states that if no two successive rotations is about the same axis, then the maximum number of rotations needed to achieve the transformation is three. Thus any rotational transformation can be represented by a sequence of three rotations about mutually independent axes. These angles are called Euler angles. Before defining an Euler angle representation, we need to fix the sequence in which the rotations are performed. If we denote rotations about the X-axis by ψ, rotations about Y by ϕ, and rotations about Z by θ, a set of Euler angles can be defined using any of the following 12 sequences:

$\psi\ \phi\ \theta$	$\phi\ \theta\ \psi$	$\theta\ \psi\ \phi$
$\psi\ \theta\ \phi$	$\phi\ \psi\ \theta$	$\theta\ \phi\ \psi$
$\psi_1\phi\ \psi_2$	$\phi_1\theta\ \phi_2$	$\theta_1\psi\ \theta_2$
$\psi_1\theta\ \psi_2$	$\phi_1\psi\ \phi_2$	$\theta_1\phi\ \theta_2$

The Euler angle sequence $\{\psi\ \phi\ \theta\}$ represents a rotation about X followed by a second rotation about Y, followed by a third rotation about the Z axis. The sequence $\{\phi_1\psi\ \phi_2\}$ gives another Euler angle representation in terms of a rotation about the Y axis, followed by a second rotation about the X axis, and then a third rotation again about the Y axis. The six sequences where each axis is used exactly once are called proper Euler angles.

The transformation matrix for the $\{\psi\ \phi\ \theta\}$ sequence is obtained by concatenating the transformation matrices as shown below.

$$
\begin{bmatrix} x' \\ y' \\ z' \\ 1 \end{bmatrix} = \begin{bmatrix} \cos\theta & -\sin\theta & 0 & 0 \\ \sin\theta & \cos\theta & 0 & 0 \\ 0 & 0 & 1 & 0 \\ 0 & 0 & 0 & 1 \end{bmatrix} \begin{bmatrix} \cos\varphi & 0 & \sin\varphi & 0 \\ 0 & 1 & 0 & 0 \\ -\sin\varphi & 0 & \cos\varphi & 0 \\ 0 & 0 & 0 & 1 \end{bmatrix} \begin{bmatrix} 1 & 0 & 0 & 0 \\ 0 & \cos\psi & -\sin\psi & 0 \\ 0 & \sin\psi & \cos\psi & 0 \\ 0 & 0 & 0 & 1 \end{bmatrix} \begin{bmatrix} x \\ y \\ z \\ 1 \end{bmatrix}
$$

$$
= \begin{bmatrix} \cos\varphi\cos\theta & \sin\psi\sin\varphi\cos\theta - \cos\psi\sin\theta & \cos\psi\sin\varphi\cos\theta + \sin\psi\sin\theta & 0 \\ \cos\varphi\sin\theta & \sin\psi\sin\varphi\sin\theta + \cos\psi\cos\theta & \cos\psi\sin\varphi\sin\theta - \sin\psi\cos\theta & 0 \\ -\sin\varphi & \sin\psi\cos\varphi & \cos\psi\cos\varphi & 0 \\ 0 & 0 & 0 & 1 \end{bmatrix} \begin{bmatrix} x \\ y \\ z \\ 1 \end{bmatrix} \tag{5.30}
$$

The above equation can be interpreted as the transformation of any point (x, y, z) to (x', y', z') in a fixed coordinate frame. This interpretation does not use any information pertaining to body-fixed axes. On the other hand, if we assume that x, y, z represent the body-fixed axes which initially coincide with the coordinate reference axes X, Y, Z, respectively, Eq. 5.30 can be viewed as the transformation of a point from the moving body frame to the fixed coordinate reference frame. The Euler angle representation described above (and shown in Fig. 5.3) used rotations

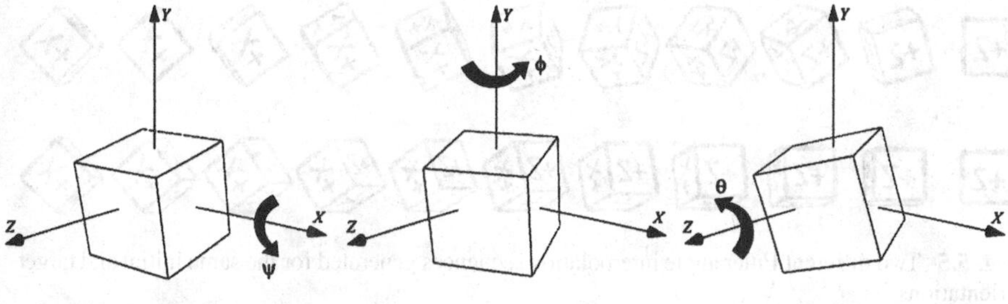

Fig. 5.3 An extrinsic composition of Euler angle rotations performed using the sequence $\{\psi, \phi, \theta\}$

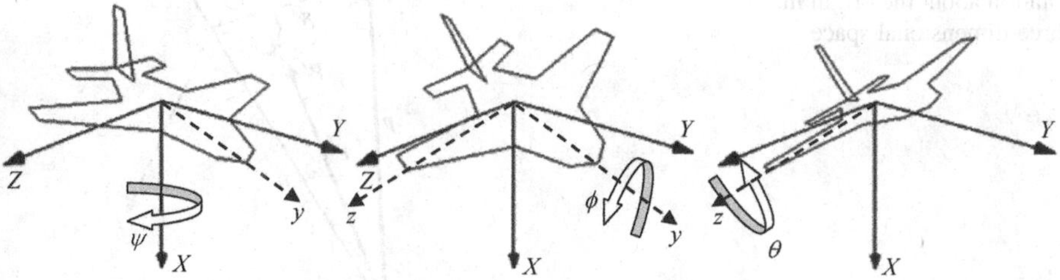

Fig. 5.4 An intrinsic composition of Euler angle rotations performed using the sequence $\{\psi, \phi, \theta\}$

that are performed about the fixed principal axes directions X, Y, Z of the reference frame. Such a transformation is called an extrinsic composition of rotations.

An intrinsic composition, on the other hand, uses rotations about body-fixed axes whose directions change in the reference frame after every rotation. For example, an aircraft orientation is defined in this manner. In Fig. 5.4, the yaw rotation ψ is performed about the x-axis, the roll rotation ϕ about the transformed body y-axis, and the pitch rotation θ about the transformed body z-axis. For this sequence of intrinsic composition of rotations, the transformation from body frame to the coordinate reference frame is given by

$$\begin{bmatrix} X \\ Y \\ Z \\ 1 \end{bmatrix} = \begin{bmatrix} 1 & 0 & 0 & 0 \\ 0 & \cos\psi & -\sin\psi & 0 \\ 0 & \sin\psi & \cos\psi & 0 \\ 0 & 0 & 0 & 1 \end{bmatrix} \begin{bmatrix} \cos\phi & 0 & \sin\phi & 0 \\ 0 & 1 & 0 & 0 \\ -\sin\phi & 0 & \cos\phi & 0 \\ 0 & 0 & 0 & 1 \end{bmatrix}$$
$$\times \begin{bmatrix} \cos\theta & -\sin\theta & 0 & 0 \\ \sin\theta & \cos\theta & 0 & 0 \\ 0 & 0 & 1 & 0 \\ 0 & 0 & 0 & 1 \end{bmatrix} \begin{bmatrix} x \\ y \\ z \\ 1 \end{bmatrix} \tag{5.31}$$

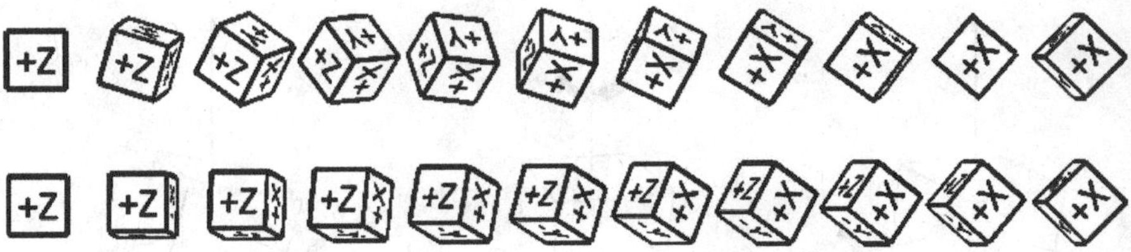

Fig. 5.5 Two different Euler angle interpolation sequences generated for the same initial and target orientations

Fig. 5.6 Transformation of a vector under a general rotation about the origin in three-dimensional space

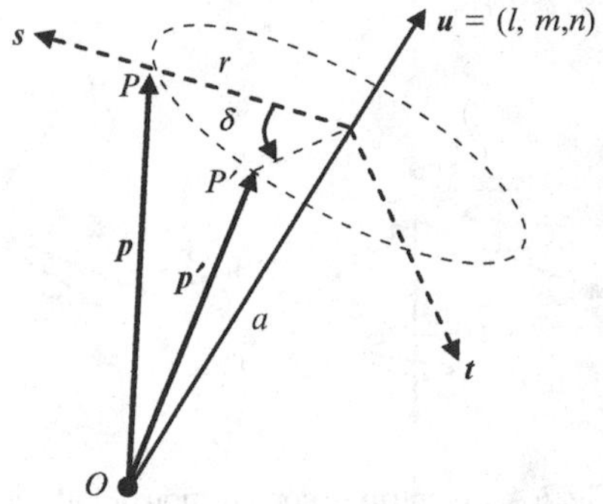

A three-dimensional orientation can be represented in different ways using different Euler angle sequences. Even if we keep the sequence fixed, certain orientations can have more than one set of Euler angles. For instance, using the same sequence $\{\psi\ \phi\ \theta\}$, both $\{-45, -80, 0\}$ and $\{135, -100, -180\}$ represent the same transformation. This can be verified by evaluating the product matrix in Eq. 5.30 for the two sets of angles. The non-uniqueness of the Euler angle representation also means that you may not get a unique interpolation path between two orientations (Fig. 5.5).

5.4.2 Angle-Axis Transformation

The Euler's theorem concerning three-dimensional rotations states that any number of rotational transformations with a single fixed point applied to an object can be replaced by a single rotation of the object about an axis passing through the fixed point. The axis is often called the equivalent axis of rotation. Any orientation of an object with the origin as a fixed point can therefore be specified using an angle of rotation δ and an axis of rotation given by a unit vector $\boldsymbol{u} = (l, m, n)$. In the following discussion, we assume that the axis of rotation passes through the origin. Figure 5.6 depicts the rotational transformation applied to a vector $\boldsymbol{p}$ (or a point P).

If we denote the projected lengths of the vector $\boldsymbol{p}$ along directions of $\boldsymbol{u}$ (axis of rotation) and $\boldsymbol{s}$ (perpendicular to axis of rotation) by a and r respectively, we can write $\boldsymbol{p} = a\boldsymbol{u} + r\boldsymbol{s}$, where $a = \boldsymbol{p}\bullet\boldsymbol{u}$. During any rotation of the vector $\boldsymbol{p}$ about the axis $\boldsymbol{u}$, both these projected distances a and r remain constant. If $\boldsymbol{t}$ denotes the vector orthogonal to both $\boldsymbol{u}$ and $\boldsymbol{s}$, the transformed vector direction $\boldsymbol{p}'$ can be written as

$$\begin{aligned} \boldsymbol{p}' &= a\boldsymbol{u} + (r \cos \delta)\boldsymbol{s} + (r \sin \delta)\boldsymbol{t} \\ &= a\boldsymbol{u} + (\boldsymbol{p} - a\boldsymbol{u})\cos \delta + (\boldsymbol{u} \times \boldsymbol{p})\sin \delta \\ &= \boldsymbol{p} \cos\delta + (1 - \cos\delta)(\boldsymbol{p} \bullet \boldsymbol{u})\boldsymbol{u} + (\boldsymbol{u} \times \boldsymbol{p})\sin \delta \end{aligned} \tag{5.32}$$

The above equation is the well-known Rodrigues' rotation formula. The matrix version of the Rodrigues' formula can be derived by defining a 3 × 3 skew-symmetric matrix $\mathbf{U_X}$ as

$$\mathbf{U_x} = \begin{bmatrix} 0 & -n & m \\ n & 0 & -l \\ -m & l & 0 \end{bmatrix}, \tag{5.33}$$

and replacing $\boldsymbol{u}, \boldsymbol{p}, \boldsymbol{p}'$ by the corresponding column vectors:

$$\mathbf{U} = \begin{bmatrix} l \\ m \\ n \end{bmatrix}, \quad \boldsymbol{p} = \begin{bmatrix} x \\ y \\ z \end{bmatrix}, \quad \boldsymbol{p}' = \begin{bmatrix} x' \\ y' \\ z' \end{bmatrix}. \tag{5.34}$$

With the above notations, the vector cross-product $\boldsymbol{u}\times\boldsymbol{p}$ has an equivalent matrix representation $(\mathbf{U_X})\,\boldsymbol{p}$. It can also be easily verified that the term $(\boldsymbol{p}\bullet\boldsymbol{u})\,\boldsymbol{u}$ in Eq. 5.32 is equivalent to the matrix $(\mathbf{UU^T})\,\boldsymbol{p}$. Thus we get

$$\boldsymbol{p}' = \left(\mathbf{I} \cos \delta + (1 - \cos \delta)\mathbf{UU^T} + \mathbf{U_X} \sin \delta\right) \boldsymbol{p} \tag{5.35}$$

Noting that

$$\mathbf{U_X^2} = \mathbf{UU^T} + \mathbf{I} \tag{5.36}$$

Equation 5.35 can be written in an alternate form as below.

$$\boldsymbol{p}' = \left(\mathbf{I} + (1 - \cos\delta)\mathbf{U_X^2} + \mathbf{U_X} \sin\delta\right) \boldsymbol{p} \tag{5.37}$$

Equation 5.35 can also be written in the expanded matrix form as follows for defining the rotational transformation of a point P expressed in homogeneous coordinates:

$$\begin{bmatrix} x' \\ y' \\ z' \\ 1 \end{bmatrix} = \begin{bmatrix} l^2(1-\cos\delta)+\cos\delta & lm(1-\cos\delta)-n\sin\delta & nl(1-\cos\delta)+m\sin\delta & 0 \\ lm(1-\cos\delta)+n\sin\delta & m^2(1-\cos\delta)+\cos\delta & mn(1-\cos\delta)-l\sin\delta & 0 \\ nl(1-\cos\delta)-m\sin\delta & mn(1-\cos\delta)+l\sin\delta & n^2(1-\cos\delta)+\cos\delta & 0 \\ 0 & 0 & 0 & 1 \end{bmatrix} \begin{bmatrix} x \\ y \\ z \\ 1 \end{bmatrix} \tag{5.38}$$

Let us consider the problem of computing the equivalent angle and axis of rotation from a transformation matrix. Given a general 4×4 rotation matrix in the form

$$\begin{bmatrix} m_{00} & m_{01} & m_{02} & 0 \\ m_{10} & m_{11} & m_{12} & 0 \\ m_{20} & m_{21} & m_{22} & 0 \\ 0 & 0 & 0 & 1 \end{bmatrix} \tag{5.39}$$

we get the following equations using the matrix elements from Eq. 5.38:

$$\begin{aligned} m_{00} + m_{11} + m_{22} &= 1 + 2\cos\delta \\ m_{21} - m_{12} &= 2l\ \sin\delta \\ m_{02} - m_{20} &= 2m\ \sin\delta \\ m_{10} - m_{01} &= 2n\sin\delta \end{aligned} \tag{5.40}$$

From the above equations, we can derive the expressions for angle and axis of rotation as follows:

$$\begin{aligned} \delta &= \tan^{-1}\left(\frac{\sqrt{(m_{21}-m_{12})^2 + (m_{02}-m_{20})^2 + (m_{10}-m_{01})^2}}{m_{00}+m_{11}+m_{22}-1}\right) \\ l &= \frac{m_{21}-m_{12}}{2\ \sin\delta} \\ m &= \frac{m_{02}-m_{20}}{2\ \sin\delta} \\ n &= \frac{m_{10}-m_{01}}{2\ \sin\delta} \end{aligned} \tag{5.41}$$

In the next section, we will establish the equivalence between an angle-axis transformation and a unit quaternion transformation of the form QPQ^* where P is a pure quaternion $(0, \boldsymbol{p})$.

5.5 Quaternion Rotations

We will now try to represent the rotational transformation in Fig. 5.6 by a unit quaternion $Q = (q_0, \boldsymbol{w})$, where the vector component $\boldsymbol{w}$ of the quaternion is along the axis of rotation. Therefore we have

$$\boldsymbol{w} = k\boldsymbol{u}, \text{ for some constant } k. \tag{5.42}$$

We saw earlier that a vector $\boldsymbol{p}$ can be transformed into another vector $\boldsymbol{p}'$ using a unit quaternion Q and the result of this transformation is given by Eq. 5.27. In the previous section, we considered an angle-axis transformation of a vector $\boldsymbol{p}$ given by Eq. 5.32. We find a striking similarity between the two equations, which suggests that the quaternion transformation in Eq. 5.27 is indeed an angle-axis transformation. Equating the corresponding terms in both the equations, we find that

$$\begin{aligned} {q_0}^2 - w^2 &= \cos\delta \\ 2q_0 k &= \sin\delta \\ 1 - \cos\delta &= 2k^2 \end{aligned} \tag{5.43}$$

From the above equations, we can see that $k = \sin(\delta/2)$, and $q_0 = \cos(\delta/2)$. Therefore the unit quaternion that represents the rotation in Fig. 5.6 is given by

$$Q = \left(\cos\frac{\delta}{2},\ l\sin\frac{\delta}{2},\ m\sin\frac{\delta}{2},\ n\sin\frac{\delta}{2}\right) \tag{5.44}$$

This result is fundamental to the theory of generalized rotations, as it provides a direct mechanism for converting angle-axis representations of three-dimensional rotations into unit quaternions. From this equation, we can also derive the relationship between the components of any unit quaternion $Q = (q_0, q_1, q_2, q_3)$ and the parameters of rotation it represents. The angle of rotation is given by

$$\delta = 2\tan^{-1}\left(\frac{\sqrt{q_1^2 + q_2^2 + q_3^2}}{q_0}\right) \tag{5.45}$$

and the unit vector along the axis of rotation (l, m, n) can be obtained as

$$\begin{aligned} l &= \frac{q_1}{\sqrt{q_1^2 + q_2^2 + q_3^2}} \\ m &= \frac{q_2}{\sqrt{q_1^2 + q_2^2 + q_3^2}} \\ n &= \frac{q_3}{\sqrt{q_1^2 + q_2^2 + q_3^2}} \end{aligned} \tag{5.46}$$

Replacing $\delta/2$ with δ in Eq. 5.44, we can summarize our discussion above as follows:

Any unit quaternion Q can be expressed in the form $Q = (\cos\delta,\ \boldsymbol{u}\sin\delta)$, and it represents a rotation by an angle 2δ about a unit vector $\boldsymbol{u}$ passing through the origin.

5.5.1 Quaternion Transformation Matrix

From the above discussion, we can conclude that if Q is a unit quaternion, then Eq. 5.27 gives a rotational transformation of a vector $\boldsymbol{p} = (x, y, z, 0)$. This transformation equation could also be written in the conventional matrix form as shown below:

$$\begin{bmatrix} x' \\ y' \\ z' \\ 0 \end{bmatrix} = \begin{bmatrix} 1-2q_2^2-2q_3^2 & 2q_1q_2-2q_0q_3 & 2q_1q_3+2q_0q_2 & 0 \\ 2q_1q_2+2q_0q_3 & 1-2q_1^2-2q_3^2 & 2q_2q_3-2q_0q_1 & 0 \\ 2q_1q_3-2q_0q_2 & 2q_2q_3+2q_0q_1 & 1-2q_1^2-2q_2^2 & 0 \\ 0 & 0 & 0 & 1 \end{bmatrix} \begin{bmatrix} x \\ y \\ z \\ 0 \end{bmatrix} \tag{5.47}$$

The same transformation matrix can be applied to transform a point $P = (x, y, z, 1)$ to another point $P' = (x', y', z', 1)$ using the quaternion Q. The quaternion transformation matrix in Eq. 5.47 is orthogonal, meaning that its inverse is the same as its transpose. The matrix also has some very useful properties. If we equate this matrix to a general 4×4 matrix given in Eq. 5.39, we can find that the following relationships hold among the matrix elements:

$$\begin{aligned} m_{00} + m_{11} + m_{22} + 1 &= 4{q_0}^2 \\ m_{21} - m_{12} &= 4q_0q_1 \\ m_{02} - m_{20} &= 4q_0q_2 \\ m_{10} - m_{01} &= 4q_0q_3 \end{aligned} \tag{5.48}$$

The above equations are useful for extracting the quaternion elements from a given 4×4 rotational transformation matrix:

$$\begin{aligned} q_0 &= \frac{\sqrt{1 + m_{00} + m_{11} + m_{22}}}{2} \\ q_1 &= \frac{m_{21} - m_{12}}{4q_0} \\ q_2 &= \frac{m_{02} - m_{20}}{4q_0} \\ q_3 &= \frac{m_{10} - m_{01}}{4q_0} \end{aligned} \tag{5.49}$$

We will choose only the positive value of the square-root for computing q_0. A negative value for q_0 will change the sign of all remaining components and yield the quaternion $-Q$ in place of Q. Shortly (Eq. 5.57) we will see that both Q and $-Q$ represent the same rotation, and therefore we can safely impose the constraint that the sign of q_0 is positive, and compute the remaining components from it. Note also that the above equations are valid only when $q_0 \neq 0$. If $q_0 = 0$, then the angle of rotation $\delta = \pm 180°$, and the matrix in Eq. 5.47 becomes a symmetric matrix. For this special case, the remaining quaternion elements can be derived as follows:

$$q_1 = sign\,(m_{21} - m_{12}) \left\{ \frac{\sqrt{1 + m_{00} - m_{11} - m_{22}}}{2} \right\}$$

$$q_2 = sign\,(m_{02} - m_{20}) \left\{ \frac{\sqrt{1 - m_{00} + m_{11} - m_{22}}}{2} \right\}$$

$$q_3 = sign\,(m_{10} - m_{01}) \left\{ \frac{\sqrt{1 - m_{00} - m_{11} + m_{22}}}{2} \right\} \tag{5.50}$$

If a point (or a vector) P is first transformed by a quaternion Q_1 and then by a quaternion Q_2, the resulting point (or vector) P' is obtained by applying the transformation formula twice:

$$P' = Q_2(Q_1 P Q_1{}^*)Q_2{}^* = (Q_2 Q_1)P(Q_2 Q_1)^* \tag{5.51}$$

The above equation shows that the composite rotation is given by the quaternion product Q_2Q_1. Generalising this result, a series of rotational transformations performed using unit quaternions $Q_1, Q_2, \ldots Q_k$ in that order, is equivalent to a single rotational transformation produced by the combined product quaternion $(Q_k \ldots Q_2Q_1)$.

5.5.2 *Quaternions and Euler Angles*

In this section, we explore the relationship between unit quaternions and Euler angles. Using Eq. 5.44, we can represent elementary rotations about X, Y, and Z axes by angles ψ, ϕ, θ respectively, as follows:

$$Q_X = \left(\cos\frac{\psi}{2},\ \sin\frac{\psi}{2},\ 0,\ 0\right) \tag{5.52}$$

$$Q_Y = \left(\cos\frac{\phi}{2},\ 0,\ \sin\frac{\phi}{2},\ 0\right) \tag{5.53}$$

$$Q_Z = \left(\cos\frac{\theta}{2},\ 0,\ 0,\ \sin\frac{\theta}{2}\right) \tag{5.54}$$

A sequence of Euler angle rotations $\{\psi, \phi, \theta\}$ is equivalent to the quaternion product $Q_ZQ_YQ_X$. We will denote this product by Q_E. Using the quaternion multiplication rule in Eq. 5.10, we can easily express the components of Q_E in terms of the Euler angles. For convenience, the four quaternion components are arranged as a column vector in the equation below.

$$Q_E = \begin{pmatrix} \cos\left(\frac{\psi}{2}\right)\cos\left(\frac{\phi}{2}\right)\cos\left(\frac{\theta}{2}\right) + \sin\left(\frac{\psi}{2}\right)\sin\left(\frac{\phi}{2}\right)\sin\left(\frac{\theta}{2}\right) \\ \sin\left(\frac{\psi}{2}\right)\cos\left(\frac{\phi}{2}\right)\cos\left(\frac{\theta}{2}\right) - \cos\left(\frac{\psi}{2}\right)\sin\left(\frac{\phi}{2}\right)\sin\left(\frac{\theta}{2}\right) \\ \cos\left(\frac{\psi}{2}\right)\sin\left(\frac{\phi}{2}\right)\cos\left(\frac{\theta}{2}\right) + \sin\left(\frac{\psi}{2}\right)\cos\left(\frac{\phi}{2}\right)\sin\left(\frac{\theta}{2}\right) \\ \cos\left(\frac{\psi}{2}\right)\cos\left(\frac{\phi}{2}\right)\sin\left(\frac{\theta}{2}\right) - \sin\left(\frac{\psi}{2}\right)\sin\left(\frac{\phi}{2}\right)\cos\left(\frac{\theta}{2}\right) \end{pmatrix} \tag{5.55}$$

Conversely, given a unit quaternion $Q = (q_0, q_1, q_2, q_3)$, we can compute the equivalent Euler angle representation by comparing the elements of the quaternion transformation matrix and the Euler angle transformation matrix. As an example, by equating the corresponding elements from only the first column and the third row of the matrices in Eqs. 5.47 and 5.30, we get the following expressions for the Euler angles ψ, ϕ, θ in terms of quaternion components:

$$\begin{aligned} \psi &= \tan^{-1}\left(\frac{2(q_0q_1 + q_2q_3)}{1 - 2q_1^2 - 2q_2^2}\right) \\ \phi &= \sin^{-1}(2q_0q_2 - 2q_1q_3) \\ \theta &= \tan^{-1}\left(\frac{2(q_0q_3 + q_1q_2)}{1 - 2q_2^2 - 2q_3^2}\right) \end{aligned} \tag{5.56}$$

There are many other ways in which the above parameters can be obtained by comparing the remaining elements of the two matrices. However, each derivation has its own set of singularities that need to be handled as special cases. For example, the unit quaternion

$$Q = \left(\frac{1}{\sqrt{2}}, 0, \frac{1}{\sqrt{2}}, 0\right)$$

presents a singularity for ψ, with both the numerator and the denominator of the first equation in Eq. 5.56 becoming zero.

5.5.3 *Negative Quaternion*

In this section, we consider another geometrical property of quaternions, taking Q_Z (Eq. 5.54) as an example. Figure 5.7 shows the plot of the first and the fourth non-zero components of Q_Z as the rotation angle θ is varied over two cycles from 0° to 720°.

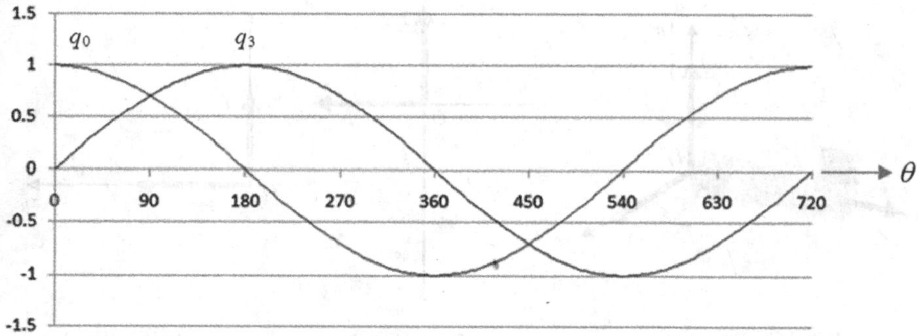

Fig. 5.7 Plot showing the variation of quaternion components with rotation angle

Figure 5.7 shows that one cycle in quaternion space takes two revolutions in the Cartesian coordinate space. This means that two rotations by angles θ and $360+\theta$ that are geometrically equivalent, can have different quaternion representations. If a unit quaternion Q is given by Eq. 5.44, then replacing δ with $360+\delta$ we get,

$$\begin{aligned} Q' &= \left(\cos\frac{360+\delta}{2},\ l\sin\frac{360+\delta}{2},\ m\sin\frac{360+\delta}{2},\ n\sin\frac{360+\delta}{2}\right) \\ &= \left(-\cos\frac{\delta}{2}, -l\sin\frac{\delta}{2}, -m\sin\frac{\delta}{2}, -n\sin\frac{\delta}{2}\right) \\ &= -Q \end{aligned} \tag{5.57}$$

The above equation shows that both Q and $-Q$ represent the same rotational transformation. In the next section, we will consider the problem of interpolating between two orientations (which we had briefly touched on while introducing Euler angles), and then use some of the properties of quaternion rotations discussed above to define quaternion based interpolation methods.

5.6 Rotation Interpolation

Animation sequences commonly use interpolated values between two poses. A pose defines the position and orientation an object. Position interpolation can be carried out either by interpolating between the corresponding coordinate values, or by fitting parametric curves (splines) through the points. However, interpolation between two orientations in three-dimensional space need not always produce a smooth transition from one orientation to another. Depending on the mechanism we use for representing rotations, we can get completely different interpolation sequences between the same initial and target orientations. Generally, one would prefer an interpolation that yields an optimal path that gives minimum rotation and uniform

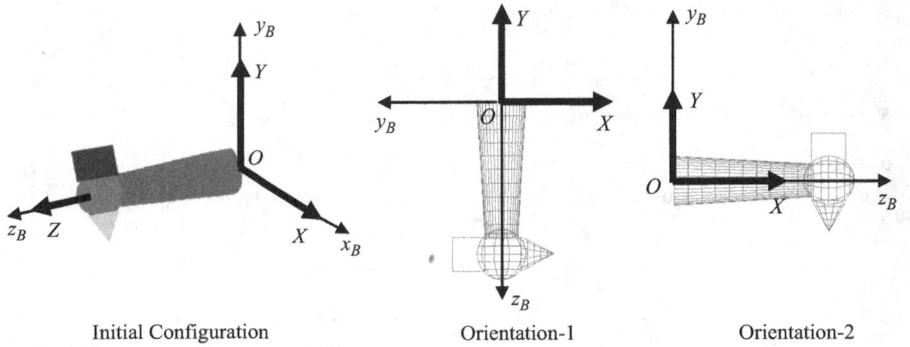

Fig. 5.8 Initial configuration and two orientations of an object

angular velocity between two configurations. In this section, we will compare different interpolation methods using different representations of rotation we have considered so far, and establish that quaternions have a clear advantage over others.

We define orientation as the result of a rotational transformation from the initial configuration of an object to its current configuration. A configuration is uniquely specified by an orthogonal system of axes fixed on the object. Some of these concepts are explained in a little more detail below with the help of an example. Figure 5.8 shows a simple model, "Hammer", constructed using four primitives, a cylinder, a cone, a sphere and a cube. The figure also shows two orientations of this model.

The initial configuration of the object defines its orientation when no rotational transformation is applied. In this configuration, an orthogonal right-handed system of body-fixed axes $Ox_By_Bz_B$ coincides with the inertially fixed coordinate reference axes *OXYZ*. Without any loss of generality, we can assume that all rotations take place about the origin. The unit vectors along body fixed axes have components $\boldsymbol{x}_B = (1, 0, 0), \boldsymbol{y}_B = (0, 1, 0), \boldsymbol{z}_B = (0, 0, 1)$ in the initial configuration. An orientation can be uniquely defined using the transformed components of these three vectors. For example, Orientation-1 in Fig. 5.8 is defined by the vectors $\boldsymbol{x}_B = (0, 0, 1)$, $\boldsymbol{y}_B = (-1, 0, 0)$, $\boldsymbol{z}_B = (0, -1, 0)$. During any rotational transformation the tips of these vectors move on a unit sphere centered at the origin (Fig. 5.9a).

The rotational transformation of an object can thus be visualized using the trace of the unit vectors along the body-fixed axes on a unit sphere. Any unit vector has a spherical parameterization in terms of its azimuth (or longitude) α, and elevation (or latitude) β (Fig. 5.9). The variation of the tip of a vector $\boldsymbol{v} = (x_v, y_v, z_v)$ on a unit sphere can be conveniently represented as a 2D-graph of the values (α, β) computed as follows:

$$\alpha = \tan^{-1}\left(\frac{x_v}{z_v}\right)$$

$$\beta = \tan^{-1}\left(\frac{y_v}{\sqrt{x_v^2 + z_v^2}}\right) \tag{5.58}$$

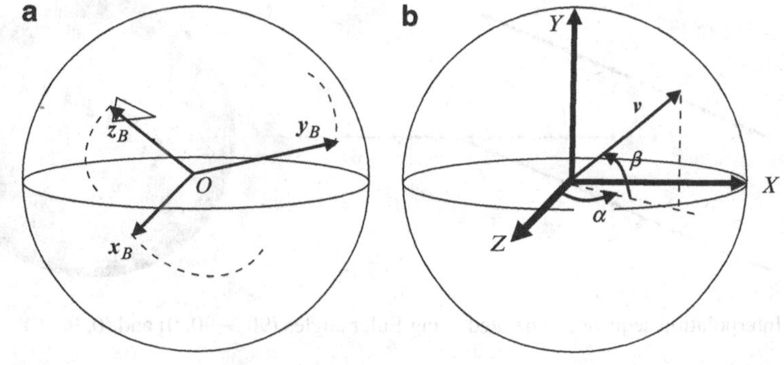

Fig. 5.9 Spherical parameterization of rotations: (**a**) Movement of unit vectors attached to body axes during a rotation of the object. (**b**) Parametric representation of unit vectors on a sphere

Table 5.1 Graph values (α,β) of the two orientations in Fig. 5.8

	Orientation-1	Orientation-2
x_B	(0, 0)	(±180, 0)
y_B	(−90, 0)	(∼, 90)
z_B	(∼, −90)	(90, 0)
Transformation matrix	$\begin{bmatrix} 0 & -1 & 0 \\ 0 & 0 & -1 \\ 1 & 0 & 0 \end{bmatrix}$	$\begin{bmatrix} 0 & 0 & 1 \\ 0 & 1 & 0 \\ -1 & 0 & 0 \end{bmatrix}$

∼indicates an indeterminate value

We call the above method of representing the three-dimensional variations of a unit vector as the $\alpha\beta$-graph method. Note that when $\beta = \pm 90°$, the value of α is indeterminate. In the following sections, we will use $\alpha\beta$-graphs of the body-fixed axes for a given interpolation sequence to compare the paths generated by different methods. For the example given in Fig. 5.8, the graph values (in degrees) of Orientation-1 and Orientation-2 are shown in Table 5.1. The variation of a graph between the two points will help us visualize how a sequence of rotational transformations operates on an object for transforming it from one orientation to the other.

Another method for visualizing three-dimensional rotations is to show a small triangle (see Fig. 5.9a) at the position of one of the body axes (say, z_B) on the unit sphere, oriented towards another axis (say y_B). The triangle uniquely represents the three-dimensional orientation of the object. Triangles displayed at equal time intervals during a rotational transformation will clearly show the movement of an axis of interest, and also indicate the spin of the object about that axis (see Fig. 5.10).

5.6.1 Euler Angle Interpolation

Let us first consider the interpolation between two orientations represented using Euler angles. For our example, we will use the Euler angle sequence $\{\psi, \phi, \theta\}$

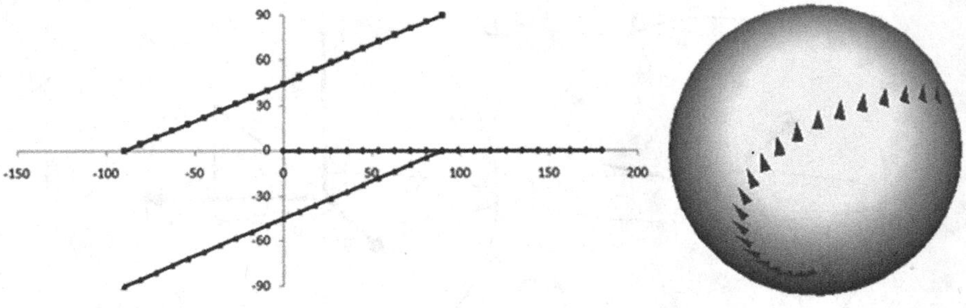

Fig. 5.10 Interpolation sequence generated using Euler angles (90, −90, 0) and (0, 90, 0)

introduced in Sect. 5.4.1. Given two sets of Euler angles $\{\psi_1, \phi_1, \theta_1\}$ and $\{\psi_2, \phi_2, \theta_2\}$, all intermediate sets can be obtained using a linear interpolation between the corresponding Euler angles:

$$\begin{aligned}\psi &= (1-t)\psi_1 + t\psi_2\\ \phi &= (1-t)\phi_1 + t\phi_2\\ \theta &= (1-t)\theta_1 + t\theta_2, 0 \le t \le 1.\end{aligned} \tag{5.59}$$

The transformation matrix in Eq. 5.30 then defines the rotation from the initial configuration to the intermediate orientation. Earlier in Fig. 5.5, we saw examples of interpolation sequences generated in this manner. For the example given in Fig. 5.8, Orientation-1 is defined by Euler angles $\{\psi_1 = 90, \phi_1 = -90, \theta_1 = 0\}$, and Orientation-2 by $\{\psi_2 = 0, \phi_2 = 90, \theta_2 = 0\}$. The $\alpha\beta$-graph for the interpolation sequence is given in Fig. 5.10. For this specific example, linear interpolation in the domain of Euler angles also generates a perfect linear interpolation in $\alpha\beta$-space, consisting of equidistant points. However, when we look at the trace of the hammer's axis from $-Y$ direction to $+X$ direction on the surface of the unit sphere, we observe that the rotational motion from the source to the destination in three-dimensional space is not uniform.

The "Hammer" example in Fig. 5.8 also presents an interesting aspect of Euler angles. Orientation-2 can have an infinite number of Euler angle representations given by $\{\psi_2 = \lambda, \phi_2 = 90, \theta_2 = \lambda\}$ where λ is any value. Thus between the same two orientations, we can have several interpolation paths using Euler angles. As an example, the interpolated values obtained using $\lambda = -170°$ give a distinctly different and curvilinear path between Orientation-1 and Orientation-2, as shown in Fig. 5.11.

5.6.2 Axis-Angle Interpolation

The equivalent angles and axes of rotation for both Orientation-1 and Orientation-2 can be computed from the corresponding transformation matrices using Eq. 5.41.

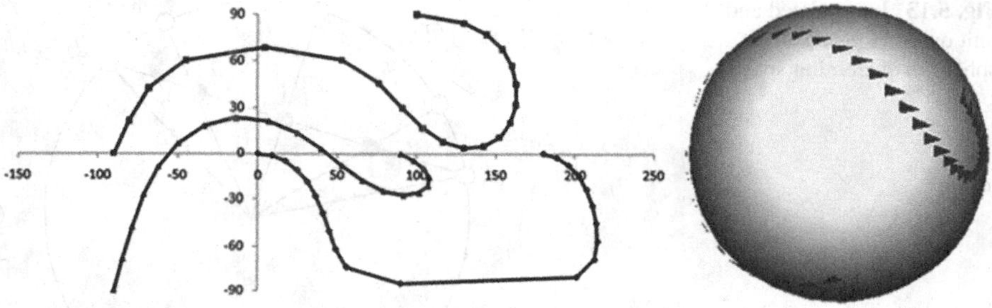

Fig. 5.11 Interpolation sequence generated using Euler angles (90, −90, 0) and (−170, 90, −170)

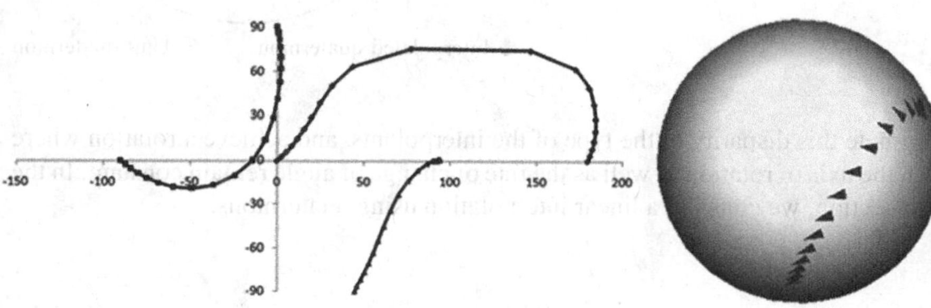

Fig. 5.12 Interpolation sequence generated using the angle-axis transformation

The parameters for Orientation-1 are $\delta_1 = 120°$, $l_1 = 0.57735$, $m_1 = -0.57735$, $n_1 = 0.57735$, and for Orientation-2 the values are $\delta_2 = 90°$, $l_2 = 0$, $m_2 = 1$, $n_2 = 0$. A straightforward linear interpolation gives

$$\begin{aligned} \delta &= (1-t)\delta_1 + t\delta_2 \\ l &= (1-t)l_1 + tl_2 \\ m &= (1-t)m_1 + tm_2 \\ n &= (1-t)n_1 + tn_2, \; 0 \le t \le 1. \end{aligned} \tag{5.60}$$

The interpolated vector will need to be normalized before constructing the transformation matrix in Eq. 5.38. The intermediate orientations generated using the above equation are shown in Fig. 5.12.

In the example shown above, the angle axis transformation generates a non-uniform motion with a large variation in the angular velocity. As can be seen from both the $\alpha\beta$-graph and the trace on the sphere, the density of points around the source and the destination points is very large compared to the middle. The parameters used in the interpolation belong to completely different domains, the angle being a scalar and the axis of rotation being a vector. Quaternions help us to

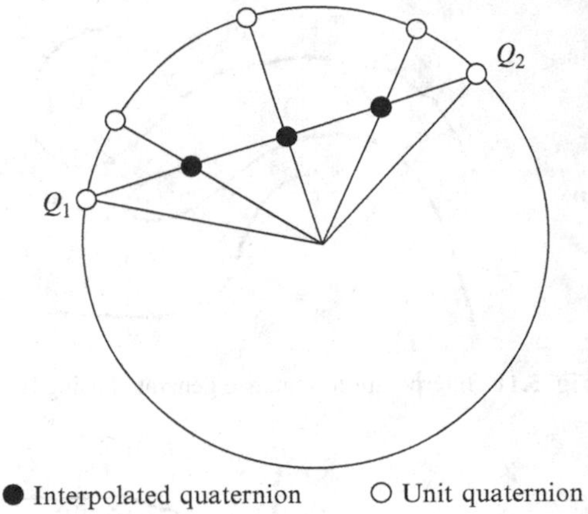

Fig. 5.13 Interpolated and unit quaternions on a unit sphere in quaternion space

eliminate this disparity in the type of the interpolants, and achieve a rotation where both the axis of rotation as well as the rate of change of angle remain constant. In the next section, we consider a linear interpolation using quaternions.

5.6.3 *Quaternion Linear Interpolation (LERP)*

Given two unit quaternions $Q_1 = \{q_0{}^{(1)}, q_1{}^{(1)}, q_2{}^{(1)}, q_3{}^{(1)}\}$ and $Q_2 = \{q_0{}^{(2)}, q_1{}^{(2)}, q_2{}^{(2)}, q_3{}^{(2)}\}$, a linear interpolation gives the quaternion

$$Q = (1-t)Q_1 + tQ_2, \quad 0 \leq t \leq 1. \tag{5.61}$$

The quaternion resulting from the above equation is converted to a unit quaternion before a transformation of the form QPQ^* is applied to all points P of the object. Every unit quaternion lies on a unit sphere in the four-dimensional space spanned by the quaternion basis (1, *i*, *j*, *k*). The interpolated quaternions obtained from Eq. 5.61 lie on a straight line between the two points Q_1 and Q_2. Converting them to unit quaternions moves each interpolated quaternion to the surface of the sphere along a radial (Fig. 5.13), resulting in an uneven distribution of points and a corresponding non-uniformity in the angular velocity of the object. The speed in the middle of the interpolation path is generally much higher than the speed at the end points. The interpolated quaternions after normalization lie on an arc of a great circle between Q_1 and Q_2.

Continuing with our "Hammer" example in Fig. 5.8, the source and the target orientations in Table 5.1 can be converted into quaternions using Eq. 5.49. For Orientation-1, the quaternion parameters are $q_0{}^{(1)} = 0.5$, $q_1{}^{(1)} = 0.5$, $q_2{}^{(1)} = -0.5$, $q_3{}^{(1)} = 0.5$, and for Orientation-2, the values are $q_0{}^{(2)} = 0.71$, $q_1{}^{(2)} = 0$, $q_2{}^{(2)} = 0.71$, $q_3{}^{(2)} = 0$. The $\alpha\beta$-graph and the trace of the hammer axis on the sphere are shown in Fig. 5.14.

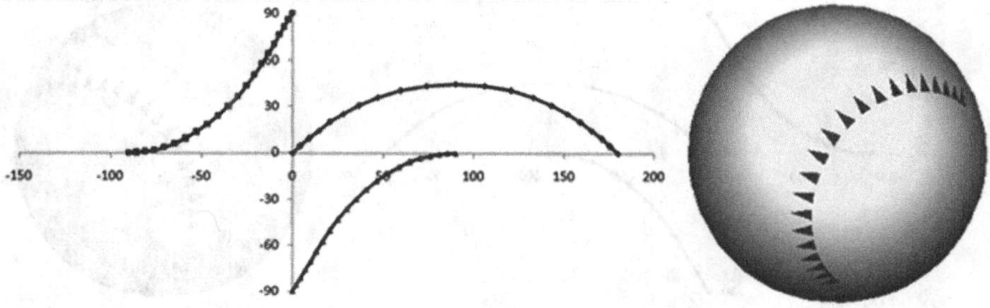

Fig. 5.14 Interpolation sequence generated using quaternion linear interpolation

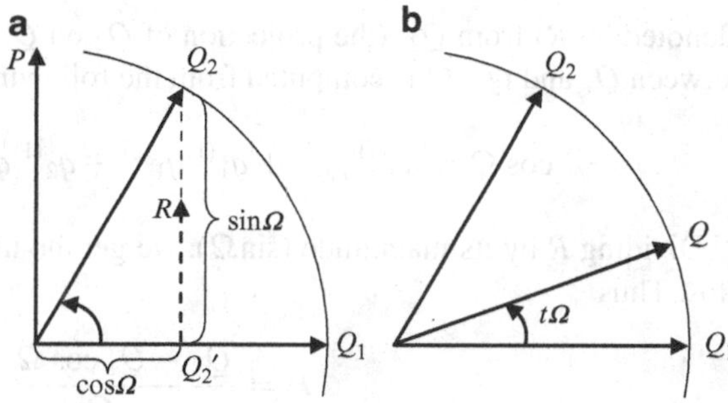

Fig. 5.15 Subdivision of the angle between unit quaternions

The interpolation path obtained using quaternions is along a circular arc between the end points, which is often the most desired path. However, the non-uniform spacing of points along the arc indicates that the angular velocity is initially smaller, then increases towards the middle and slows down again towards the target.

5.6.4 Quaternion Spherical Linear Interpolation (SLERP)

In the previous section we saw that linear interpolation generates intermediate quaternions along a chord between Q_1 and Q_2 (Fig. 5.13) on the unit sphere in quaternion space. If we subdivide the angle between Q_1 and Q_2 uniformly, then we will get an even distribution of points on the sphere. Such a distribution will also yield a smooth rotation of the object from one orientation to another with nearly constant angular velocity. The spherical linear interpolation (SLERP) technique uses this approach to compute intermediate quaternions.

Figure 5.15 shows the geometrical constructions needed to derive the SLERP formula. In the figure, $Q_1 = \{q_0^{(1)}, q_1^{(1)}, q_2^{(1)}, q_3^{(1)}\}$ and $Q_2 = \{q_0^{(2)}, q_1^{(2)}, q_2^{(2)}, q_3^{(2)}\}$ are any two unit quaternions and P is another unit quaternion that is orthogonal to Q_1. Treating them as vectors in quaternion space, $Q_2 - Q_1\cos\Omega$ is a vector

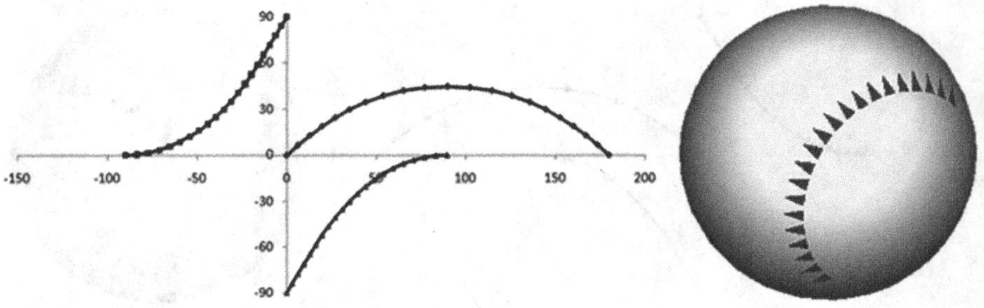

Fig. 5.16 Interpolation sequence generated using quaternion spherical linear interpolation

(denoted by R) from Q_2' (the projection of Q_2 on Q_1) to Q_2, where Ω is the angle between Q_1 and Q_2. Ω is computed from the following formula:

$$\cos\Omega = q_0^{(1)}q_0^{(2)} + q_1^{(1)}q_1^{(2)} + q_2^{(1)}q_2^{(2)} + q_3^{(1)}q_3^{(2)} \tag{5.62}$$

Dividing R by its magnitude ($\sin\Omega$), we get the unit quaternion in the direction of R. Thus

$$P = \frac{Q_2 - Q_1\cos\Omega}{\sin\Omega} \tag{5.63}$$

Figure 5.15 shows the angle between Q_1 and Q_2 subdivided using an interpolation parameter t ($0 \leq t \leq 1$), and the interpolated unit quaternion Q generated using this subdivision. Resolving Q along the orthogonal unit directions of Q_1 and P we get

$$Q = Q_1\cos(t\Omega) + P\sin(t\Omega) \tag{5.64}$$

Substituting Eq. 5.63 and simplifying we get

$$Q = \frac{Q_1\sin((1-t)\Omega) + Q_2\sin(t\Omega)}{\sin(\Omega)} \tag{5.65}$$

The above equation has a singularity when $\Omega = 0$ or $\pm180°$. When $\Omega = 0$, both the initial and final quaternions are the same, and therefore no interpolation is necessary. When $\Omega = \pm180°$, $Q_2 = -Q_1$. From Eq. 5.57 we know that this condition also corresponds to the situation where both orientations are the same.

The interpolated sequence generated by Eq. 5.65 for the "Hammer" example is shown in Fig. 5.16. Compared with the results obtained from previously discussed forms of interpolation, the smoothness of the interpolating curves as well as the uniformity in the distribution of points along them are noticeable. Spherical linear interpolation yields an optimal angle interpolation between two orientations with a constant axis of rotation. If the interpolation parameter is incremented in constant steps, spherical linear interpolation will generate a motion with constant angular velocity.

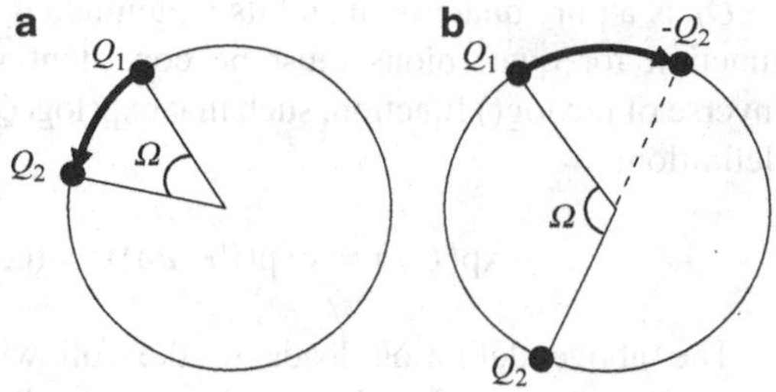

Fig. 5.17 Two different interpolation paths on the quaternion sphere

When interpolating between two quaternions Q_1 and Q_2, we have to make sure that the interpolation is performed along the shorter arc on the great circle through the two points on the quaternion sphere. If the angle Ω between Q_1 and Q_2 is less than 90°, we interpolate between the two quaternions (Fig. 5.17), otherwise we interpolate between Q_1 and $-Q_2$ (Fig. 5.17). In other words, if $Q_1 \bullet Q_2 = \cos\Omega < 0$, we negate the sign of Q_2. The value of $\cos\Omega$ is computed using the formula in Eq. 5.62.

The following sections discuss a few more applications of quaternions for representing transformations in a three-dimensional space.

5.7 Quaternion Exponentiation

We will extend the notion of exponentiation from the field of complex numbers to the domain of quaternions and also define the associated logarithmic function that is consistent with exponentiation. However, there are some subtle differences between the way in which these operations are performed on real and complex numbers and the way they are applied to quaternions.

From Eq. 5.6 we know that a unit complex number can be expressed as $z = (\cos\delta, \sin\delta)$. The same complex number has an alternate representation in the form $z = e^{i\delta}$. This is the well known Euler's formula in complex numbers. We know that a unit quaternion can also be written as $Q = (\cos\delta, \boldsymbol{u} \sin\delta)$. Similar to complex numbers, an exponential notation for unit quaternions can be introduced as follows:

$$Q = (\cos\delta, \boldsymbol{u} \sin\delta) = e^{\boldsymbol{u}\delta} \tag{5.66}$$

where $\boldsymbol{u} = (l, m, n)$ is a unit vector in three-dimensional space. For the time being, we will treat the above equation as only an alternate representation of unit quaternions. We will see the formal definition of the exponential function and how it is related to the above notation immediately after the next equation. The logarithm of the unit quaternion in Eq. 5.66 is defined as

$$Q_L = \log(Q) = \log(e^{\boldsymbol{u}\delta}) = (0, \boldsymbol{u}\delta) = (0, l\delta, m\delta, n\delta) \tag{5.67}$$

Q_L is a pure quaternion and its magnitude is δ. The definition of an exponential function for quaternions must be consistent with the above operation and the inverse of the log() function, such that $\exp(\log(Q)) = Q$. We thus have the following definition:

$$\exp(Q_L) = \exp((0,\ \boldsymbol{u}\delta)) = (\cos\delta, \boldsymbol{u}\ \sin\delta) = e^{\boldsymbol{u}\delta}. \tag{5.68}$$

The above definition leads to the following important result for any unit quaternion $Q = (\cos\delta,\ \boldsymbol{u}\ \sin\delta)$, and any real value t:

$$Q^t = \exp(t\log(Q)) = \exp((0, \boldsymbol{u}t\delta)) = (\cos(t\delta), \boldsymbol{u}\ \sin(t\delta)) \tag{5.69}$$

Note that the operations Q^t and $\exp(Q_L)$ both return unit quaternions. As a special case, when $t = 0$, we have

$$Q^0 = (1, 0, 0, 0) \text{ for any unit quaternion } Q. \tag{5.70}$$

Since quaternion multiplication is non-commutative, it immediately follows that $Q^a Q^b \neq Q^b Q^a$ and, $\log(PQ) \neq \log(P) + \log(Q)$. However, the following equations are valid for all unit quaternions Q:

$$\begin{aligned} Q^a Q^b &= Q^{a+b} \\ (Q^a)^b &= Q^{ab} \end{aligned} \tag{5.71}$$

We know that the unit quaternion Q given in Eq. 5.66 represents a rotation by an angle 2δ about the unit vector $\boldsymbol{u}$ passing through the origin. From Eq. 5.69, we see that raising Q to the power of t effectively changes the angle of rotation. Thus if $0 \leq t \leq 1$, then Q^t gives a unit quaternion that represents a partial rotation $2t\delta$. This result is useful for interpolating between orientations. In the next section, we will define the relative quaternion between two orientations, and then apply Eq. 5.69 to perform incremental rotations along a path from the source orientation to the target orientation. As a result, we will get another equation for the quaternion spherical linear interpolation using the exponential notation.

5.8 Relative Quaternions

In Sect. 5.6, we defined the three-dimensional orientation of an object using the parameters of rotation that transforms the object from its initial configuration to the current. This rotation can be represented by a unit quaternion. Thus two independent orientations of an object can be represented by two unit quaternions Q_1 and Q_2 (Fig. 5.18). In the following, we try to find the relative quaternion that performs

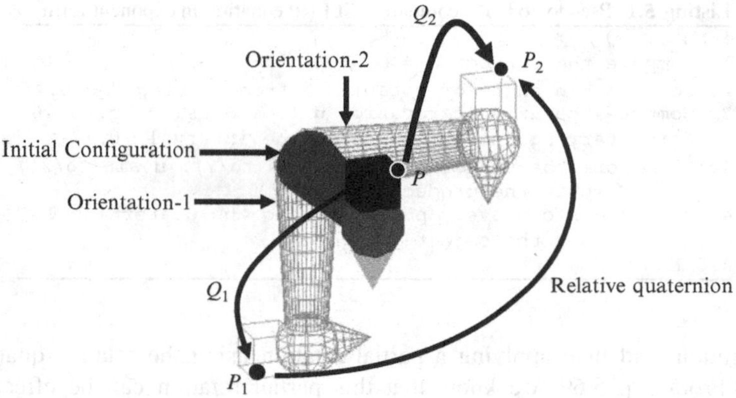

Fig. 5.18 The relative quaternion transforms an object from one orientation to another

a rotation from the first orientation to the second. This relative quaternion can be easily obtained by noting how Q_1 and Q_2 transform points from one frame to another.

In Fig. 5.18, the point P_1 in Orientation-1 corresponds to the point P in the initial configuration. In other words, the quaternion Q_1 transforms P into P_1. Similarly the quaternion Q_2 transforms P into P_2 in Orientation-2. Therefore,

$$\begin{aligned} P_1 &= Q_1 P Q_1{}^* \\ P_2 &= Q_2 P Q_2{}^* \end{aligned} \tag{5.72}$$

Now we seek a quaternion that transforms P_1 into P_2. From the first equation above, we get the inverse transformation,

$$P = Q_1{}^* P_1 Q_1 \tag{5.73}$$

Substituting in the second equation, we have

$$\begin{aligned} P_2 &= Q_2 Q_1{}^* P_1 \; Q_1 Q_2{}^* \\ &= (Q_2 Q_1{}^*) P_1 \; (Q_2 \, Q_1{}^*)^* \end{aligned} \tag{5.74}$$

The above equation shows that the quaternion $Q_2Q_1{}^*$ transforms the point P_1 into P_2, and therefore represents the transformation from Orientation-1 to Orientation-2. Note that $Q_2Q_1{}^*$ is a unit quaternion. $Q_2Q_1{}^*$ is called the relative quaternion between Q_1 and Q_2.

We now revisit the problem of interpolating between Orientation-1 and Orientation-2. Any intermediate orientation in the above example can be obtained by first applying the unit quaternion Q_1 to get to Orientation-1 from the initial

Listing 5.1 Pseudo-code for computing SLERP equation in exponent form

```
Inputs:  Q1, Q2
1. Compute the product S = Q2(Q1*)
2. Compute the angle of rotation δ from S using Eq. 5.45
3. Compute the axis of rotation u from S using Eq. 5.46
4. For t varying uniformly within the interval [0, 1]
4.1     Form the quaternion St = (cos(tδ/2), u sin(tδ/2))
4.2     Compute the product T = StQ1
4.3     Transform every point P using the quaternion T
4.4     Render the object
4.5 End
```

configuration, and then applying a partial rotation using the relative quaternion $Q_2Q_1{}^*$. From Eq. 5.69, we know that this partial rotation can be effected by $(Q_2Q_1{}^*)^t$, where, $0 < t < 1$. Combining the two transformations together, we get the quaternion $(Q_2Q_1{}^*)^t Q_1$. By varying t uniformly between 0 and 1, we get the quaternions that interpolate between the two orientations. What we have just obtained is another form for the quaternion spherical interpolation (SLERP) formula using the exponent function. The pseudo-code in Listing 5.1 outlines this method for rotation interpolation. When $t = 0$, $(Q_2Q_1{}^*)^t Q_1$ becomes Q_1, and when $t = 1$, the interpolated quaternion becomes identical to Q_2.

5.9 Dual Quaternions

In previous sections we saw applications of unit quaternions in representing rotational transformations. Dual quaternions generalize the notion of quaternions to an 8-tuple, and provide a convenient tool for representing rigid body transformations containing both rotations and translations in three-dimensional space. The mathematical structure of dual quaternions uses two quaternions that are combined using the algebra of dual numbers. Before considering the theoretical aspects of dual quaternions, we will look at the definition and properties of dual numbers.

5.9.1 *Dual Numbers*

The structure and the algebra of dual numbers are very similar to complex numbers. Given two real numbers a and b, a dual number can be written as $a + \varepsilon\, b$, where $\varepsilon^2 = 0$. The number a is then called the real part, and b the dual part. ε is often referred to as the dual unit. As in the case of complex numbers, we can use a tuple notation $\boldsymbol{d} = (a, b)$ to represent a dual number. The algebra of dual numbers satisfies the following rules for addition and multiplication:

$$(a_1, b_1) \pm (a_2, b_2) = (a_1 \pm a_2, b_1 \pm b_2) \tag{5.75}$$

$$(a_1, b_1)(a_2,\ b_2) = (a_1 a_2,\ a_1 b_2 + a_2 b_1) \tag{5.76}$$

$$c(a, b) = (ca, cb),\ \text{for any real number } c. \tag{5.77}$$

Using the multiplication rule in Eq. 5.76 we find that

$$(a, b)\left(\frac{1}{a},\ \frac{-b}{a^2}\right) = (1,\ 0) \tag{5.78}$$

Therefore, the second term in the product above is the multiplicative inverse of (a, b), provided $a \neq 0$. The conjugate of a dual number $\boldsymbol{d} = (a, b)$ is defined in a way similar to that of a complex number:

$$\boldsymbol{d}^* = (a, -b) \tag{5.79}$$

Using Eq. 5.76, it can be verified that $\boldsymbol{dd}^* = a^2$. We also note that $(a, b)^2 = (a^2, 2ab)$. Hence,

$$\left(\sqrt{a},\ \frac{b}{2\sqrt{a}}\right)^2 = (a,\ b) \tag{5.80}$$

The above equation directly leads to the definition of the square-root of a dual number:

$$\sqrt{(a, b)} = \left(\sqrt{a},\ \frac{b}{2\sqrt{a}}\right) \tag{5.81}$$

In the next section, we will extend the concepts introduced above to the algebra of dual quaternions. For notational convenience, dual numbers will often be written as $(a, \tilde{a})$.

5.9.2 *Algebra of Dual Quaternions*

A dual quaternion is a quaternion constructed using dual numbers as its components: $\boldsymbol{Q} = (\boldsymbol{q}_0, \boldsymbol{q}_1, \boldsymbol{q}_2, \boldsymbol{q}_3)$, where $\boldsymbol{q}_i = (q_i, \tilde{q}_i)$, $i = 0, \ldots 3$. Equivalently, we can also define a dual quaternion as a dual number whose components are quaternions: $\boldsymbol{Q} = (Q, \tilde{Q})$ where $Q = (q_0, q_1, q_2, q_3)$, and $\tilde{Q} = (\tilde{q}_0, \tilde{q}_1, \tilde{q}_2, \tilde{q}_3)$. $\boldsymbol{Q}$ is a pure dual quaternion if $\boldsymbol{q}_0 = 0$, or equivalently if $q_0 = \tilde{q}_0 = 0$. We can also represent any dual quaternion $\boldsymbol{Q}$ as an 8-tuple $(q_0, q_1, q_2, q_3, \tilde{q}_0, \tilde{q}_1, \tilde{q}_2, \tilde{q}_3)$. The following representation of $\boldsymbol{Q}$ reveals the products of quaternion units and the dual units that are associated with each component of the 8-tuple.

$$\boldsymbol{Q} = q_0 + i q_1 + j q_2 + k q_3 + \varepsilon \tilde{q}_0 + \varepsilon\, i\, \tilde{q}_1 + \varepsilon\, j\, \tilde{q}_2 + \varepsilon\, k\, \tilde{q}_3 \tag{5.82}$$

Table 5.2 Multiplication table for dual quaternion units

	1	i	j	k	ε	εi	εj	εk
1	1	i	j	k	ε	εi	εj	εk
i	i	-1	k	$-j$	εi	$-\varepsilon$	εk	$-\varepsilon j$
j	j	$-k$	-1	i	εj	$-\varepsilon k$	$-\varepsilon$	εi
k	k	j	$-i$	-1	εk	εj	$-\varepsilon i$	$-\varepsilon$
ε	ε	εi	εj	εk	0	0	0	0
εi	εi	$-\varepsilon$	εk	$-\varepsilon j$	0	0	0	0
εj	εj	$-\varepsilon k$	$-\varepsilon$	εi	0	0	0	0
εk	εk	εj	$-\varepsilon i$	$-\varepsilon$	0	0	0	0

The following dual quaternions form a mutually orthogonal set of basis vectors for the entire 8-dimensional space of dual quaternions.

$$\begin{aligned}
\boldsymbol{i}_0 &= 1 = (1,0,0,0,0,0,0,0)\\
\boldsymbol{i}_1 &= i = (0,1,0,0,0,0,0,0)\\
\boldsymbol{i}_2 &= j = (0,0,1,0,0,0,0,0)\\
\boldsymbol{i}_3 &= k = (0,0,0,1,0,0,0,0)\\
\boldsymbol{i}_4 &= \varepsilon = (0,0,0,0,1,0,0,0)\\
\boldsymbol{i}_5 &= \varepsilon i = (0,0,0,0,0,1,0,0)\\
\boldsymbol{i}_6 &= \varepsilon j = (0,0,0,0,0,0,1,0)\\
\boldsymbol{i}_7 &= \varepsilon k = (0,0,0,0,0,0,0,1)
\end{aligned} \tag{5.83}$$

Any dual quaternion is a linear combination of the above basis vectors:

$$\boldsymbol{Q} = \sum_{k=0}^{7} \boldsymbol{i}_k q_k \tag{5.84}$$

Using the multiplication rule for quaternion basis, we observe that $i(\varepsilon j) = \varepsilon k$, $(\varepsilon k)j = -\varepsilon i$, $(\varepsilon i)(\varepsilon j) = 0$ etc. Note also that $\varepsilon i = i\varepsilon$. The complete multiplication table is given in Table 5.2. The multiplication rule for dual numbers given in Eq. 5.76 can be extended to quaternions:

$$\boldsymbol{PQ} = (P,\ \tilde{P})\ (Q,\ \tilde{Q}) = (P\ Q,\ \tilde{P}Q + P\tilde{Q}) \tag{5.85}$$

We can also multiply a dual quaternion $\boldsymbol{P}$ by a quaternion Q:

$$\boldsymbol{P}Q = (P,\ \tilde{P})\ Q = (P\ Q,\ \tilde{P}\ Q) \tag{5.86}$$

The conjugate of a dual quaternion is defined in three different ways, as discussed below.

Conjugate type 1: As mentioned in the beginning of this section, we can treat a dual quaternion $\boldsymbol{Q}$ as a quaternion with dual number components $(\boldsymbol{q}_0, \boldsymbol{q}_1, \boldsymbol{q}_2, \boldsymbol{q}_3)$. Applying the rule for a quaternion conjugate, we get $\boldsymbol{Q}^* = (\boldsymbol{q}_0, -\boldsymbol{q}_1, -\boldsymbol{q}_2, -\boldsymbol{q}_3)$, hence

$$\boldsymbol{Q}^* = (Q^*,\ \tilde{Q}^*) = (q_0, -q_1, -q_2, -q_3,\ \tilde{q}_0, -\tilde{q}_1, -\tilde{q}_2, -\tilde{q}_3) \tag{5.87}$$

This definition satisfies the following property:

$$\begin{aligned} \boldsymbol{Q}\boldsymbol{Q}^* &= (QQ^*, \tilde{Q}Q^* + Q\tilde{Q}^*) \\ &= \left({q_0}^2 + {q_1}^2 + {q_2}^2 + {q_3}^2,\ 2(q_0\tilde{q}_0 + q_1\tilde{q}_1 + q_2\tilde{q}_2 + q_3\tilde{q}_3)\right) \\ &= \boldsymbol{Q}^*\boldsymbol{Q} \end{aligned} \tag{5.88}$$

In the above derivation, note that $\boldsymbol{Q}\boldsymbol{Q}^* = (|Q|^2,\ 2\ Q\bullet\tilde{Q})$, where • indicates the dot product between the two quaternions. It can also be easily verified that $(\boldsymbol{P}\boldsymbol{Q})^* = \boldsymbol{Q}^*\boldsymbol{P}^*$, for any two dual quaternions $\boldsymbol{P}$, $\boldsymbol{Q}$. This property is useful for combining two or more successive transformations (see Eq. 5.51). The norm of a dual quaternion can now be defined as follows:

$$||\boldsymbol{Q}|| = \sqrt{\boldsymbol{Q}\boldsymbol{Q}^*} = \sqrt{(|Q|^2,\ 2(Q\bullet\tilde{Q}))} = \left(|Q|,\ \frac{2(Q\bullet\tilde{Q})}{|Q|}\right) \tag{5.89}$$

The above derivation is based on the definition of the square-root of a dual number as given in Eq. 5.81. A unit dual quaternion $\boldsymbol{Q}$ satisfies the condition $||\boldsymbol{Q}|| = 1$. From Eq. 5.89, we see that $\boldsymbol{Q} = (Q,\ \tilde{Q})$ is a unit dual quaternion if and only if $|Q| = 1$ (*i.e.*, Q is a unit quaternion) and $Q\bullet\tilde{Q} = 0$ (*i.e.*, Q is orthogonal to $\tilde{Q}$ in quaternion space, or $\tilde{Q}=0$).

Conjugate type 2: If we treat $\boldsymbol{Q}$ as a dual number $(Q,\ \tilde{Q})$, then the application of the rule in Eq. 5.79 gives the following definition:

$$\boldsymbol{Q}^* = (Q, -\tilde{Q}) = (q_0,\ q_1,\ q_2,\ q_3, -\tilde{q}_0, -\tilde{q}_1, -\tilde{q}_2, -\tilde{q}_3) \tag{5.90}$$

The main drawback of the above definition is that it does not lead to a convenient definition for the unit norm. Further, it does not satisfy the condition $(\boldsymbol{P}\boldsymbol{Q})^* = \boldsymbol{Q}^*\boldsymbol{P}^*$.

Conjugate type 3: Here we combine both the above definitions to form a new type of conjugate as given below:

$$\boldsymbol{Q}^* = (Q^*, -\tilde{Q}^*) = (q_0, -q_1, -q_2, -q_3 - \tilde{q}_0,\ \tilde{q}_1, \tilde{q}_2, \tilde{q}_3) \tag{5.91}$$

The above definition satisfies the properties $(\boldsymbol{P}\boldsymbol{Q})^* = \boldsymbol{Q}^*\boldsymbol{P}^*$, and $(\boldsymbol{Q}^*)^* = \boldsymbol{Q}$. The norm in this case is defined as

$$||\boldsymbol{Q}|| = \sqrt{\boldsymbol{Q}\boldsymbol{Q}^{*}} = \sqrt{\left(|Q|^2,\ \tilde{Q}Q^* - (\tilde{Q}Q^*)^*\right)} = \left(|Q|,\ \frac{\tilde{Q}Q^* - (\tilde{Q}Q^*)^*}{|Q|}\right) \tag{5.92}$$

With the above norm, a unit dual quaternion $\boldsymbol{Q}$ must have a unit quaternion Q for its real part, and $\tilde{Q}Q^*$ must be a real quaternion. In the next section, we will use the above definition (type 3) of the conjugate to construct dual quaternions that represent rigid body transformations.

5.9.3 Transformations Using Dual Quaternions

Recall that any unit quaternion Q can be used to perform a rotational transformation of a vector $\boldsymbol{p} = (x, y, z)$ in three-dimensional space using the quaternion product QPQ^* where P is the quaternion $(0, \boldsymbol{p})$. We can also represent the vector $\boldsymbol{p}$ by the dual quaternion $\boldsymbol{P} = (1, P) = (1, 0, 0, 0, 0, x, y, z)$. $\boldsymbol{P}$ is a unit dual quaternion. Similarly, if Q is a unit quaternion, then $\boldsymbol{Q} = (Q, 0)$ is a unit dual quaternion. Then

$$\begin{aligned} \boldsymbol{QPQ^*} &= (Q,0)(1,P)(Q^*,0) = (Q,QP)Q^* = (1,QPQ^*) \\ &= (1,P') = \boldsymbol{P'} \end{aligned} \tag{5.93}$$

where P' is the quaternion $(0, \boldsymbol{p}')$ that represents the transformed (rotated) vector. The above result is valid for all types of dual quaternion conjugates described in the previous section. It shows that for every unit quaternion there exists a corresponding unit dual quaternion that performs exactly the same rotational transformation of vectors. We now ask the question: does such a transformation exist for translations in three-dimensional space?

Given a translation vector $\boldsymbol{t} = (t_1, t_2, t_3)$, let us construct a quaternion T in the form $(0, \boldsymbol{t}/2)$, and from it, a dual quaternion $\boldsymbol{T}$ as

$$\boldsymbol{T} = (1,\ T) = \left(1, 0, 0, 0, 0, \frac{t_1}{2}, \frac{t_2}{2}, \frac{t_3}{2}\right) \tag{5.94}$$

Note the division of the vector components by 2 in T, similar to that of a rotation angle in a unit quaternion (see Eq. 5.44). Using conjugate type 3,

$$\boldsymbol{T^*} = (1, -T^*) = (1, T) = \boldsymbol{T} \tag{5.95}$$

Applying a transformation of $\boldsymbol{P}$ using $\boldsymbol{T}$ similar to Eq. 5.93,

$$\boldsymbol{TPT^*} = (1,T)(1,P)(1,T^*) = (1, P + 2T) = \boldsymbol{P'} \tag{5.96}$$

The above equation shows that a point $\boldsymbol{p} = (x, y, z)$ gets transformed into the point $\boldsymbol{p}' = (x + t_1, y + t_2, z + t_3)$ if $\boldsymbol{p}$ was embedded in a quaternion as $P = (0, \boldsymbol{p})$, the quaternion itself embedded in a dual quaternion $\boldsymbol{P}$ as $(1, P)$. Thus we can use $\boldsymbol{T}$ as a dual quaternion representing spatial translations. We will now use the above results to construct a dual quaternion that represents the most general rigid body transformation: a rotation by an angle δ about an arbitrary vector (l, m, n) through the origin, followed by a displacement by a translation vector (t_1, t_2, t_3). Let $\boldsymbol{Q} = (Q, 0)$, $\boldsymbol{T} = (1, T)$ represent rotation and translation respectively. The composite transformation is then represented by the dual quaternion $\boldsymbol{G} = (Q, TQ)$ as seen in the following derivation:

$$\begin{aligned}\boldsymbol{GPG}^* &= (Q, TQ)(1, P)(Q,\ TQ)^* = (Q, QP + TQ)(Q^*, -Q^*\ T^*)\\ &= (QQ^*, QPQ^* + TQQ^* - QQ^*T^*) = (1, QPQ^* + 2T) = \boldsymbol{P}'\end{aligned} \tag{5.97}$$

The quaternion $QPQ^* + 2T$ gives the transformed point after the required rotation and translation.

5.10 Summary

This chapter gave an overview of the quaternion algebra including the properties that are useful for graphics applications. Unit quaternions represent rotations about the origin. Composite rotations can be represented by a product of quaternions. The multiplicative inverse of a unit quaternion is the same as its conjugate. A unit quaternion with all of its components negated represents the same orientation as the original quaternion.

Computer graphics animations generally involve several rotation interpolations. This chapter compared the effects produced by Euler angle interpolation, axis-angle interpolation and quaternion interpolation. The spherical linear interpolation of rotations using unit quaternions produced optimal rotation with uniform angular velocity. Methods for visualising three-dimensional rotation sequences were discussed.

This chapter also presented the algebra of dual quaternions which has recently found applications in graphics. Dual quaternions are defined based on the concept of dual numbers, and they can be viewed as 8-dimensional vectors. The conjugate of a dual quaternion can be defined in three different ways. The property of dual numbers that is important from the point of view of computer graphics is that the most general rigid-body transformation in three-dimensional space can be represented by unit dual quaternions.

The next chapter further analyses three-dimensional motion using forward and inverse kinematics equations. In this chapter, we will revisit quaternion representation of rotations to define angular velocity components of motion.

5.11 Supplementary Material for Chap. 5

The folder `Chapter5/Code` on the companion website contains the definition and implementation files for both the quaternion and the dual quaternion classes. It also contains the following programs demonstrating the effects of different types of interpolation methods on rotational transforms.

1. **Quaternion.cpp**

Additional files:
```
Quaternion.h
Point3.h
Matrix.h
Point3.cpp
Matrix.cpp
```

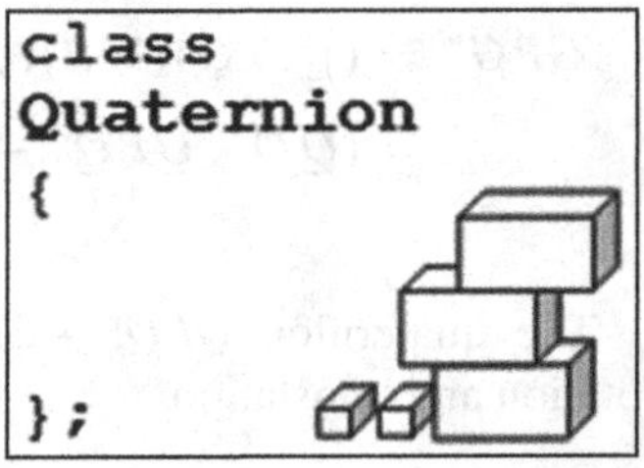

The quaternion class defines methods for performing quaternion operations, and representing three-dimensional rotations using quaternions. The class also has methods for both linear and spherical linear interpolation of rotations using quaternions. The class documentation can be found in Appendix D.

2. **DualQuat.cpp**

Additional files:
```
DualQuat.h
Quaternion.h
Quaternion.cpp
```

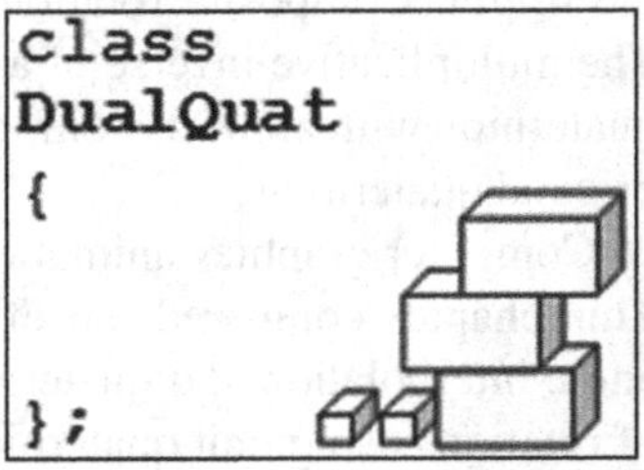

This class is used for the construction of dual quaternions and for performing basic operations and transformations using them. The class documentation can be found in Appendix D.

3. **EulerInterp.cpp**

Additional files:
```
tga.h
tga.cpp
xn.tga, xp.tga
yn.tga, yp.tga
zn.tga, zp.tga
```

The program displays a texture mapped cube with its orientation clearly shown using the markings of initial direction on each face. For a given set of initial and final orientations specified using Euler angles, the program generates the display of ten intermediate orientations using Euler angle interpolation.

4. **RotationInterp1.cpp**

Additional files:
`Quaternion.h`
`Quaternion.cpp`

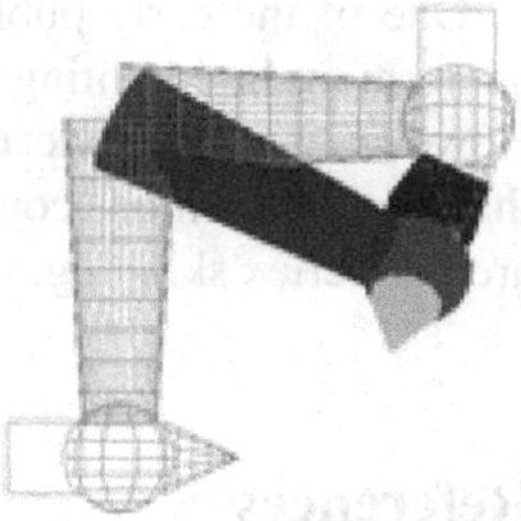

The program uses the object model in Fig. 5.8, and two orientations as given in Table 5.1 to compare the paths taken by Euler, quaternion and angle-axis interpolations. Pressing key '1' selects Euler, '2' angle-axis, and '3' quaternion interpolation. Pressing space bar shows the motion of the object through the interpolated sequence.

5. **RotationInterp2.cpp**

Additional files:
`Quaternion.h`
`Quaternion.cpp`

The program displays an interpolation sequence using triangles placed on a sphere. Different parts of the sphere can be viewed by rotating it using the arrow keys. The initial, final and the interpolated values are also displayed in text form. Pressing key 1 selects Euler interpolation, key 2 selects angle-axis interpolation, and key 3 selects quaternion interpolation.

5.12 Bibliographical Notes

The algebra of quaternions was first discovered by the Irish mathematician Sir William Rowan Hamilton (1805–1865). Most of his work on the quaternion group were later published as a book (Hamilton and Joly 1899). A detailed description of the quaternion algebra including definitions, properties and proofs of theorems are given in Kuipers (1999) and Hanson (2006). An in-depth theoretical analysis of the quaternion group, associative algebras and higher dimensional structures can be found in Conway and Smith (2003), Ward (1997), Kamberov (2002).

Shoemake's paper (Shoemake 1985) established the effectiveness of quaternions as a powerful mathematical tool in graphics applications. Several books on computer graphics such as Eberly (2007), Foley (1996), Watt and Policarpo (2003) describe the applications of quaternions in rotational transformations of objects.

One of the early publications containing references to dual numbers and dual quaternions highlighting their importance in kinematics is Bottema and Roth (1979). However, it is a more recent publication by Ladislav Kavan et al. (2007) that showed that dual quaternions could indeed be used in computer graphics, particularly in the area of vertex skinning, for representing rotations combined with displacements.

References

Bottema, O., & Roth, B. (1979). *Theoretical kinematics*. Amsterdam/Oxford: North-Holland Publishing Co.

Conway, J. H., & Smith, D. A. (2003). *On quaternions and octonions: Their geometry, arithmetic, and symmetry*. Natick: AK Peters.

Eberly, D. H. (2007). *3D game engine design: A practical approach to real-time computer graphics* (2nd ed.). Amsterdam/London: Morgan Kaufmann.

Foley, J. D. (1996). *Computer graphics: Principles and practice* (2nd ed.). Reading/Wokingham: Addison-Wesley.

Hamilton, W. R. S. (1899). *Elements of quaternions* (2nd ed.), 2 vols. London: Longmans, Green & Co.

Hanson, A. (2006). *Visualizing quaternions*. San Francisco/London: Morgan Kaufmann.

Kamberov, G. (2002). *Quaternions, spinors and surfaces*. Providence/Great Britain: American Mathematical Society.

Kavan, L., Collins, S., Zara, J., & O'Sullivan, C. (2007). *Skinning with dual quaternions*. Proceedings of the 2007 symposium on Interactive 3D graphics and games, Seattle, WA.

Kuipers, J. B. (1999). *Quaternions and rotation sequences: a primer with applications to orbits, aerospace, and virtual reality*. Princeton/Chichester: Princeton University Press.

Shoemake, K. (1985). Animating rotation with quaternion curves. *SIGGRAPH Computer Graphics, 19*(3), 245–254.

Ward, J. P. (1997). *Quaternions and cayley numbers: Algebra and applications*. Dordrecht/London: Kluwer.

Watt, A. H., & Policarpo, F. (2003). *3D games: Animation and advanced real-time rendering*. Harlow: Addison-Wesley.

Chapter 6
Kinematics

Overview

The term "kinematics" refers to the study of the translational and rotational motion of objects without reference to mass, force or torque. Kinematics equations are used to describe three-dimensional motion of a multi-body system in terms of translational and rotational motions, and optionally, linear and angular velocities. Kinematics analysis becomes important in the animation of articulated models and skeletal structures containing serial chains of joints and links.

To set the context for developing the kinematics equations for graphics applications, we first give an outline of robot manipulators comprising a chain of joints. Both forward and inverse kinematics equations of joint chains are then discussed in detail. Iterative numerical algorithms for computing joint angles for a given target position are also presented. These methods are useful for performing goal-directed motion in an animation sequence.

6.1 Robot Manipulators

In a system containing several interconnected links, it is often required to find the global position of the end-point of the last link. This end-point is called the end effector. In an animated character model that performs a certain task, this could be the tip of a finger. In a robot manipulator, knowing the end effector position is important to carry out tasks such as inspection, picking, welding, painting, etc. Robot manipulators usually contain many links and different types of joints. In such systems, the motion of the end effector becomes exceedingly complex, as it depends on many joint parameters.

The Programmable Universal Machine for Assembly (PUMA) is a classic example of a robot manipulator arm. A graphics model of the PUMA robot is shown in Fig. 6.1. It consists of a chain of links and joints, with the end effector

R. Mukundan, *Advanced Methods in Computer Graphics: With examples in OpenGL*, DOI 10.1007/978-1-4471-2340-8_6, © Springer-Verlag London Limited 2012

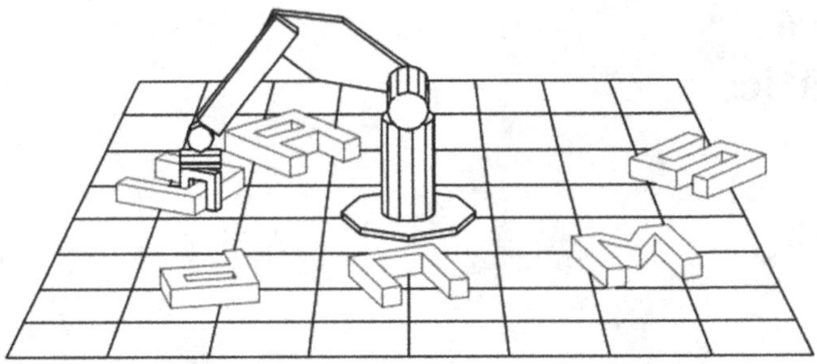

Fig. 6.1 A graphics model of a PUMA robot

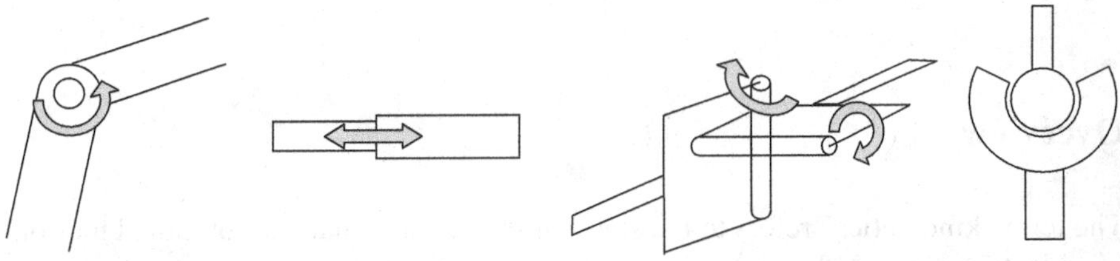

Fig. 6.2 Commonly used joints in robot manipulator arms

or the gripping device forming the last link. The other end of the joint chain is fixed to the base. This link forms the root of the tree that represents the hierarchy of transformations applied to the links. This hierarchical structure is the same as that of the scene graph we saw in Chap. 3. The transformations depend on the rotation and displacement of each link relative to its parent. The joint types as well as physical mounting constraints dictate the degrees of freedom of a particular configuration. The range of allowable angular and linear displacements at a joint also depends on the joint type.

Several types of joints can be found in robot manipulators. The most common is the revolute joint that is used for a simple rotation of a link about a fixed axis, providing one degree of freedom. A prismatic joint, on the other hand allows a translation or displacement of a link with respect to its parent. Compound rotations about two orthogonal axes can be performed using a Cardan joint or a Hooke's joint. A Hooke's joint can be modelled by two revolute joints whose axes intersect. A more sophisticated type of joint providing three axes rotation is the spherical joint, also known as the ball and socket joint. Sample illustrations of these joints are given in Fig. 6.2.

For graphics applications, joint chains with only rotational transformations are commonly used. Some examples of such systems were given earlier in Chaps. 3 and 4. Generalised rotations with multiple degrees of freedom can be easily modelled using either Euler angles or quaternions as described in the previous chapter. In the next section, we consider the problem of finding the global position of the end effector, given the joint angle parameters.

6.2 Forward Kinematics

The term forward kinematics refers to the movement of a joint chain, given all the information about the relative position and orientation of each link with respect to its parent, and absolute position of the root joint. Forward kinematics equations are used to determine the position of the end effector in the world coordinate system for a given set of joint angles.

6.2.1 Joint Chain in Two Dimensions

Consider a 3-link chain shown in Fig. 6.3, that is constrained to move on a two-dimensional *xy*-plane. Assume that the absolute position of the base link is specified by the point $A = (x_a, y_a)$, and that the link lengths d_1, d_2, d_3, and the joint angles θ_1, θ_2, θ_3 are given. These parameters completely specify the configuration of the joint chain. Note that the joint angles are defined relative to the parent link. Using this information, we seek the coordinates of the end effector E.

For a planar motion, the angles are simply summed up from the base link to the current link to find the absolute orientation of that link. In the example given above, angles θ_1, θ_2 are positive while θ_3 is negative. The coordinates of the points B, C, E can be computed in a sequence starting from the base as follows:

$$
\begin{aligned}
x_b &= x_a + d_1 \cos(\theta_1) \\
y_b &= y_a + d_1 \sin(\theta_1) \\
x_c &= x_b + d_2 \cos(\theta_1 + \theta_2) \\
y_c &= y_b + d_2 \sin(\theta_1 + \theta_2) \\
x_e &= x_c + d_3 \cos(\theta_1 + \theta_2 + \theta_3) \\
&= d_3\cos(\theta_1 + \theta_2 + \theta_3) + d_2\cos(\theta_1 + \theta_2) + d_1\cos(\theta_1) + x_a \\
y_e &= y_c + d_3 \sin(\theta_1 + \theta_2 + \theta_3) \\
&= d_3\sin(\theta_1 + \theta_2 + \theta_3) + d_2\sin(\theta_1 + \theta_2) + d_1\sin(\theta_1) + y_a
\end{aligned}
\tag{6.1}
$$

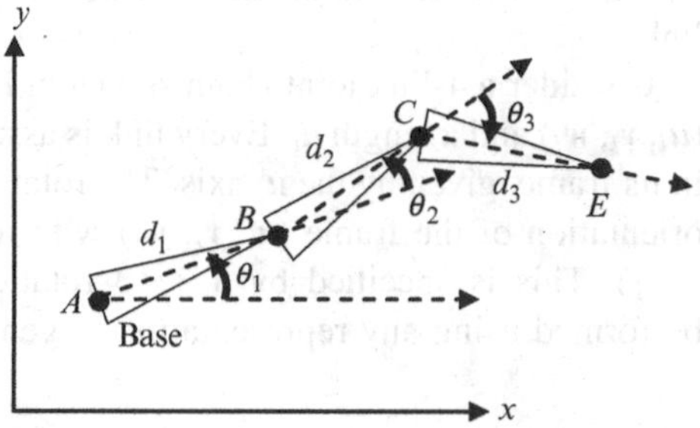

Fig. 6.3 A planar motion of a three-link joint chain

Fig. 6.4 A 4-link joint chain in three-dimensional space

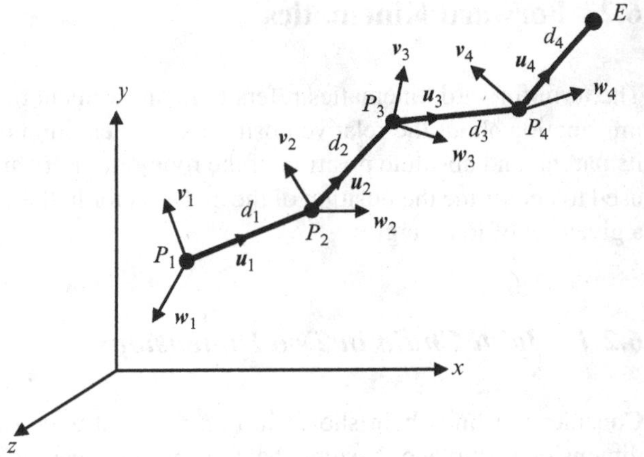

The above sequence can be extended to any number of links and joint angles:

$$x_n = x_{n-1} + d_n \cos\left(\sum_{i=1}^{n} \theta_i\right)$$
$$y_n = y_{n-1} + d_n \sin\left(\sum_{i=1}^{n} \theta_i\right) \tag{6.2}$$

where (x_n, y_n) is the position of the nth link, and d_n its length. If n is the index of the last link containing the end effector, then its direction is given by the unit vector$(\cos(\sum_{i=1}^{n} \theta_i), \sin(\sum_{i=1}^{n} \theta_i))$.

6.2.2 *Joint Chain in 3D Space*

In a three-dimensional coordinate system, we should be able to apply the most general rotational transformation to every link of the joint chain. We can then simulate the movement of links connected by a revolute joint, a Hooke's joint, or a spherical joint. In order to define the relative orientation of a link with respect to its parent, we will need to define an orthogonal right-handed body-fixed frame on each link.

Consider a 4-link joint chain shown in Fig. 6.4. A link i has a body-fixed frame $(\boldsymbol{u}_i, \boldsymbol{v}_i, \boldsymbol{w}_i)$ and a length d_i. Every link is assumed to be aligned along the x-direction in its frame, given by the $\boldsymbol{u}_i$ axis. The rotation of the link i is defined by the relative orientation of the frame $(\boldsymbol{u}_i, \boldsymbol{v}_i, \boldsymbol{w}_i)$ with respect to its parent's frame $(\boldsymbol{u}_{i-1}, \boldsymbol{v}_{i-1}, \boldsymbol{w}_{i-1})$. This is specified by a 3×3 rotation matrix $\mathbf{R}_i$. The rotation matrix can be formed using any representation of generalized rotations such as Euler angles, angle-axis parameters, or quaternions. The end effector is denoted by the point E. The position of link i is indicated by the point P_i. The forward kinematics solution for this joint chain attempts to find the coordinates (x_e, y_e, z_e) of the point E in the world coordinate system, given the position of the base link $P_1 = (x_1, y_1, z_1)$, lengths of the links $d_1..d_4$, and rotation matrices $\mathbf{R}_1..\mathbf{R}_4$.

Note that the matrix $\mathbf{R}_1$ represents the rotational transformation of the first link's local frame $(\boldsymbol{u}_1, \boldsymbol{v}_1, \boldsymbol{w}_1)$ in the world coordinate space. Therefore,

$$\boldsymbol{u}_1 = \mathbf{R}_1 \begin{bmatrix} 1 \\ 0 \\ 0 \end{bmatrix}, \quad \boldsymbol{v}_1 = \mathbf{R}_1 \begin{bmatrix} 0 \\ 1 \\ 0 \end{bmatrix}, \quad \boldsymbol{w}_1 = \mathbf{R}_1 \begin{bmatrix} 0 \\ 0 \\ 1 \end{bmatrix}. \tag{6.3}$$

The position of the point P_2 can be determined as

$$\begin{bmatrix} x_2 \\ y_2 \\ z_2 \end{bmatrix} = \mathbf{R}_1 \begin{bmatrix} d_1 \\ 0 \\ 0 \end{bmatrix} + \begin{bmatrix} x_1 \\ y_1 \\ z_1 \end{bmatrix} \tag{6.4}$$

The matrix $\mathbf{R}_2$ gives the rotation of the frame $(\boldsymbol{u}_2, \boldsymbol{v}_2, \boldsymbol{w}_2)$ with respect to the frame $(\boldsymbol{u}_1, \boldsymbol{v}_1, \boldsymbol{w}_1)$. The position of the point P_3 can be obtained in terms of the coordinates of P_2 as follows:

$$\begin{bmatrix} x_3 \\ y_3 \\ z_3 \end{bmatrix} = \mathbf{R}_1\mathbf{R}_2 \begin{bmatrix} d_2 \\ 0 \\ 0 \end{bmatrix} + \begin{bmatrix} x_2 \\ y_2 \\ z_2 \end{bmatrix} \tag{6.5}$$

Continuing as above, the coordinates of the end effector E are obtained as shown below.

$$\begin{bmatrix} x_e \\ y_e \\ z_e \end{bmatrix} = \mathbf{R}_1\mathbf{R}_2\mathbf{R}_3\mathbf{R}_4 \begin{bmatrix} d_4 \\ 0 \\ 0 \end{bmatrix} + \begin{bmatrix} x_4 \\ y_4 \\ z_4 \end{bmatrix} \tag{6.6}$$

The above equation can be expanded and expressed in terms of the known parameters:

$$\begin{bmatrix} x_e \\ y_e \\ z_e \end{bmatrix} = \mathbf{R}_1\mathbf{R}_2\mathbf{R}_3\mathbf{R}_4 \begin{bmatrix} d_4 \\ 0 \\ 0 \end{bmatrix} + \mathbf{R}_1\mathbf{R}_2\mathbf{R}_3 \begin{bmatrix} d_3 \\ 0 \\ 0 \end{bmatrix} + \mathbf{R}_1\mathbf{R}_2 \begin{bmatrix} d_2 \\ 0 \\ 0 \end{bmatrix} + \mathbf{R}_1 \begin{bmatrix} d_1 \\ 0 \\ 0 \end{bmatrix} + \begin{bmatrix} x_1 \\ y_1 \\ z_1 \end{bmatrix} \tag{6.7}$$

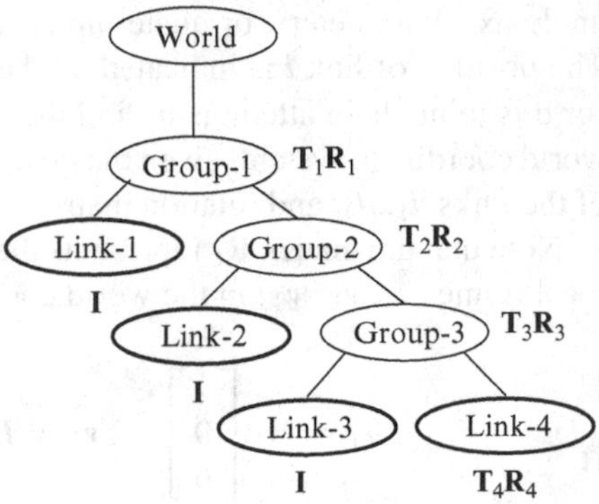

Fig. 6.5 A scene graph based representation of the transformations applied to the links of the joint chain in Fig. 6.4

The orientation of the frame of the end effector in the world coordinate system is given by the product matrix $\mathbf{R}_1\mathbf{R}_2\mathbf{R}_3\mathbf{R}_4$. The sequence of derivations given above can be extended to form an iterative algorithm for computing the end effector position of a general n-link joint chain.

We can use a scene graph to represent the transformations of the joint chain as shown in Fig. 6.5. Using this scene graph model, the coordinates of the end effector in the root node's reference frame is given by

$$\begin{bmatrix} x_e \\ y_e \\ z_e \end{bmatrix} = \mathbf{T}_1\mathbf{R}_1\mathbf{T}_2\mathbf{R}_2\mathbf{T}_3\mathbf{R}_3\mathbf{T}_4\mathbf{R}_4 \begin{bmatrix} d_4 \\ 0 \\ 0 \end{bmatrix} \tag{6.8}$$

In the above equation,

$$\mathbf{T}_i = \begin{bmatrix} d_{i-1} \\ 0 \\ 0 \end{bmatrix}, \quad i = 2, 3, 4, \text{and} \quad \mathbf{T}_1 = \begin{bmatrix} x_1 \\ y_1 \\ z_1 \end{bmatrix}. \tag{6.9}$$

The equivalence of Eqs. 6.7 and 6.8 can be readily established.

6.3 Linear and Angular Velocity

In addition to the position and the orientation, the velocity of the end effector is also an important parameter in many applications involving a serial chain. For example, an articulated character model may be required to move an object with constant velocity. The velocity of the end effector is a combination of the linear velocity of the chain itself and the angular velocity introduced by the joint rotations.

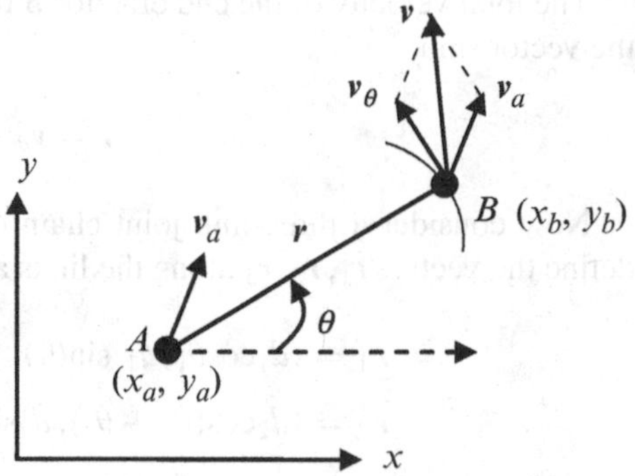

Fig. 6.6 Velocity vectors on a single link in two-dimensional space

6.3.1 Velocity in Two Dimensions

First, we consider a single link AB that can move on the xy-plane, and rotate about the point A (Fig. 6.6). The position of the link at any instant is defined by the coordinates (x_a, y_a) of the point A. The point B takes the role of the end effector. The orientation of the link is measured by the angle θ made by the link with the direction of the x-axis. The linear velocity of the link is the instantaneous speed with which it is moved from its current position A. If $(\Delta x, \Delta y)$ denote the change in the position of the link from A in an infinitesimal interval of time Δt, the linear velocity components are given by

$$v_a = \lim_{t\to 0}\left(\frac{\Delta x}{\Delta t}, \frac{\Delta y}{\Delta t}\right) \tag{6.10}$$

The angular velocity ω of the link is defined as the instantaneous change in the rotation angle θ :

$$\omega = \dot{\theta} = \lim_{t\to 0}\left(\frac{\Delta\theta}{\Delta t}\right) \tag{6.11}$$

The direction of angular velocity is perpendicular to the xy-plane. If $\boldsymbol{k}$ is a unit vector along the z-direction, the angular velocity vector is

$$\boldsymbol{\omega} = \omega \boldsymbol{k} \tag{6.12}$$

The linear velocity $\boldsymbol{v}_\theta$ of the point B induced by the above rotation is tangential to the circular arc with radius r at B (Fig. 6.6). This velocity is relative to the point A. If $\boldsymbol{r}$ denotes the vector from A to B given by $(x_b - x_a, y_b - y_a)$, then $\boldsymbol{v}_\theta$ is defined as the following vector cross product:

$$\boldsymbol{v}_\theta = \boldsymbol{\omega} \times \boldsymbol{r} = (y_a - y_b, x_b - x_a)\,\dot{\theta} \tag{6.13}$$

The total velocity of the end effector B relative to the coordinate frame is simply the vector sum

$$\boldsymbol{v} = \boldsymbol{v}_a + \boldsymbol{v}_\theta \tag{6.14}$$

Now consider a three-link joint chain on the xy-plane, shown in Fig. 6.3. We define the vectors $\boldsymbol{r}_1, \boldsymbol{r}_2, \boldsymbol{r}_3$ along the links as follows:

$$\begin{aligned}
\boldsymbol{r}_1 &= (d_1\cos\theta_1, d_1\ \sin\theta_1) \\
\boldsymbol{r}_2 &= (d_2\cos(\theta_1 + \theta_2), d_2\sin(\theta_1 + \theta_2)) \\
\boldsymbol{r}_3 &= (d_3\cos(\theta_1 + \theta_2 + \theta_3), d_3\ \sin(\theta_1 + \theta_2 + \theta_3))
\end{aligned} \tag{6.15}$$

The linear velocity $\boldsymbol{v}_\theta$ of the end effector E induced by the three joint angle rotations is given by

$$\boldsymbol{v}_\theta = (\boldsymbol{\omega}_1 \times (\boldsymbol{r}_1 + \boldsymbol{r}_2 + \boldsymbol{r}_3)) + (\boldsymbol{\omega}_2 \times (\boldsymbol{r}_2 + \boldsymbol{r}_3)) + (\boldsymbol{\omega}_3 \times \boldsymbol{r}_3) \tag{6.16}$$

where $\boldsymbol{\omega}_1 = \dot{\theta}_1\boldsymbol{k}$, $\boldsymbol{\omega}_2 = \dot{\theta}_2\boldsymbol{k}$, $\boldsymbol{\omega}_3 = \dot{\theta}_3\boldsymbol{k}$, and $\boldsymbol{k}$ is a unit vector along the z-axis. Therefore

$$\begin{aligned}
\boldsymbol{v}_\theta = &(-d_1\ \sin(\theta_1) - d_2\ \sin(\theta_1 + \theta_2) - d_3\sin(\theta_1 + \theta_2 + \theta_3), \\
&d_1\cos(\theta_1) + \ d_2\cos(\theta_1 + \theta_2) + d_3\cos(\theta_1 + \theta_2 + \theta_3))\,\dot{\theta}_1 \\
&+ (-d_2\sin(\theta_2) - d_3\sin(\theta_2 + \theta_3), d_2\cos(\theta_2) + d_3\cos(\theta_2 + \theta_3))\,\dot{\theta}_2 \\
&+ (-d_3\ \sin(\theta_3), d_3\cos(\theta_3))\,\dot{\theta}_3
\end{aligned} \tag{6.17}$$

The total velocity of the end effector E is $\boldsymbol{v}_\theta + \boldsymbol{v}_a$ where $\boldsymbol{v}_a$ is the velocity of the chain induced by the translational movement of the base A. As a particular case of Eq. 6.13, if $\boldsymbol{p}$ is a vector from A to B that undergoes only a rotational motion about A, then the linear velocity of the point B is given by

$$\dot{\boldsymbol{p}} = \boldsymbol{\omega} \times \boldsymbol{p} \tag{6.18}$$

6.3.2 Velocity Under Euler Angle Transformations

The animation of a general serial chain in a three-dimensional space can be performed using Euler angle rotations (see Eq. 5.30) applied at the joints. In an extrinsic composition of rotations, the axes of rotation are fixed relative to the joint chain. In such a case, if the Euler angle sequence is given by $\{\psi, \phi, \theta\}$ as described in Sect. 5.4.1, the angular rate vector has the following form:

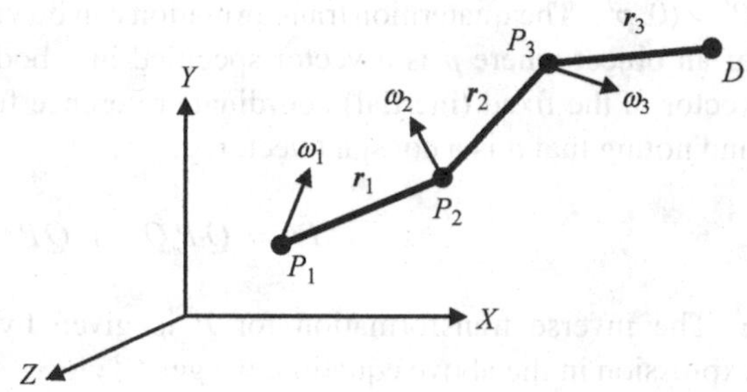

Fig. 6.7 Angular velocity vectors on a joint chain in three-dimensional space

$$\boldsymbol{\omega} = \begin{bmatrix} \dot{\psi} \\ \dot{\phi} \\ \dot{\theta} \end{bmatrix} \tag{6.19}$$

Let us now consider a joint chain that is transformed using Euler angle rotations, as shown in Fig. 6.7.

Each joint P_i ($i = 1, 2, 3$) has a set of Euler angles $\{\psi_i\ \phi_i\ \theta_i\}$ from which we can construct a rotational transformation matrix $\mathbf{R}_i$ using Eq. 5.30, and an angular velocity vector $\boldsymbol{\omega}_i$ using Eq. 6.19. If d_i is the length of ith link, the vectors $\boldsymbol{r}_i$ along the link directions can be computed as

$$\boldsymbol{r}_1 = \mathbf{R}_1 \begin{bmatrix} d_1 \\ 0 \\ 0 \end{bmatrix}$$

$$\boldsymbol{r}_2 = \mathbf{R}_1\mathbf{R}_2 \begin{bmatrix} d_2 \\ 0 \\ 0 \end{bmatrix}$$

$$\boldsymbol{r}_3 = \mathbf{R}_1\mathbf{R}_2\mathbf{R}_3 \begin{bmatrix} d_3 \\ 0 \\ 0 \end{bmatrix} \tag{6.20}$$

The linear velocity $\boldsymbol{v}_\theta$ of the end effector E resulting from the changes in the Euler angles can now be computed using Eq. 6.16. We add this velocity to the translational velocity of the joint chain at the base P_1 to get the total velocity of the end effector E with respect to the reference frame.

6.3.3 Quaternion Velocity

We know that if $P = (0, \boldsymbol{p})$ is a pure quaternion, and Q a unit quaternion, then the equation $P' = QPQ^*$ gives a rotational transformation of the vector $\boldsymbol{p}$, where

$P' = (0, \boldsymbol{p}')$. The quaternion transformation can be viewed as defining the orientation of an object where $\boldsymbol{p}$ is a vector specified in a body-fixed frame, and $\boldsymbol{p}'$ the same vector in the fixed (inertial) coordinate reference frame. Differentiating both sides and noting that $\boldsymbol{p}$ is a constant vector,

$$\dot{P}' = \dot{Q}PQ^* + QP\dot{Q}^* \tag{6.21}$$

The inverse transformation for P is given by $P = Q^*P'Q$. Substituting this expression in the above equation, we get

$$\dot{P}' = \dot{Q}Q^*P'QQ^* + QQ^*P'Q\dot{Q}^* \tag{6.22}$$

Since Q is a unit vector, $QQ^* = 1$. Therefore,

$$\dot{P}' = \dot{Q}Q^*P' + P'Q\dot{Q}^* \tag{6.23}$$

Differentiating both sides of the equation $QQ^* = 1$, we also find that

$$\dot{Q}Q^* + Q\dot{Q}^* = 0 \tag{6.24}$$

The above equation shows that $\dot{Q}Q^* + (\dot{Q}Q^*)^* = 0$. In other words, the real part of the quaternion $\dot{Q}Q^*$ is zero. Hence $\dot{Q}Q^*$can be expressed in the form $(0, \boldsymbol{v})$. With these observations, Eq. 6.23 becomes

$$(0, \dot{\boldsymbol{p}}') = (0,\ \boldsymbol{v})(0,\ \boldsymbol{p}') - (0,\ \boldsymbol{p}')(0,\ \boldsymbol{v}) \tag{6.25}$$

Using the quaternion multiplication rule in Eq. 5.11, we get

$$\dot{\boldsymbol{p}}' = 2(\boldsymbol{v} \times \boldsymbol{p}') \tag{6.26}$$

Since we consider only rotational motion of the vector $\boldsymbol{p}'$, its linear velocity is given by Eq. 6.18. Comparing both equations, we find that $\boldsymbol{\omega} = 2\boldsymbol{v}$. Hence we can write

$$\dot{Q}Q^* = \left(0,\ \frac{\boldsymbol{\omega}}{2}\right) \tag{6.27}$$

where $\boldsymbol{\omega}$ is the angular rate. Conversely, if a vector is rotated using a unit quaternion Q, the angular rate is given by the vector part of the quaternion product $2\dot{Q}Q^*$. Using Eq. 5.13, we can write this relationship in matrix form as given below.

$$\begin{bmatrix} 0 \\ \omega_1 \\ \omega_2 \\ \omega_3 \end{bmatrix} = 2 \begin{bmatrix} q_0 & q_1 & q_2 & q_3 \\ -q_1 & q_0 & -q_3 & q_2 \\ -q_2 & q_3 & q_0 & -q_1 \\ -q_3 & -q_2 & q_1 & q_0 \end{bmatrix} \begin{bmatrix} \dot{q}_0 \\ \dot{q}_1 \\ \dot{q}_2 \\ \dot{q}_3 \end{bmatrix} \tag{6.28}$$

Note that Q is a quaternion of the type given in Eq. 5.44. Accordingly, $\dot{Q}$ takes the form

$$\dot{Q} = \left(-\sin\frac{\delta}{2},\ l\cos\frac{\delta}{2},\ m\cos\frac{\delta}{2},\ n\cos\frac{\delta}{2}\right)\frac{\dot{\delta}}{2} \tag{6.29}$$

As expected, the above equations yield the result

$$\boldsymbol{\omega} = (l,\ m,\ n)\ \dot{\delta} \tag{6.30}$$

6.3.4 The Jacobian

In general, we can assume that the end effector position $E = (x_e, y_e, z_e)$ of an n-link joint chain can be expressed as a function of joint angles θ_i for $i = 1,...,n$, (for example, see Eq. 6.1). Thus we can write

$$\begin{aligned} x_e &= x_e(\theta_1, \theta_2, \ldots, \theta_n) \\ y_e &= y_e(\theta_1, \theta_2, \ldots, \theta_n) \\ z_e &= z_e(\theta_1, \theta_2, \ldots, \theta_n) \end{aligned} \tag{6.31}$$

If $\Delta\theta_i$ denotes an infinitesimal change in the joint angles θ_i for $i = 1,...,n$, and $(\Delta x_e, \Delta y_e, \Delta z_e)$ the corresponding change in the end effector position during a small time interval Δt, we have,

$$\begin{aligned} x_e + \Delta x_e &= x_e(\theta_1 + \Delta\theta_1, \theta_2 + \Delta\theta_2, \ldots, \theta_n + \Delta\theta_n) \\ y_e + \Delta y_e &= y_e(\theta_1 + \Delta\theta_1, \theta_2 + \Delta\theta_2, \ldots, \theta_n + \Delta\theta_n) \\ z_e + \Delta z_e &= z_e(\theta_1 + \Delta\theta_1, \theta_2 + \Delta\theta_2, \ldots, \theta_n + \Delta\theta_n) \end{aligned} \tag{6.32}$$

Assuming that joint angle perturbations are small, we can use Taylor's first order approximation to express the above set of equations in matrix form as follows:

$$\begin{bmatrix} \Delta x_e \\ \Delta y_e \\ \Delta z_e \end{bmatrix} = \begin{bmatrix} \frac{\partial x_e}{\partial \theta_1} & \frac{\partial x_e}{\partial \theta_2} & \cdots & \frac{\partial x_e}{\partial \theta_n} \\ \frac{\partial y_e}{\partial \theta_1} & \frac{\partial y_e}{\partial \theta_2} & \cdots & \frac{\partial y_e}{\partial \theta_n} \\ \frac{\partial z_e}{\partial \theta_1} & \frac{\partial z_e}{\partial \theta_2} & \cdots & \frac{\partial z_e}{\partial \theta_n} \end{bmatrix} \begin{bmatrix} \Delta\theta_1 \\ \Delta\theta_2 \\ \vdots \\ \Delta\theta_n \end{bmatrix} \tag{6.33}$$

From the above equation, it follows that

$$v_e = \dot{\mathbf{E}} = \mathbf{J}\dot{\boldsymbol{\theta}} \tag{6.34}$$

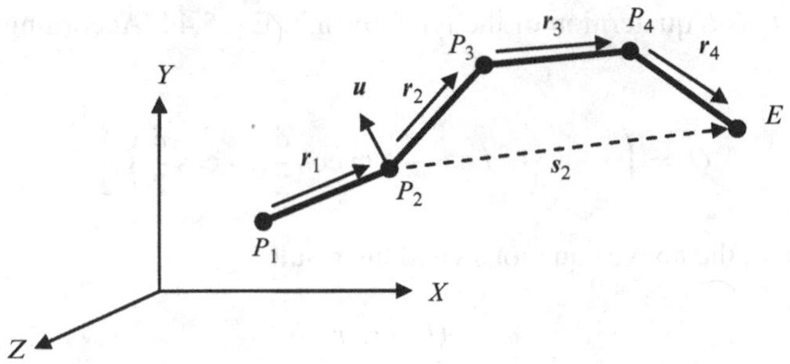

Fig. 6.8 The Jacobian matrix can be constructed using the axis of rotation of each link and a vector from that link to the end effector

where

$$\dot{\mathbf{E}} = \begin{bmatrix} \dot{x}_e \\ \dot{y}_e \\ \dot{z}_e \end{bmatrix}, \qquad \dot{\boldsymbol{\theta}} = \begin{bmatrix} \dot{\theta}_1 \\ \dot{\theta}_2 \\ \vdots \\ \dot{\theta}_n \end{bmatrix} \tag{6.35}$$

The $3 \times n$ matrix $\mathbf{J}$ is called the Jacobian of the transformation in Eq. 6.31.

As an example, consider the end effector position of a 3-link chain given in Eq. 6.1. The Jacobian in this case is a 2×3 matrix containing the partial derivatives of x_e and y_e with respect to the three joint angles. It can be easily verified that the expressions for the velocity components obtained using Eq. 6.34 are the same as those given in Eq. 6.17.

The ith column of the Jacobian in Eq. 6.33 can also be obtained using the axis of rotation of the ith link and the vector from that link to the end effector. Figure 6.8 shows an example, where the second link's general rotational transformation has an equivalent axis of rotation given by the unit vector $\boldsymbol{u}$. The vector from the second link to the end effector is $E - P_2$ denoted by $\boldsymbol{s}_2$.

The second column of the 3×4 Jacobian matrix for the above example can be computed using the vector cross product $\boldsymbol{u} \times \boldsymbol{s}_2$. Note that $\boldsymbol{s}_2 = \boldsymbol{r}_2 + \boldsymbol{r}_3 + \boldsymbol{r}_4$.

6.4 Inverse Kinematics

Inverse kinematics (IK) deals with the process of computing the joint angles, given the world coordinates of the end effector. Inverse kinematics solutions are needed for animating an articulated figure using only the desired positions of end points as inputs. Two examples are shown in Fig. 6.9, where the known end effector position is indicated by the point E.

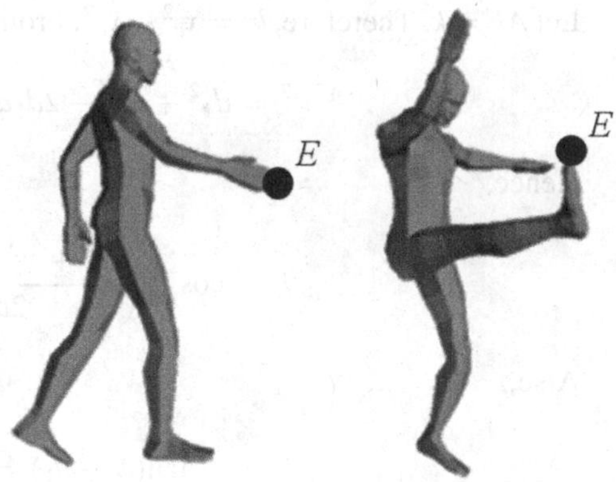

Fig. 6.9 Inverse kinematics solutions try to find the joint angles of a serial chain given the position of the end effector

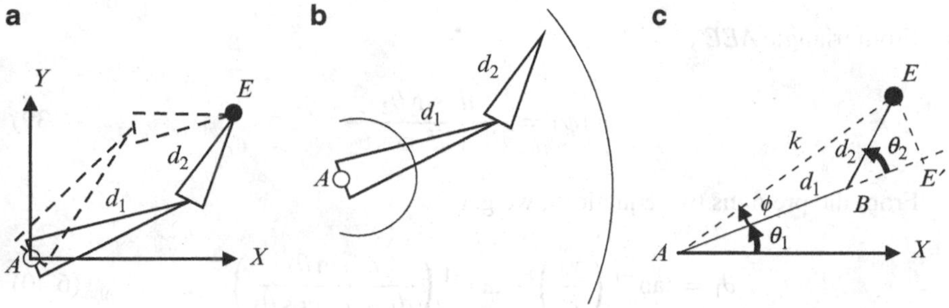

Fig. 6.10 (**a**) Multiple solutions may exist for the inverse kinematics problem for a 2-link chain. (**b**) A solution exists only when the target point is between the inner and outer circles. (**c**) A simple geometric construction used for an inverse kinematics solution

In the absence of joint angle constraints, multiple solutions may exist for a two link joint chain as shown in Fig. 6.10a. On the other hand, a solution may not exist for certain other positions of the end effector. In Fig. 6.10b, a solution cannot be found if the target position is either inside the inner circle of radius $d_1 - d_2$, or outside the outer circle of radius $d_1 + d_2$.

Without loss of generality, we can assume that the base of the joint chain A is fixed at the origin. We can also assume that there are no joint angle constraints. In the following sections, we will discuss methods for arriving at inverse kinematics solutions with these assumptions.

6.4.1 2-Link Inverse Kinematics

We can easily develop an analytical solution for the 2-link inverse kinematics problem for the configuration shown in Fig. 6.10c. If the coordinates (x_e, y_e) of the end point E are given, the joint angles θ_1, θ_2 can be determined as follows:

Let $AE = k$. Therefore, $k^2 = {x_e}^2 + {y_e}^2$. From triangle ABE we get,

$$k^2 = {d_1}^2 + {d_2}^2 - 2d_1d_2\cos(\pi - \theta_2) \quad (6.36)$$

Hence,

$$\theta_2 = \cos^{-1}\left(\frac{x_e^2 + y_e^2 - d_1^2 - d_2^2}{2d_1d_2}\right) \quad (6.37)$$

Also,

$$\tan(\phi + \theta_1) = \frac{y_e}{x_e} \quad (6.38)$$

From triangle AEE',

$$\tan(\phi) = \frac{d_2 \sin\theta_2}{d_1 + d_2\cos\theta_2} \quad (6.39)$$

From the previous two equations, we get

$$\theta_1 = \tan^{-1}\left(\frac{y_e}{x_e}\right) - \tan^{-1}\left(\frac{d_2\sin\theta_2}{d_1 + d_2\cos\theta_2}\right) \quad (6.40)$$

Equation 6.37 is valid only if

$$(d_1 - d_2)^2 \le {x_e}^2 + {y_e}^2 \le (d_1 + d_2)^2 \quad (6.41)$$

The above condition corresponds to the situation shown in Fig. 6.10b.

6.4.2 n-Link Inverse Kinematics

For a general n-link configuration, the problem of estimating the joint angles $\theta_1, \theta_2, \ldots, \theta_n$, given only the end effector coordinates (x_e, y_e, z_e), clearly leads to an under-determined system of equations when $n > 3$. Such a system is called a redundant manipulator, implying that more than one set of joint angles could possibly lead to the same end effector position. A non-redundant manipulator in three-dimensional space contains only three links.

Suppose we are required to move the end effector from its current position E to a desired target location given by $T = (x_t, y_t, z_t)$. The inverse kinematics problem can be rephrased as follows: Determine the change in joint angles required to produce a change in the end effector position from E to T. If we denote this displacement of the end effector by the vector $\Delta\mathbf{E} = T - E$, and the joint angle perturbation vector by $\Delta\boldsymbol{\theta}$, then from Eq. 6.33 we know that

$$\Delta\mathbf{E} = \mathbf{J}\,\Delta\boldsymbol{\theta} \tag{6.42}$$

where $\mathbf{J}$ is the $3 \times n$ Jacobian matrix. $\mathbf{J}$ is invertible only for a non-redundant manipulator ($n = 3$). Generally when $n > 3$, $\mathbf{J}$ is not a square invertible matrix, and therefore we cannot directly obtain $\Delta\boldsymbol{\theta}$ from the above equation. However, pre-multiplying both sides by the transpose $\mathbf{J}^{\mathrm{T}}$, we can form a symmetric, square and invertible matrix $(\mathbf{J}^{\mathrm{T}}\mathbf{J})$, and then obtain a solution for $\Delta\boldsymbol{\theta}$ as

$$\Delta\boldsymbol{\theta} = \mathbf{J}^{+}\,\Delta\mathbf{E} \tag{6.43}$$

where

$$\mathbf{J}^{+} = (\mathbf{J}^{\mathrm{T}}\mathbf{J})^{-1}\,\mathbf{J}^{\mathrm{T}} \tag{6.44}$$

The above matrix is called the left pseudo-inverse of $\mathbf{J}$. For an n-link chain, $(\mathbf{J}^{\mathrm{T}}\mathbf{J})$ is an $n \times n$ matrix. One could use Singular Value Decomposition (SVD) to compute the pseudo-inverse of $\mathbf{J}$. If $\mathbf{J}$ has a decomposition of the form $\mathbf{USV}^{\mathrm{T}}$, then the pseudo-inverse of $\mathbf{J}$ is given by

$$\mathbf{J}^{+} = \mathbf{VS}^{+}\mathbf{U}^{\mathrm{T}} \tag{6.45}$$

In the above matrix equation, $\mathbf{U}$ is a 3×3 orthogonal matrix, $\mathbf{S}$ is a $3 \times n$ diagonal matrix, and $\mathbf{V}$ is a $n \times n$ orthogonal matrix. Columns of $\mathbf{U}$ are orthonormal eigenvectors of $\mathbf{JJ}^{\mathrm{T}}$, and the columns of $\mathbf{V}$ are orthonormal eigenvectors of $\mathbf{J}^{\mathrm{T}}\mathbf{J}$. The matrix $\mathbf{S}$ contains square-roots of eigenvalues of either $\mathbf{JJ}^{\mathrm{T}}$ or $\mathbf{J}^{\mathrm{T}}\mathbf{J}$. Its inverse $\mathbf{S}^{+}$ can be readily obtained by transposing $\mathbf{S}$ and taking the reciprocals of the diagonal elements. Denoting the columns of $\mathbf{U}$ by vectors $\boldsymbol{u}_i$ ($i = 1..3$), and the columns of $\mathbf{V}$ by vectors $\boldsymbol{v}_i$ ($i = 1..n$), we have

$$\mathbf{J} = \begin{bmatrix} \boldsymbol{u}_1 \; \boldsymbol{u}_2 \; \boldsymbol{u}_3 \end{bmatrix} \begin{bmatrix} \sqrt{\sigma_1} & 0 & 0 & \cdots & 0 \\ 0 & \sqrt{\sigma_2} & 0 & \cdots & 0 \\ 0 & 0 & \sqrt{\sigma_3} & \cdots & 0 \end{bmatrix} \begin{bmatrix} \boldsymbol{v}_1^T \\ \boldsymbol{v}_2^T \\ \vdots \\ \boldsymbol{v}_n^T \end{bmatrix} \tag{6.46}$$

and

$$\mathbf{J}^{+} = \begin{bmatrix} \boldsymbol{v}_1 \; \boldsymbol{v}_2 \cdots \boldsymbol{v}_n \end{bmatrix} \begin{bmatrix} \frac{1}{\sqrt{\sigma_1}} & 0 & 0 \\ 0 & \frac{1}{\sqrt{\sigma_2}} & 0 \\ 0 & 0 & \frac{1}{\sqrt{\sigma_3}} \\ \vdots & \vdots & \vdots \\ 0 & 0 & 0 \end{bmatrix} \begin{bmatrix} \boldsymbol{u}_1^T \\ \boldsymbol{u}_2^T \\ \boldsymbol{u}_3^T \end{bmatrix} \tag{6.47}$$

where σ_i denotes the ith eigenvalue of the square matrix $\mathbf{JJ}^{\mathrm{T}}$, and $\sigma_1 \geq \sigma_2 \geq \sigma_3$. Substituting the above expression in Eq. 6.43 and simplifying,

$$\begin{bmatrix} \Delta\theta_1 \\ \Delta\theta_2 \\ \vdots \\ \Delta\theta_n \end{bmatrix} = \begin{bmatrix} \frac{1}{\sqrt{\sigma_1}}\mathbf{v}_1 & \frac{1}{\sqrt{\sigma_2}}\mathbf{v}_2 & \frac{1}{\sqrt{\sigma_3}}\mathbf{v}_3 \end{bmatrix} \begin{bmatrix} \mathbf{u}_1^T \\ \mathbf{u}_2^T \\ \mathbf{u}_3^T \end{bmatrix} \begin{bmatrix} x_t - x_e \\ y_t - y_e \\ z_t - z_e \end{bmatrix} \tag{6.48}$$

Note that the sizes of the three matrices on the right-hand side of the above equation are $n \times 3$, 3×3, and 3×1 respectively. In the following sections, we discuss iterative numerical methods that try to move the end effector through a sequence of points to the desired target position.

6.5 Gradient Descent

The inverse kinematics solution for computing $\Delta\boldsymbol{\theta}$ as outlined in the previous section is based on an important assumption that both $\Delta\mathbf{E}$ (the distance from the current end effector position to the target) and $\Delta\boldsymbol{\theta}$ (joint angle perturbations) are small. Many practical situations violate these conditions. The two-dimensional analogue of the situation where the distance between the end effector and target is large is shown in Fig. 6.11a. The y-axis represents the end effector position whose dependency on the joint angle θ is given by the function $y = f(\theta)$. The desired target position is indicated by the ordinate T.

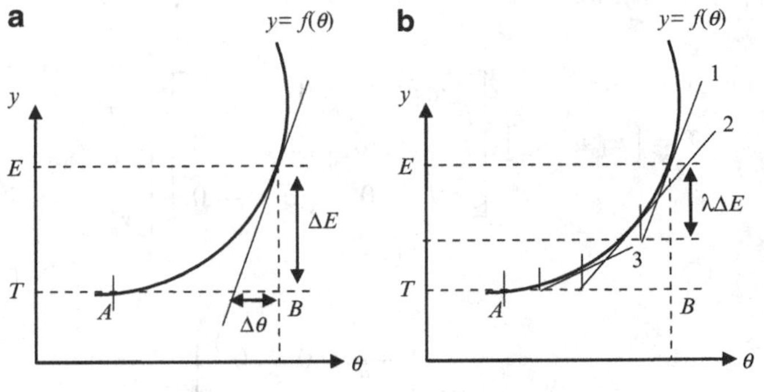

Fig. 6.11 (**a**) Computing Δθ from the derivative alone can lead to significant errors if ΔE is large. (**b**) The iterative convergence of the gradient descent algorithm

Listing 6.1 Pseudo code for the gradient descent algorithm

```
1.   Input:  λ          //A value between 0 and 1.
2.   Input:  T          //Target position
3.   Input:  ε          //Error threshold
4.   Input:  kmax       //Maximum number of iterations
5.   Input:  θ1         //Initial joint angles
6.   k = 1              //iteration number
7.   Compute E(θk)      //End effector position
8.   IF (|T-E|<ε)STOP   //Reached target
9.   Compute J          //Jacobian
10.  Compute J+         //Jacobian pseudo inverse
11.  Compute Δθk        //Using Eq. (6.51)
12.  k = k+1            //Increment iteration count
13.  Compute θk         //Upadate equation in Eq. (6.51)
14.  IF (k>kmax)STOP    //Maximum iterations exceeded
15.  GOTO Step 7
```

The solution given in Eq. 6.43 is equivalent to computing $\Delta\theta$ in the above example using the formula

$$\Delta\theta = \frac{\Delta E}{\left(\frac{df(\theta)}{d\theta}\right)} \tag{6.49}$$

As can be seen from Fig. 6.11a, there is a large error in the value obtained for $\Delta\theta$, the solution giving only a fraction of the required change in θ given by the distance *AB*. If $\Delta \mathbf{E}$ is large, we will need to approach the target in smaller steps. This is done by scaling $\Delta \mathbf{E}$ by a factor λ $(0 < \lambda < 1)$, each time updating the end effector position and the derivative. This approach is called the gradient descent method, and is shown in Fig. 6.11b. The following equation computes the value of incremental changes in θ for each iteration step *k*, and updates the function value and its derivative.

$$\Delta\theta_k = \frac{\lambda\,(T - f(\theta_k))}{\left(\frac{df(\theta)}{d\theta}\right)_k}, \quad \theta_{k+1} = \theta_k + \Delta\theta_k \tag{6.50}$$

We can employ the gradient descent method for iteratively computing $\Delta\boldsymbol{\theta}$ after introducing the scaling factor λ in Eq. 6.43. The modified equation is given below.

$$\Delta\boldsymbol{\theta}_k = \lambda \mathbf{J}_k{}^{+}(T - E_k), \quad \boldsymbol{\theta}_{k+1} = \boldsymbol{\theta}_k + \Delta\boldsymbol{\theta}_k \tag{6.51}$$

where $\boldsymbol{\theta}_k$ is a column vector of joint angles updated in the *k*th iteration. The gradient descent algorithm for computing the joint angles for a *n*-link chain is given in Listing 6.1.

6.6 Cyclic Coordinate Descent

The Cyclic Coordinate Descent (CCD) algorithm is a well-known method used for inverse kinematics solutions in computer graphics applications involving joint chains and moving targets. CCD performs a series of rotations on the links of a joint chain, starting with the last link, each time trying to move the end effector closer to the target.

A sequence of rotations performed by the CCD algorithm for a 4-link chain on a two-dimensional plane is shown in Fig. 6.12. The joints of the links are denoted by P_1, P_2 ... etc., the target by T, and the end effector position by E. The last link is rotated first by an angle θ_4 about P_4, where θ_4 is the angle between end

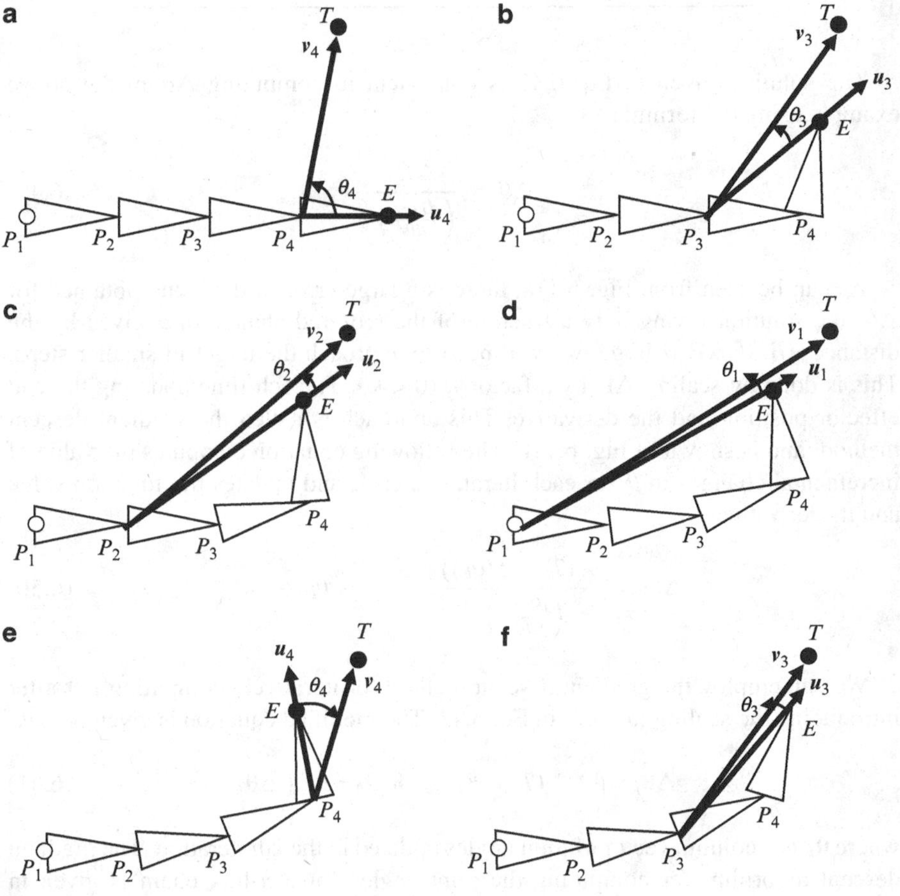

Fig. 6.12 Sequence of rotations performed by CCD algorithm on a 4-link joint chain

Listing 6.2 Pseudo code for the CCD algorithm

```
1.  Inputs:  P1..Pn,T,E,n
2.  Input:  ε              //Error threshold
3.  Input:  kmax            //Maximum number of iterations
4.  i = n                  //Link index.  Start from last link
5.  k = 1                  //Iteration count
6.  Compute ui, vi         //Vectors E-Pi, T-Pi
7.  Compute ωi             //Using Eq. (6.52)
8.  Compute δi             //Using Eq. (6.53)
9.  Perform angle-axis rotation (δi, ωi) of link i
10. Compute the new position of E
11. IF(|T-E|<ε)STOP  //Reached target
12. i = i-1          //Next link
13. IF(i<1) THEN {k = k+1;  i = n}  //Start again
14. IF(k>kmax)STOP   //Maximum iterations exceeded
15. GOTO Step 6
```

effector vector $\boldsymbol{u}_4 = E - P_4$ and the target vector $\boldsymbol{v}_4 = T - P_4$ (Fig. 6.12a). This rotation brings the end effector E to a point on the target vector. The second rotation is performed about the next link position P_3, by an angle θ_3 between the end effector and target vectors at that point (Fig. 6.12b). This process of rotating links is continued till the first link P_1 is reached (Fig. 6.12d), and then repeated over, starting again from the last link P_4 (Fig. 6.12e). In three-dimensional space, the axis of rotation for the ith link at position P_i is calculated as

$$\boldsymbol{\omega}_i = \frac{\boldsymbol{u}_i \times \boldsymbol{v}_i}{|\boldsymbol{u}_i \times \boldsymbol{v}_i|} \tag{6.52}$$

where $\boldsymbol{u}_i = E - P_i$, and $\boldsymbol{v}_i = T - P_i$. The angle of rotation about the unit vector $\boldsymbol{\omega}_i$ is

$$\delta_i = \cos^{-1}\left(\frac{\boldsymbol{u}_i \cdot \boldsymbol{v}_i}{|\boldsymbol{u}_i|\ |\boldsymbol{v}_i|}\right) \tag{6.53}$$

The general algorithm for a n-link joint chain is given in Listing 6.2.

The terminating condition for the iterative algorithm can be defined based on the distance TE between the end effector and the target, and also the number of iterations performed. Physical systems using a set of joints, such as robotic manipulator arms, have joint angle constraints and other physical limitations that should be taken into account while designing an inverse kinematics solution. The CCD algorithm can generate large angle rotations that may violate joint angle constraints. In some cases, particularly when the target is located close to the base, the CCD algorithm causes a chain to form a loop, intersecting itself (Fig. 6.13a). Similarly, for certain target positions, the algorithm can take a large number of iterations resulting in a slow zigzag motion of the end effector (Fig. 6.13b). The method discussed in the next section is designed to overcome these drawbacks.

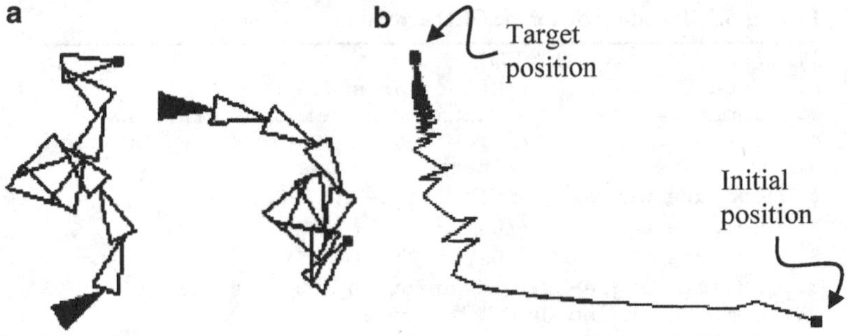

Fig. 6.13 (**a**) Two examples showing entangled configurations of a 10-link joint chain generated by the CCD algorithm. (**b**) The path showing the convergence of the end effector position towards a target location

6.7 Circular Alignment Algorithm

The circular alignment algorithm tries to place the given joint chain along a circular arc between the base and the target position, provided the target is reachable. With such a placement of the chain, joint angles will automatically assume values in an acceptable range, and there is no possibility of the chain to intersect itself. This method has some key advantages over the CCD algorithm:

1. This algorithm is significantly faster than the CCD algorithm. All joint angles have the same value based on a single solution.
2. The algorithm does not generate large angle rotations.
3. The algorithm does not generate entangled configurations of chains with large number of links.

The algorithm, however, requires all links to have the same length in order to use a simple inverse kinematics solution. The algorithm works on a two-dimensional plane containing the base of the link and the target. A general three-dimensional problem is thus reduced to two dimensions, assuming that the base link can be rotated in such a way that the whole chain is reoriented towards the target with all links constrained to move on a single plane. We will first consider the problem on the *xy*-plane, and later discuss how it could be generalized into three dimensions.

We assume that each link of an n-link chain has length d, and the total length of the chain is $L = nd$. The distance of the target T from the base P_1 of the joint chain is denoted by D (Fig. 6.13). If the target is reachable ($0 < D < L$) then the joints of the link can be made to align along a circular path such that the end effector coincides with the target. There are two possible scenarios as shown in Fig. 6.13.

We first compute the angle β subtended by the arc P_1T, and then derive the radius, coordinates of the centre, and joint angle parameters from it. The angle β is acute if the length L of the chain is less than $\pi D/2$, otherwise it is obtuse. In either case, we have

$$\frac{\sin\left(\frac{\beta}{2n}\right)}{\sin\left(\frac{\beta}{2}\right)} = \frac{d}{D} \tag{6.54}$$

We seek the solution of the above equation for β, by defining the function

$$f(\beta) = d\sin\left(\frac{\beta}{2}\right) - D\sin\left(\frac{\beta}{2n}\right). \tag{6.55}$$

The function has a derivative

$$f'(\beta) = \left(\frac{d}{2}\right)\cos\left(\frac{\beta}{2}\right) - \left(\frac{D}{2n}\right)\cos\left(\frac{\beta}{2n}\right) \tag{6.56}$$

The solution for β can be obtained using Newton-Raphson iteration:

$$\beta_{k+1} = \beta_k - \frac{f(\beta_k)}{f'(\beta_k)}, \tag{6.57}$$

with the initial condition

$$\beta_0 = 2\pi/n. \tag{6.58}$$

The Newton-Raphson method yields fast convergence for the parameter β, from which all joint angles can be computed as described below. The radius R of the circle and the perpendicular distance S (Fig. 6.15) can be obtained as

$$R = \frac{D}{2\sin\left(\frac{\beta}{2}\right)}, \quad S = \frac{D}{2\tan\left(\frac{\beta}{2}\right)} \tag{6.59}$$

Without loss of generality, we can assume that the base of the link P_1 is located at the origin of the coordinate system. If the target T has coordinates (x_t, y_t), the centre of the circle is selected among two possible values (Fig. 6.15) as

$$\begin{aligned} C = (x_c, y_c) &= \left(\frac{x_t}{2} - \frac{y_t S}{D}, \ \frac{y_t}{2} + \frac{x_t S}{D}\right), \ \text{if} \ \ L \le \pi D/2 \\ &= \left(\frac{x_t}{2} + \frac{y_t S}{D}, \ \frac{y_t}{2} - \frac{x_t S}{D}\right), \ \text{if} \ \ L > \pi D/2 \end{aligned} \tag{6.60}$$

The above choice causes the chain to orient along an anticlockwise circular path towards the target, and to have positive values for the joint angles for both the cases shown in Fig. 6.14.

The joint angles for the two-dimensional case are computed as follows. The base link's joint angle θ_1 is measured with respect to the x-axis, and is given by

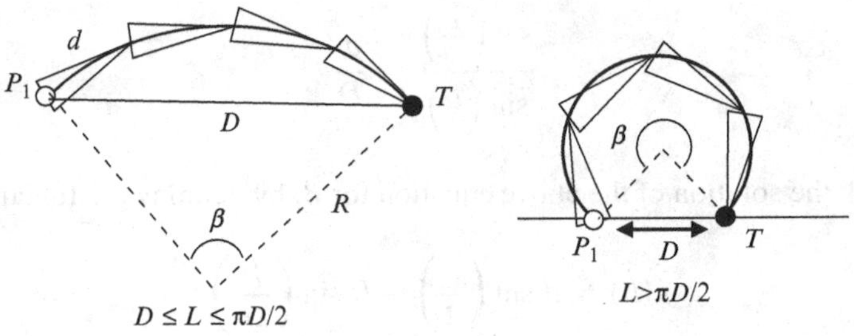

Fig. 6.14 Circular alignment of joints

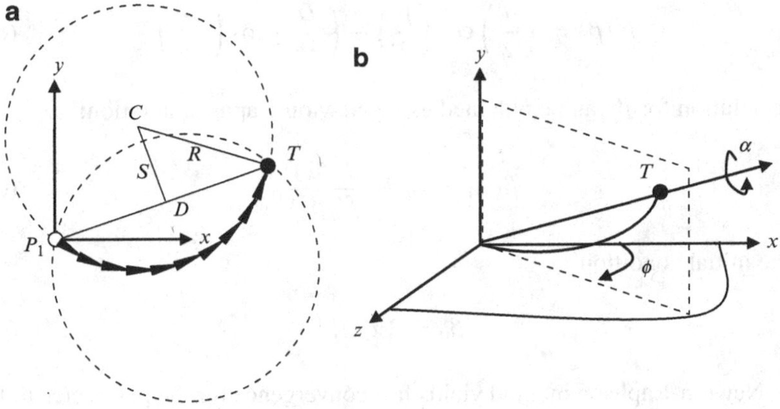

Fig. 6.15 (**a**) Two possible orientations of the joint chain for a given target position. (**b**) Extension of the inverse kinematics solution to three dimensions

$$\theta_1 = \tan^{-1}\left(\frac{y_c}{x_c}\right) + \frac{\beta}{2n} - \frac{\pi}{2} \tag{6.61}$$

All remaining joint angles have the same value given by

$$\theta_i = \beta/n,\ i = 2 \ldots n. \tag{6.62}$$

The approach detailed above can be extended to three dimensions where the target position is given by $T = (x_t,\ y_t,\ z_t)$. The problem is first reduced to two dimensions by transforming the target location to the *xy*-plane, and computing the joint angles as described previously. The transformed target position is

$$\begin{aligned} x'_t &= \sqrt{x_t^2 + z_t^2} \\ y'_t &= y_t \end{aligned} \tag{6.63}$$

After computing the joint angles, the whole chain is rotated about the y-axis by an angle $-\phi$ as shown in Fig. 6.15b to achieve the desired configuration. The rotation angle ϕ can be computed as $\tan^{-1}(z_t/x_t)$. This rotation can be combined with the joint angle rotation of the base link P_1. We can add one more degree of freedom to the link by allowing the chain to rotate about the line joining the base and the target, thus varying the direction in which the end effector approaches the target.

6.8 Summary

This chapter discussed forward and inverse kinematics equations for serial links containing only revolute or spherical joints. Such joint chains are commonly used in computer graphics for skeletal animation. Forward kinematics equations are used to compute the position of the end effector, given the joint angles. The chapter presented methods for computing the linear velocity of the end effector as a function of angular velocities of the joints. Both Euler angle and quaternion based definitions of rotations were considered. In the most general case, when the end effector coordinates are expressed as functions of joint angles, the Jacobian matrix defines the relationship between the linear and angular velocities.

Inverse kinematics (IK) solutions can have singularities for redundant manipulators. The inverse Jacobian in the general IK solution is calculated in terms of the pseudo-inverse obtained using methods such as the singular value decomposition. If the distance between the end effector position and target is large, iterative numerical techniques are often used for a more accurate solution that converges to the target position. This chapter also outlined the cyclic coordinate descent and the circular alignment algorithms that are useful for animating joint chains.

The next chapter introduces parametrically generated curves and surfaces and discusses their applications in computer graphics.

6.9 Supplementary Material for Chap. 6

The folder `Chapter6/Code` on the companion website contains the following programs demonstrating the working of inverse kinematics algorithms.

1. **IK_CCD.cpp**

Additional files:
`none`

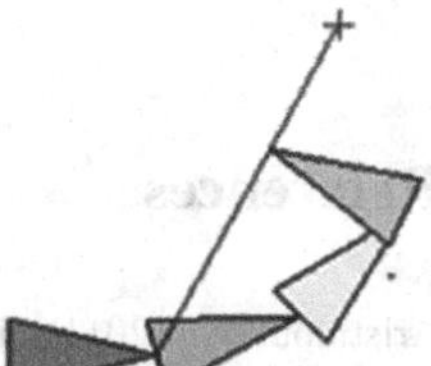

The program shows the working of the cyclic coordinate descent algorithm (Sect. 6.6) in transforming a 4-link chain. Target positions can be interactively specified using mouse clicks. Pressing the space bar updates the display, showing the next step in the sequence of rotations performed on the joint chain. The target vector and the end effector vectors are also drawn to show the amount of rotation in each step.

2. **IK_CAA.cpp**

Additional files:
`none`

The program displays a 10-link joint chain that aligns along a circular path to reach a target position. Target positions can be interactively specified using mouse clicks. The circular alignment algorithm was discussed in Sect. 6.7.

6.10 Bibliographical Notes

Kinematic analysis is an integral part of robotic systems, and most of the important references on the topic can be found in the area of serial manipulators and multi-body systems. Bottema and Roth (1979), Crane and Duffy (1998), and Jazar (2010) are just a few among many excellent books that provide a detailed description of the theory of kinematic manipulators, forward kinematics equations, and several types of inverse kinematic solutions. Orin and Schrader (1984), Maciejewski and Klein (1989) discuss the solutions based on Jacobian inverses.

In early 1980s, Korein and Badler (1982) proposed inverse kinematics solutions for goal directed motion of articulated character models. A comprehensive coverage of kinematics algorithms that are useful in computer animation of character models can be found in Parent (2002) and Yamane (2010). The cyclic coordinate descent (CCD) algorithm was introduced by Chris Welman in his Masters thesis (Welman 1989). An overview of this algorithm and its implementation can also be found in Lander (1998). An fast iterative solver for animating character models was recently introduced by A. Aristidou (2011). The circular alignment algorithm was also recently introduced by O. Cardwell (2011).

References

Aristidou, A. (2011). FABRIK: A fast iterative solver for the inverse kinematics problem. *Graphical Models, 73*(5), 243–260.

Bottema, O., & Roth, B. (1979). *Theoretical kinematics*. Amsterdam/Oxford: North-Holland Publishing Co.

Cardwell, O., & R. Mukundan. (2011). *Visualization and analysis of inverse kinematics algorithms using performance metric maps*. The 19th international conference in Central Europe on computer graphics, visualization and computer vision, WSCG-2011, Czech Republic.

Crane, C. D., & Duffy, J. (1998). *Kinematic analysis of robot manipulators*. Cambridge: Cambridge University Press.

Jazar, R. N. (2010). *Theory of applied robotics: Kinematics, dynamics, and control* (2nd ed.). New York: Springer.

Korein, J. U., & Badler, N. I. (1982). Techniques for generating the goal-directed motion of articulated structures. *IEEE Computer Graphics and Applications, 2*(9), 71–81.

Lander, J. (1998, November). Making kine more flexible. *Game Developer, 5(3)*, 15–22.

Maciejewski, A. A., & Klein, C. A. (1989). The singular value decomposition: Computation and applications to robotics. *International Journal of Robotics Research, 8*, 63–79.

Orin, D. E., & Schrader, W. W. (1984). Efficient computation of the Jacobian for robot manipulators. *International Journal of Robotics Research, 3*, 66–75.

Parent, R. (2002). *Computer animation: Algorithms and techniques*. San Francisco/London: Morgan Kaufmann Publishers.

Welman, C. (1989). *Inverse kinematics and geometric constraints for articulated figure manipulation*. Master of Science thesis, Simon Fraser University.

Yamane, K. (2010). *Simulating and generating motions of human figures*. Berlin/Heidelberg: Springer.

Chapter 7
Curves and Surfaces

Overview

In computer graphics, blending curves and surfaces are widely used for both interpolation and approximation. We have previously seen the application of Hermite polynomials in vertex blending, and Catmull-Rom splines for keyframe interpolation. Spline curves and surfaces also find applications in the interactive design of three-dimensional models.

This chapter gives an overview of polynomial interpolation methods, and the construction of splines using different types of piecewise cubic polynomial curves. Design aspects such as local control, flexibility and parametric continuity are discussed in detail. Surface design techniques using two-dimensional Bezier and B-spline surface patches are also presented. Extensions of these methods using rational basis functions are then outlined.

7.1 Polynomial Interpolation

Suppose we are given n points (x_i, y_i), $i = 1 \ldots n$, on the xy-plane where all x_is are distinct. The polynomial interpolation theorem states that there is a unique polynomial $f(x)$ of degree $n - 1$ such that

$$f(x_i) = y_i, \quad i = 1...n. \tag{7.1}$$

The above equation shows that the polynomial curve given by $y = f(x)$ passes through all the n points. Such a curve that passes through all input points is called an interpolating curve. On the other hand, a curve that passes through only a few of the input points is called an approximating curve. The Bezier spline (see Box 2.4, Sect. 2.7) is an example of an approximating curve.

R. Mukundan, *Advanced Methods in Computer Graphics: With examples in OpenGL*,
DOI 10.1007/978-1-4471-2340-8_7, © Springer-Verlag London Limited 2012

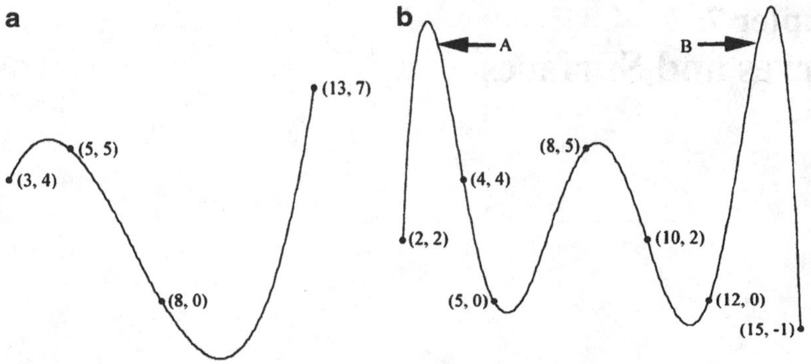

Fig. 7.1 Polynomial interpolation curves of (**a**) degree 3, and (**b**) degree 6

Consider the polynomial of degree $n - 1$ given by

$$c_1(x) = \frac{(x - x_2)(x - x_3)...(x - x_n)}{(x_1 - x_2)(x_1 - x_3)...(x_1 - x_n)} \tag{7.2}$$

The above function attains a value 1 if $x = x_1$, and 0 if $x = x_2, \ldots, x_n$. We can therefore combine such polynomials to form the required interpolating polynomial $f(x)$:

$$f(x) = c_1(x)y_1 + c_2(x)y_2 + ... + c_n(x)y_n \tag{7.3}$$

The polynomials $c_i(x)$ are the Lagrange polynomials of degree $n - 1$ given by

$$c_i(x) = \prod_{\substack{k=1 \\ k \neq i}}^{n} \frac{(x - x_k)}{(x_i - x_k)} \tag{7.4}$$

As an example, four points (3, 4), (5, 5), (8, 0), (13, 7) are used to construct a cubic polynomial curve in Fig. 7.1a. Another interpolating curve through seven points is shown in Fig. 7.1b.

Interpolation curves of degree higher than three can potentially have large overshoots (marked 'A' in Fig. 7.1b), or undesirable oscillations (marked 'B' in Fig. 7.1b). Such curves, even though they pass through all the user input points, may not describe the shape represented by those points. Piecewise polynomial curves of a low degree are therefore commonly used for approximating shapes.

The system of equations in Eq. 7.1 can also be written as a matrix equation $\mathbf{Y} = \mathbf{VA}$:

$$\begin{bmatrix} y_1 \\ y_2 \\ \vdots \\ y_n \end{bmatrix} = \begin{bmatrix} 1 & x_1 & \cdots & x_1^{n-1} \\ 1 & x_2 & \cdots & x_2^{n-1} \\ \vdots & \vdots & \cdots & \vdots \\ 1 & x_n & \cdots & x_n^{n-1} \end{bmatrix} \begin{bmatrix} a_0 \\ a_1 \\ \vdots \\ a_{n-1} \end{bmatrix} \tag{7.5}$$

where the polynomial is assumed to have the form

$$f(x) = a_0 + a_1 x + a_2 x^2 + \ldots + a_{n-1} x^{n-1} \tag{7.6}$$

The coefficients a_i of the polynomial can be obtained by taking the matrix inverse: $\mathbf{A} = \mathbf{V}^{-1}\mathbf{Y}$. The $n \times n$ matrix $\mathbf{V}$ is called the Vandermonde matrix. Since x_is are all distinct, this matrix is invertible.

We now look at a simple and efficient method for evaluating polynomials of the form in Eq. 7.6. If we use the formula $x^k = x.x^{k-1}$ to compute the powers of x for evaluating the terms of the polynomial from left to right, we need to perform $2(n-1)$ multiplications and $n-1$ additions. The Horner's method is used to reduce the number of multiplications by rearranging the polynomial as a nested set of expressions:

$$f(x) = a_0 + x(a_1 + x(a_2 + \ldots + x(a_{n-2} + x a_{n-1}) \ldots)) \tag{7.7}$$

Each nested sub-expression in the above equation requires one multiplication and one addition. Evaluating the polynomial from the innermost expression requires a total of only $n-1$ multiplications.

7.2 Cubic Parametric Curves

Cubic polynomials have the advantage that they can be easily evaluated and used to generate small curve segments of an interpolating spline with sufficient flexibility. A cubic polynomial curve can meet four constraints simultaneously such as the requirement to pass through four distinct points, or a requirement to pass through two points and have user specified tangent directions at those points. Splines commonly use parametric representations of piecewise cubic curves defined using three polynomials in a single parameter t:

$$\begin{aligned} x(t) &= a_0 + a_1 t + a_2 t^2 + a_3 t^3 \\ y(t) &= b_0 + b_1 t + b_2 t^2 + b_3 t^3 \\ z(t) &= c_0 + c_1 t + c_2 t^2 + c_3 t^3 \end{aligned} \tag{7.8}$$

The above polynomials are called the x-polynomial, y-polynomial and z-polynomial respectively. The parameter t usually varies from 0 to 1, with each value of t corresponding to a single point $P(t) = (x(t), y(t), z(t))$ on the curve. The polynomials thus define a mapping from an interval in the one-dimensional parameter space to a set of points in the three-dimensional space. A common example is where t represents time, and $P(t)$ the position of a moving point at that instant. The equation for $x(t)$ given above can be re-written as follows:

$$x(t) = \begin{bmatrix} 1 & t & t^2 & t^3 \end{bmatrix} \begin{bmatrix} a_0 \\ a_1 \\ a_2 \\ a_3 \end{bmatrix} = \mathbf{TA} \tag{7.9}$$

The polynomial coefficients a_i, b_i, c_i are computed using a set of control points and continuity constraints. As an example, consider the requirement that the cubic curve needs to pass through four distinct points $P_i = (x_i, y_i, z_i)$, $i = 1 \ldots 4$. If t_i denotes the values of the parameter t corresponding to the four control points, we have

$$\begin{bmatrix} x_1 \\ x_2 \\ x_3 \\ x_4 \end{bmatrix} = \begin{bmatrix} 1 & t_1 & t_1^2 & t_1^3 \\ 1 & t_2 & t_2^2 & t_2^3 \\ 1 & t_3 & t_3^2 & t_3^3 \\ 1 & t_4 & t_4^2 & t_4^3 \end{bmatrix} \begin{bmatrix} a_0 \\ a_1 \\ a_2 \\ a_3 \end{bmatrix} \tag{7.10}$$

This equation is the cubic version of Eq. 7.5. The 4×4 Vandermonde matrix is invertible if all t_is are distinct. We write this equation in a concise form as $\mathbf{G}_x = \mathbf{VA}$, or equivalently as $\mathbf{A} = \mathbf{V}^{-1}\mathbf{G}_x$, where $\mathbf{G}_x$ is a column vector containing only the x-coordinates of the control points. The inverse $\mathbf{V}^{-1}$ of the Vandermonde matrix can be computed as the product $\mathbf{UL}$, where $\mathbf{U}$ is the following upper triangular matrix

$$\mathbf{U} = \begin{bmatrix} 1 & -t_1 & t_1 t_2 & -t_1 t_2 t_3 \\ 0 & 1 & -(t_1 + t_2) & t_1 t_2 + t_2 t_3 + t_3 t_1 \\ 0 & 0 & 1 & -(t_1 + t_2 + t_3) \\ 0 & 0 & 0 & 1 \end{bmatrix} \tag{7.11}$$

and **L** is a lower triangular matrix given by

$$\mathbf{L}=\begin{bmatrix} 1 & 0 & 0 & 0 \\ \left(\frac{1}{t_1-t_2}\right) & \left(\frac{1}{t_2-t_1}\right) & 0 & 0 \\ \left(\frac{1}{(t_1-t_2)(t_1-t_3)}\right) & \left(\frac{1}{(t_2-t_1)(t_2-t_3)}\right) & \left(\frac{1}{(t_3-t_1)(t_3-t_2)}\right) & 0 \\ \left(\frac{1}{(t_1-t_2)(t_1-t_3)(t_1-t_4)}\right) & \left(\frac{1}{(t_2-t_1)(t_2-t_3)(t_2-t_4)}\right) & \left(\frac{1}{(t_3-t_1)(t_3-t_2)(t_3-t_4)}\right) & \left(\frac{1}{(t_4-t_1)(t_4-t_2)(t_4-t_3)}\right) \end{bmatrix} \tag{7.12}$$

For example, if the parametric values are equally spaced in the interval [0, 1], so that $t_1 = 0$, $t_2 = 1/3$, $t_3 = 2/3$, $t_4 = 1$, then we have the following values for **V** and $\mathbf{V}^{-1}$:

$$\mathbf{V}=\begin{bmatrix} 1 & 0 & 0 & 0 \\ 1 & \left(\frac{1}{3}\right) & \left(\frac{1}{9}\right) & \left(\frac{1}{27}\right) \\ 1 & \left(\frac{2}{3}\right) & \left(\frac{4}{9}\right) & \left(\frac{8}{27}\right) \\ 1 & 1 & 1 & 1 \end{bmatrix}, \mathbf{V}^{-1}=\begin{bmatrix} 1 & 0 & 0 & 0 \\ \left(\frac{-11}{2}\right) & 9 & \left(\frac{-9}{2}\right) & 1 \\ 9 & \left(\frac{-45}{2}\right) & 18 & \left(\frac{-9}{2}\right) \\ \left(\frac{-9}{2}\right) & \left(\frac{27}{2}\right) & \left(\frac{-27}{2}\right) & \left(\frac{9}{2}\right) \end{bmatrix} \tag{7.13}$$

From Eq. 7.9, we now have

$$x(t) = \mathbf{T}\mathbf{V}^{-1}\,\mathbf{G}_x \tag{7.14}$$

The product $\mathbf{TV}^{-1}$ is a row vector containing four functions of the parameter t. Thus the above equation can be rewritten as

$$x(t) = [f_1(t),\, f_2(t),\, f_3(t),\, f_4(t)]\mathbf{G}_x \tag{7.15}$$

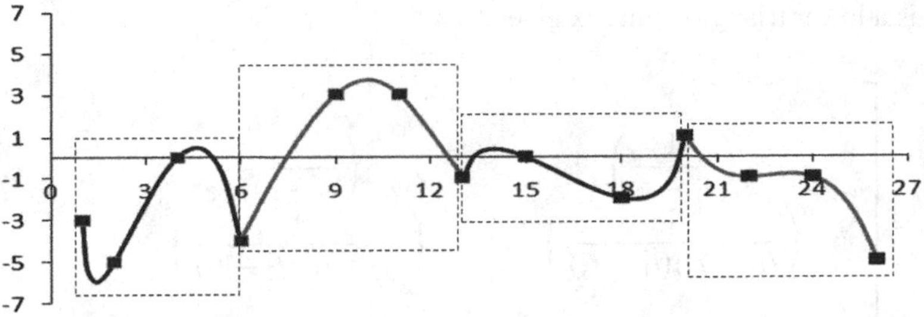

Fig. 7.2 Piecewise cubic interpolation polynomials constructed using groups of four points

For the example in Eq. 7.13, we have

$$\begin{aligned} f_1(t) &= 1 - \left(\frac{11}{2}\right)t + 9t^2 - \left(\frac{9}{2}\right)t^3 \\ f_2(t) &= 9t - \left(\frac{45}{2}\right)t^2 + \left(\frac{27}{2}\right)t^3 \\ f_3(t) &= -\left(\frac{9}{2}\right)t + 18t^2 - \left(\frac{27}{2}\right)t^3 \\ f_4(t) &= t - \left(\frac{9}{2}\right)t^2 + \left(\frac{9}{2}\right)t^3 \end{aligned} \tag{7.16}$$

The functions $f_i(t)$ are called blending polynomials. Note that the sum of the above functions is 1 for all values of t. Generalising Eq. 7.15, and since the blending polynomials are common for x, y, and z axes, we find that

$$P(t) = [f_1(t), f_2(t), f_3(t), f_4(t)] \begin{bmatrix} P_1 \\ P_2 \\ P_3 \\ P_4 \end{bmatrix} \tag{7.17}$$

We can thus write the parametric equation for the cubic curve as a combination of the control points:

$$P(t) = f_1(t)P_1 + f_2(t)P_2 + f_3(t)P_3 + f_4(t)P_4, \quad 0 \le t \le 1. \tag{7.18}$$

Figure 7.2 shows a set of points joined together using piecewise cubic polynomial curves through groups of four points, constructed using the above equation. Each cubic polynomial curve is called a segment.

The matrix $\mathbf{V}^{-1}$ is sometimes denoted by $\mathbf{M}$, and referred to as the basis matrix. With this notation, the blending functions and the basis matrix are related as follows:

$$[f_1(t), f_2(t), f_3(t), f_4(t)] = \mathbf{TM} \tag{7.19}$$

The points where the polynomial curves meet are called knots. It is often desirable to have tangential and higher order continuity at the knots. Such curves are called splines. In the next section, we discuss different orders of continuity constraints that can be used in the design of interpolating curves and surfaces.

7.3 Parametric Continuity

In the previous section we saw an example (Fig. 7.2) of a set of piecewise cubic curves joined together to form a single "continuous" curve. Clearly we require higher levels of continuity at the points where two curves meet, in order to get a smooth transition from one polynomial curve on to another.

A parametric curve defined using cubic polynomials as in Eq. 7.8 has the property that the first and second order derivatives exist and are continuous over the interval in which the curve is defined. Two parametric curves $P_A(t) = (x_A(t), y_A(t), z_A(t))$ and $P_B(t) = (x_B(t), y_B(t), z_B(t))$ are said to have C^0 continuity if they meet at a common point M (Fig. 7.3). That is, there exits valid parametric values t_1, t_2 such that

$$M = (x_A(t_1),\ \ y_A(t_1), z_A(t_1)) = (x_B(t_2), y_B(t_2), z_B(t_2)) \tag{7.20}$$

If the tangents to the two curves at M also coincide, then the curves have C^1 continuity. The tangent direction at M is obtained by differentiating the cubic polynomials with respect to t, and substituting the parametric value for the knot M. We use the following notation for the derivatives of the x-polynomial in Eq. 7.8:

$$\begin{aligned} x_A{}'(t_1) &= \left(\frac{dx_A(t)}{dt}\right)_{t=t_1} = a_1 + 2a_2t_1 + 3a_3{t_1}^2 \\ x_A{}''(t_1) &= \left(\frac{d^2x_A(t)}{dt^2}\right)_{t=t_1} = 2a_2 + 6a_3t_1 \end{aligned} \tag{7.21}$$

with similar notations for the y-polynomial and the z-polynomial. The vector $(x_A{}'(t),$ $y_A{}'(t), z_A{}'(t))$ gives the tangent direction on the curve A at point $P(t)$. If t denotes time, then this vector represents the velocity of the point P as it moves along the curve A. C^1 continuity implies that the velocity of P considered as a point on the curve A at the knot M is the same as its velocity when considered as a point on the curve B:

$$(x_A{}'(t_1), y_A{}'(t_1), z_A{}'(t_1)) = (x_B{}'(t_2), y_B{}'(t_2), z_B{}'(t_2)) \tag{7.22}$$

If two curves are joined with C^1 continuity, the point $P(t)$ will have at most finite acceleration as it crosses the knot M. Second order continuity denoted by C^2 requires that the second derivatives of both curves at M are equal. That is,

$$(x_A{}''(t_1), y_A{}''(t_1), z_A{}''(t_1)) = (x_B{}''(t_2), y_B{}''(t_2), z_B{}''(t_2)) \tag{7.23}$$

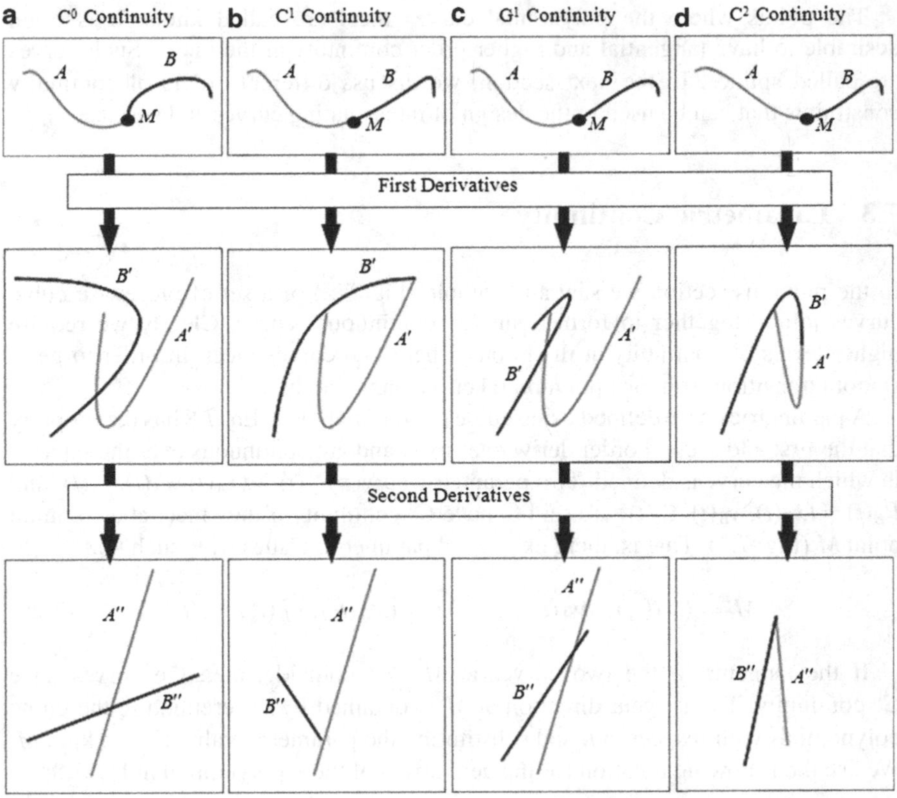

Fig. 7.3 Examples of piecewise cubic curves with different orders of parametric and geometric continuity

The above vectors represent the curvature at M, or equivalently acceleration of the point $P(t)$ if t denotes time. The continuity constraints discussed above are often relaxed to just smoothness constraints that define only the important shape characteristics used for constructing splines. For example, the requirement in Eq. 7.22 to have the same tangent vector for both curves at the joint can be relaxed to the condition that the tangent vectors are just parallel, with possibly unequal magnitudes. The modified constraint can be written as

$$(x_A{}'(t_1), y_A{}'(t_1), z_A{}'(t_1)) = \beta(x_B{}'(t_2), y_B{}'(t_2), z_B{}'(t_2)) \qquad (7.24)$$

for some constant β. Two curves satisfying the above equation are said to have a geometric continuity G^1 at the common point M. Note that we can always re-parameterize the curve A by substituting $t = \beta u$ in its equation, and the resultant tangent vectors at M would still be equal, satisfying the C^1 continuity constraint. The geometric continuity G^2 is also similarly defined by introducing a constant of proportionality in Eq. 7.23. The difference between parametric and geometric continuity is illustrated through an example in Fig. 7.3.

In column (a) of Fig. 7.3, the curves A and B meet at M with C^0 continuity. The first and the second derivatives of the curves do not meet at the corresponding point. Column (b) shows the curves with C^1 continuity at M where the tangent vectors are equal. Correspondingly, the first derivatives of the curves meet at a point. The curves formed using second derivatives are discontinuous. Column (c) shows the curves with G^1 continuity where the tangent vectors at M are only parallel but unequal in magnitude. The first derivatives of the curves therefore do not meet at the corresponding point. In column (d), the curves meet with C^2 continuity at M. In this case, the first derivatives meet at a common point with C^1 continuity. The second derivatives of the curves also meet with C^0 continuity. Note that the second derivatives of cubic polynomial curves are always straight lines.

7.4 Hermite Splines

Hermite splines are cubic polynomial interpolation curves passing through two control points $P_1 = (x_1, y_1, z_1)$ and $P_2 = (x_2, y_2, z_2)$, with the additional requirement that the curve is tangential to the specified directions at the two end points (Fig. 7.4).

In Fig. 7.4a, the required tangent directions at the end points are denoted by $\boldsymbol{m}_1$ and $\boldsymbol{m}_2$ with components $(x_1{}', y_1{}', z_1{}')$ and $(x_2{}', y_2{}', z_2{}')$ respectively. For the interpolating curve, we use the parametric equation given in Eq. 7.8. The control point P_1 corresponds to the parameter value of 0, and P_2 corresponds to $t = 1$. The tangent vector components at t are given by

$$
\begin{aligned}
x'(t) &= a_1 + 2a_2t + 3a_3t^2 \\
y'(t) &= b_1 + 2b_2t + 3b_3t^2 \\
z'(t) &= c_1 + 2c_2t + 3c_3t^2
\end{aligned}
\tag{7.25}
$$

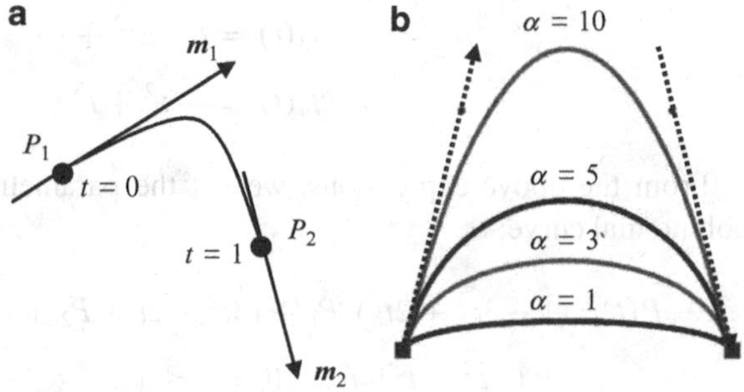

Fig. 7.4 Hermite polynomial interpolation

Similar to Eq. 7.10, we can now write an equation using position coordinates and tangent vector components:

$$\begin{bmatrix} x_1 \\ x_2 \\ x'_1 \\ x'_2 \end{bmatrix} = \begin{bmatrix} 1 & t_1 & t_1^2 & t_1^3 \\ 1 & t_2 & t_2^2 & t_2^3 \\ 0 & 1 & 2t_1 & 3t_1^2 \\ 0 & 1 & 2t_2 & 3t_2^2 \end{bmatrix} \begin{bmatrix} a_0 \\ a_1 \\ a_2 \\ a_3 \end{bmatrix} \tag{7.26}$$

Substituting the parameter values for the end points in the above equation, we have

$$\begin{bmatrix} x_1 \\ x_2 \\ x'_1 \\ x'_2 \end{bmatrix} = \begin{bmatrix} 1 & 0 & 0 & 0 \\ 1 & 1 & 1 & 1 \\ 0 & 1 & 0 & 0 \\ 0 & 1 & 2 & 3 \end{bmatrix} \begin{bmatrix} a_0 \\ a_1 \\ a_2 \\ a_3 \end{bmatrix} \tag{7.27}$$

The basis matrix for Hermite polynomial interpolation is the inverse of the 4 × 4 matrix in the above equation, and is given by

$$\mathbf{M}_H = \begin{bmatrix} 1 & 0 & 0 & 0 \\ 0 & 0 & 1 & 0 \\ -3 & 3 & -2 & -1 \\ 2 & -2 & 1 & 1 \end{bmatrix} \tag{7.28}$$

Pre-multiplying the above matrix by $\mathbf{T} = [1, t, t^2, t^3]$, we get the blending functions $f_i(t)$ (see Eq. 7.19):

$$\begin{aligned} f_1(t) &= 1 - 3t^2 + 2t^3 \\ f_2(t) &= 3t^2 - 2t^3 \\ f_3(t) &= t - 2t^2 + t^3 \\ f_4(t) &= -t^2 + t^3 \end{aligned} \tag{7.29}$$

From the above expressions, we get the parametric equation for the Hermite polynomial curve:

$$\begin{aligned} P(t) = {} & (1 - 3t^2 + 2t^3)\, P_1 + (3t^2 - 2t^3)\, P_2 + (t - 2t^2 + t^3)\, \boldsymbol{m}_1 \\ & + (-t^2 + t^3)\boldsymbol{m}_2, \quad (0 \le t \le 1). \end{aligned} \tag{7.30}$$

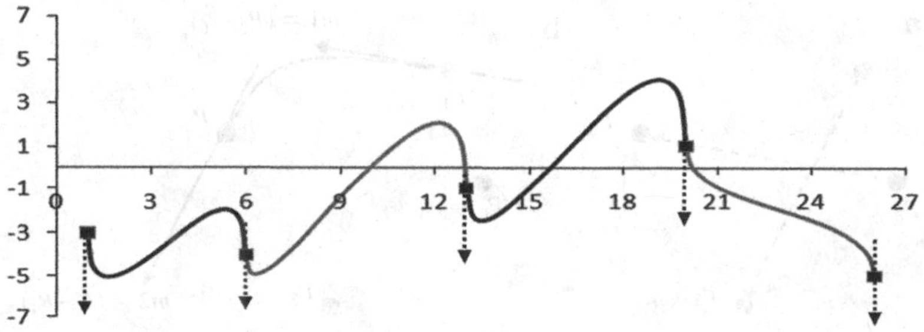

Fig. 7.5 Hermite interpolation spline

The tangent vectors $\boldsymbol{m}_1$ and $\boldsymbol{m}_2$ can have arbitrary magnitude if we require only G^1 continuity at the end points when two curves are joined together. Increasing the magnitude causes the curve to align closer to the tangent direction. A scale parameter $\alpha > 0$ for the tangents is introduced into this equation to control the shape of the cubic curve:

$$P(t) = (1 - 3t^2 + 2t^3)P_1 + (3t^2 - 2t^3)P_2 + (t - 2t^2 + t^3)\alpha\boldsymbol{m}_1 + (-t^2 + t^3)\alpha\boldsymbol{m}_2 \tag{7.31}$$

α is sometimes referred to as the tension parameter of the curve. An example with four different values of α is shown in Fig. 7.4b. Note that when $\alpha = 0$, the above equation represents a linear interpolation between P_1 and P_2.

Given n points ($n > 2$), we can develop an interpolating spline that passes through all the points by constructing Hermite cubic curves for every consecutive pair of points. The tangent direction at each knot must be carefully specified by the user in such a way that it corresponds to the tangents to curves on both sides of the knot.

In Fig. 7.5, piecewise Hermite polynomial curves are fitted through a set of points. The points are the same as the knots of the interpolation curve shown in Fig. 7.2. The common tangent vectors are all defined as parallel to negative y-axis.

7.5 Cardinal Splines

A cardinal spline is a smooth piecewise cubic polynomial curve that passes through every point except the first and the last in a given set of control points, maintaining first-order continuity at every point. A cardinal spline works very much like a Hermite spline with the exception that the tangent directions are not specified by the user but derived from the control points themselves.

Consider a set of four control points P_0, P_1, P_2, P_3 as shown in Fig. 7.6. The tangent at P_1 is specified in the direction of the vector $P_2 - P_0$, and the tangent at P_2 in the direction of the vector $P_3 - P_1$. We can now use Eq. 7.31 with $\boldsymbol{m}_1 = P_2 - P_0$,

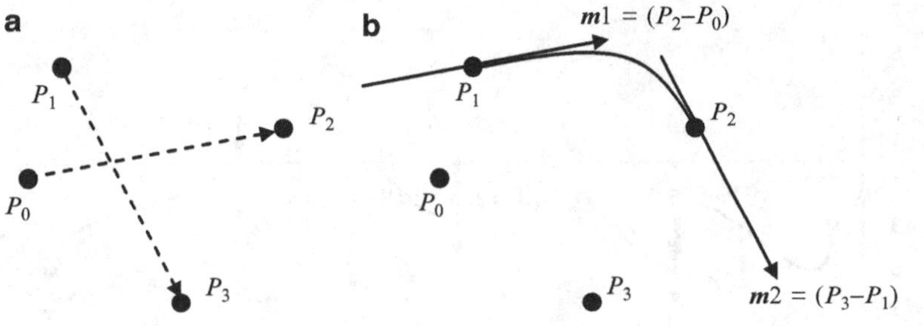

Fig. 7.6 A cardinal spline definition using four points

and $\boldsymbol{m}_2 = P_3 - P_1$ to generate a Hermite cubic polynomial curve between P_1 and P_2. The scaling parameter α controls the tension of the curve. Without any reference to the tangent directions, the curve's equation can be rewritten as a function of the control points alone as below.

$$\begin{aligned}P(t) &= (-t + 2t^2 - t^3)\alpha P_0 + (1 + (\alpha - 3)t^2 + (2 - \alpha)t^3)P_1 \\ &\quad +(\alpha t + (3 - 2\alpha)t^2 + (\alpha - 2)t^3)P_2 + (-t^2 + t^3)\alpha P_3 \end{aligned} \tag{7.32}$$

Writing the coefficients of 1, t, t^2, t^3 of each blending function in the above equation as columns of a 4 × 4 matrix, we obtain the basis matrix for cardinal splines:

$$\mathbf{M}_c = \begin{bmatrix} 0 & 1 & 0 & 0 \\ -\alpha & 0 & \alpha & 0 \\ 2\alpha & \alpha - 3 & 3 - 2\alpha & -\alpha \\ -\alpha & 2 - \alpha & \alpha - 2 & \alpha \end{bmatrix}, \quad \alpha > 0. \tag{7.33}$$

Given a set of $n+2$ control points $\{P_0, P_1, \ldots, P_n, P_{n+1}\}$, $n > 1$, we can fit a cubic curve with the above basis matrix to every pair of consecutive control points (P_k, P_{k+1}), $1 \le k < n$, with tangent vectors defined as $\boldsymbol{m}_k = P_{k+1} - P_{k-1}$, and $\boldsymbol{m}_{k+1} = P_{k+2} - P_k$. In other words we need to process overlapping blocks of four control points $[P_{k-1}, P_k, P_{k+1}, P_{k+2}]$, with only the middle two points used for interpolation at a time.

When $\alpha = 0.5$, we get a special case of cardinal splines called Catmull-Rom splines. It directly follows from Eq. 7.33 that Catmull-Rom splines are given by the parametric equation:

$$P(t) = \begin{bmatrix} 1 & t & t^2 & t^3 \end{bmatrix} \begin{bmatrix} 0 & 1 & 0 & 0 \\ -0.5 & 0 & 0.5 & 0 \\ 1 & -2.5 & 2 & -0.5 \\ -0.5 & 1.5 & -1.5 & 0.5 \end{bmatrix} \begin{bmatrix} P_0 \\ P_1 \\ P_2 \\ P_3 \end{bmatrix} \tag{7.34}$$

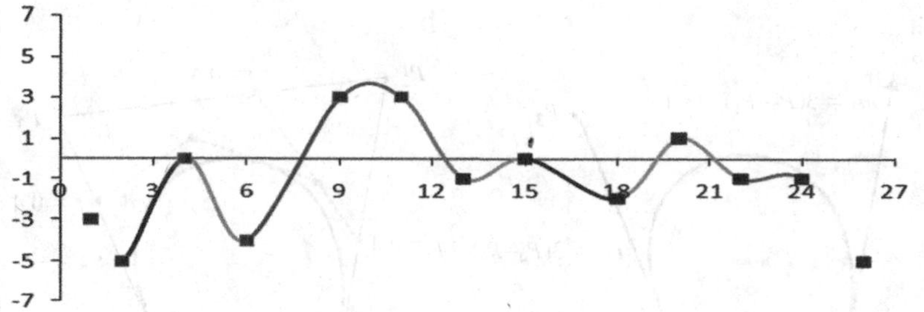

Fig. 7.7 A Catmull-Rom spline through a set of control points

Figure 7.7 shows a Catmull-Rom spline generated using a set of control points. Compare this figure with the piecewise cubic spline in Fig. 7.2 where the same set of control points was used.

7.6 Bezier Curves

Bezier splines are approximating curves generated using Bernstein polynomials as the blending functions (see Box 2.4, Sect. 2.7). Denoting $n+1$ control points by $P_1 \ldots P_{n+1}$, the parametric representation of the nth degree Bezier curve is given by

$$P(t) = \sum_{i=0}^{n} \beta_{i,n}(t) P_{i+1}. \tag{7.35}$$

where, $\beta_{i,n}(t)$ denotes Bernstein polynomials of degree n. Since Bernstein polynomials always yield non-negative values for $0 \le t \le 1$, and form a partition of unity, every point on a Bezier curve is a convex combination of the control points. In this section, we discuss the construction of piecewise cubic splines using Bezier curves, and outline an important algorithm that will be later extended to develop the framework for B-splines.

7.6.1 *Cubic Bezier Splines*

The parametric equation of the cubic Bezier curve is given by

$$\begin{aligned} P(t) =& (1-t)^3 P_1 + 3t(1-t)^2 P_2 + 3t^2(1-t) P_3 + t^3 P_4, \quad 0 \le t \le 1. \\ =& (1 - 3t + 3t^2 - t^3) P_1 + (3t - 6t^2 + 3t^3) P_2 + (3t^2 - 3t^3) P_3 + t^3 P_4 \end{aligned} \tag{7.36}$$

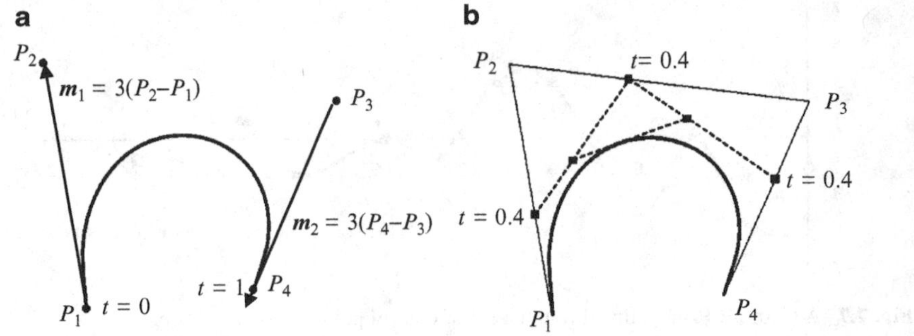

Fig. 7.8 Cubic Bezier curves

where $P_1 \ldots P_4$ are the control points. The Bezier spline interpolates between the first and the last control points. The two middle control points are used to define the tangent directions at the end points. In the matrix form, the cubic Bezier curve is given as

$$P(t) = \begin{bmatrix} 1 & t & t^2 & t^3 \end{bmatrix} \begin{bmatrix} 1 & 0 & 0 & 0 \\ -3 & 3 & 0 & 0 \\ 3 & -6 & 3 & 0 \\ -1 & 3 & -3 & 1 \end{bmatrix} \begin{bmatrix} P_1 \\ P_2 \\ P_3 \\ P_4 \end{bmatrix} \tag{7.37}$$

Differentiating Eq. 7.36 with respect to t, we get the tangent directions on the Bezier curve:

$$P'(t) = (-3 + 6t - 3t^2)P_1 + (3 - 12t + 9t^2)\ P_2 + (6t - 9t^2)P_3 + 3t^2 P_4 \tag{7.38}$$

From the above equation, the tangent directions at P_1 and P_4 are obtained as follows:

$$\begin{aligned} P'(0) &= 3(P_2 - P_1) \\ P'(1) &= 3(P_4 - P_3) \end{aligned} \tag{7.39}$$

The control points and the tangent directions are shown in Fig. 7.8a. Clearly, the Bezier cubic curve is a special case of the Hermite polynomial curve where $\boldsymbol{m}_1 = 3(P_2 - P_1)$ and $\boldsymbol{m}_2 = 3(P_4 - P_3)$. The following equation relates the input vector $[P_1, P_2, \boldsymbol{m}_1, \boldsymbol{m}_2]$ of a Hermite curve as given in Eq. 7.30, with the input vector $[P_1, P_2, P_3, P_4]$ of the Bezier curve, so that the resulting splines coincide.

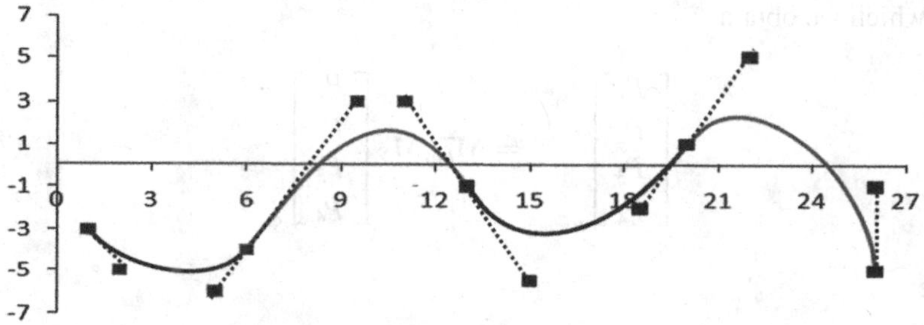

Fig. 7.9 A Bezier spline passing through a set of control points

$$\begin{bmatrix} P_1 \\ P_2 \\ \boldsymbol{m}_1 \\ \boldsymbol{m}_2 \end{bmatrix}_{Hermite} = \begin{bmatrix} 1 & 0 & 0 & 0 \\ 0 & 0 & 0 & 1 \\ -3 & 3 & 0 & 0 \\ 0 & 0 & -3 & 3 \end{bmatrix} \begin{bmatrix} P_1 \\ P_2 \\ P_3 \\ P_4 \end{bmatrix}_{Bezier} \tag{7.40}$$

Given a set of n control points $P_1, \ldots P_n$, the Bezier spline consisting of piecewise cubic polynomial curves can be made to pass through the first and every fourth point P_{3k+1}, $k = 0, 1, 2 \ldots$. The remaining points are used for specifying tangent directions. For G^1 continuity of the spline, we need to make sure that the three points P_{3k}, P_{3k+1}, P_{3k+2} are collinear for $k = 1, 2, \ldots$. An example of a piecewise cubic Bezier spline satisfying this condition is shown in Fig. 7.9. The knot positions are the same as those used earlier in Figs. 7.2 and 7.5.

Bezier splines are widely used in computer graphics and therefore graphics packages commonly support methods for creating Bezier curves of different orders. We could also make use of the functionality provided by such libraries for generating other types of splines (Hermite, Catmull-Rom etc.), if we can compute the Bezier equivalent set of control points for the required spline. As an example, by computing the inverse of the 4 × 4 matrix in Eq. 7.40, we can obtain the Bezier control points for the required Hermite curve as follows:

$$\begin{bmatrix} P_1 \\ P_2 \\ P_3 \\ P_4 \end{bmatrix}_{Bezier} = \begin{bmatrix} 1 & 0 & 0 & 0 \\ 1 & 0 & \left(\frac{1}{3}\right) & 0 \\ 0 & 1 & 0 & -\left(\frac{1}{3}\right) \\ 0 & 1 & 0 & 0 \end{bmatrix} \begin{bmatrix} P_1 \\ P_2 \\ \boldsymbol{m}_1 \\ \boldsymbol{m}_2 \end{bmatrix}_{Hermite} \tag{7.41}$$

In a general case, we express the parametric curve $P(t)$ in terms of the required spline's basis (denoted by $\mathbf{M}_S$) as well as the Bezier basis as

$$P(t) = \mathbf{TM}_{Bez} \begin{bmatrix} P_1 \\ P_2 \\ P_3 \\ P_4 \end{bmatrix}_{Bezier} = \mathbf{TM}_S \begin{bmatrix} P_1 \\ P_2 \\ P_3 \\ P_4 \end{bmatrix}_S \tag{7.42}$$

from which we obtain

$$\begin{bmatrix} P_1 \\ P_2 \\ P_3 \\ P_4 \end{bmatrix}_{Bezier} = \mathbf{M}_{Bez}^{-1}\mathbf{M}_S \begin{bmatrix} P_1 \\ P_2 \\ P_3 \\ P_4 \end{bmatrix}_S \tag{7.43}$$

where

$$\mathbf{M}_{Bez}^{-1} = \begin{bmatrix} 1 & 0 & 0 & 0 \\ 1 & \left(\frac{1}{3}\right) & 0 & 0 \\ 1 & \left(\frac{2}{3}\right) & \left(\frac{1}{3}\right) & 0 \\ 1 & 1 & 1 & 1 \end{bmatrix} \tag{7.44}$$

The above matrix is the inverse of the 4×4 matrix in Eq. 7.37.

7.6.2 de-Casteljau's Algorithm

The de-Casteljau's algorithm provides an alternative representation of a Bezier curve in terms of a combination of linear interpolation functions. Given three control points P_1, P_2, P_3, we can construct parametric equations of two straight lines

$$\begin{aligned} P_{11}(t) &= (1-t)P_1 + tP_2 \\ P_{21}(t) &= (1-t)P_2 + tP_3 \end{aligned} \tag{7.45}$$

For each parameter value $t \in [0, 1]$, the above equations give two points. We now further interpolate between these two points using the same parameter value:

$$P(t) = (1-t)P_{11} + tP_{21} \tag{7.46}$$

The resulting point will lie on the quadratic Bezier curve generated using the control points P_1, P_2 and P_3. This can be easily proved by substituting for P_{11} and P_{21} from Eq. 7.45 in the above equation:

$$\begin{aligned} P(t) =& (1-t)\{(1-t)P_1 + tP_2\} + t\{(1-t)P_2 + tP_3\} \\ =& (1-t)^2 P_1 + 2t(1-t)P_2 + t^2 P_3 \end{aligned} \tag{7.47}$$

Figure 7.10 shows the geometrical interpretation of the above equation. Using the same method, we can obtain the cubic Bezier curve from four control points (Fig. 7.8b). Using a parameter value in the range [0, 1], we interpolate between consecutive pairs of control points to get three points, further interpolate between

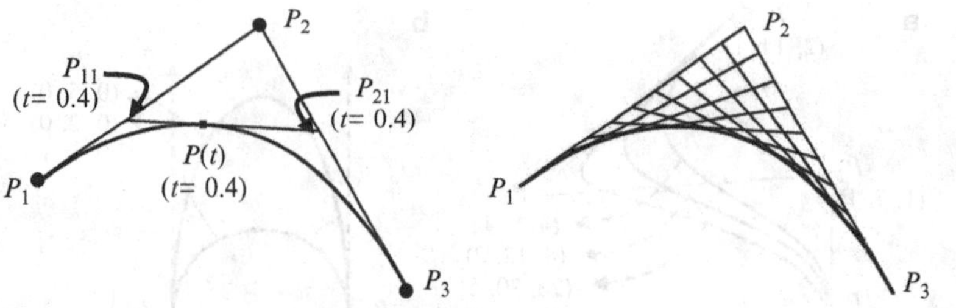

Fig. 7.10 Interpolation between three control points using de-Casteljau's algorithm

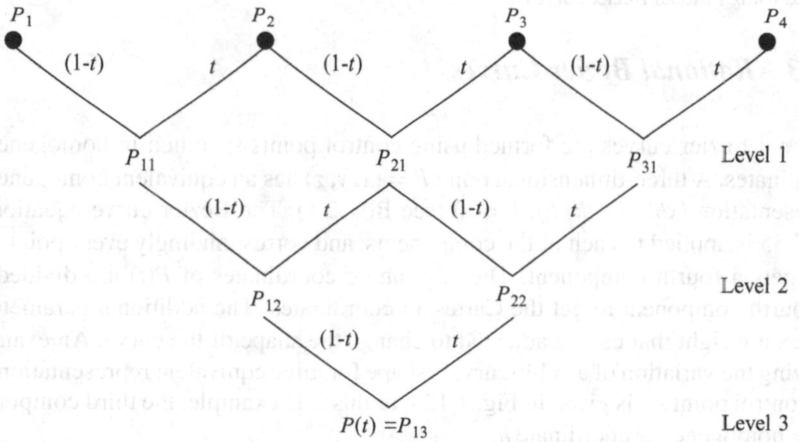

Fig. 7.11 Iteration sequence for de-Casteljau's algorithm with four control points

them to get two points, and again interpolate between the two points to get a single point on the cubic curve. This interpolation sequence is shown in Fig. 7.11. The whole process is repeated for the next parameter value.

The de-Casteljau's algorithm for a general $n - 1$ degree Bezier curve with control points $P_1 \ldots P_n$ can be written as follows:

$$\begin{aligned} P_{k,d}(t) &= (1-t)P_{k,d-1}(t) + tP_{k+1,d-1}(t) \qquad 0 \le t \le 1, k = 1..n-d. \\ P_{k,0}(t) &= P_k, \qquad k = 1..n. \\ P(t) &= P_{1,n-1}. \end{aligned} \tag{7.48}$$

For the above iteration, the index d is varied from 1 to $n - 1$, and for each d the index k is varied from 1 to $n - d$. After each level of iteration (see Fig. 7.11), the number of points reduces by one. At level $n - 1$, we get a single point $P_{1,n-1}$ which lies on the Bezier curve $P(t)$ of degree $n - 1$.

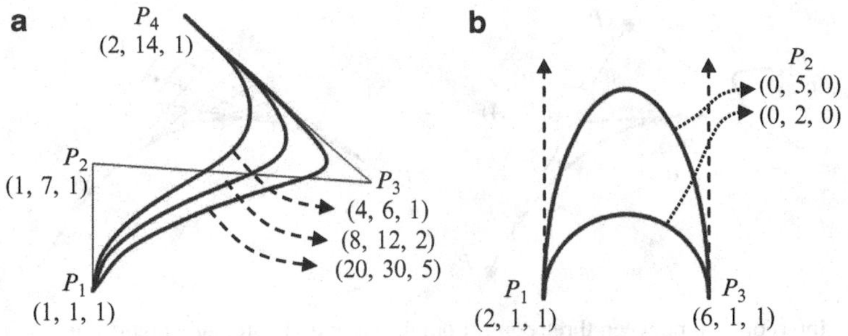

Fig. 7.12 (**a**) Effect of varying homogeneous coordinates on Bezier curve. (**b**) Conic sections formed using rational Bezier curves

7.6.3 Rational Bezier Curves

Rational Bezier curves are formed using control points specified in homogeneous coordinates. A three-dimensional point $P = (x, y, z)$ has an equivalent homogeneous representation (xh, yh, zh, h), $h \neq 0$ (see Box 2.1). The Bezier curve equation in Eq. 7.35 is applied to each of the components, and correspondingly every point $P(t)$ also gets a fourth component. The x, y, and z coordinates of $P(t)$ are divided by its fourth component to get the Cartesian coordinates. The additional parameter h acts as a weight that can be adjusted to change the shape of the curve. An example showing the variation of a cubic curve's shape for three equivalent representations of the control point P_3 is given in Fig. 7.12a. In this 2-D example, the third component is the homogeneous coordinate h.

The homogeneous coordinate system also allows the representation of points at infinity, by setting the last component to zero. Defining a control point at infinity causes the control polygonal line to have disjoint and parallel edges. This feature is useful for the generation of conic sections using Bezier curves. Figure 7.12b shows a semi-circular arc and a semi-ellipsoidal arc formed using quadratic Bezier curves. Among the three control points P_1, P_2, P_3, the point P_2 is at infinity along the $+y$ direction. The control polygonal line therefore degenerates into two parallel vertical lines meeting at P_2.

7.7 Polynomial Interpolants

The parametric curves introduced in previous sections were all based on piecewise cubic polynomials and the points on each segment were generated by varying the parameter t from 0 to 1. In this section, we will develop the framework of a more general class of interpolating splines where t can have an arbitrary range. First, we consider interpolating polynomials of degree one, two and three, and then generalize our results to an $n - 1$ degree polynomial passing through n control points. The ability to specify parameter values at control points provides added flexibility to the design of splines.

Given two points $P_1 = (x_1, y_1, z_1)$, $P_2 = (x_2, y_2, z_2)$, and two values t_1, t_2 of the parameter t such that $t_1 < t_2$, the linear equation of the interpolating line between the points can be written as

$$P_{11}(t) = \frac{t_2 - t}{t_2 - t_1} P_1 + \frac{t - t_1}{t_2 - t_1} P_2, \qquad t_1 \le t < t_2 \tag{7.49}$$

We denote the above polynomial as $g_1(P_1, P_2; t_1, t_2; t)$ with the control points and parameter values included in the function argument. The suffix of g indicates the degree of the polynomial. The first suffix of $P_{11}(t)$ indicates the starting point on the spline (P_1), and the second suffix the degree of the polynomial. Using this notation, the point P_1 itself can be represented as P_{10} or a polynomial $g_0(P_1; t_1; t)$. If we now add a third point P_3 to the set of control points, with an associated parameter t_3 ($t_1 < t_2 < t_3$), we can construct a quadratic curve that passes through the three points as follows: Similar to the previous equation, we first perform a linear interpolation between P_2 and P_3:

$$g_1(P_2, P_3; t_2, t_3; t) = P_{21}(t) = \frac{t_3 - t}{t_3 - t_2} P_2 + \frac{t - t_2}{t_3 - t_2} P_3, \qquad t_2 \le t < t_3 \tag{7.50}$$

Then we combine the points $P_{11}(t)$ and $P_{21}(t)$ using a third interpolation formula with t varying from t_1 to t_3:

$$P_{12}(t) = \frac{t_3 - t}{t_3 - t_1} P_{11} + \frac{t - t_1}{t_3 - t_1} P_{21}, \qquad t_1 \le t < t_3 \tag{7.51}$$

Substituting the expressions for P_{11} and P_{21} in the above equation, we get a quadratic polynomial which we denote as $g_2(P_1, P_2, P_3; t_1, t_2, t_3; t)$:

$$\begin{aligned} g_2(P_1, P_2, P_3; t_1, t_2, t_3;\, t) &= P_{12}(t), \qquad t_1 \le t < t_3 \\ &= \frac{(t_2 - t)(t_3 - t)}{(t_2 - t_1)(t_3 - t_1)} P_1 + \frac{(t_1 - t)(t_3 - t)}{(t_1 - t_2)(t_3 - t_2)} P_2 + \frac{(t_1 - t)(t_2 - t)}{(t_1 - t_3)(t_2 - t_3)} P_3 \end{aligned} \tag{7.52}$$

Note that the above algorithm is a generalized version of the de-Casteljau's method outlined in the previous section. For Bezier curves, we used only values between 0 and 1. In the above equation, however, the parameter is allowed to vary over the range $[t_1, t_3)$, which is the union of the two intervals $[t_1, t_2)$ and $[t_2, t_3)$ that were used to generate the line segments. Since the intervals are disjoint, this would mean that any value of the parameter will always be outside the range of one of the intervals. This situation is shown in Fig. 7.13. Compare this process with that shown in Fig. 7.10, where the parameter value is restricted to the range [0, 1] along each interpolated direction.

Figure 7.14 shows three quadratic splines generated using Eq. 7.52, all with the same set of control points $P_1 = (1, 4)$, $P_2 = (3, 1)$, $P_3 = (6, 2)$. For the first curve (a), the parametric values used were $t_1 = 2$, $t_2 = 5$, and $t_3 = 8$. Since the spacing of

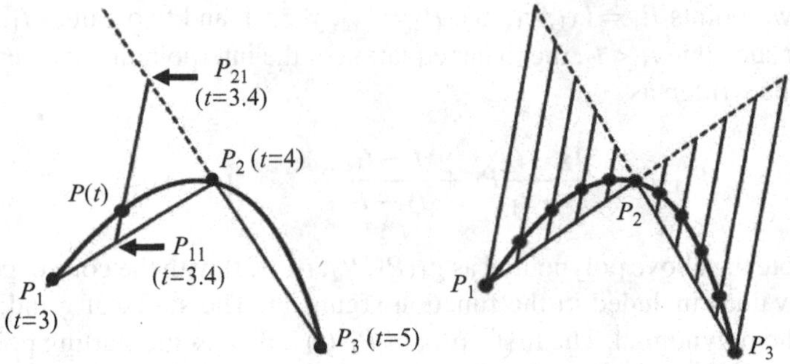

Fig. 7.13 A quadratic interpolating polynomial curve passing through three control points

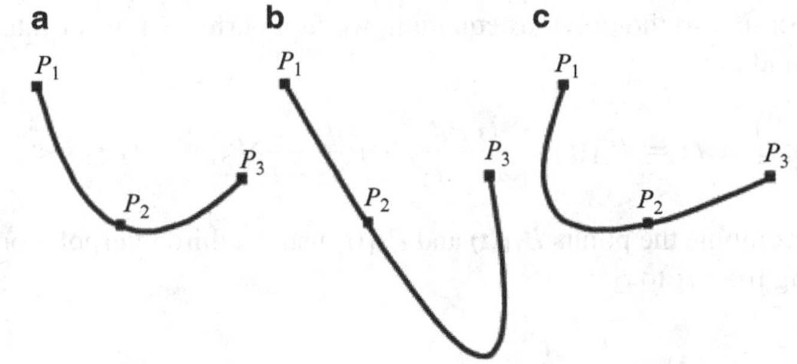

Fig. 7.14 Quadratic polynomial splines for different parameter values, but with the same control points

values was uniform, the curve also has a nearly uniform tension across the points. In the second figure (b), the parameters were changed to $t_1 = 2$, $t_2 = 3$, and $t_3 = 8$. The reduced spacing between t_1 and t_2 is seen as a higher tension of the curve between P_1 and P_2, closely approximating a straight line. Similarly, in the third figure (c), we reduced the spacing between t_2 and t_3 by choosing $t_1 = 2$, $t_2 = 6.5$, and $t_3 = 8$.

The process outlined above can be extended to a larger set of n control points $P_1 \ldots P_n$ and n parameter values $t_1 \ldots t_n$ ($t_1 < t_2 < \ldots < t_n$). We start by combining every consecutive pair of control points as shown in Eq. 7.49, to form linear equations P_{11}, P_{21}, $\ldots P_{n-1,1}$. We then combine consecutive pairs of these polynomials as in Eq. 7.51 to form quadratic polynomials $P_{12}, P_{22}, \ldots P_{n-2,2}$. This process is iteratively continued till we get the polynomial $P_{1,n-1}$ of degree $n-1$. By evaluating this polynomial by varying t from t_1 to t_n, we get the coordinates of points along the spline that passes through all the control points. The iterative procedure for four control points is illustrated in Fig. 7.15.

Note that $P_{k,d}(t)$ denotes a polynomial of degree d. There are $n - d$ polynomials of degree d on level d (Fig. 7.15). The polynomial $P_{k,d}(t)$ is formed by combining two polynomials from the previous level.

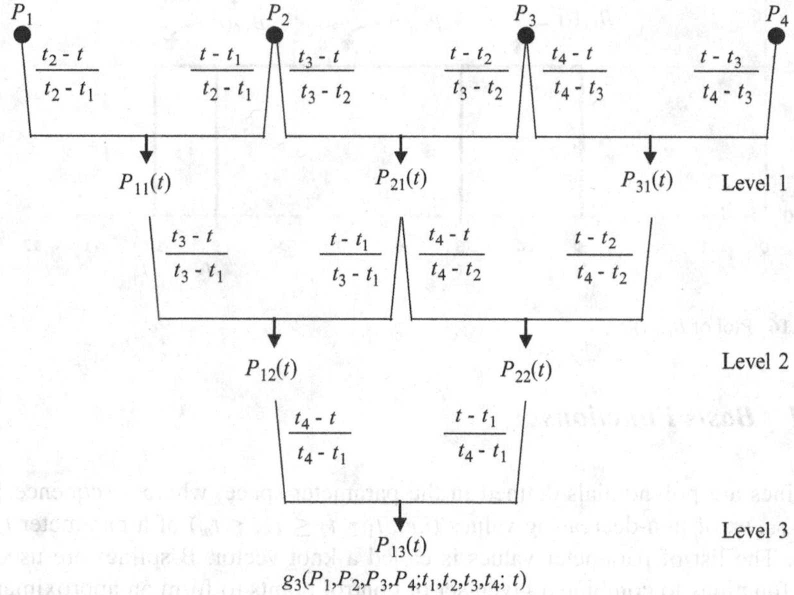

Fig. 7.15 Computation of a third degree interpolating spline using four control points

$$P_{k,d}(t) = \frac{t_{k+d} - t}{t_{k+d} - t_k} P_{k,d-1} + \frac{t - t_k}{t_{k+d} - t_k} P_{k+1,d-1}, \quad t_k \le t < t_{k+d} \tag{7.53}$$

For the above iteration, d varies from 0 to $n - 1$, and for each d, k varies from 1 to $n - d$. The initial conditions are set as

$$P_{k,0} = P_k, \quad k = 1 \ldots n. \tag{7.54}$$

The $n - 1$ degree parametric curve generated as above passes through all control points. Being a polynomial, it is differentiable up to order $n - 1$, and therefore has C^{n-1} continuity at all points. However, the curve does not lie within the convex hull of the control points, as clearly seen from Fig. 7.14. In the next section, we introduce a popular approximating spline called B-spline, that satisfies the convex hull property, but does not pass through all control points.

7.8 B-Splines

In Fig. 7.14 we observed that interpolating polynomial curves of degree d use a union of parameter intervals used by the component polynomials of degree $d - 1$, causing points to fall outside the convex hull of the control points. Basis splines or B-splines are commonly used in CAD systems to create approximating splines that are entirely contained in the convex hull of the control points. In addition, B-splines of degree d provide C^{d-1} continuity at the knots.

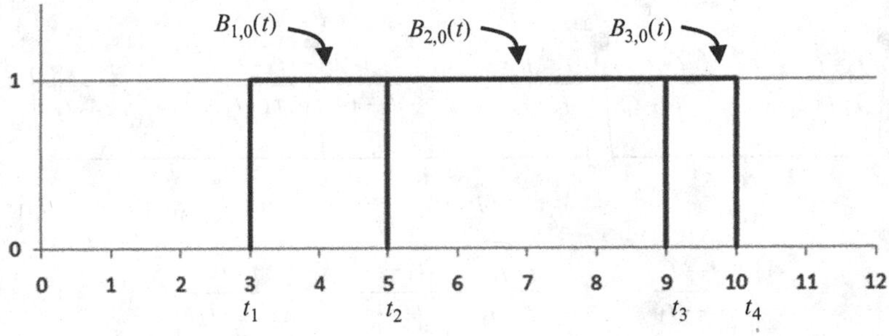

Fig. 7.16 Plot of $B_{i,o}(t)$

7.8.1 Basis Functions

B-splines are polynomials defined in the parameter space, where a sequence $\{t_i\}$, $i = 1, \ldots m$, of non-decreasing values (*i.e.*, $t_1 \leq t_2 \leq \ldots \leq t_m$) of a parameter t are given. The list of parameter values is called a knot vector. B-splines are used as basis functions to combine a given set of control points to form an approximating spline. First, we will look at some important characteristics of B-splines. B-splines of the lowest degree are constant step functions defined using two parameter values as below.

$$B_{i,0}(t) = \begin{cases} 1, & \textit{if } t_i \leq t < t_{i+1} \\ 0, & \textit{otherwise.} \end{cases} \tag{7.55}$$

The plot of $B_{i,0}(t)$ for the knot vector {3, 5, 9,10} is shown in Fig. 7.16.

The second subscript d of the B-spline $B_{i,d}$ (t) denotes the degree of the polynomial. Basis polynomials of degree 1 and higher are defined using the following Cox de Boor recurrence formula:

$$B_{i,d}(t) = \frac{t - t_i}{t_{i+d} - t_i} B_{i,d-1}(t) + \frac{t_{i+d+1} - t}{t_{i+d+1} - t_{i+1}} B_{i+1,d-1}(t), \quad t_i \leq t \leq t_{i+d+1} \tag{7.56}$$

To avoid division by zero, the conditions when $t_{i+d} = t_i$ and $t_{i+d+1} = t_{i+1}$ are considered separately as follows:

$$\begin{aligned} B_{i,d}(t) &= \frac{t_{i+d+1} - t}{t_{i+d+1} - t_{i+1}} B_{i+1,d-1}(t), \qquad \textit{if } t_i = t_{i+d} \\ &= \frac{t - t_i}{t_{i+d} - t_i} B_{i,d-1}(t), \qquad \textit{if } t_{i+1} = t_{i+d+1} \end{aligned} \tag{7.57}$$

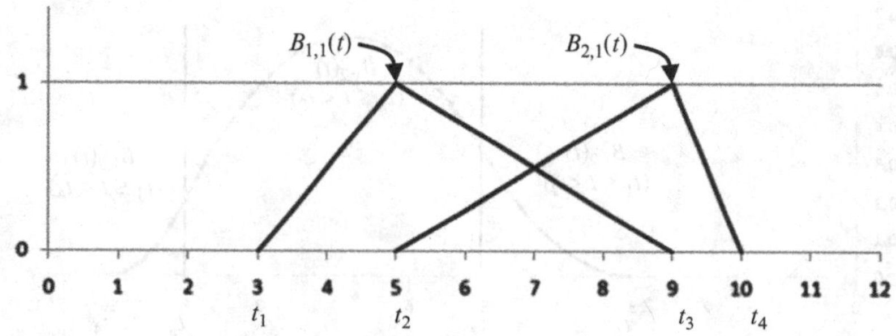

Fig. 7.17 Plot of $B_{i,1}(t)$

The above conditions do not arise in uniform B-splines where the knots are all equally spaced. From Eq. 7.56, we obtain the definition of first degree basis splines as follows:

$$B_{i,1}(t) = \begin{cases} \left(\dfrac{t - t_i}{t_{i+1} - t_i}\right), & \textit{if } t_i \le t < t_{i+1} \\ \left(\dfrac{t_{i+2} - t}{t_{i+2} - t_{i+1}}\right), & \textit{if } t_{i+1} \le t < t_{i+2} \\ 0, & \textit{otherwise.} \end{cases} \tag{7.58}$$

Note that $B_{i,1}(t)$ requires three knot values for each i, and is non-zero only in the interval $[t_i, t_{i+2})$. A plot of B-splines of degree one with the knot vector $\{3, 5, 9, 10\}$ is shown in Fig. 7.17.

From Eq. 7.56, we get the following equation for second degree B-splines:

$$B_{i,2}(t) = \frac{t - t_i}{t_{i+2} - t_i} B_{i,1}(t) + \frac{t_{i+3} - t}{t_{i+3} - t_{i+1}} B_{i+1,1}(t) \tag{7.59}$$

Substituting the values from Eq. 7.58 into the above equation, and taking into account the intervals where $B_{i,1}(t)$ and $B_{i+1,1}(t)$ are non-zero, we get

$$B_{i,2}(t) = \begin{cases} \dfrac{(t - t_i)^2}{(t_{i+2} - t_i)(t_{i+1} - t_i)}, & \textit{if } t_i \le t < t_{i+1} \\ \dfrac{(t - t_i)(t_{i+2} - t)}{(t_{i+2} - t_i)(t_{i+2} - t_{i+1})} + \dfrac{(t - t_{i+1})(t_{i+3} - t)}{(t_{i+3} - t_{i+1})(t_{i+2} - t_{i+1})}, & \textit{if } t_{i+1} \le t < t_{i+2} \\ \dfrac{(t_{i+3} - t)^2}{(t_{i+3} - t_{i+1})(t_{i+3} - t_{i+2})}, & \textit{if } t_{i+2} \le t < t_{i+3} \\ 0, & \textit{otherwise.} \end{cases} \tag{7.60}$$

The three non-zero sections of $B_{1,2}(t)$ as defined above, are shown in Fig. 7.18. The knot vector used for generating this figure is again $\{3, 5, 9, 10\}$.

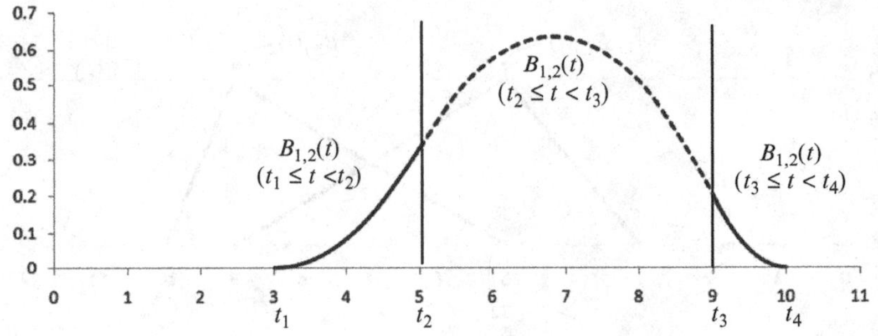

Fig. 7.18 Plot of $B_{i,2}(t)$

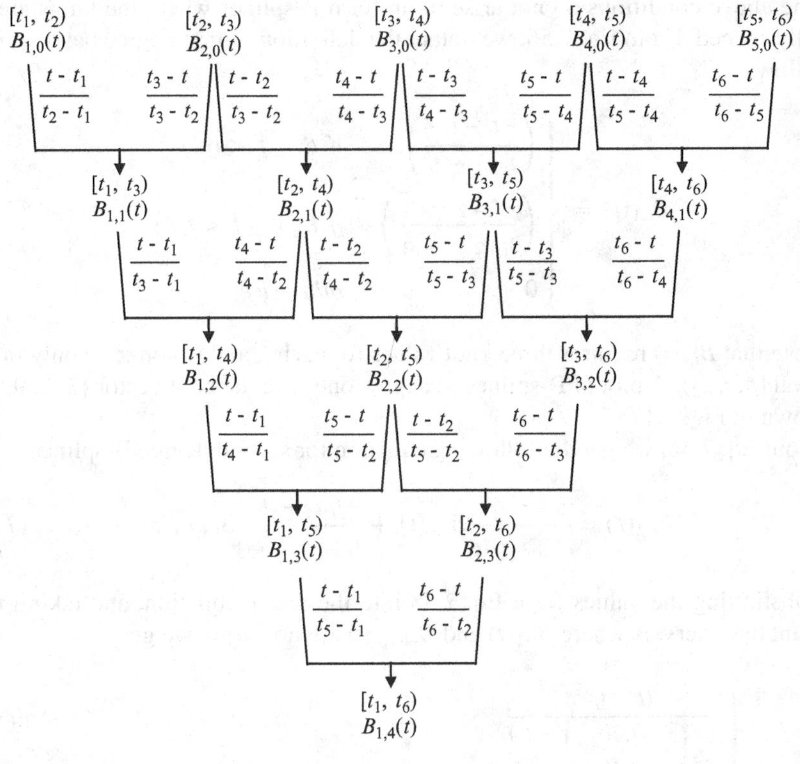

Fig. 7.19 Recursive computation of $B_{1,4}(t)$ in terms of B-splines of lower degrees

In general, a B-spline $B_{i,d}$ of degree d is defined using a non-decreasing sequence of $d+2$ knots $\{t_i, t_{i+1}, \ldots, t_{i+d+1}\}$ and is non-zero only in the interval $[t_i, t_{i+d+1})$. The interval in which a function is non-zero is called its support. The diagram in Fig. 7.19 shows the recursive computation of $B_{i,4}(t)$, and also the support of every intermediate polynomial that is evaluated. Comparing this diagram with Fig. 7.15, we see that the computations performed are very similar to those used by polynomial interpolants.

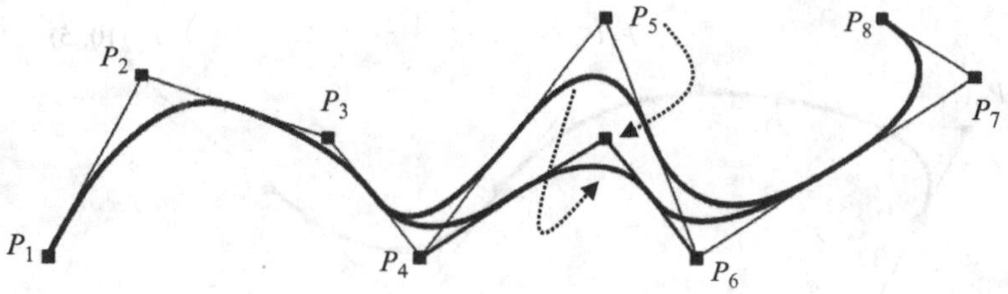

Fig. 7.20 Effect of movement of a control point on the approximating curve

7.8.2 *Approximating Curves*

We shall now look at ways of constructing approximating curves using a set of n control points $P_1 \ldots P_n$, and B-splines as the blending functions. Since the curve is not required to pass through all control points, we have a selection of polynomials of different degrees for blending functions. A parametric curve of degree d can be formed using n B-splines of degree d as follows:

$$P(t) = \sum_{i=1}^{n} P_i B_{i.d}(t), \qquad t_{d+1} \leq t \leq t_{n+1} \tag{7.61}$$

As seen earlier, the B-spline $B_{i,d}(t)$ requires a knot vector consisting of a non-decreasing sequence of $d+2$ knots $\{t_i, t_{i+1}, \ldots, t_{i+d+1}\}$. Therefore, the summation in Eq. 7.61 requires $n+d+1$ knots $\{t_1, t_2, \ldots, t_{n+d+1}\}$. Note that the parametric curve is generated by varying t within the closed subinterval $[t_{d+1}, t_{n+1}]$ only, even though other knot values outside this range may be required for computing the polynomial values. The end point of the parametric curve $t = t_{n+1}$ is a special point in the sense that the definition of $B_{n,0}(t)$ is modified to accommodate the point as follows:

$$B_{n,0}(t_{n+1}) = 1. \tag{7.62}$$

The values of the knots can be adjusted while maintaining the non-decreasing order, to make fine local changes to the shape of the resulting curve. Another advantage of using B-splines as blending functions is that due to their local support, changes made to a control point will affect the curve only in the neighbourhood of the point. As an example, consider the situation when the control point P_5 is changed in Eq. 7.61. Since P_5 is multiplied by $B_{5,d}$ which is zero outside the interval $[t_5, t_{6+d})$, any change in the position of P_5 will not affect the curve outside this interval. This property is depicted in Fig. 7.20, where a second degree approximating curve is generated using eight control points, and the position of P_5 is shifted vertically downward by a small distance. The corresponding localized shift in the curve can be clearly observed in the figure.

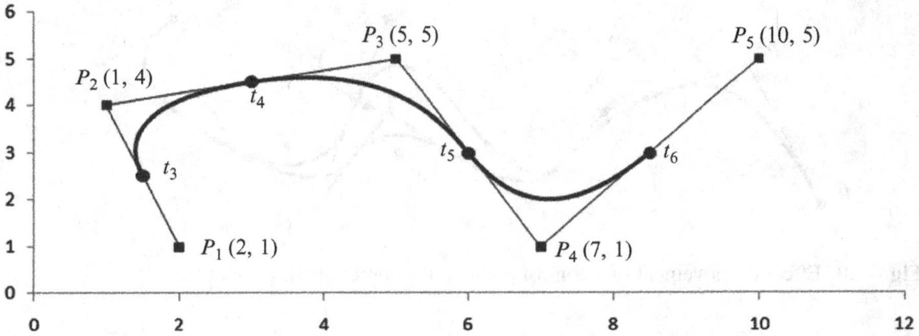

Fig. 7.21 A second degree approximating curve through five control points

We shall now look at the geometrical characteristics of shapes and the effects produced by varying knot positions. Given two points P_1 and P_2, and setting $d = 1$, Eq. 7.61 gives the following equation for the interpolating line:

$$P(t) = \left(\frac{t - t_1}{t_2 - t_1} B_{1,0}(t) + \frac{t_3 - t}{t_3 - t_2} B_{2,0}(t)\right) P_1 + \left(\frac{t - t_2}{t_3 - t_2} B_{2,0}(t) + \frac{t_4 - t}{t_4 - t_3} B_{3,0}(t)\right) P_2 \tag{7.63}$$

Note that the parameter t varies from t_2 to t_3 only (see Eq. 7.61). Therefore, the first term containing $B_{1,0}(t)$ and the last term containing $B_{3,0}(t)$ vanish from the above equation, and $B_{2,0}(t) = 1$. Thus we get the desired equation of the straight line connecting the two points:

$$P(t) = \frac{t_3 - t}{t_3 - t_2} P_1 + \frac{t - t_2}{t_3 - t_2} P_2 \tag{7.64}$$

In this case, the knots t_2, t_3 do not affect the shape of the parametric line. We shall now consider another example with five control points $P_1 \ldots P_5$ on a two-dimensional plane as shown in Fig. 7.21, and an approximating spline generated using second degree B-splines. Since we require a knot vector containing eight values, let us choose a uniformly spaced knot vector $\{10, 20, \ldots, 80\}$. The parameter interval for the curve is $[t_3, t_6]$ (see Eq. 7.61). The points where the parameter t attains the knot values on the curve are also indicated in the figure. These points are called knot points. Knot t_2 is required for computing $B_{1,2}$, and t_7 is needed for $B_{5,2}$. The remaining knots t_1 and t_8 do not affect the shape of the curve.

A knot can be repeated multiple times in a knot vector. In the above example, the curve does not pass through the first and the last control points. However, for a closer approximation of the control polygonal line, it is often required to have the curve pass through the end points, and also have the corresponding line segments tangential to the curve. We saw earlier that Bezier curves satisfy this requirement. If the first and the last knots have multiplicity $d + 1$, then the approximating curve of

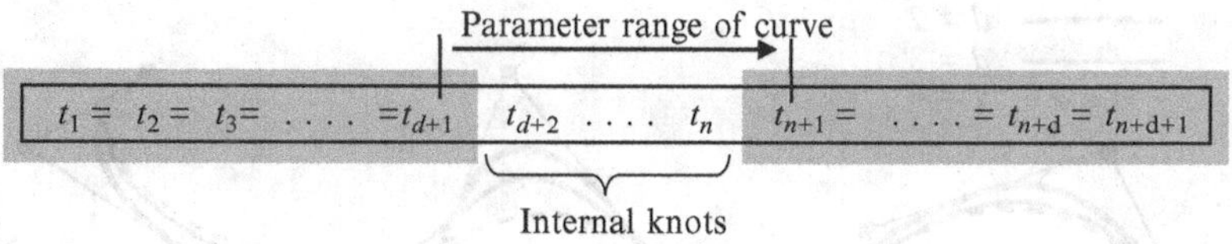

Fig. 7.22 Clamped knot vector

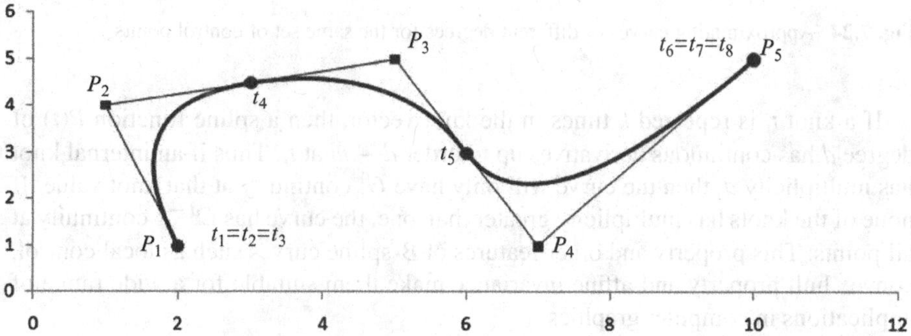

Fig. 7.23 A second degree curve generated using a clamped knot vector. Compare this with the curve in Fig. 7.21

degree d generated using B-splines also meets this requirement. The knot vector of such a curve is said to be clamped (Fig. 7.22).

If the knots have values in the range [0, 1], then the first $d+1$ values are usually clamped to 0, and the last $d+1$ values to 1. If the knot vector is clamped, it can be easily verified that

$$B_{1,d}(t_{d+1}) = B_{2,d-1}(t_{d+1}) = \ldots = B_{d+1,0}(t_{d+1}) = 1 \quad (7.65)$$

and hence $P(t_{d+1}) = P_1$. Similarly, making use of the special condition in Eq. 7.62 we can show that $P(t_{n+1}) = P_n$. The curve therefore passes through the first and the last control points. Figure 7.23 shows the modified version of the curve in Fig. 7.21, generated using the clamped knot vector {30, 30, 30, 40, 50, 60, 60, 60}.

As the degree d of the curve is increased, it tends to move further away from the control points. However, the curve always remains within the convex hull of the control points. Figure 7.24 gives an example with eight control points and clamped knot vectors for three different values of d. As d is increased, the number of internal knots $(n-d-1)$ in the clamped knot vector reduces, and eventually becomes zero when $d = n-1$. At this point, the B-spline curve degenerates into a Bezier curve. Specifically, a B-spline curve of degree d with $d+1$ control points and $2(d+1)$ knots is actually a Bezier curve of degree d if the knot vector is clamped such that

$$\begin{aligned} t_i &= 0, \quad \textit{if} \quad 1 \le i \le d+1 \\ &= 1, \quad \textit{if} \quad d+2 \le i \le 2(d+1) \end{aligned} \quad (7.66)$$

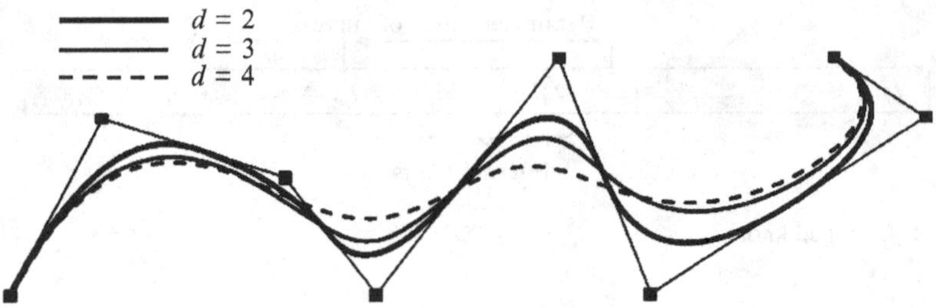

Fig. 7.24 Approximating curves of different degrees for the same set of control points

If a knot t_i is repeated k times in the knot vector, then a spline function $P(t)$ of degree d has continuous derivatives up to order $d - m$ at t_i. Thus if an internal knot has multiplicity d, then the curve will only have C^0 continuity at that knot value. If none of the knots has multiplicity greater than one, the curve has C^{d-1} continuity at all points. This property and other features of B-spline curves such as local control, convex hull property and affine invariance make them suitable for a wide range of applications in computer graphics.

7.8.3 NURBS

Similar to rational Bezier curves (Sect. 7.6.3), the control points for a B-spline curve can be expressed in the homogeneous coordinate system, each containing an additional scale factor h. This modification causes the approximating curve's equation to have a rational form. Further, if the knot vector does not contain uniformly spaced values, then we have a Non-Uniform Rational Basis Spline, or NURBS, as it is commonly known in computer graphics literature. In the homogeneous coordinate space, control points $P_i = (x_i,\ y_i,\ z_i)$ can be expressed as $(x_ih_i,\ y_ih_i,\ z_ih_i,\ h_i)$, $h_i \neq 0$. The term h_i acts as a scalar weight for each point, providing an extra level of control over the shape of the spline curve. The parametric equation of the spline curve in Eq. 7.61 now becomes

$$P(t) = \frac{\sum_{i=1}^{n} h_i P_i B_{i.d}(t)}{\sum_{i=1}^{n} h_i B_{i.d}(t)}, \qquad t_{d+1} \le t \le t_{n+1} \tag{7.67}$$

If the knot vector is clamped as given in Eq. 7.66, then the above equation yields a rational Bezier curve. As an example, a circular arc that subtends an angle 2θ at the centre can be generated by representing the middle control point P_2 in homogeneous coordinates with $h = \cos\theta$. Suppose we require an arc between two points $P_1 = (1, 0)$ and $P_3 = (3, 0)$, so that the subtended angle is 60° ($\theta = 30°$). The

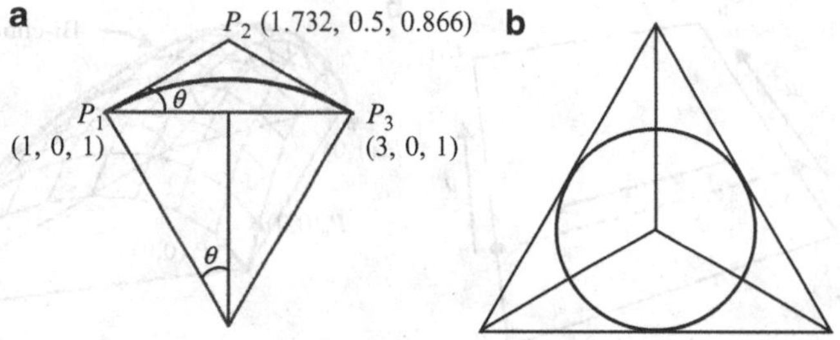

Fig. 7.25 Generation of circular arcs using NURBS

Fig. 7.26 The surface of a light bulb modelled by revolving a B-spline curve about the *y*-axis

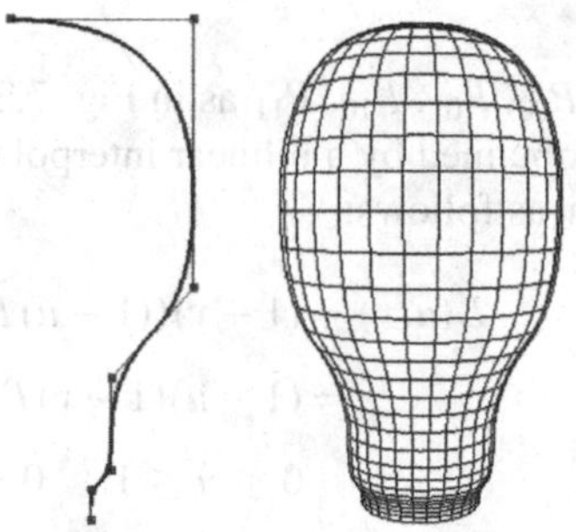

second control point P_2 must be at the position where the two tangents to the curve meet. Therefore, in this case, $P_2 = (2, \tan\theta)$. The NURBS curve in Fig. 7.25a is generated by specifying the control points in homogeneous coordinates as (1, 0, 1), $(2\cos\theta, \sin\theta, \cos\theta)$, and (3, 0, 1). Three circular arcs, each subtending an angle of 120° at the centre, can be combined as shown in Fig. 7.25b to form a complete circle.

B-splines and NURBS are widely used in the design of surfaces. A simple surface design method is to first model a spline curve on the *xy*-plane, and then revolve the curve about the *y*-axis to generate a surface of revolution (Fig. 7.26). The following sections discuss some of the important spline based surface generation techniques used in computer graphics.

7.9 Surface Patches

Surface patches are two-parameter analogues of curve segments that are defined using blending functions in two independent parameters and a set of control points. Linear, quadratic and cubic interpolation methods used for generating curve segments can be extended to bilinear, biquadratic and bicubic polynomial interpolation methods for constructing surface patches. Given four control points

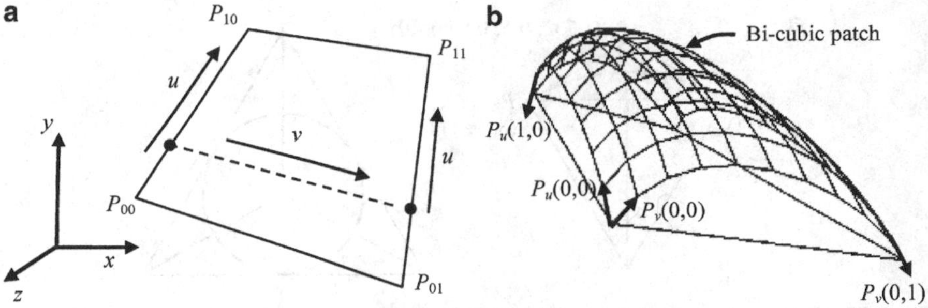

Fig. 7.27 (**a**) A bilinear surface patch. (**b**) A bi-cubic patch formed using four control points

$P_{00}, P_{01}, P_{10}, P_{11}$ as in Fig. 7.27, a polygonal surface passing through them can be obtained by a bilinear interpolation between the points using two parameters u and v as follows:

$$\begin{aligned} L(u,v) &= (1-v)((1-u)P_{00} + uP_{10}) + v((1-u)P_{01} + uP_{11}) \\ &= (1-u)(1-v)P_{00} + u(1-v)P_{10} + (1-u)vP_{01} + uvP_{11}, \\ &\quad 0 \le u \le 1, \quad 0 \le v \le 1. \end{aligned} \tag{7.68}$$

The interpolating patch in this case is simply a quadrilateral surface element with straight edges connecting the control points. Hence the above equation is not very useful in surface design applications.

We can use a general bi-cubic polynomial equation as given below for constructing an interpolating surface that passes through four control points:

$$P(u,v) = \sum_{i=0}^{3}\sum_{j=0}^{3} c_{ij}u^i v^j, \quad 0 \le u \le 1, \quad 0 \le v \le 1. \tag{7.69}$$

The above equation has 16 unknowns c_{ij}, and requires 16 boundary conditions to provide a unique solution for the coefficients. These boundary conditions are formed using the four control points, the four tangent vectors along the u-direction at the points, the four tangent vectors along the v-direction, and the four twist vectors. We use the following notations for the partial derivatives of $P(u, v)$. The first two derivatives give the tangent vectors along parametric directions, and the third gives the twist vector at any point (a, b):

$$P_u(a,b) = \left(\frac{\partial P}{\partial u}\right)_{\substack{u=a\\v=b}}, \; P_v(a,b) = \left(\frac{\partial P}{\partial v}\right)_{\substack{u=a\\v=b}}, \; P_{uv}(a,b) = \left(\frac{\partial^2 P}{\partial u \partial v}\right)_{\substack{u=a\\v=b}} \tag{7.70}$$

With the above notation, the boundary conditions can be written as follows:

$$
\begin{aligned}
P(0,0) &= c_{00} = P_{00} \\
P(0,1) &= c_{00} + c_{01} + c_{02} + c_{03} = P_{01} \\
P(1,0) &= c_{00} + c_{10} + c_{20} + c_{30} = P_{10} \\
P(1,1) &= \sum_{i=0}^{3}\sum_{j=0}^{3} c_{ij} = P_{11} \\
P_u(0,0) &= c_{10} \\
P_u(0,1) &= c_{10} + c_{11} + c_{12} + c_{13} \\
P_u(1,0) &= c_{10} + 2c_{20} + 3c_{30} \\
P_u(1,1) &= \sum_{i=0}^{3} c_{1i} + 2\sum_{i=0}^{3} c_{2i} + 3\sum_{i=0}^{3} c_{3i} \\
P_v(0,0) &= c_{01} \\
P_v(0,1) &= c_{01} + 2c_{02} + 3c_{03} \\
P_v(1,0) &= c_{01} + c_{11} + c_{21} + c_{31} \\
P_v(1,1) &= \sum_{i=0}^{3} c_{i1} + 2\sum_{i=0}^{3} c_{i2} + 3\sum_{i=0}^{3} c_{i3} \\
P_{uv}(0,0) &= c_{11} \\
P_{uv}(0,1) &= c_{11} + 2c_{12} + 3c_{13} \\
P_{uv}(1,0) &= c_{11} + 2c_{21} + 3c_{31} \\
P_{uv}(1,1) &= c_{11} + 4c_{22} + 9c_{33} + 2c_{21} + 2c_{12} + 3c_{31} + 3c_{13} + 6c_{23} + 6c_{32}
\end{aligned}
\tag{7.71}
$$

The bi-cubic surface patch obtained by solving the above linear system of equations is given by

$$
P(u,v) = \begin{bmatrix} f_1(u) & f_2(u) & f_3(u) & f_4(u) \end{bmatrix}
\begin{bmatrix}
P(0,0) & P(0,1) & P_v(0,0) & P_v(0,1) \\
P(1,0) & P(1,1) & P_v(1,0) & P_v(1,1) \\
P_u(0,0) & P_u(0,1) & P_{uv}(0,0) & P_{uv}(0,1) \\
P_u(1,0) & P_u(1,1) & P_{uv}(1,0) & P_{uv}(1,1)
\end{bmatrix}
\begin{bmatrix} f_1(v) \\ f_2(v) \\ f_3(v) \\ f_4(v) \end{bmatrix}
\tag{7.72}
$$

where the blending functions $f_i(u)$ are the Hermite polynomials given in Eq. 7.29. Figure 7.27b shows an example of a bi-cubic surface patch.

7.10 Coons Patches

The interpolation methods discussed in the previous section use positions and derivatives defined at the control points as boundary conditions. A surface patch may be required to have curves with known equations along its four edges. Suppose four edge curves forming the boundary of a region are given by parametric functions $C_1(u)$, $C_2(u)$, $D_1(v)$, $D_2(v)$ as shown in Fig. 7.28. All four curves are defined over the same interval [0, 1].

At the corner points, the curves satisfy the conditions $P_{00} = C_1(0) = D_1(0)$, $P_{10} = C_1(1) = D_2(0)$, $P_{01} = C_2(0) = D_1(1)$, and $P_{11} = C_2(1) = D_2(1)$. By linearly interpolating between corresponding points of $C_1(u)$ and $C_2(u)$ using the second parameter v, we get the following ruled surface:

$$R_C(u, v) = (1 - v)C_1(u) + vC_2(u), \qquad 0 \le v \le 1 \tag{7.73}$$

Similarly, interpolating between $D_1(v)$ and $D_2(v)$ using the parameter u, we get another ruled surface:

$$R_D(u, v) = (1 - u)D_1(v) + uD_2(v), \qquad 0 \le u \le 1 \tag{7.74}$$

Figure 7.29a shows four Bezier curves surrounding a region in three-dimensional space. The corresponding ruled surfaces generated by the two equations given above are shown in Fig. 7.29b, c. Each ruled surface follows the shape of the bounding curves along one parametric direction.

The bilinear Coons patch bounded by the four parametric curves is obtained by adding together the above two ruled surfaces and subtracting the surface obtained from Eq. 7.68:

$$P(u, v) = R_C(u, v) + R_D(u, v) - L(u, v), \qquad 0 \le u \le 1, \quad 0 \le v \le 1 \tag{7.75}$$

Figure 7.30 shows the surface patch produced by applying the above equation in the example given in Fig. 7.29.

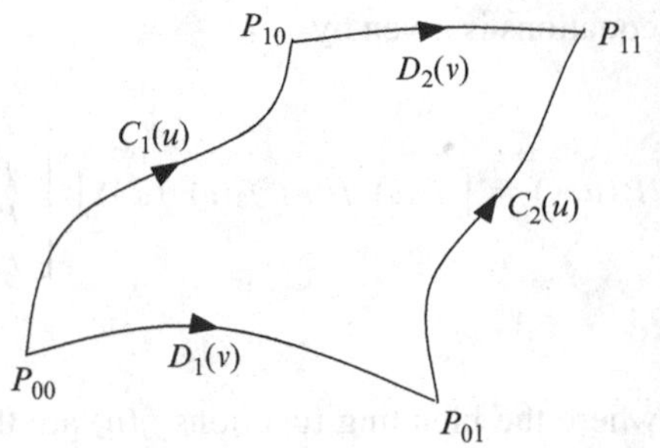

Fig. 7.28 A region for a surface patch specified using four bounding curves

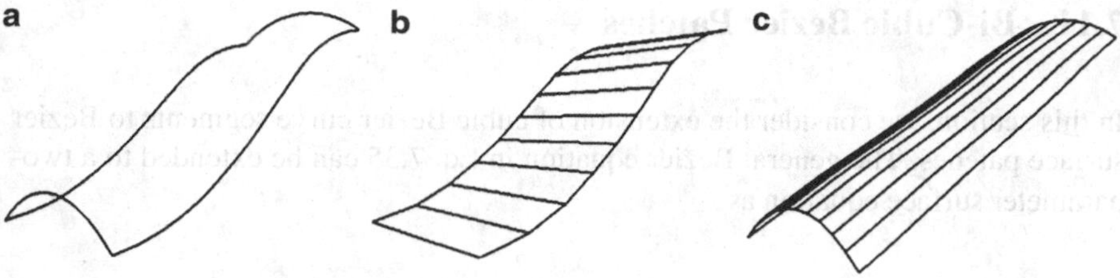

Fig. 7.29 (**a**) A region specified by four bounding curves. (**b**) Ruled surface $R_C(u,v)$. (**c**) Ruled surface $R_D(u,v)$

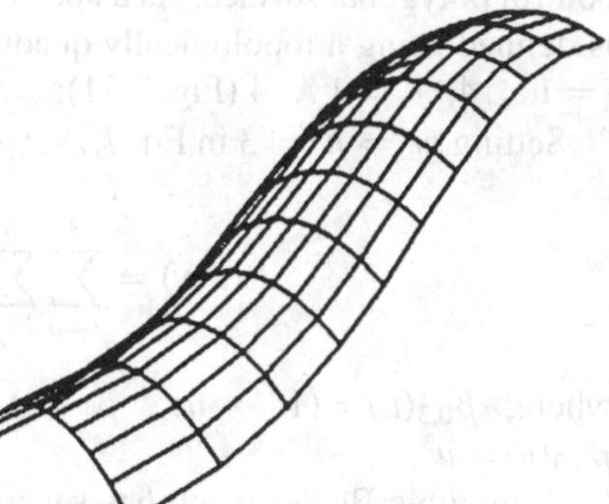

Fig. 7.30 Bilinear Coons patch corresponding to the set of curves in Fig. 7.29a

It can be easily verified that the surface patch $P(u, v)$ satisfies the desired boundary conditions:

$$P(u,0) = C_1(u),\ P(u,1) = C_2(u),\ P(0,v) = D_1(v),\ P(1,v) = D_2(v) \quad (7.76)$$

Generally the derivatives along the parametric directions of bilinear Coons patches are not always continuous, and hence the surface patches do not join smoothly along a common edge curve. Bi-cubic interpolants are used to obtain first order geometric continuity along joining curves. A bi-cubic Coons patch is a smooth blending surface created by using Hermite polynomials (see Eq. 7.29) instead of linear interpolants:

$$\begin{aligned} P(u,v) =& f_1(v)C_1(u) + f_2(v)C_2(u) + f_1(u)D_1(v) + f_2(u)D_2(v), \\ &- f_1(v)\left(f_1(u)P_{11} + f_2(u)P_{12}\right) - f_2(v)\left(f_1(u)P_{21} + f_2(u)P_{22}\right) \end{aligned} \quad (7.77)$$

where, $f_1(u) = 1 - 3u^2 + 2u^3$, and $f_2(u) = 3u^2 - 2u^3$.

7.11 Bi-Cubic Bezier Patches

In this section, we consider the extension of cubic Bezier curve segments to Bezier surface patches. The general Bezier equation in Eq. 7.35 can be extended to a two-parameter surface equation as

$$P(u,v) = \sum_{i=0}^{n}\sum_{j=0}^{m} \beta_{i,n}(u)\beta_{j,m}(v)P_{i+1,j+1}, \qquad 0 \le u \le 1, \quad 0 \le v \le 1. \quad (7.78)$$

The two-dimensional array of points P_{ij}, $i = 1 \ldots n+1, j = 1 \ldots m+1$ forms a control polygonal surface. As a special case of the above, the bi-cubic Bezier patch is defined using a topologically quadrilateral arrangement of 16 control points P_{ij}, $i = 1 \ldots 4,\ j = 1 \ldots 4$ (Fig. 7.31):

Setting $m = n = 3$ in Eq. 7.78, we get

$$P(u,v) = \sum_{i=0}^{3}\sum_{j=0}^{3} \beta_{i,3}(u)\beta_{j,3}(v)P_{i+1,j+1} \qquad (7.79)$$

where, $\beta_{0,3}(u) = (1-u)^3$, $\beta_{1,3}(u) = 3u(1-u)^2$, $\beta_{2,3}(u) = 3u^2(1-u)$ and $\beta_{3,3}(u) = u^3$.

A bi-cubic Bezier patch has several desirable properties that makes it suitable for surface design applications (Fig. 7.32). From Eq. 7.78, it can be seen that $P(0,0) = P_{11}$, $P(1,0) = P_{41}$, $P(0,1) = P_{14}$, and $P(1,1) = P_{44}$. Thus, the four corner points of the control polygonal surface lie on the Bezier patch. It can also be observed that

$$P(u,0) = \sum_{i=0}^{3} \beta_{i,3}(u)P_{i+1,1}, \qquad 0 \le u \le 1. \qquad (7.80)$$

The above equation shows that $P(u, 0)$ is a cubic Bezier curve formed using the control points P_{11}, P_{21}, P_{31} and P_{41}. Similarly, we can prove that the remaining edge curves of the surface patch are also Bezier curves. In fact, for any constant c, both $P(u, c)$ and $P(c, v)$ are cubic Bezier curves.

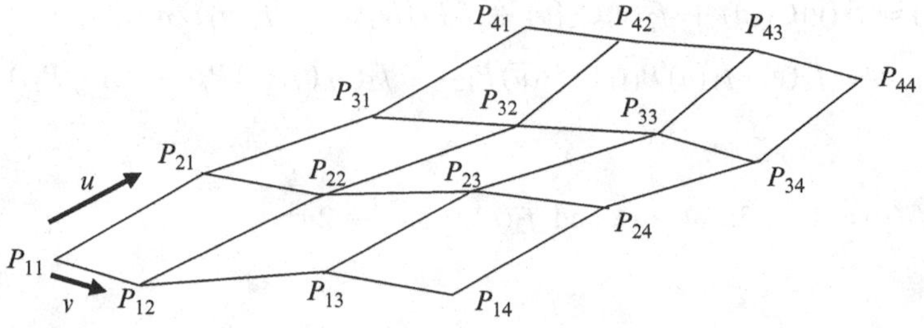

Fig. 7.31 A control polygonal surface for a bi-cubic Bezier patch

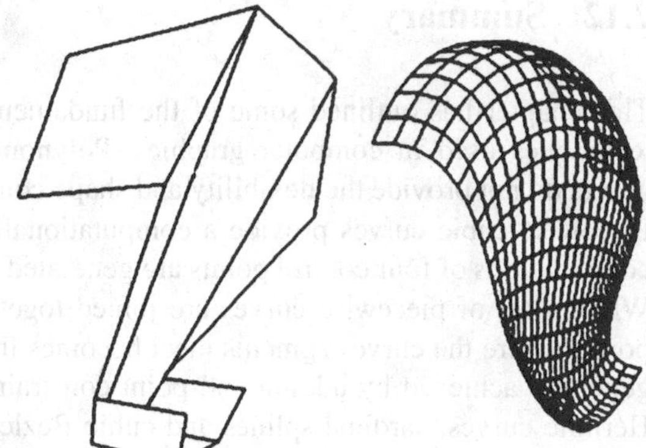

Fig. 7.32 A Bezier control polygonal surface and wireframe model of its cubic Bezier patch

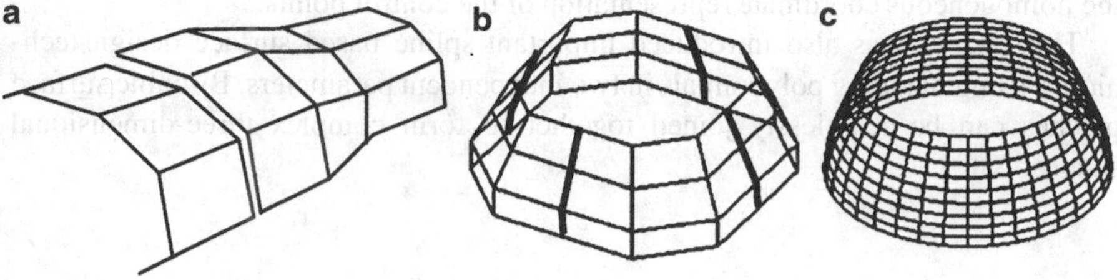

Fig. 7.33 (**a**) Polygonal elements along a common edge must be coplanar to ensure first-order continuity. (**b**) Control polygonal surfaces joined together to form a closed surface. (**c**) The resulting Bezier patches have first order continuity

Since Eq. 7.78 defines a convex combination of the control points, the Bezier surface patch lies within the convex hull of the control points. Another important property useful in computer graphics is the affine invariance of Bezier patches. For any affine transformation given by a matrix **T**, the transformed Bezier surface can be obtained as

$$P(u,v) = \mathbf{T}\ P(u,v) = \sum_{i=0}^{n}\sum_{j=0}^{m} \beta_{i,n}(u)\beta_{j,m}(v)(\mathbf{T}P_{i+1,j+1}) \qquad (7.81)$$

which shows that the transformed patch can also be obtained by computing the Bezier surface of the transformed control points.

When several Bezier patches are joined together to form complex shapes, it becomes necessary to have at least first-order geometric continuity along the edges where two patches join. A sufficient condition for meeting this requirement is the co-planarity of polygonal elements of the corresponding control surfaces that share a common edge (Fig. 7.33a).

The surface of the Utah Teapot is specified using 32 control polygonal surfaces. A section of the main body consisting of four control surfaces is shown in Fig. 7.33b. The bold lines show the edges where the surfaces meet. The Bezier patches form a continuous surface as shown in Fig. 7.33c.

7.12 Summary

This chapter has outlined some of the fundamental curve and surface generation techniques used in computer graphics. Polynomial interpolation curves of high orders do not provide the flexibility and shape control needed in many applications. Piecewise cubic curves provide a computationally simple solution where convex combinations of four control points are generated using a set of blending functions. When a set of piecewise curves are joined together, parametric continuity at the points where the curve segments meet becomes important. Tangential continuity is generally achieved by adding end-point constraints for the first order derivatives. Hermite curves, cardinal splines and cubic Bezier curves are all generated in this fashion. Piecewise curves with higher order continuity can be generated using B-splines. Rational Bezier curves and rational B-spline curves are constructed using the homogeneous coordinate representation of the control points.

This chapter has also introduced important spline based surface design techniques using blending polynomials in two independent parameters. Bi-cubic surface patches can be seamlessly joined together to form complex three-dimensional shapes.

7.13 Supplementary Material for Chap. 7

The section `Chapter7/Code` on the companion website contains the following programs demonstrating the curve and surface generation techniques discussed in this chapter.

1. **PolyInterp.cpp**

Additional files:
`none`

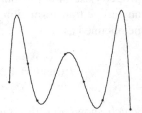

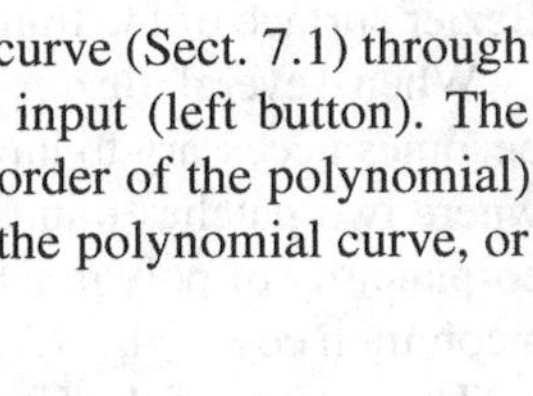

The program generates an interpolating polynomial curve (Sect. 7.1) through a set of points. The points are specified using mouse input (left button). The maximum number of points (and hence the maximum order of the polynomial) is set to 7. After defining the points, press ‘p’ to draw the polynomial curve, or ‘c’ to clear the screen and start over again.

2. **CatmullRom.cpp**

Additional files:
`none`

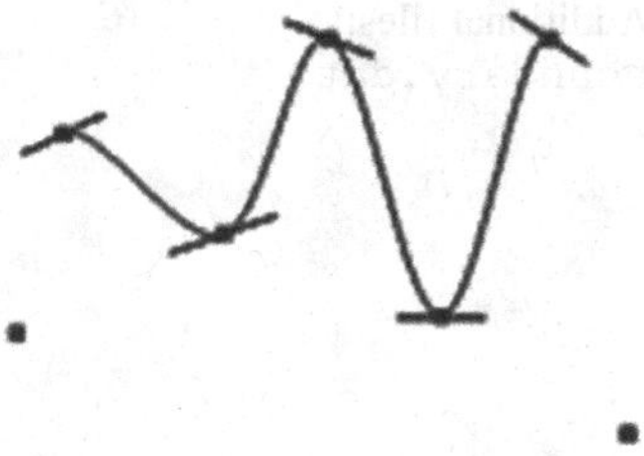

The program generates a Catmull-Rom spline (Sect. 7.5) through a set of points interactively specified using mouse input (left button). The curve is updated as and when a new point is input. The tangent directions at each input point are also shown. A point's position can be changed by clicking on it and dragging it with the right mouse button pressed. Press 'c' to clear the screen and start over.

3. **Bezier2D.cpp**

Additional files:
`none`

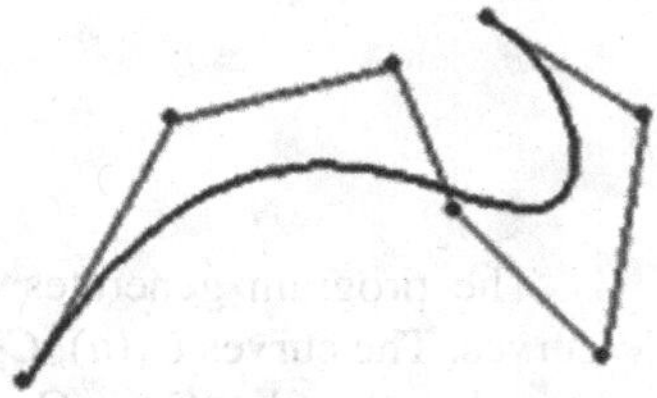

The program uses the OpenGL evaluator functions for drawing a two-dimensional Bezier curve (Sect. 7.6) for a given set of points specified interactively using mouse input. The control polygonal line and the corresponding Bezier curve are updated as and when a new point is input. Press 'c' to clear the screen and start over.

4. **Bezier3D.cpp**

Additional files:
`teapot.dat`
`teacup.dat`
`teaspoon.dat`

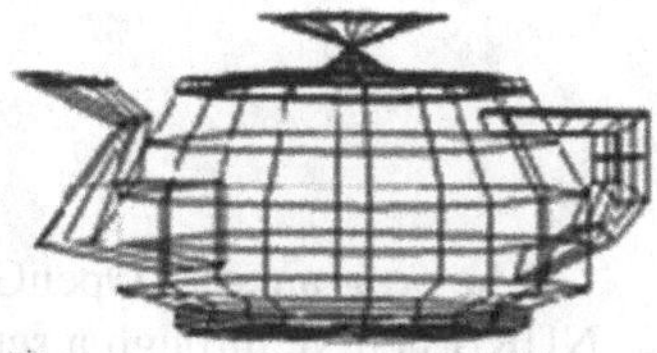

The program uses OpenGL evaluator functions to generate three-dimensional Bezier patches for the control polyhedra stored in an input file. The program reads three input files that contain polyhedral data for the Utah teapot, teacup and teaspoon. Select '1' for the teapot, '2' for the teacup and '3' for the teaspoon. Pressing the space bar toggles between the displays of the control polyhedral surface and the Bezier surface. Pressing 'n' increases the number of subdivisions. The arrow keys are used to change the view direction.

5. **Bicubic.cpp**

Additional files:
`boundary.dat`

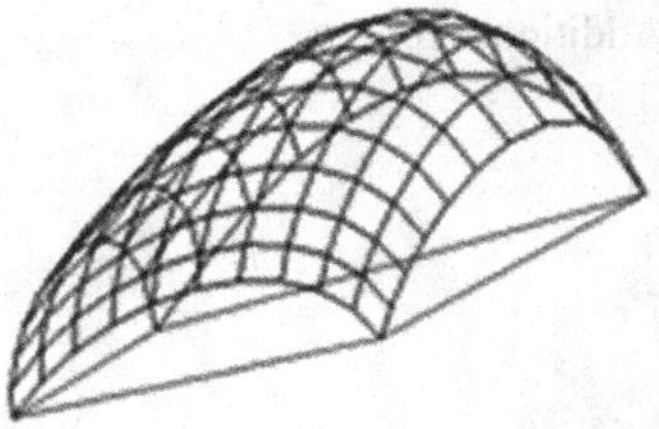

The program generates a bi-cubic patch (Sect. 7.9) on a set of 4 control points. The control points and the boundary conditions for the patch are read in from the file "boundary.dat". Use left or right arrow keys to change the view direction.

6. **Coons.cpp**

Additional files:
`CurveCoeffs.dat`

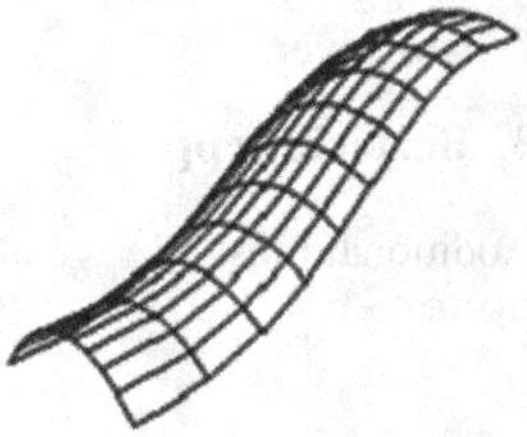

The program generates a Coons patch (Sect. 7.10) using four parametric curves. The curves $C_1(u)$, $C_2(u)$, $D_1(v)$, $D_2(v)$ are specified using the coefficients stored in the file "CurveCoeffs.dat". Use left or right arrow keys to change the view direction.

7. **SurfRevln.cpp**

Additional files:
`none`

The program uses OpenGL evaluator functions to generate a two-dimensional NURBS curve through a set of user defined points. The points are interactively specified using mouse clicks. Pressing 's' key generates a surface by revolving the curve about the y-axis. Press 'c' to clear the screen and start over again.

7.14 Bibliographical Notes

Curve and surface design techniques are generally discussed in detail in text books on computer-aided design and geometric modelling (e.g., Farin (2001), Goldman (2009), Olfe (1995)). Some computer graphics texts also give an excellent coverage of the mathematical and implementation aspects of spline curves and parametric surfaces (e.g., Buss (2003), McConnell (2006), Watt and Watt (1992), Salomon (2006)).

The notions of parametric and geometric continuity are clearly explained in the fundamental paper by Barsky and Tony (1989). Surface construction techniques using NURBS, Coons patches and ruled surfaces are covered in Piegl and Tiller (1997). A comprehensive analysis of rational Bezier curves and surfaces, and quadric surfaces can be found in Farin (1999). Bezier and B-spline curves and surfaces are also discussed in detail in Prautzsch et al. (2002).

References

Barsky, B. A., & Tony, D. (1989). Geometric continuity of parametric curves. *IEEE Computer Graphics & Applications, 9*(6), 60–69.

Buss, S. R. (2003). *3-D computer graphics: A mathematical introduction with OpenGL*. New York: Cambridge University Press.

Farin, G. (1999). *NURBS: From projective geometry to practical use* (2nd ed.). Natick: A K Peters.

Farin, G. E. (2001). *Curves and surfaces for CAGD: A practical guide* (5th ed.). San Francisco: Morgan Kaufmann.

Goldman, R. (2009). *An integrated introduction to computer graphics and geometric modeling*. Boca Raton: CRC Press.

McConnell, J. J. (2006). *Computer graphics: Theory into practice*. Boston/London: Jones and Bartlett Publishers.

Olfe, D. B. (1995). *Computer graphics for design: From algorithms to AutoCAD*. Englewood Cliffs/London: Prentice Hall.

Piegl, L. A., & Tiller, W. (1997). *The NURBS book* (2nd ed.). Berlin/London: Springer.

Prautzsch, H., Boehm, W., & Paluszny, M. (2002). *Bézier and B-spline techniques*. Berlin/New York: Springer.

Salomon, D. (2006). *Curves and surfaces for computer graphics*. New York/London: Springer.

Watt, A. H., & Watt, M. (1992). *Advanced animation and rendering techniques: Theory and practice*. New York/Wokingham/Reading: ACM Press/Addison-Wesley Pub.

Chapter 8
Mesh Processing

Overview

In computer graphics applications, three-dimensional models are almost always represented using polygonal meshes. A mesh in its simplest form consists of a set of vertices, polygons, and optionally a number of additional vertex and polygonal attributes. The complexity of a mesh can vary from low to very high depending on requirements such as rendering quality, speed and resolution. A wide spectrum of mesh processing algorithms is used by graphics and game developers for a variety of applications such as generating, simplifying, smoothing, remapping and transforming meshes. Several types of data structures and file formats are also used to store mesh data.

This chapter discusses the geometrical and topological aspects related to three-dimensional meshes and their processing. It also presents important data structures and algorithms used for operations such as mesh simplification, mesh subdivision, planar embedding, and polygon triangulation.

8.1 Mesh Representation

A polygonal mesh is a set of vertices and polygonal elements that collectively define a three-dimensional geometrical shape. The simplest mesh representation thus consists of a vertex list and a polygon list as shown in Fig. 8.1. Polygons are often defined in terms of triangular elements. Since triangles are always both planar and convex, they can be conveniently used in several geometrical computations such as point inclusion tests, area and normal calculations and interpolation of vertex attributes.

The vertex list contains the three-dimensional coordinates of the mesh vertices defined in a suitable coordinate frame, and the polygon list contains integer values that index into the vertex list. An anticlockwise ordering of vertices with respect

R. Mukundan, *Advanced Methods in Computer Graphics: With examples in OpenGL*,
DOI 10.1007/978-1-4471-2340-8_8, © Springer-Verlag London Limited 2012

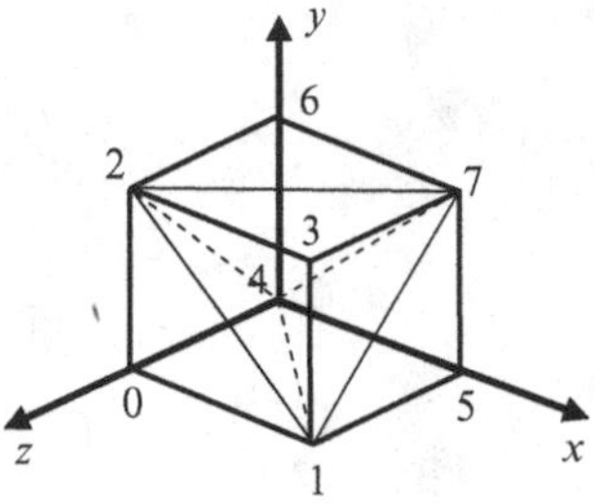

Vertex List		
x	y	z
0.0	0.0	1.0
1.0	0.0	1.0
0.0	1.0	1.0
1.0	1.0	1.0
0.0	0.0	0.0
1.0	0.0	0.0
0.0	1.0	0.0
1.0	1.0	0.0

Triangle List		
i	j	k
0	1	2
1	3	2
2	3	7
2	7	6
1	7	3
1	5	7
6	7	4
7	5	4
0	4	1
1	4	5
2	6	4
0	2	4

Fig. 8.1 A cube and its mesh definition using vertex and polygon lists

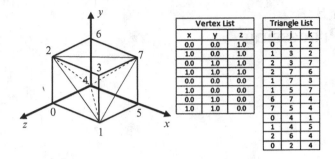

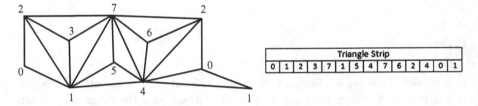

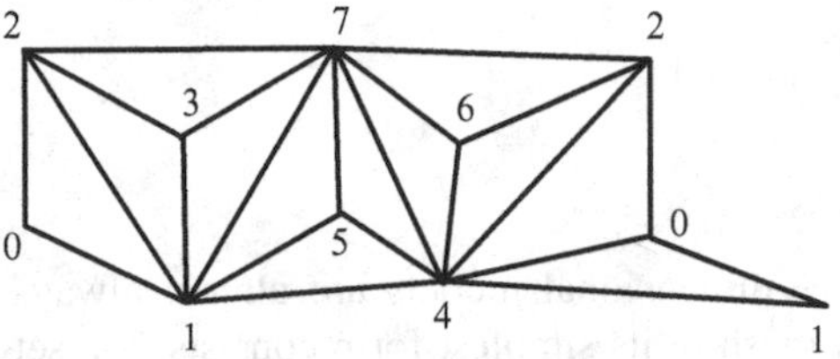

Triangle Strip													
0	1	2	3	7	1	5	4	7	6	2	4	0	1

Fig. 8.2 The cut-open view of the cube in Fig. 8.1 showing its representation as a triangle strip

to the outward face normal direction is commonly used to indicate the front facing side of each polygon. The distinction between the front and the back faces of a polygon becomes important in lighting computations and culling operations. If the polygon list represents a set of connected triangles as in Fig. 8.1, a more efficient and compact data structure called a triangle strip may be used. The first three indices in a triangle strip specify the first triangle. The fourth index along with the previous two indices represents the second triangle. In this fashion, each remaining index represents a triangle that is defined by that index and the previous two indices.

The representation of a cube as a triangle strip is given in Fig. 8.2. The triangle strip is decoded as the set of 12 triangles {012, 123, 237, 371, 715, 154, 547, 476, 762, 624, 240, 401}. Note that the orientation of triangles alternates between clockwise and anticlockwise in this representation. The change of orientation is corrected by reversing the direction of every alternate triangle in the list, starting from the second triangle. Thus the above list would be correctly interpreted as {012, 213, 237, 731, 715, 514, 547, 746, 762, 264, 240, 041}. If the first triangle is defined in the anticlockwise sense, then all triangles in the corrected list will have the same orientation.

Several file formats are used in graphics applications for storing and sharing mesh data. A number of such file formats represent values in binary and compressed forms for minimizing storage space. In this section, we review some of the popular ASCII file formats that allows easy viewing and editing of mesh data. The Object (.OBJ) format was developed by Wavefront technologies. This format allows the definition

Box 8.1 OBJ File Format

Comments start with the symbol #

e.g., `# 3D Model definition`

A vertex definition starts with the symbol v and is followed by 3 or 4 floating point values. Each vertex is implicitly assigned an index. The first vertex has an index 1.

```
e.g.,  v  −1.53   2.06   3.82
       v  6.98   -11.3   -0.008  1.0
```

Texture coordinates are specified by the symbol vt followed by two or three floating point values in the range [0, 1]. Texture coordinates are mapped to vertex coordinates through the face ('f') command. The first set of texture coordinates have an index 1.

```
e.g.,  vt  0.25  0.90
       vt  0.0   0.5   0.5
```

Vertex normals are specified using the vn command. The normal components are assigned to a vertex through the face ('f') command. The first set of normal components is assigned an index 1.

```
e.g.,  vn  −0.256  0.1888  -0.756
```

A polygon definition uses a face command that starts with the symbol f and followed by a list of positive integers that are valid vertex indices.

```
e.g.,  f  2     3  6
       f  15 8  1  22
```

The above face command has a more general form f v/vt/vn v/vt/vn v/vt/vn ... that can be used to combine texture and normal attributes with vertices. Both/vt and/vn fields are optional.

```
e.g.,  f  2/3/1  3/5/2  6/1/7
       f  15/2   8/3    1/5    22/9
       f  6//1   7//6   2//12
```

The first example above defines a triangle including references to the texture and normal coordinates at the vertices. The second example attaches only texture coordinate references to each vertex, while the third example uses only the normal vectors.

of vertices in terms of either three-dimensional Cartesian coordinates or four-dimensional homogeneous coordinates. Polynomials can have more than three vertices. In addition to the basic set of commands supporting simple polygonal mesh data (Box 8.1), the .OBJ format also supports a number of advanced features such as grouping of polygons, material definitions and the specification of free-form surface geometries including curves and surfaces.

Box 8.2 OFF File Format

The first line should contain the header keyword OFF
This line can be followed by optional comment lines starting with the character #

e.g., `# Model file for a cube`

The first non-comment line should have three integer values n_v, n_f, n_e denoting the total number of vertices, faces and edges. The number of edges (n_e) is always set to 0

e.g., `8 6 0`

The above line is followed by the vertex list. The number of vertices in the list must match the number n_v. The first vertex is assigned the index 0, and the last vertex the index n_v-1.

e.g.,
```
-1.2   -1.5   -1.3
1.1    -1.9   -1.7
...
```

Vertices can also be specified using four coordinates in homogeneous form. In this case, the header keyword should be changed to 4OFF.
The vertex list is followed by the face list. Each line contains a set of integers n, i_1, i_2, $\ldots i_n$, where the first integer n gives the number of vertices of that face and the remaining integers give the face indices.

e.g.,
```
3  2     0    1
4  1021  558  632  717
```

Color values in either RGB or RGBA representation can be optionally added to each face as 3 or 4 integer values in the range [0, 255] or floating point values in the range [0, 1].

e.g.,
```
3  1   0   5   255  255  0    0
4  15  26  78  9    0.5  0.1  0.25
```

The Object File Format (.OFF) is another convenient ASCII format for storing 3D model definitions. It uses simple vertex-list and face-list structures for specifying a polygonal model. Unlike the .OBJ format, this format does not intersperse commands with values on every line, and therefore can be easily parsed to extract vertex coordinates and face indices. This format also allows users to specify vertices in homogeneous coordinates, faces with more than three vertex indices, and optional colour values for every vertex or face (Box 8.2).

The Polygon File Format (.PLY) also organises mesh data as a vertex list and a face list with the addition of several optional elements. The format is also called the Stanford Triangle Format. Elements can be assigned a type (`int, float, double, uint` etc.), and a number of values that are stored against each element.

Box 8.3 PLY File Format

The first line in the header should contain the keyword `ply`. The second line specifies the file format using the `format` keyword.

e.g., `format ascii 1.0`

Comments begin with the keyword `comment`

e.g., `comment Model definition for a cube`

The total number of vertices, polygons etc. in the model definition is specified using the `element` keyword.

```
e.g.,  element vertex 8
       element face 6
```

The type of each element is specified using the `property` keyword. The following commands specify the types of vertex coordinates.

```
e.g.,  property float x
       property float y
       property float z
```

The polygon data is usually defined using a set of vertex indices. The type specification is included in the header as

```
property int vertex_index
```

The keyword `end_header` is used to delimit the header information. The vertex and face lists follow this keyword. The first vertex has the index 0.

```
e.g.,
end_header
0.5 0.5 0.5
1.0 0.5 0.5
..
0 1 2 3
1 0 4 5
....
```

Such information is specified using a list of properties as part of the header (Box 8.3). This file format supports several types of elements and data, and the complete specification is included in the header. Parsing a PLY file is therefore considerably complex than parsing an OBJ or OFF file.

8.2 Polygonal Manifolds

The model definition files introduced in the previous section contain information about vertices, polygons, colour values, texture coordinates and possibly many other vertex and face related attributes that collectively specify the mesh geometry. As

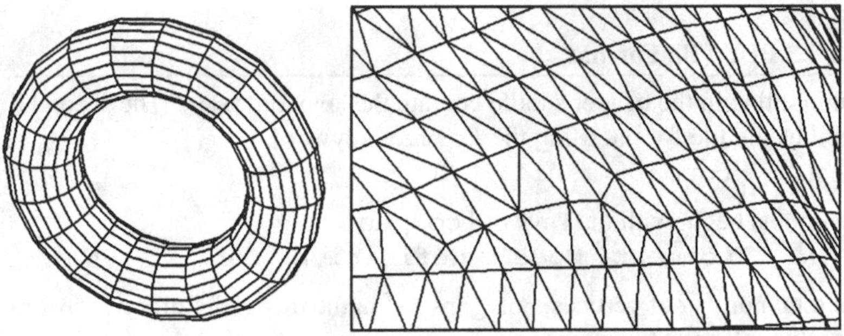

Fig. 8.3 Examples of manifold meshes

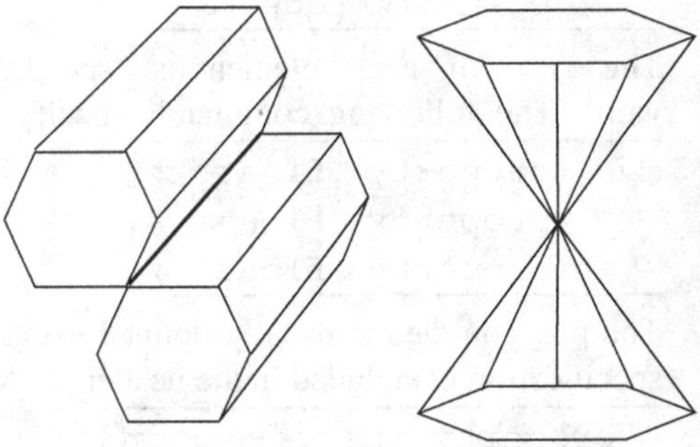

Fig. 8.4 Examples of non-manifold meshes

seen from the examples, list based mesh definitions often do not store any neighbourhood or connectivity information. The adjacency and incidence relationships between mesh elements define the topology of the mesh and are heavily used by several mesh processing algorithms. This section introduces some of the general and desirable topological characteristics of meshes.

A common assumption in the construction of mesh data structures and related algorithms is that the given mesh is a polygonal manifold. A polygonal manifold is defined as a mesh that satisfies two conditions: (i) no edge is shared by more than two faces, and (ii) the faces sharing a vertex can be ordered in such a way that their vertices excluding the shared vertex form a simple chain (Fig. 8.3).

A non-manifold mesh may contain edges shared by more than two polygons, or vertices with more than one chain of neighbouring vertices (Fig. 8.4). In a non-manifold mesh, the neighbourhood of a point may not be topologically equivalent to a disc, which makes local adjustments surrounding that vertex difficult in many mesh processing algorithms. The methods discussed in this chapter assume that the given mesh satisfies the conditions of a polygonal manifold.

The chain of vertices surrounding a vertex in a polygonal manifold is closed if the vertex is an interior vertex, otherwise the vertex is a boundary vertex. In a triangular mesh, the triangles sharing a common vertex form a closed triangle fan for interior vertices, and an open triangle fan for boundary vertices (Fig. 8.5). An interior vertex

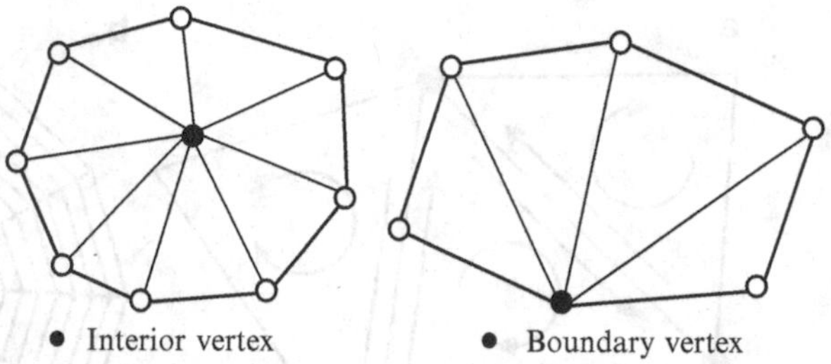

Fig. 8.5 An interior and a boundary vertex on a polygonal manifold

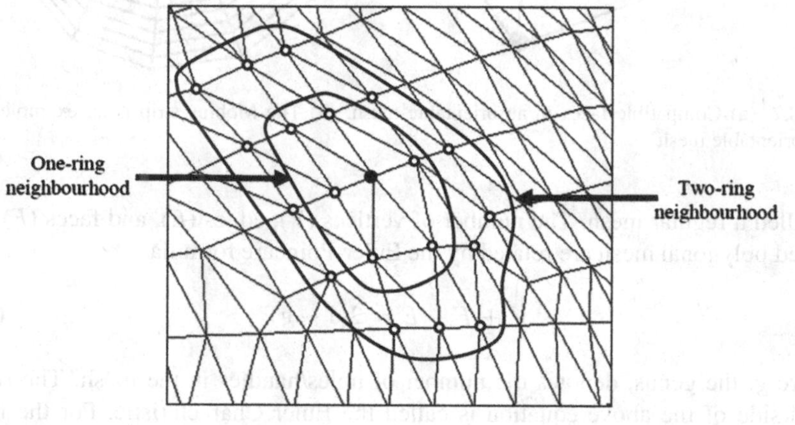

Fig. 8.6 One-ring and two-ring neighbours of a vertex on a manifold mesh

is also commonly called a simple vertex. A closed manifold that does not contain any boundary vertices is called a polyhedron.

Two vertices are adjacent if they are connected by an edge of a polygon. As seen in Fig. 8.5, the set of vertices that are adjacent to a vertex $\boldsymbol{v}$ in a closed manifold forms a ring. This set is called the one-ring neighbourhood of the vertex $\boldsymbol{v}$. The union of one-ring neighbourhoods of every vertex in this set is called the two-ring neighbourhood of $\boldsymbol{v}$ (Fig. 8.6).

The orientation of the faces of a polygonal manifold is determined by the way in which its vertices are ordered. An anticlockwise ordering of vertices generally corresponds to the front face of a polygon. If two adjacent faces have the same orientation, they are said to be compatible. In this case, a common edge will have opposite directions in the two faces that share the edge (Fig. 8.7a). If every pair of adjacent faces is compatible, the mesh is said to be orientable.

The number of edges incident on a vertex is called its valence. A mesh in which every face has the same number of edges, and every vertex has the same valence

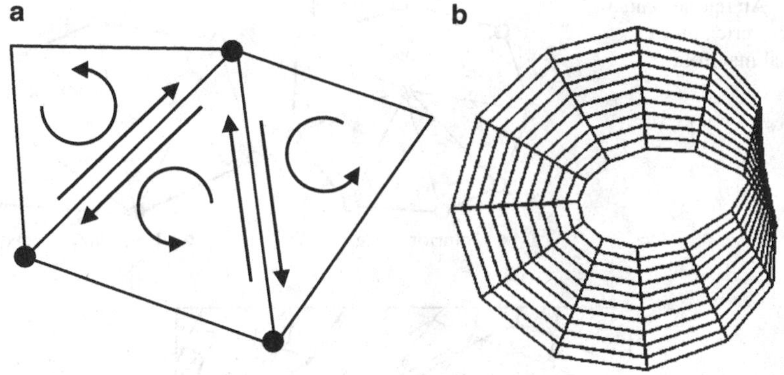

Fig. 8.7 (**a**) Compatible faces in an orientable mesh. (**b**) The Möbius strip is an example of a non-orientable mesh

is called a regular mesh. The number of vertices (V), edges (E), and faces (F) in a closed polygonal mesh are related by the Euler-Poincare formula

$$V + F - E = 2(1 - g) \tag{8.1}$$

where g, the genus, denotes the number of holes/handles in the mesh. The right-hand side of the above equation is called the Euler Characteristic. For the torus in Fig. 8.3 and the Möbius strip in Fig. 8.7b, $g = 1$, and hence $V + F = E$. For polyhedral objects without any holes, $V + F = E + 2$. This equation is generally referred to as the Euler's formula. In a triangular mesh without holes, the average valence of a vertex is six, and we can get an estimate of the number of faces and edges in terms of the vertices as

$$\begin{aligned} F &\approx 2V \\ E &\approx 3V \end{aligned} \tag{8.2}$$

Also in a triangular mesh, every face has three edges, and every edge is counted twice while counting the number of faces. Therefore the number of faces and edges are connected by the equation $E = 3\,F/2$.

8.3 Mesh Data Structures

Mesh data structures are designed to provide information about both mesh geometry and topology so that they could be used for fast traversal and processing of meshes. A large number of mesh operations extensively use information about mesh connectivity and local orientation around vertices. Mesh data structures also support efficient processing of incidence and adjacency queries. In this section, we consider one face-based and two edge-based data structures.

```
struct Triangle
{
    Vertex *p1, *p2, *p3;
    Triangle *t1, *t2, *t3;
};
```

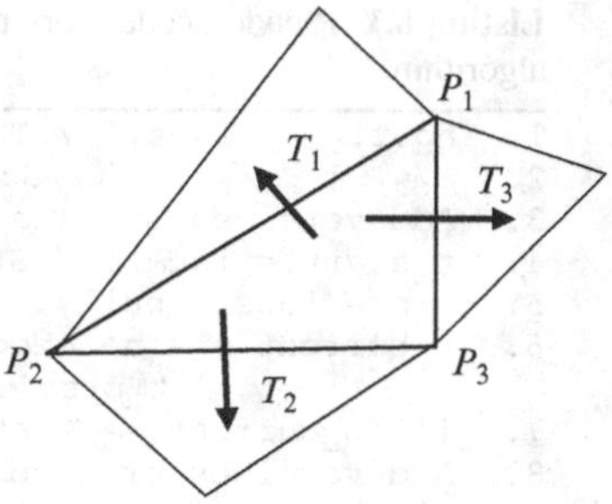

Fig. 8.8 A face based data structure for a triangle showing references to its neighbouring faces

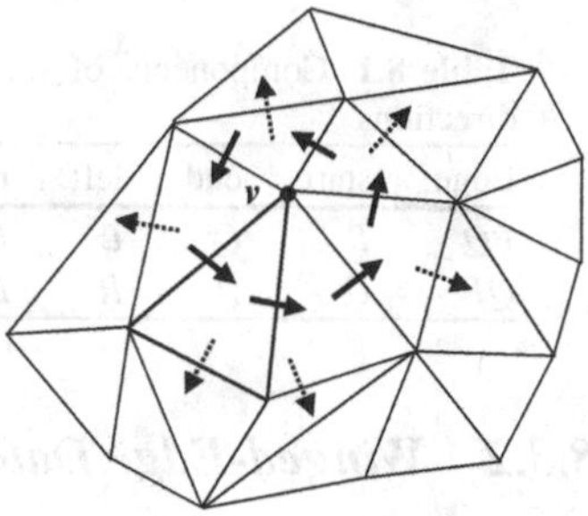

Fig. 8.9 Traversal of the one-ring neighbourhood of a vertex using a face-based data structure

8.3.1 Face-Based Data Structure

Face-based data structures are primarily used for triangular meshes where both the number of edges and number of vertices per face have a constant value 3. In an ordinary mesh file, each triangle is defined using the indices of its three vertices. A face-based data structure additionally stores references to its three neighbouring triangles (Fig. 8.8). Because of its simple structure, a face data structure can be easily constructed from a vertex list and a face list. This data structure does not store any edge related information, and hence is not particularly suitable for edge operations such as edge collapse, edge flipping or edge traversal.

Assuming that every polygonal face in a mesh is a triangle, the face-based data structure provides a convenient mechanism to obtain information about all triangles surrounding a vertex. Using this information, we could perform the traversal of the one-ring neighbourhood of a vertex in constant time. The inputs for the algorithm are a vertex ***v*** and a triangle containing that vertex. The algorithm iteratively visits the neighbouring triangles, each time checking if the triangle has ***v*** as one of its vertices and has not been visited previously. In Fig. 8.9, the triangles indicated by dotted arrows are not visited as they do not have ***v*** as a vertex. The vertices of the visited triangles are added to the set of one-ring neighbours of ***v***. A pseudo-code of this method is given in Listing 8.1.

Listing 8.1 Pseudo code for the one-ring neighbourhood traversal algorithm

```
1. Input:  v, face    //The triangle has v as a vertex
2.   S = {}          //Solution set
3.   Add vertices of face other than v to S
4.   t_start = face    //Starting triangle
5.   t_previous = null
6.   t_current = a neighbour of face different from
                 t_previous, which has v as a vertex
7.   if (t_current == t_start) STOP
8.   Add vertices of t_current other than v, and not
     already in S, to S
9.   t_previous = face
10.  face = t_current
11.  GOTO 6
```

Table 8.1 Components of the wing-edge structure for the same edge in opposite directions

Edge	start	end	left	right	left_prev	left_next	right_prev	right_next
PQ	*P*	*Q*	*L*	*R*	*a*	*b*	*c*	*d*
QP	*Q*	*P*	*R*	*L*	*c*	*d*	*a*	*b*

8.3.2 *Winged-Edge Data Structure*

The winged-edge data structure is one of the powerful representations of an orientable mesh that could be used for a variety of edge-based query processing and manipulation of a mesh. In this representation, each face has a clockwise ordering of its vertices and edges. The structure stores several interconnected information pertaining to the neighbourhood of every edge in the form of three substructures: an edge table, a vertex table and a face table.

An edge *PQ* and its adjacent faces are shown in Fig. 8.10. The direction of the edge is specified by the start and end vertices, and it enables us to define the left and right sides of the edge. The corresponding references to the polygon *L* on its left, and *R* on its right are stored. The edge structure also stores the preceding and succeeding edges of *PQ* with respect to each of these faces. The preceding edge on the left is the edge *a*, and the succeeding edge on the left is the edge *b*. Similarly, the preceding edge on the right is *c*, and the succeeding edge on the right *d*. Note that on each face, a clockwise ordering of the edges is used. Table 8.1 shows how the component values change when the direction of the same edge is reversed.

The winged-edge structure also requires two additional tables or structures, as shown in Fig. 8.10. The vertex table stores the coordinates of each vertex and one of the edges incident to that vertex. The face table maps each face to one of the edges of that face. These tables provide the entry points to the edge structure via either a vertex or a face. For example, if we are required to find all edges that end at a given vertex ***v***, we first use the vertex table to find one of the edges incident at ***v***, and then use the winged-edge structure to iteratively find the remaining edges. Care must be

```
struct W_edge
{
   Vertex *start, *end;
   Face   *left,  *right;
   W_edge *left_prev,   *left_next;
   W_edge *right_prev,  *right_next;
};
struct Vertex
{
    float x, y, z;
    W_edge *edge;
};
struct Face
{
    W_edge *edge;
};
```

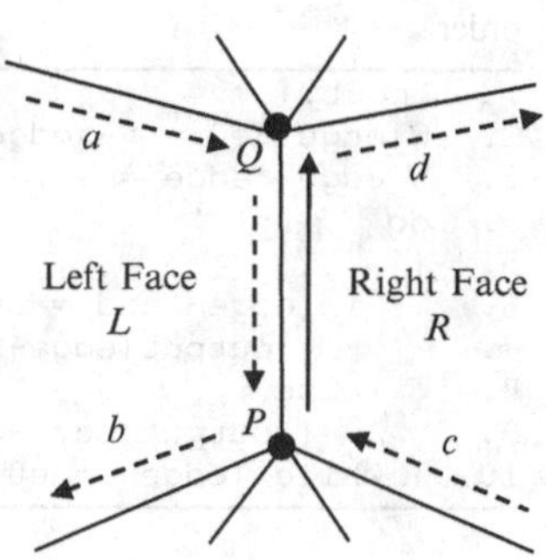

Fig. 8.10 The winged-edge data structure

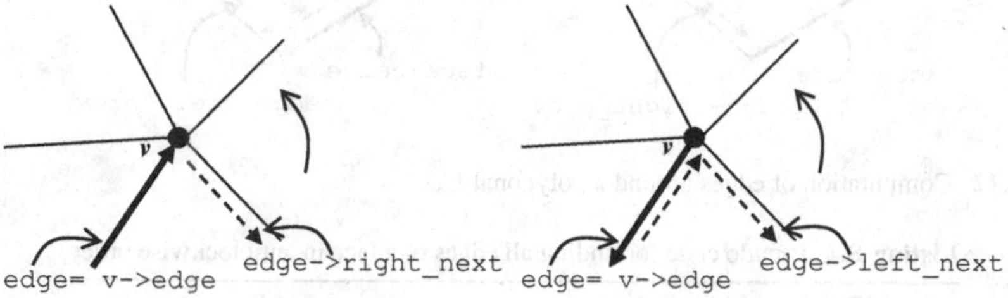

Fig. 8.11 Computation of all edges incident at a vertex. Both directions of an edge should be considered in algorithms using the winged-edge data structure

Listing 8.2 Pseudo code for finding all edges through a vertex in anticlockwise order

```
Input:  v                                  //A vertex
W_edge *e0 = v->edge;                      //Initial edge
W_edge *edge = e0;
do
{
     if(edge->end == v) edge = edge -> right_next;
                  else  edge = edge -> left_next;
     output(edge);
} while (edge != e0);
```

taken to use the right orientation of an edge; the edge entry for a vertex ***v*** in the vertex table may have ***v*** as the either the start vertex or the end vertex. Similarly an edge in the face table may have the face as either its left face or the right face of the edge.

The algorithm to find all edges incident at a vertex ***v*** considers both the cases discussed above, and enumerates the edges surrounding ***v*** in an anticlockwise order (Fig. 8.11). The pseudo-code for the algorithm is given in Listing 8.2.

Listing 8.3 Pseudo code for finding all faces that share a vertex in anticlockwise order

```
Input:  v                                    //A vertex
W_edge *e0 = v->edge;                        //Initial edge
W_edge *edge = e0;
do
{
   if(edge->end == v)
     { output(edge->right); edge = edge->right_next; }
   else
     { output(edge->left);  edge = edge->left_next;  }
} while (edge != e0);
```

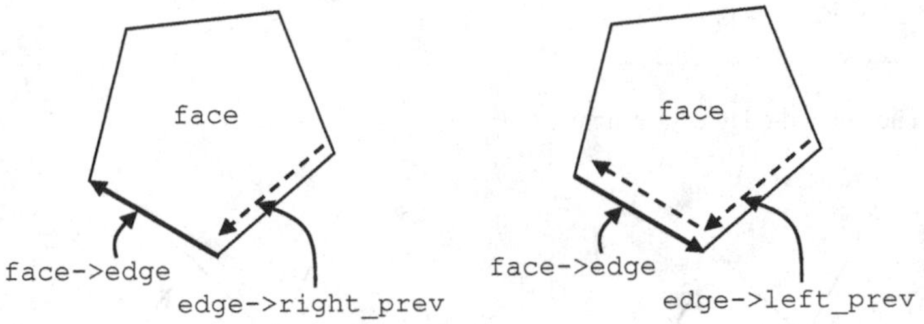

Fig. 8.12 Computation of edges around a polygonal face

Listing 8.4 Pseudo code for finding all edges of a face in anticlockwise order

```
Input:  face
W_edge *e0 = face->edge;                  //Initial edge
W_edge *edge = e0;
do
{
    if(edge->right == face) edge = edge->right_prev;
                       else edge = edge->left_prev;
    output(edge);
} while (edge != e0);
```

A slight modification of the above algorithm can yield a method to output all faces sharing a common vertex ***v*** in an anticlockwise order (Listing 8.3).

The algorithm to compute all edges of a given polygonal face in anticlockwise order uses an approach similar to the ones given above. The iteration starts from the initial edge retrieved from the face table, and proceeds to the next edge based on the orientation of the current edge (Fig. 8.12). The pseudo-code for the algorithm is in Listing 8.4.

8.3.3 Half-Edge Data Structure

The algorithm implementations discussed in the previous section show a limitation of the winged-edge data structure – the ambiguity regarding the direction of an edge

```
struct H_edge
{
   Vertex *vert;
   Face   *face;
   H_edge *prev, *next ;
   H_edge *pair;
};
struct Vertex
{
    float x, y, z;
    H_edge   *edge;
};
struct Face
{
    H_edge *edge;
};
```

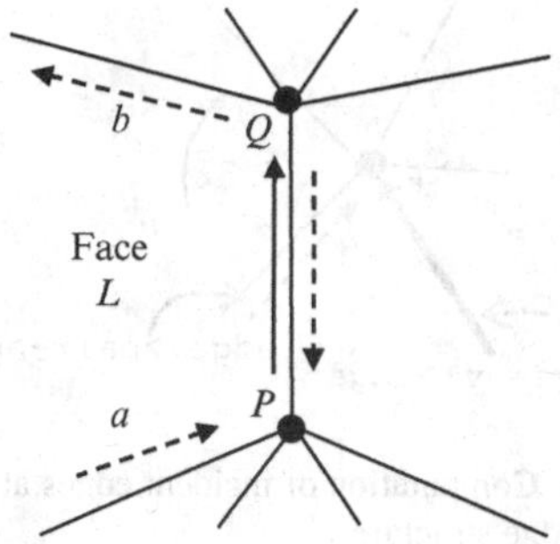

Fig. 8.13 The half-edge data structure

will need to be resolved every time an edge is processed, and this is commonly done using an if-else block to deal with the two possible directions of every edge. The half-edge data structure resolves the ambiguity by splitting every edge and storing it as two half-edges, each with a unique direction. A half-edge belongs to only a single face, which is the face on its left side. A half-edge structure stores references to the unique vertex the edge points to, the unique face it belongs to, the successor of the edge belonging to the same face, and the pair of the half-edge having the opposite direction and belonging to the adjacent face (Fig. 8.13). The half-edge structure is essentially a doubly linked list and hence is also known as the Doubly Connected Edge List (DCEL).

The components of the half-edge *PQ* in Fig. 8.13 are the references to the ending vertex *Q*, the face *L* on its left side, the next edge *b* on the same face, and the pair which is the half-edge *QP* in the opposite direction. Edge processing algorithms often use references to the previous edge (e.g., the method shown in Fig. 8.14), and this information may also be stored in the edge structure. As in the case of the winged-edge structure, two additional tables/structures are used to obtain a half-edge from either a vertex or a face. The vertex table contains for each vertex, its coordinates and a half-edge incident at that vertex. The face table contains for each face, a half-edge that belongs to that face. From the definition of the half-edge structure, it is clear that for a given half-edge `edge`, the end and start points are given by `edge->vert`, and `edge->pair->vert` respectively. Similarly, the two faces that border an edge are given by `edge->face` and `edge->pair->face`.

We will now consider the algorithm for computing all edges incident at a given vertex ***v***. Using a half-edge data structure, the edges can be unambiguously retrieved using a simple iteration (Fig. 8.14). The modified version of the pseudo-code in Listing 8.2 using the half-edge data structure is given in Listing 8.5. In this case, the algorithm is simpler without any case distinction, and returns edges that *end at* the given vertex in anticlockwise order.

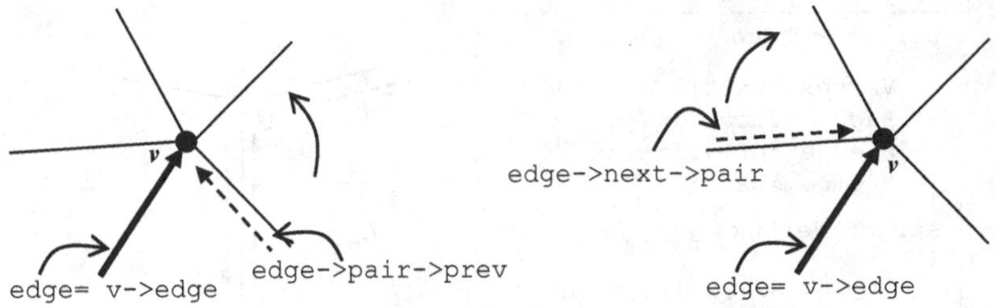

Fig. 8.14 Computation of incident edges at a vertex in anticlockwise and clockwise orders using the half-edge structure

Listing 8.5 Pseudo code for finding all edges that end at a vertex in anticlockwise order

```
Input:  v                               //A vertex
H_edge *e0 = v->edge;                   //Initial edge
H_edge *edge = e0;
do
{
    edge = edge -> pair -> prev;
    output(edge);
} while (edge != e0);
```

Listing 8.6 Pseudo code for finding all faces adjacent to a face

```
Input: face
H_edge *e0 = face->edge;                //Initial edge
H_edge *edge = e0;
do
{
    edge = edge -> next;
    output(edge->pair->face);
} while (edge != e0);
```

In Listing 8.5, if we replace the output statement with `output (edge->pair->vert)`, we get all the vertices in the one-ring neighbourhood of the given vertex. Likewise, the method with `output(edge->face)` returns all faces that share the vertex. The half-edge data structure provides a convenient tool for enumerating all faces that are adjacent to a given face (Listing 8.6).

An edge data structure links together adjacency information pertaining to vertices, faces and neighbouring edges. The removal of an edge from a polygon calls for an update of this information by way of readjusting references to the deleted edge and adjacent faces. As an example, if the edge *PQ* of the polygonal face shown in Fig. 8.15 is removed, several edges along the boundary of the resulting polygon will need to be updated. Listing 8.7 provides the list of "tidy-up" operations required after removing *PQ*. Even though the edges marked '*a*', '*b*', '*c*', '*d*' in Fig. 8.15 can be indirectly referenced through either e_1 or e_2, separate variable declarations for each of these edges are used in Listing 8.7 for better clarity.

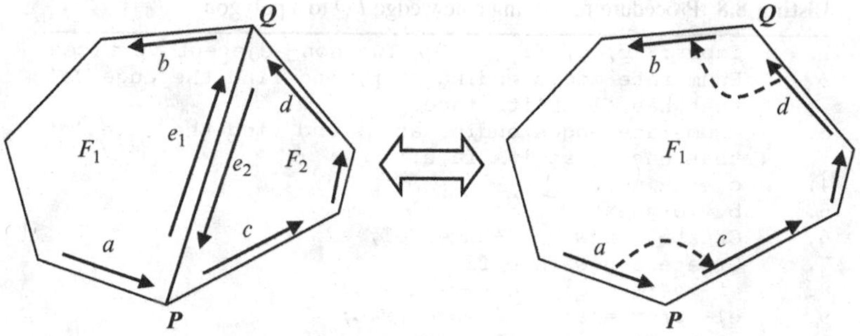

Fig. 8.15 Readjustments to pointers/references are required when an edge is removed

Listing 8.7 Pseudo code for finding all edges through a vertex in anticlockwise order

```
1.     Input:   e1      //The edge and its pair to be removed
2.     e2 = e1->pair;
3.     f1 = e1->face;
4.     f2 = e2->face;
5.     a = e1->prev;
6.     b = e1->next;
7.     c = e2->next;
8.     d = e2->prev;
9.     q = e1->vert;
10.    p = e2->vert;
11.    a->next = c;
12.    c->prev = a;
13.    b->prev = d;
14.    d->next = b;
15.    p->edge = a;
16.    q->edge = d;
17.    if(f1->edge == e1) f1->edge = a;
18.    if(p->edge == e2) p->edge = a;
19.    if(q->edge == e1) q->edge = d;
20.    edge = a;
21.    while (edge != d)
22.    {
23.        edge = edge->next;
24.        edge->face = f1;
25.    }
```

We now consider the inverse of the process discussed above, where a new edge is introduced into a polygon, splitting the polygon into two separate polygons. This process is commonly used for incrementally triangulating an arbitrary polygon. With reference to Fig. 8.15, the sequence of operations required for adding a new edge *PQ* is given in Listing 8.8.

In the following sections, we consider more complex mesh processing algorithms that use different types of adjacency information.

Listing 8.8 Procedure for adding a new edge *PQ* to a polygon

```
Input:   p, q, f1        //Two non-adjacent vertices
Enumerate edges ending at p, and find the edge 'a'
that has f1 as its face.
Enumerate edges ending at q, and find the edge 'd'
that has f1 as its face.
c = a->next
b = d->next
Create 2 new half-edges e1, e2
Create a new face f2
e1->vert = q;     e2->vert = p;
e1->prev = a;     e2->prev = d;
e1->next = b;     e2->next = c;
e1->face = f1;    e2->face = f2;
e1->pair = e2;    e2->pair = e1;
f2->edge = d;
a->next = e1;   d->next = e2;
b->prev = e1;   c->prev = e2;
edge = c;
do
{
    edge->face = f2;
    edge = edge->next;
} while (edge != e2);
```

8.4 Mesh Simplification

Mesh simplification algorithms aim to reduce the geometric complexity of a mesh without altering the essential shape characteristics. These methods are designed to take meshes containing a large number of polygons and convert them into meshes with a relatively smaller number of polygons. Mesh simplification is commonly used in the construction of level-of-detail representations of objects with a high polygon count. Most of the algorithms try to preserve the topology of the mesh by making sure that the resulting mesh has the same Euler characteristic (Eq. 8.1). In this section, we outline two important methods based on the local simplification strategy that progressively remove vertices or edges until the required level of simplification is achieved. In general, simplification methods will use a cost function to select the most appropriate vertex or edge for removal, and also have a set of constraints which the selected item is required to satisfy.

8.4.1 Vertex Decimation

The vertex decimation algorithm iteratively removes vertices from a triangular mesh, at the same time trying to preserve the topology and the shape of the original mesh. When a vertex is removed, its one-ring neighbourhood will need to be re-triangulated. The selection of a vertex for removal is generally based on a decimation criterion that ensures that important shape features of the mesh are not affected.

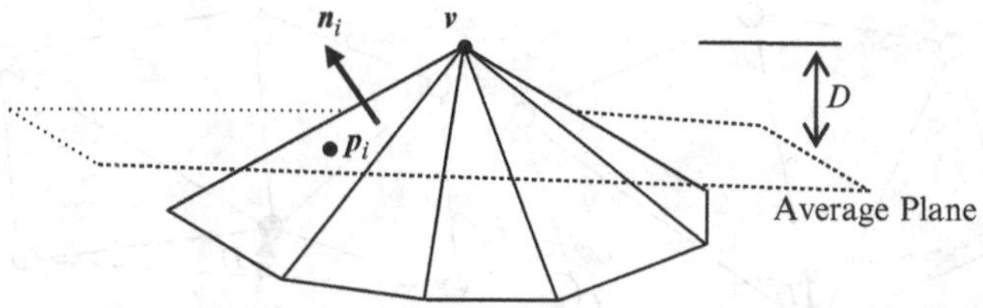

Fig. 8.16 Definition of the average plane of a set of triangles sharing a vertex

One of the commonly used criteria for vertex decimation is the near-planarity of the neighbourhood of a vertex. A nearly planar region could be represented by a few large triangular elements covering the region instead of several small triangles. Consider an interior vertex $\boldsymbol{v}$ surrounded by a closed triangle fan as shown in Fig. 8.16. The planarity of the surface region around the vertex can be measured as a distance d of the vertex from an average plane of its neighbourhood. The average plane is formed by the local area-weighted average of the surface normal vectors $\boldsymbol{n}_i$ and the centroids $\boldsymbol{p}_i$ of all triangles sharing the vertex $\boldsymbol{v}$. If there are k triangles that have a common vertex $\boldsymbol{v}$, and if A_i, $\boldsymbol{n}_i$, $\boldsymbol{p}_i$ denote the area, normal vector and the centroid respectively of the ith triangle, then the area-weighted average normal and point are computed as follows:

$$\boldsymbol{n}_{avg} = \frac{\sum_{i=1}^{k} A_i \boldsymbol{n}_i}{\sum_{i=1}^{k} A_i} \tag{8.3}$$

$$\boldsymbol{p}_{avg} = \frac{\sum_{i=1}^{k} A_i \boldsymbol{p}_i}{\sum_{i=1}^{k} A_i} \tag{8.4}$$

The average plane is then defined as the plane passing through the point $\boldsymbol{p}_{avg}$, having a normal direction $\boldsymbol{n}_{avg}$. Its equation can be obtained as given in Eq. 2.21, and the shortest distance D of the vertex $\boldsymbol{v}$ to the plane can be computed using Eq. 2.24. The value of D can be used as the cost function for selecting a vertex.

If $\boldsymbol{v}$ is a boundary vertex, the deviation of the boundary segments containing $\boldsymbol{v}$ from a straight line can be used as the error function (Fig. 8.17). This is measured as the shortest distance D of the vertex from an imaginary line connecting the two opposite neighbours of the vertex along the boundary. These neighbouring vertices are connected to $\boldsymbol{v}$ by edges that have only one bordering face, and can be identified using either a winged-edge or half-edge based ring traversal algorithm. The shortest distance D can then be obtained using Eq. 2.16. D is the altitude of the triangle formed by $\boldsymbol{v}$ and its two neighbours (Fig. 8.17).

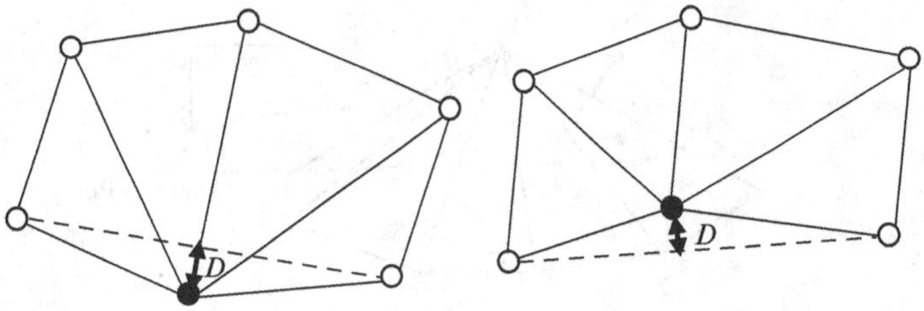

Fig. 8.17 The error metric for a boundary vertex can be defined as the distance of the vertex from the *dotted line* connecting its neighbours on the boundary

The vertex decimation algorithm uses a greedy approach, iteratively selecting the vertex with the current minimum value of the error metric D for decimation. An upper threshold for D prevents all vertices with values greater than the threshold from being deleted. When a vertex is removed, all edges that end at the vertex are also removed and the components of the edges of the resulting polygon are adjusted as previously shown in Fig. 8.15 and Listing 8.7. Two important steps remain in the vertex decimation process before proceeding to the next iteration where another vertex is chosen: the polygon resulting from the removal of the current vertex must to be triangulated (Fig. 8.18), and the error metrics for its vertices must be updated. The one-ring neighbourhood of the deleted vertex will in general form the boundary of a star-shaped polygon. Algorithms for the triangulation of such polygons are discussed later in this chapter. Convex polygons are special types of star-shaped polygons where every internal angle is at most 180°. Convex polygons can be easily triangulated from any vertex, but such a triangulation may not always give the optimal value for the minimum angle of the triangles.

8.4.2 Edge Collapse Operation

An edge collapse is a relatively simpler operation compared to vertex decimation. Here, a local curvature based cost function is associated with every edge, and used for selecting an edge for removal. The edge and its two incident faces are removed by moving one of the edge's end points towards the other, and deleting the second vertex. The result of an edge collapse operation is illustrated in Fig. 8.19, where the edge PQ is collapsed and the vertex Q deleted. Note that the new position of P may in general be somewhere in between the original positions of P and Q. Commonly adopted methods for positioning P are: (a) keep P in its original position, (b) move P to coincide with Q (c) move P to the midpoint of PQ.

An edge collapse operation can be implemented using an edge-based data structure such as the winged-edge or the half-edge. We use the half-edge structure, as it helps in minimizing the amount of restructuring operations needed to the surrounding mesh elements. All references to the vertex P are retained, while

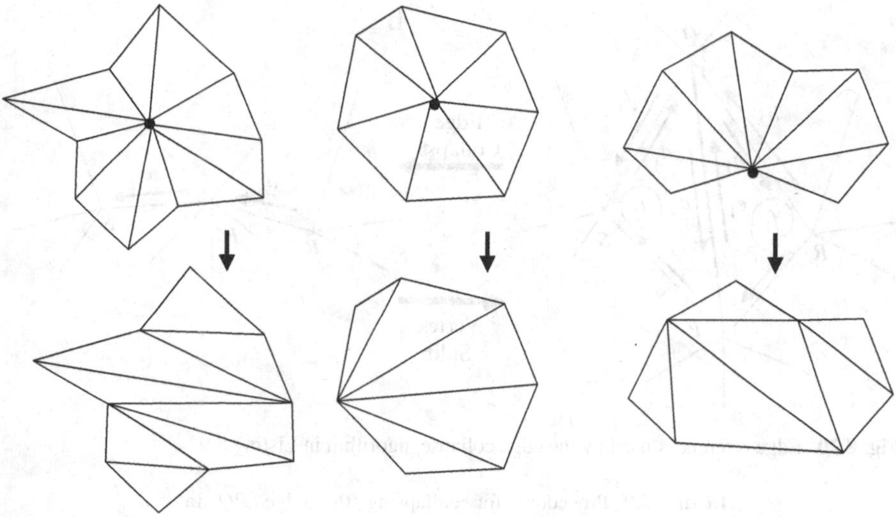

Fig. 8.18 Removal of internal and boundary vertices and the triangulation of the resulting polygons

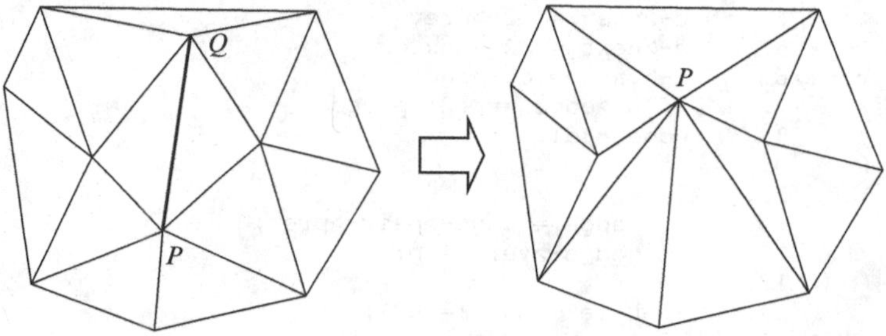

Fig. 8.19 An edge collapse operation performed by moving the vertex *P* towards *Q*

those to *Q* are replaced with *P*. The sequence of steps required by the edge collapse operations are given in Listing 8.9. The references to edges and faces used in the code are shown in Fig. 8.20. The new position of *P* is indicated by the point *P′*.

An interesting aspect of the edge collapse operation is that it is totally invertible. With reference to Fig. 8.20b, given the original positions of *P*, *Q* and also the locations of *R*, *S*, we can reconstruct the edge *PQ* and its two adjacent triangles as in Fig. 8.20a. The inverse process is called the vertex split operation.

The main topological restrictions used by the edge collapse algorithm in selecting edges are shown in Fig. 8.21. The bottom row of the figure shows the result of the edge collapse operation in each of the following cases:

(a) The edge belongs to a triangle whose other two edges are boundary edges. Collapsing this edge results in a topologically inconsistent configuration that contains an isolated vertex.

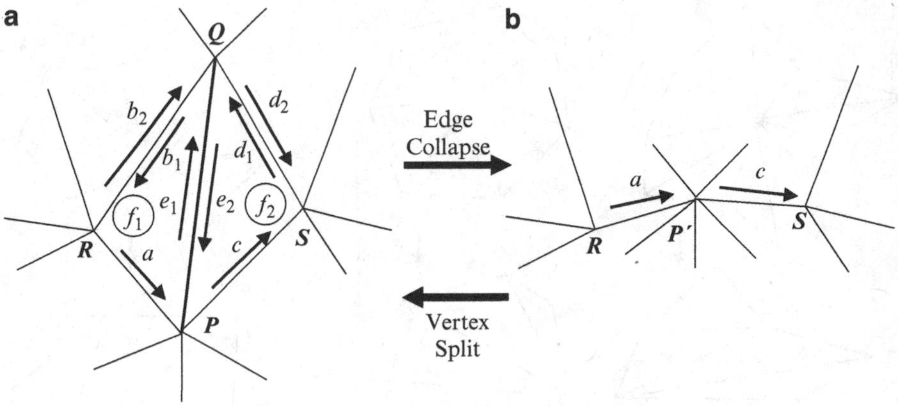

Fig. 8.20 Edge references used by the edge collapse algorithm in Listing 8.9

Listing 8.9 Procedure for collapsing the edge *PQ* in Figs. 8.18 and 8.19.

```
a->prev = b2->prev
a->next = b2->next
a->face = b2->face
c->prev = d2->prev
c->next = d2->next
c->face = d2->face
if(p->edge == e2) p->edge = a;
edge = d1;
do
{
      edge = edge->pair->prev;
      edge->vert = p;

} while (edge != b2);
b2->prev->next = a;
d2->prev->next = c;
d2->next->prev = c;
b2->next->prev = a;
b2->face->edge = a;
d2->face->edge = c;
b2->prev->vert->edge = b2->prev;
c->vert->edge = c;
Update the position of p as required
```

(b) Both vertices of the edge are boundary vertices, but the edge is not a boundary edge. Collapsing this edge results in a non-manifold vertex.

(c) The intersection of the one-ring neighbourhoods of vertices *P* and *Q* normally contains only the opposite vertices *A*, *B* of the edge *PQ*. In the special case shown in the figure, the intersection contains vertices *A*, *B*, *C*, *D*. Collapsing the edge *PQ* removes six faces instead of just two. In a more general case, when *AC* or *BD* is not perpendicular to *PQ*, the operation results in the folding of triangles.

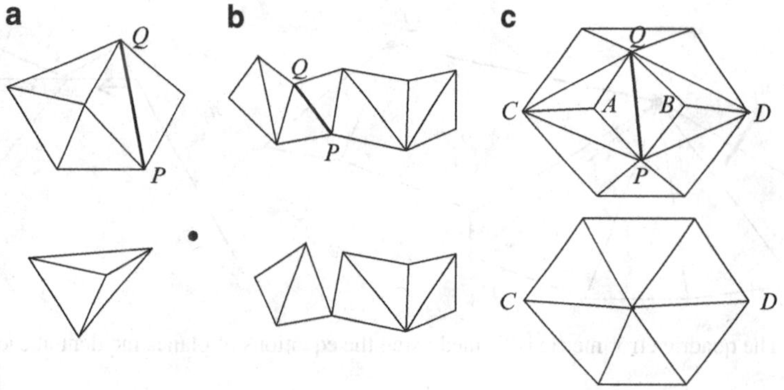

Fig. 8.21 Configurations not suitable for the edge collapse operation

As with the vertex decimation algorithm, we require a cost function for assigning a priority value to edges for removal. The cost function is often designed as a measure of the local curvature and represents the geometric error introduced by the edge collapse operation. A simple cost function is a linear combination of the dihedral angle between the two triangles bordering the edge and the length of the edge:

$$Cost(P,\ Q) = k_1 \cos^{-1}(\boldsymbol{m}_1 \bullet \boldsymbol{m}_2) + k_2|P - Q| \tag{8.5}$$

where $\boldsymbol{m}_1$, $\boldsymbol{m}_2$ are the unit normal vectors of the two triangles and k_1, k_2 are user specified constants. The computation of inverse cosine in the above equation can be eliminated by replacing the function with a mapping of the value of $\boldsymbol{m}_1 \bullet \boldsymbol{m}_2$ from the range $[-1, +1]$ to $[+1, 0]$:

$$Cost(P,\ Q) = k_1 \left(\frac{1 - \boldsymbol{m}_1 \bullet \boldsymbol{m}_2}{2} \right) + k_2\,|P - Q| \tag{8.6}$$

The cost function proposed by Melax (1998) uses the product of the edge length and the local curvature. The local curvature here is defined as the largest dihedral angle between the triangles incident at P and the face of the edge PQ that is on the same side as the triangle. The mapping in the above equation is again used as the approximation of the dihedral angle. If the unit surface normal vectors of the faces incident at P are denoted by $\boldsymbol{n}_i$, $i = 1..N$, and $\boldsymbol{m}_1$, $\boldsymbol{m}_2$ denote the unit normal vectors of the two triangles adjacent to the edge PQ, then

$$Cost(P,\ Q) = |P - Q| \cdot \max_{i=1..N} \left\{ \min_{j=1,2} \left(\frac{1 - \boldsymbol{m}_j \bullet \boldsymbol{n}_i}{2} \right) \right\} \tag{8.7}$$

Another cost function that has been found particularly useful for edge collapse operations is the quadric error metric (QEM). The primary advantage of this method is that the error function parameters can be pre-computed for the original vertices of the mesh, and later used to obtain the cost associated with any edge PQ. This cost

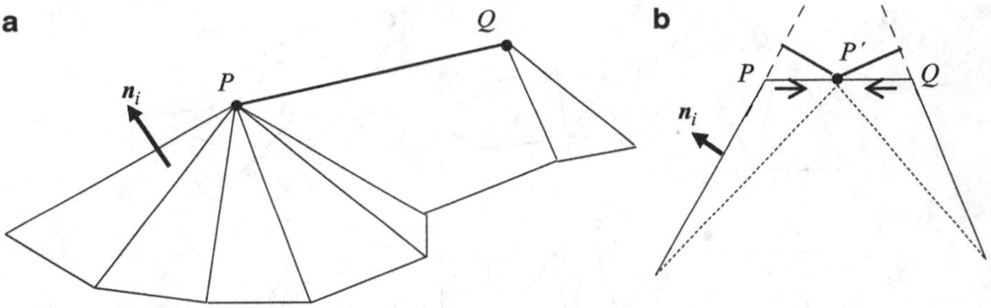

Fig. 8.22 The quadric error metric is defined using the equations of planes incident at each vertex

function is simply the sum of the error metrics at the end points P, Q evaluated using the new position of the vertex P. The following paragraphs describe the computation of this cost function.

Consider an edge PQ as in Fig. 8.22, and assume that this edge is collapsed and P moved to a new position P'. The value of the cost function at P' is the sum of squares of the distances of P' to the planes adjacent to both P and Q (Fig. 8.22b). If $\boldsymbol{n}_i$ denotes the unit surface normal vector of a triangle incident at the point P (x_p, y_p, z_p), then the equation of the plane of that triangle can be written as (see Eq. 2.22)

$$a_i x + b_i y + c_i z + d_i = 0, \tag{8.8}$$

where $(a_i, b_i, c_i) = \boldsymbol{n}_i$, and $d_i = -a_i x_p - b_i y_p - c_i z_p$. The shortest distance of a point $V(x_v, y_v, z_v)$ to this plane is given by (see Eq. 2.25)

$$D_i(V) = a_i x_v + b_i y_v + c_i z_v + d_i = \mathbf{A}_i{}^{\mathrm{T}}\mathbf{V} \tag{8.9}$$

where,

$$\mathbf{A}_i = \begin{bmatrix} a_i \\ b_i \\ c_i \\ d_i \end{bmatrix}, \text{ and } \mathbf{V} = \begin{bmatrix} x_v \\ y_v \\ z_v \\ 1 \end{bmatrix}.$$

The square of the distance of V to the plane is therefore

$$D_i{}^2(V) = (\mathbf{A}_i{}^{\mathrm{T}}\mathbf{V})^{\mathrm{T}}(\mathbf{A}_i{}^{\mathrm{T}}\mathbf{V}) = \mathbf{V}^{\mathrm{T}}(\mathbf{A}_i\mathbf{A}_i{}^{\mathrm{T}})\mathbf{V} \tag{8.10}$$

Thus the sum of squares of distances of V to all planes adjacent to P is given by

$$D_p{}^2(V) = \mathbf{V}^{\mathrm{T}}\left(\sum_{i \in N_p} \mathbf{A}_i\mathbf{A}_i^T\right)\mathbf{V} \tag{8.11}$$

In the above equation N_p denotes the set of all triangles incident at P. The right-hand side of the equation is a quadratic polynomial, hence the name Quadric Error Metric (Garland 1999). The summation within the brackets can be pre-computed for every vertex P and stored. We are now in a position to define the cost function using QEM. If the edge PQ is removed, and if P' is the new position of P, then

$$Cost(P, Q) = D_p{}^2(P') + D_Q{}^2(P') \tag{8.12}$$

In the next section we consider the inverse problem of mesh simplification, and look at a few important subdivision algorithms.

8.5 Mesh Subdivision

Mesh subdivision methods increase the polygon density of a mesh by iteratively splitting polygons and applying a set of rules for repositioning the vertices. Every subdivision step increases the number of edges, vertices and polygons in a mesh without grossly distorting the overall shape or topological characteristics. Mesh subdivision algorithms are used for geometric modelling of complex surfaces from simple coarse meshes through successive refinement, smoothing and approximation. Subdivision algorithms provide us the capability to alter the level of detail of a polygonal mesh from very coarse to highly tessellated and smooth object models. Such methods are therefore also called scalable geometry techniques.

Before considering subdivision algorithms for polygonal meshes, we review the fundamental aspects of iterative polygonal line subdivision.

8.5.1 *Subdivision Curves*

An iterative refinement of a control polygon can be made to converge to a parametric curve by suitably defining the transformations associated with points at each level. Consider a polygonal line formed using four control points as shown in Fig. 8.23. We denote this set as $S^0 = \{P_0{}^0, P_1{}^0, P_2{}^0, P_3{}^0\}$. The superscript indicates the subdivision level, and the subscript the index of the point within the set. At the next level, this set is refined into $S^1 = \{P_0{}^1, P_1{}^1, \ldots P_6{}^1\}$ by adding a new point in between every consecutive pair of points, and also transforming the existing points. Points $P_{2i}{}^1 \in S^1$ with an even index correspond to existing points $P_i{}^0 \in S^0$ at the previous level, while points with an odd index in S^1 are newly inserted points. Figure 8.23 also shows the next level of subdivision S^2. The points at a level $j+1$ are generated from the points belonging to the previous level according to the following equations, also known as refinement rules:

Transformation of existing points:

$$p_{2i}^{j+1} = \left(\frac{1}{8}\right) p_{i-1}^{j} + \left(\frac{6}{8}\right) p_{i}^{j} + \left(\frac{1}{8}\right) p_{i+1}^{j}, \quad i = 1, \ldots N_j - 2. \tag{8.13}$$

Insertion of new points:

$$p_{2i+1}^{j+1} = \left(\frac{1}{2}\right) p_{i}^{j} + \left(\frac{1}{2}\right) p_{i+1}^{j}, \quad i = 0, \ldots N_j - 2, \tag{8.14}$$

where N_j is the number of points in S^j. The number of points in S^{j+1} is then $2N_j-1$. For the example in Fig. 8.23, $N_0 = 4$, $N_1 = 7$, and $N_2 = 13$. The end points of the polygonal line are kept fixed throughout the subdivision process:

$$p_0^{j+1} = p_0^j, \quad p_{2(N_j-1)}^{j+1} = p_{N_j-1}^j. \tag{8.15}$$

As can be seen from Fig. 8.23, when the level number increases, the set of points converges to a continuous parametric curve.

Figure 8.24 shows how three consecutive points at level $j+1$ are computed using three points at level j. The dotted lines correspond to the transformation in Eq. 8.13, and the solid lines to Eq. 8.14. This correspondence between three points can be expressed as the following equation:

$$\begin{bmatrix} p_{2i-1}^{j+1} \\ p_{2i}^{j+1} \\ p_{2i+1}^{j+1} \end{bmatrix} = \frac{1}{8} \begin{bmatrix} 4 & 4 & 0 \\ 1 & 6 & 1 \\ 0 & 4 & 4 \end{bmatrix} \begin{bmatrix} p_{i-1}^{j} \\ p_{i}^{j} \\ p_{i+1}^{j} \end{bmatrix} \tag{8.16}$$

The above transformation matrix can be extended to a 5×5 matrix for five consecutive points. In the above example, each of the existing points was transformed using a convex combination of three points. The transformations can be further generalized using convex combinations of k points:

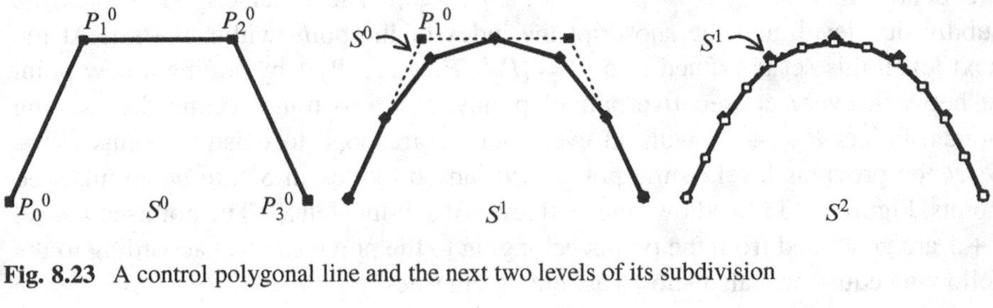

Fig. 8.23 A control polygonal line and the next two levels of its subdivision

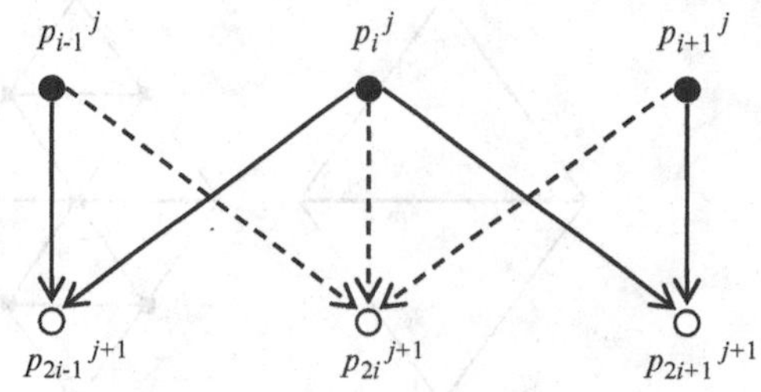

Fig. 8.24 Correspondence between three consecutive points at levels j and $j+1$

$$p_{2i}^{j+1} = \sum_{u=-k}^{k} a_u p_{i+u}^{j},$$

$$p_{2i+1}^{j+1} = \sum_{u=-k}^{k} b_u p_{i+u}^{j}. \tag{8.17}$$

The coefficient sets $\{a_u\}$, $\{b_u\}$ are called subdivision masks. A subdivision mask is said to be stationary if its values do not vary with the subdivision level j. Each set also forms a partition of unity:

$$\sum_{u=-k}^{k} a_u = 1., \qquad \sum_{u=-k}^{k} b_u = 1. \tag{8.18}$$

In the next section, we extend the concepts outlined above to subdivision surfaces.

8.5.2 The Loop Subdivision Algorithm

The subdivision of a triangular polygonal manifold can be performed in a manner similar to the method given in the previous section, by adding a new vertex at the midpoint of each edge, and transforming the existing vertices. The triangular subdivision scheme without the coordinate transformation is shown in the Fig. 8.25. As the subdivision level increases, the mesh immediately tends to become a regular mesh where the valence of every internal vertex is 6. Internal vertices where the valence is not equal to 6 are called extraordinary vertices.

The coordinates of the subdivided mesh vertices are computed using two subdivision masks as seen in the previous section. The first mask computes the coordinates of a new vertex based on a convex combination of existing neighbouring vertices. The second mask transforms every existing vertex using another convex combination of its one-ring neighbours. The Loop subdivision scheme is primarily

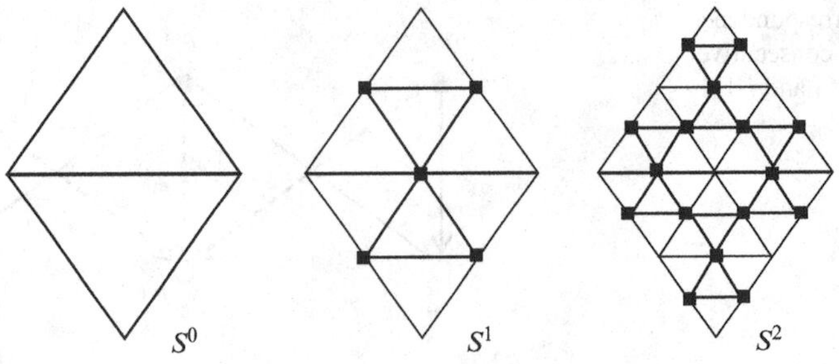

Fig. 8.25 Triangular subdivision scheme

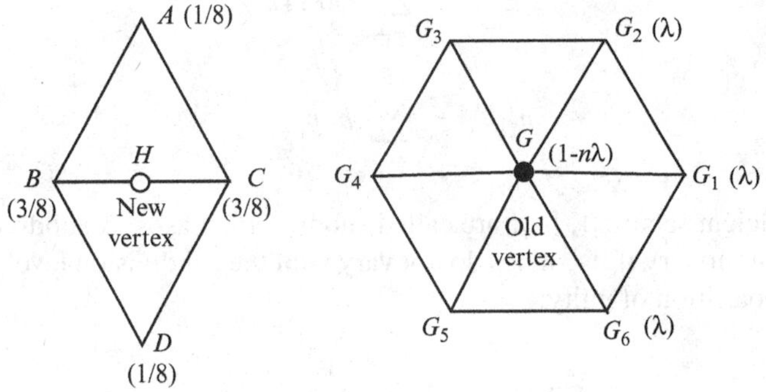

Fig. 8.26 Masks used by the Loop subdivision algorithm

designed for triangular meshes and it uses the subdivision masks shown in Fig. 8.26. Correspondingly, the update equations for points at subdivision level $j+1$ can be written as follows:

Insertion of new vertices:

$$p_H^{j+1} = \left(\frac{1}{8}\right) p_A^j + \left(\frac{3}{8}\right) p_B^j + \left(\frac{3}{8}\right) p_C^j + \left(\frac{1}{8}\right) p_D^j \tag{8.19}$$

Transformation of existing vertices:

$$p_G^{j+1} = (1-n\lambda)\, p_G^j + \lambda \sum_{i=1}^{n} p_{G_i}^j \tag{8.20}$$

where G_i, $i = 1,..n$ are the one-ring neighbours (at level j) of an existing vertex G. The factor λ is chosen such that

$$\lambda < \frac{1}{2n}. \tag{8.21}$$

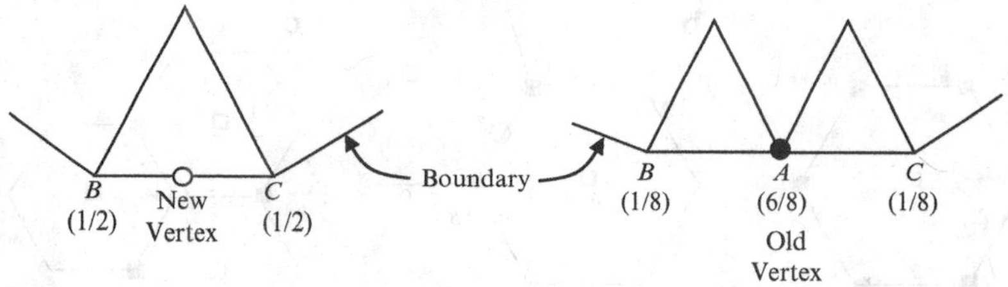

Fig. 8.27 Loop subdivision masks for boundary vertices

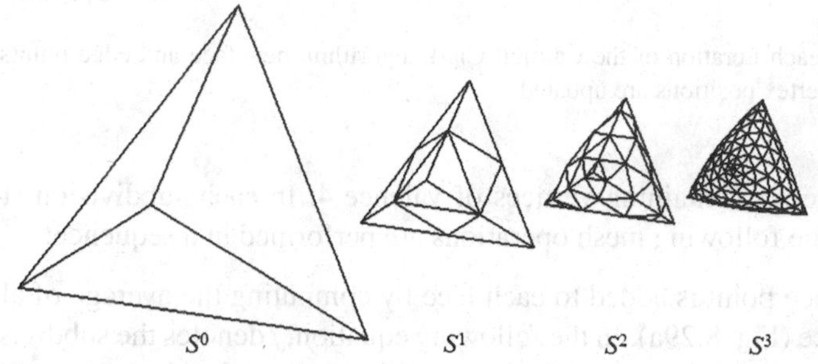

Fig. 8.28 Subdivision of a tetrahedron using the Loop algorithm

The above condition ensures that the weight $(1-n\lambda)$ assigned to the current vertex is greater than the sum of weights $n\lambda$ assigned to its one-ring neighbours.

For a regular vertex ($n = 6$), λ is given a value 1/16. Equation 8.20 then becomes

$$p_G^{j+1} = \left(\frac{10}{16}\right) p_G^j + \left(\frac{1}{16}\right) \sum_{i=1}^{6} p_{G_i}^j \tag{8.22}$$

For boundary vertices, the subdivision masks in Fig. 8.26 are appropriately modified as shown in Fig. 8.27.

The Loop subdivision algorithm can be implemented using a model definition based on vertex and face lists, and a data structure such as the half-edge for obtaining the one-ring neighbours of vertices. The result of the application of the Loop subdivision algorithm on a tetrahedral object is shown in Fig. 8.28. Note that the original vertices of the tetrahedron are the only extraordinary vertices of the mesh as they have a constant valence 3 throughout the subdivision process. All new vertices are regular vertices with valence 6.

8.5.3 *Catmull-Clark Subdivision*

The Catmull-Clark subdivision scheme can be applied to meshes with arbitrary topology, but unlike the previous method, it produces a mesh that consists primarily

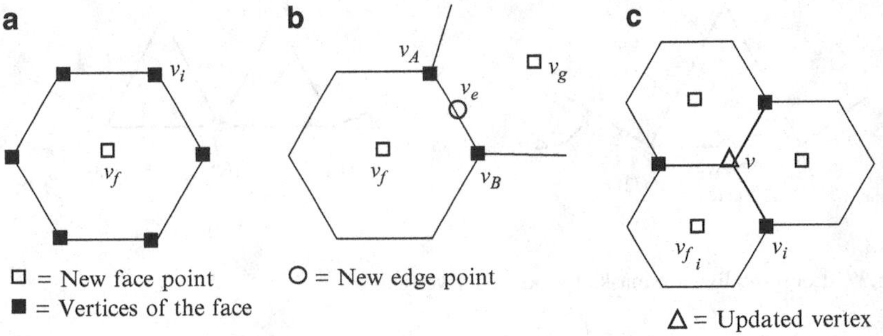

Fig. 8.29 In each iteration of the Catmull-Clark algorithm, new face and edge points are added and existing vertex positions are updated

of quadrilaterals containing vertices of valence 4. In each subdivision step of the algorithm, the following mesh operations are performed in a sequence:

- A new face point is added to each face by computing the average of all vertices of the face (Fig. 8.29a). In the following equation, j denotes the subdivision level, f a face, and n_f the number of vertices of that face, and v_i the vertices of the face. v_f denotes the new face point.

$$v_f^{j+1} = \frac{1}{n_f} \sum_{i=1}^{n_f} v_i^j \tag{8.23}$$

- A new edge point is added to each edge by computing the average of the end points of the edge and the new face points of the edge's neighbouring faces (Fig. 8.29b). In the following equation, the new edge point is denoted by v_e. The edge has end points v_A, v_B, and adjacent faces f and g.

$$v_e^{j+1} = \frac{v_f^{j+1} + v_g^{j+1} + v_A^j + v_B^j}{4} \tag{8.24}$$

- After adding new face and edge points, the position of every old vertex is updated as follows. Let n_v be the number of edges incident at a vertex v, v_i the one-ring neighbours of the vertex v, and v_{f_i} the new face points on the faces surrounding v (Fig. 8.29c). Q_v and R_v denote the average of the new face points and the edge midpoints respectively. The superscript j denotes the subdivision level.

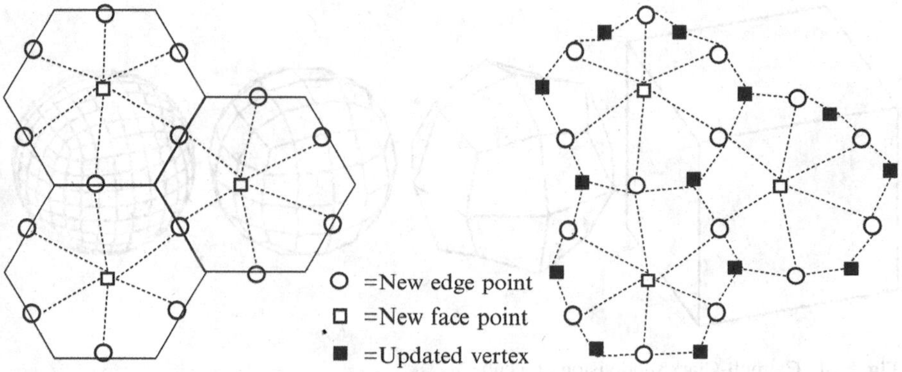

Fig. 8.30 Mesh tessellation after one iteration of the Catmull-Clark algorithm

$$Q_v = \frac{1}{n_v}\sum_{i=1}^{n_v} v_{f_i}^{j+1}$$

$$R_v = \frac{1}{n_v}\sum_{i=1}^{n_v}\left(\frac{v^j + v_i^j}{2}\right)$$

$$v^{j+1} = \frac{Q + 2R + (n_v - 3)v^j}{n_v} \tag{8.25}$$

The vertex update equation in Eq. 8.25 can be viewed as a convex combination of three points Q, R and v^j, with weights 0.25, 0.5, 0.25 for a regular vertex. For a vertex of valence 3, the weights are 0.33, 0.67 and 0.

On completion of the steps outlined above, the mesh is re-tessellated. New faces and edges are added to the mesh by connecting each new face point to every new edge point located around that face (Fig. 8.30a). Insertion of new edge points also splits existing edges. Coordinates of existing vertices as well as the definitions of edges incident at those vertices are updated (Fig. 8.30b).

As seen in Fig. 8.30b, the newly added faces are all quadrilaterals, and all new edge points will have valence 4. Vertices that have a valence other than 4 after the first iteration will continue to have a valence other than 4 in subsequent iterations, and will therefore become extraordinary vertices. The Catmull-Clark subdivision of a cube is shown in Fig. 8.31. The original vertices of the cube always have a valence 3, while all other vertices have a valence 4.

8.5.4 Root-3 Subdivision

The $\sqrt{3}$-subdivision scheme combines a triangle split operation and an edge flip operation to generate a smooth surface from a triangular mesh. The iterative algorithm performs the following two steps in every iteration.

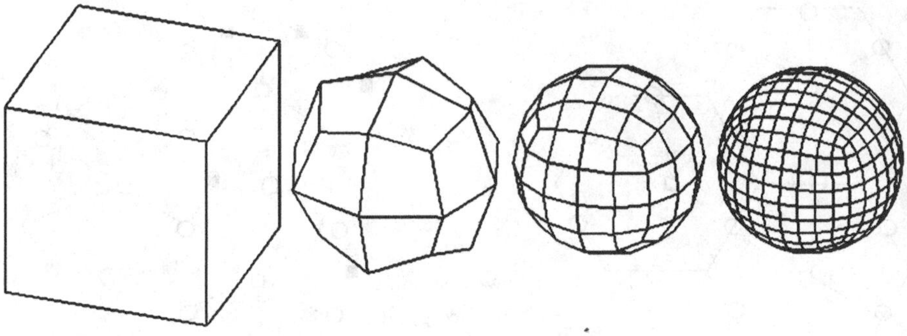

Fig. 8.31 Catmull-Clark subdivision of a cube

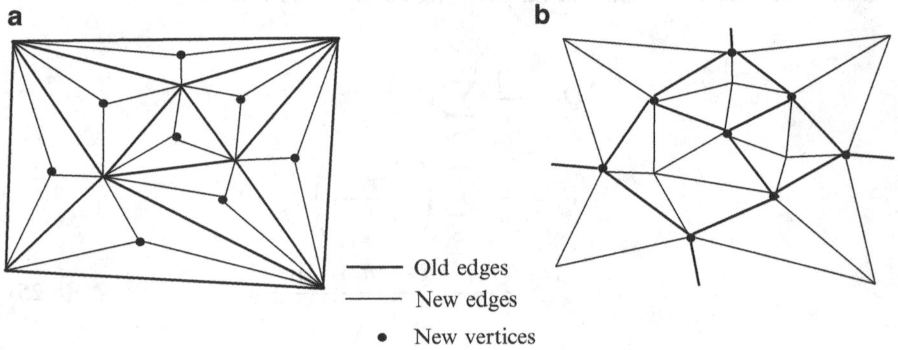

Fig. 8.32 The $\sqrt{3}$-subdivision algorithm divides every triangle into three triangles and flips every old edge

- For each triangle, insert a new vertex at its centroid, and split the triangle into three triangles as in Fig. 8.32a. This operation performs the subdivision of the mesh, increasing the number of triangles by a factor of three in a single subdivision step. The operation also introduces three new edges, one from each vertex to the centroid, along the direction of a median.
- Flip the old edges as shown in Fig. 8.32b. This operation contributes to the smoothing of the mesh.

Applying the subdivision operator twice causes the tri-section of every original edge. The method is therefore referred to as the $\sqrt{3}$-subdivision scheme. An edge data structure which is both non-recursive and much simpler compared to the half-edge structure, containing only references to the incident vertices v_1, v_2, and adjacent triangles f_1, f_2, is particularly useful for this algorithm (Listing 8.10). The edge flip operation can be implemented by simply traversing the edge list, and for each edge (`edge`) creating two new faces (`faceNew1`, `faceNew2`) as in Listing 8.11. After traversing the list of edges, the old face list is deleted and replaced with the list of new faces.

Listing 8.10 Data structure for the $\sqrt{3}$-Subdivision algorithm.

```
struct Edge
{
     Vertex *v1, *v2;     //start and end vertices
     Face   *f1, *f2;     //left and right faces
};
struct Vertex
{
      float x, y, z;
};
struct Face
{
      Vertex *v1, *v2, *v3, *v4;
      Vertex *mid;
};
```

Listing 8.11 The edge-flip operation.

```
Input:  An edge from the list of edges
Output: Two new faces faceNew1, faceNew2
faceNew1->v1 = edge->v1;
faceNew1->v2 = edge->f2->mid;
faceNew1->v3 = edge->f1->mid;
faceNew2->v1 = edge->f1->mid;
faceNew2->v2 = edge->f2->mid;
faceNew2->v3 = edge->v2;
```

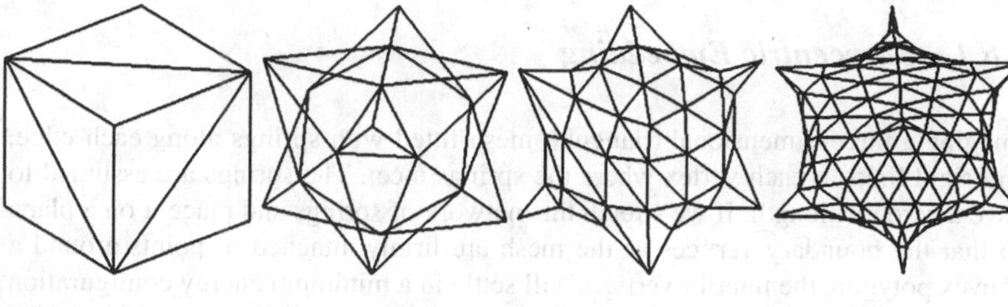

Fig. 8.33 Three iterations of the application of $\sqrt{3}$-subdivision algorithm on a cube model

The application of the $\sqrt{3}$-subdivision method on the triangular mesh model of a cube is shown in Fig. 8.33.

8.6 Mesh Parameterization

Mesh parameterization can be broadly defined as the process of generating a mapping of points in a three-dimensional mesh to points belonging to a simpler parametric domain. A parameterization typically associates a unique two-dimensional point to every vertex, thus establishing a mapping from a subset of $\Re^3$ to a subset of $\Re^2$. The two-dimensional domain could simply be a region of a plane, or in a more general case a set of parametric coordinates defined on another surface such as a sphere. The mesh is then said to be parametrically embedded in that domain. Mesh parameterization finds several applications in computer graphics such as texture mapping, mesh morphing and re-meshing.

One of the primary goals of parameterization is to achieve a one-to-one and invertible mapping (a bijection). Some parameterizations additionally preserve angles and areas. Angle preserving mappings are called conformal, while area preserving mappings are known as authalic. Triangular meshes that are topologically equivalent to a disc have a simple planar parameterization using piecewise linear mappings. If we can find a one-one correspondence of the vertices $P_i = (x_i, y_i, z_i)$, $i = 1..3$, of a triangle to points $S_i = (u_i, v_i)$, $i = 1..3$ in a plane, then the map f of any point (x, y, z) *within* the triangle is given by the linear function

$$f(x, y, z) = \lambda_1 S_1 + \lambda_2 S_2 + \lambda_3 S_3 \tag{8.26}$$

where $(\lambda_1, \lambda_2, \lambda_3)$ are the barycentric coordinates of the point (x, y, z) with respect to the triangle $P_1P_2P_3$ (Eq. 2.48). The above linear mapping is also shown in Fig. 2.12. The problem of planar embedding for a triangular mesh therefore reduces to the problem of determining the mapping for just the vertices of the triangles. We consider below a physics-based method for obtaining this mapping for an open mesh.

8.6.1 Barycentric Embedding

Imagine a three-dimensional triangular mesh fitted with springs along each edge, and rigid links at each vertex where the springs meet. The springs are assumed to have a zero rest length. If we stretch this network of springs and place it on a plane so that the boundary vertices of the mesh are firmly attached to points around a convex polygon, the interior vertices will settle in a minimum energy configuration (Fig. 8.34). We then have a planar embedding of the mesh without any fold-over of triangles.

We denote the map of a vertex V_i (x_i, y_i, z_i) on the mesh by P_i (u_i, v_i), $i = 1..n$. The potential energy of the spring attached to the edge P_iP_j is proportional to the square of the displacement:

$$E_{ij} = \frac{1}{2} K_{ij} \left\| P_i - P_j \right\|^2 \tag{8.27}$$

where K_{ij} is the spring constant. For any point P_i, if N_i denotes the set of indices of its one-ring neighbours, the sum of potential energies of all edges incident at P_i is given by

$$E(P_i) = \frac{1}{2} \sum_{j \in N_i} K_{ij} \left\| P_i - P_j \right\|^2, \; i = 1 \ldots n. \tag{8.28}$$

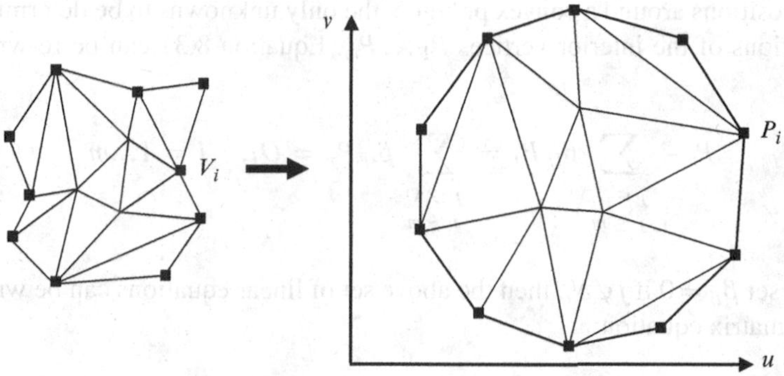

Fig. 8.34 Planar embedding of a mesh

The total potential energy of the system is obtained by adding up the above values for every vertex. We note that every edge is counted twice in the summation and therefore we further multiply the result by half.

$$E = \frac{1}{4} \sum_{i} \sum_{j \in N_i} K_{ij} \left\| P_i - P_j \right\|^2 \tag{8.29}$$

For the minimum energy configuration, the partial derivatives of the above expression with respect to the variable P_i must be zero. Hence

$$\sum_{j \in N_i} K_{ij} (P_i - P_j) = 0. \tag{8.30}$$

From the above equation, we get

$$P_i = \sum_{j \in N_i} \beta_{ij} P_j, \; i = 1 \ldots n. \tag{8.31}$$

where

$$\beta_{ij} = \frac{K_{ij}}{\sum\limits_{r \in N_i} K_{ir}} \tag{8.32}$$

Since K_{ij}s are all positive and there are at least two edges incident at a vertex, we have $0 < \beta_{ij} < 1$ for all $j \in N_i$. Thus Eq. 8.31 expresses P_i as a convex combination of its one-ring neighbours in the planar domain. Let the boundary vertices be given by $P_{m+1}, \ldots P_n$ for some value of $m < n$. Since these vertices are fixed at known positions around a convex polygon, the only unknowns to be determined are the locations of the interior vertices $P_1 \ldots P_m$. Equation 8.31 can be re-written as follows:

$$P_i - \sum_{\substack{j \in N_i \\ j \le m}} \beta_{ij} P_j = \sum_{\substack{j \in N_i \\ j > m}} \beta_{ij} P_j = Q_i, \quad i = 1, ..m. \tag{8.33}$$

If we set $\beta_{ij} = 0$ if $j \notin N_i$, then the above set of linear equations can be written as a single matrix equation:

$$\begin{bmatrix} 1 & -\beta_{12} & \cdots & -\beta_{1m} \\ -\beta_{21} & 1 & \cdots & -\beta_{2m} \\ \cdots & \cdots & \cdots & \cdots \\ -\beta_{m1} & -\beta_{m2} & \cdots & 1 \end{bmatrix} \begin{bmatrix} P_1 \\ P_2 \\ \vdots \\ P_m \end{bmatrix} = \begin{bmatrix} Q_1 \\ Q_2 \\ \vdots \\ Q_m \end{bmatrix} \tag{8.34}$$

The above equation in fact represents two equations in u and v coordinates of the interior points P_i. Since $0 \le \beta_{ij} < 1$, the $m \times m$ matrix in the above equation is diagonally dominant as well as non-singular. The planar locations of the interior points are therefore given by

$$\begin{bmatrix} P_1 \\ P_2 \\ \vdots \\ P_m \end{bmatrix} = \begin{bmatrix} 1 & -\beta_{12} & \cdots & -\beta_{1m} \\ -\beta_{21} & 1 & \cdots & -\beta_{2m} \\ \cdots & \cdots & \cdots & \cdots \\ -\beta_{m1} & -\beta_{m2} & \cdots & 1 \end{bmatrix}^{-1} \begin{bmatrix} Q_1 \\ Q_2 \\ \vdots \\ Q_m \end{bmatrix} \tag{8.35}$$

Box 8.4 Commonly Used Expressions for Spring Constants (Edge Weights) K_{ij}

Wachspress Metric:

$$K_{ij} = \frac{\cot \psi_{ji} + \cot \phi_{ij}}{r_{ij}^2}$$

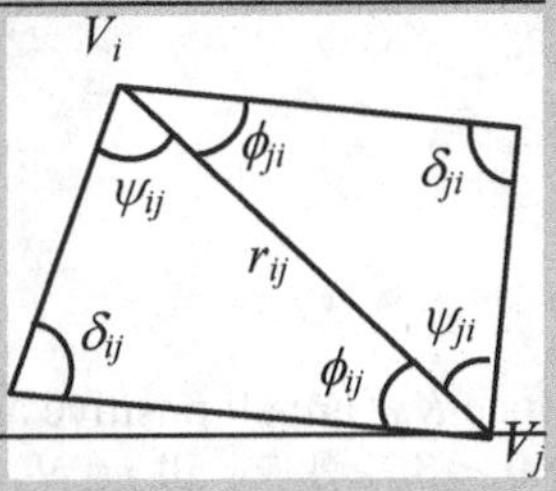

Discrete Harmonic Metric:

$$K_{ij} = \cot\delta_{ij} + \cot\delta_{ji}$$

Mean Value Metric:

$$K_{ij} = \frac{\tan\left(\frac{\psi_{ij}}{2}\right) + \tan\left(\frac{\phi_{ji}}{2}\right)}{r_{ij}}$$

The values of $Q_1, \ldots Q_m$ can be pre-computed using Eq. 8.33. A simple choice for β_{ij} is

$$\beta_{ij} \begin{cases} 0, & if \;\; j \notin N_i \\ \frac{1}{|N_i|}, & if \;\; j \in N_i \end{cases} \tag{8.36}$$

The above setting is equivalent to assigning a unit value for all spring constants ($K_{ij} = 1$, for $j \in N_i$, for all i). This also implies that for a given i, the value of β_{ij}s are all equal and independent of j. The position of a vertex relative to its neighbours is thus ignored. In fact, Eq. 8.31 places P_i at the barycentric centre of the closed polygon formed by its one-ring neighbours. Also note that the definition of β_{ij} is not symmetric, i.e., $\beta_{ij} \neq \beta_{ji}$. A few other commonly used metrics for K_{ij} are listed in Box 8.4. These metrics capture information about the geometry of the mesh surrounding an edge using distances and angles within the triangles that border the edge. For each metric, the values of K_{ij} are further normalized using Eq. 8.32 to obtain the corresponding values of β_{ij}. The metrics are defined using the angles within the adjacent triangles of the edge V_iV_j of the original mesh.

The inverse of the matrix in Eq. 8.35 can be computed easily for simple meshes only, when m is small. For large values of m, we can solve the system iteratively by either Jacobi or Gauss-Seidel methods. Rewriting Eq. 8.33 as an update equation for P_i in the $(k+1)^{\text{th}}$ iteration in terms of the values of P_j in the previous iteration k, we have the following solution based on the Jacobi method:

$$P_i^{(k+1)} = Q_i + \sum_{\substack{j \in N_i \\ j \leq m}} \beta_{ij} P_j^{(k)}, \quad i = 1, ..m, \quad k = 0, 1, \ldots \tag{8.37}$$

The Gauss-Seidel method uses the updated values of $P_1, \ldots, P_{i-1}$ and the previous values $P_{i+1}, \ldots P_m$ to update P_i:

$$P_i^{(k+1)} = Q_i + \sum_{\substack{j \in N_i \\ j < i \leq m}} \beta_{ij} P_j^{(k+1)} + \sum_{\substack{j \in N_i \\ i < j \leq m}} \beta_{ij} P_j^{(k)}, \; i = 1, ..m, \; k = 0, 1, \ldots \tag{8.38}$$

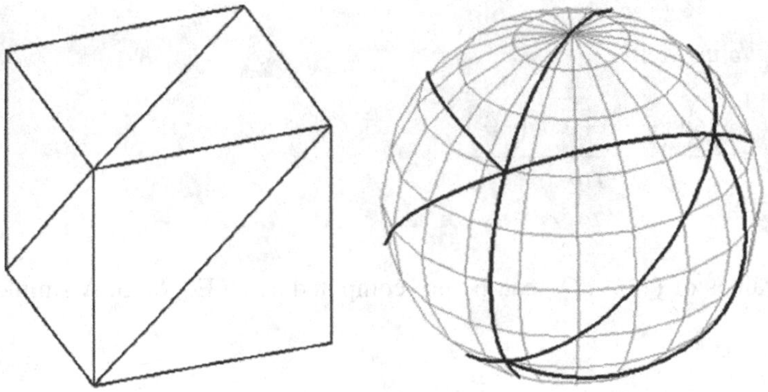

Fig. 8.35 Spherical embedding of a triangular mesh

The advantage of the Gauss-Seidel method over Jacobi method is that the values of P_i can be sequentially updated in place within the same list without having to maintain two separate lists for the previous and the updated values. In both the above cases, a convergence criterion is used to determine when the iteration must stop:

$$\left| P_i^{(k+1)} - P_i^{(k)} \right| < \varepsilon \qquad i = 1, ..m, \quad k = 0, 1, \ldots \tag{8.39}$$

where ε is a user specified threshold that is independent of i.

8.6.2 Spherical Embedding

The methods presented in the previous section are suitable for open manifold meshes. A closed manifold mesh, on the other hand, is topologically equivalent to a sphere, and therefore the natural parameterization domain for such meshes is a sphere. A spherical embedding generates a mapping of vertices of a closed mesh to points on a sphere. As a consequence, triangles of the mesh get mapped to spherical triangles (Fig. 8.35). For a triangular mesh, the mapped set of spherical triangles must form a partition of the sphere. The embedding associates a pair of spherical coordinates (α, δ), $0 \le \alpha \le 2\pi$, $-\pi/2 \le \delta \le \pi/2$, with every three-dimensional vertex of the mesh.

For geometrically simple closed meshes centred at the origin, the vertices can be directly projected to the surface of a unit sphere using coordinate normalization. The spherical coordinates are then extracted from the normalized coordinates (u_i, v_i, w_i) using the following equations:

$$\alpha_i = \tan^{-1}\left(\frac{u_i}{w_i}\right)$$

$$\delta_i = \tan^{-1}\left(\frac{v_i}{\sqrt{u_i^2 + w_i^2}}\right) \tag{8.40}$$

The above values can be further transformed into the range [0, 1] if they are to be used as texture coordinates. For a general triangular mesh, the iterative solution for the minimum energy equation in Eq. 8.31 can be extended for a mapping onto a unit sphere as follows:

$$P_i^{(k+1)} = (1-\lambda)P_i^{(k)} + \lambda \sum_{j \in N_i} \beta_{ij} P_j, \quad |P_i|| = 1. \tag{8.41}$$

where $P_i = (u_i, v_i, w_i)$, $i = 1..\ n$ are points on the unit sphere, and λ is a damping parameter. The value of λ is usually set to 0.5. The weights β_{ij} are computed using Eq. 8.36. The Gauss-Seidel solver provides the following iterative solution for the above equation:

$$S_i = (1-\lambda)P_i^{(k)} + \lambda \sum_{\substack{j \in N_i \\ j < i}} \beta_{ij} P_j^{(k+1)} + \lambda \sum_{\substack{j \in N_i \\ j < i}} \beta_{ij} P_j^{(k)}, \quad P_i^{(k+1)} = \frac{S_i}{|S_i|}. \tag{8.42}$$

In the next section, we give an outline of another important class of mesh processing algorithms, namely polygon triangulation.

8.7 Polygon Triangulation

Triangles have the property of being the simplest convex and planar polygonal regions. For this reason, triangular meshes are generally preferred to more complex polygonal meshes by applications involving both processing and rendering of meshes. In this section, we consider two important classes of triangulation algorithms:

- Polygon triangulation.
- Point set triangulation.

Polygon triangulation is the process of decomposing a polygon into a set of triangles such that the vertices of the triangles are the same as the vertices of the polygon, and no two triangles intersect. In a triangulation of a polygon, the union of all triangles is the complete polygon. An implicit assumption in all polygon triangulation algorithms is the fact that every simple polygon (see next section) can be triangulated. Indeed, every simple polygon with n vertices can be decomposed into a set of $n-2$ triangles.

Point set triangulation is a relatively complex problem of triangulating the convex hull of a given set of points on a two-dimensional plane. The vertices of the convex hull as well as the interior points of the hull are included in the triangulation. We impose the planar restriction here since in a general three-dimensional space, four points can be connected together to form tetrahedral regions that enclose a volume.

8.7.1 Polygon Types

Polygons are the most fundamental blocks in the construction and processing of meshes. The geometric operations that can be performed on a mesh heavily depend on the type of polygons used. In this section, we look at some of the important polygon classes and their commonly used properties.

As mentioned in the previous section, mesh algorithms often restrict polygons to simple polygons. A simple polygon is defined as a closed polygon without self-intersections, and is thus topologically equivalent to a circle. A convex polygon is a simple polygon that satisfies several properties. Every line segment connecting two points within a convex polygon lies entirely within the polygon. The interior angles of a convex polygon are all less than or equal to 180°. Every anticlockwise traversal of a convex polygon either continues straight, or turns left at every vertex. Point inclusion tests and convex hull algorithms use this property. Convex polygons admit simple and straightforward solutions to many processing algorithms. For example, a convex polygon can be easily triangulated from any vertex (the resulting triangulation may not be angle-optimal, though). A regular polygon is a special type of convex polygon that is both equiangular (all angles are equal) and equilateral (all sides are equal). A regular polygon is an approximation of a circle in the sense that as the number of sides is increased, the shape of the polygon tends to that of a circle.

A star-shaped polygon is characterized by the property that there exists at least one point within or on the polygon which is visible to every other point inside the polygon. Specifically, if Γ is a polygon and if there exists a point Q either on or inside Γ, such that for every other point $P \in \Gamma$, the line segment PQ lies entirely within Γ, then the polygon is star-shaped. The set of all points Q satisfying the above condition is called the kernel of the polygon (Fig. 8.36a). A star-shaped polygon can thus be defined as a polygon with a non-empty kernel. The kernel of a star-shaped polygon is always a convex polygon formed by the intersection of the half-planes of all the edges directed towards the interior of the polygon. If the kernel is the interior of the whole polygon, then the polygon is obviously convex. Conversely, for every convex polygon, the kernel is the interior of polygon itself.

We saw earlier in Sect. 8.4.1 that the vertex decimation algorithm generates star-shaped polygons that require triangulation after the removal of a vertex (Fig. 8.18).

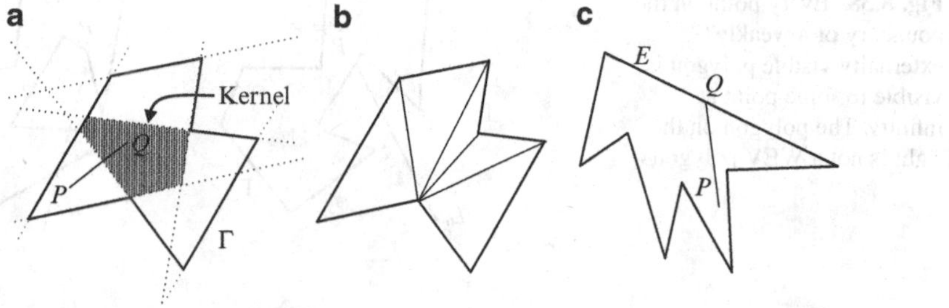

Fig. 8.36 (**a**) The kernel of a star-shaped polygon and (**b**) its triangulation from a vertex inside the kernel. (**c**) An edge visible polygon

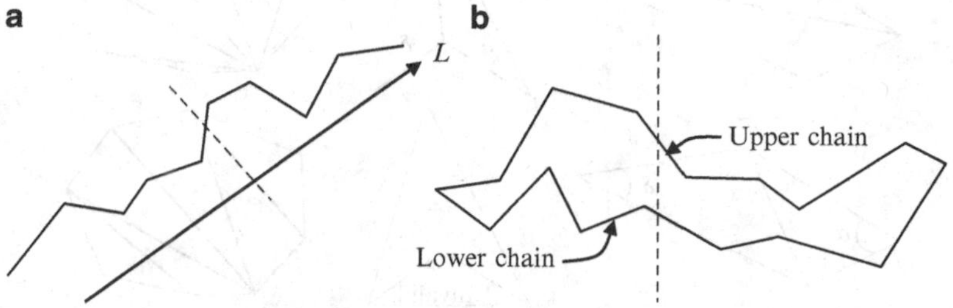

Fig. 8.37 (**a**) A monotone polygonal chain with respect to the line L. (**b**) A x-monotone polygon

If the kernel of a polygon contains a vertex, then the polygon can be triangulated from that vertex (Fig. 8.36b). A convex polygon can therefore be triangulated from any of its vertices. A polygon is said to be edge-visible if there exists an edge E of the polygon such that for any point P within the polygon, there exists a point $Q \in E$ such that the line segment PQ lies entirely within the polygon (Fig. 8.36c).

A polygonal line is called a monotone polygonal chain with respect to a line L if every line perpendicular to L intersects the chain at most once (Fig. 8.37a). A simple polygon is monotone with respect to L if any line orthogonal to L intersects the polygon at most twice. A convex polygon is always monotone with respect to any line on the plane of the polygon. An x-monotone polygon can be subdivided into upper and lower x-monotone chains. The two chains meet at the leftmost and the rightmost points of the polygon (Fig. 8.37b). Starting from the leftmost point, the x-coordinates of the vertices monotonically increase along each chain.

A polygon is called a weakly externally visible (WEV) polygon if and only if for every point P on the boundary of the polygon, there exists a semi-half line L_p that does not intersect the polygon anywhere else. In other words, every point on the boundary of a WEV polygon is visible to some point at infinity (Fig. 8.38). Star-shaped and monotone polygons are clearly externally visible.

Fig. 8.38 Every point on the boundary of a weakly externally visible polygon is visible to some point at infinity. The polygon on the right is not a WEV polygon

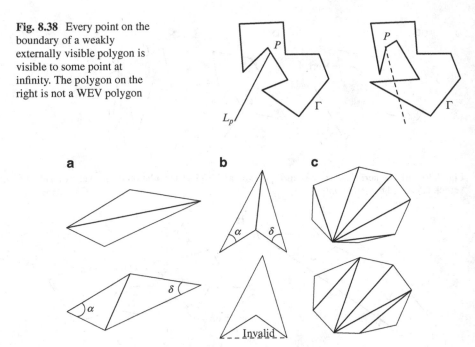

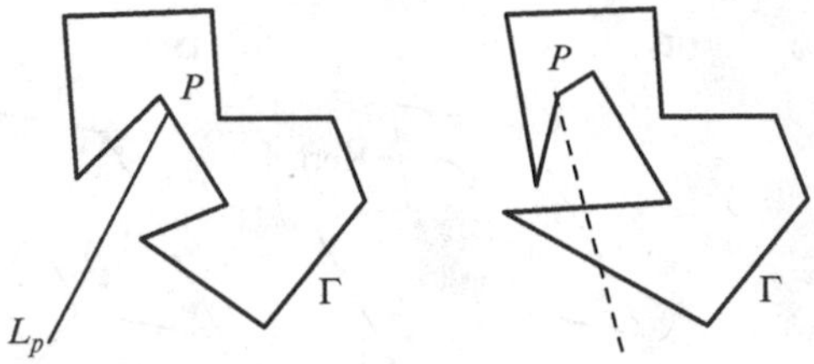

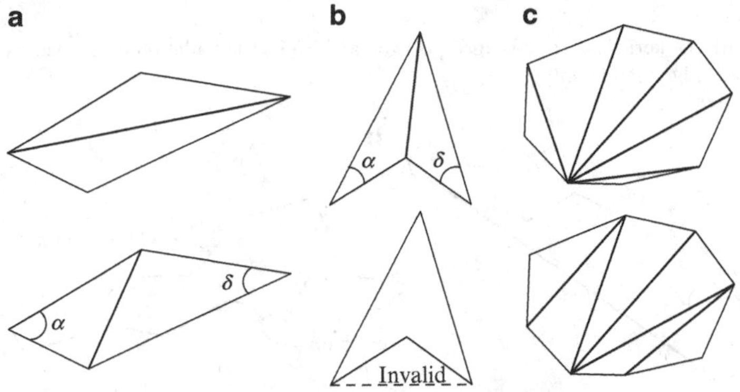

Fig. 8.39 The edge flip operation can be used for producing locally angle-optimal triangulation

8.7.2 Edge-Flip Algorithm

A quadrilateral can be triangulated in at most two possible ways. The triangulation that gives the maximum value for the minimum angle among the two triangles is called angle-optimal (Fig. 8.39a). One triangulation can be obtained from the other by flipping the dividing edge while making sure that the quadrilateral does not contain a reflex vertex. If a vertex is reflex, flipping the edge results in an invalid triangulation (Fig. 8.39b). We saw earlier that a convex polygon can be triangulated from any vertex. To obtain an angle-optimal triangulation we consider every pair of adjacent triangles and flip the common edge if the resulting configuration gives a higher value for the minimum angle (Fig. 8.39c).

In an angle-optimal triangulation, the sum of opposite angles $\alpha + \delta$ is always less than 180° (Fig. 8.39a, b). Such a pair of triangles is said to meet the Delaunay condition. Then, the triangles also satisfy the condition that interiors of the circumcircles of both triangles are point-free. The edge flipping method outlined above can be extended to get an optimal triangulation (known as the Delaunay triangulation) of a set of points. The algorithm incrementally adds points to a set and re-triangulates the set using the edge-flip operation. If a point is added to the interior of an existing triangle, the triangle is split into three, and all adjacent triangles are checked if they satisfy the Delaunay condition (Fig. 8.40a). If the new point falls on the edge of an existing triangle, it is connected to its opposite vertices and the Delaunay condition is checked for the four pairs of triangles surrounding the vertex

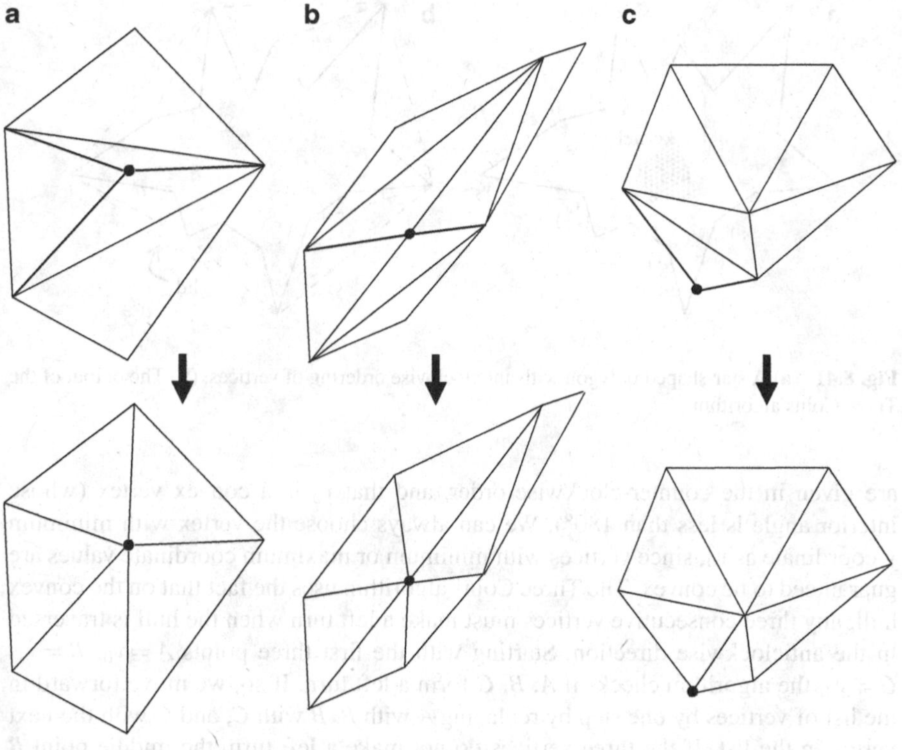

Fig. 8.40 Three different cases of the incremental Delaunay triangulation algorithm

(Fig. 8.40b). If the new point is outside all existing triangles, it is joined to the visible vertices of the convex hull of the set and the affected regions are re-triangulated (Fig. 8.40c). At any stage, the algorithm thus produces the convex hull of the points added so far, along with an angle-optimal triangulation of the hull.

8.7.3 Three Coins Algorithm

The Three Coins algorithm is a versatile and easy to implement method that can be used for finding both the convex hull and the triangulation of a star-shaped polygon. The iterative backtracking algorithm is based on the orientation of three vertices (hence the name "three coins") of a polygon. In a general three-dimensional space, the orientation of three points A, B, C is defined according to Eq. 2.10. On the other hand, if the points are two-dimensional, we use Eq. 2.11 to determine if three points make a left turn.

Let us first consider the algorithm for obtaining the convex hull of a star-shaped polygon with n vertices $v_0, v_1, \ldots, v_{n-1}$ (Fig. 8.41). Assume that the vertices

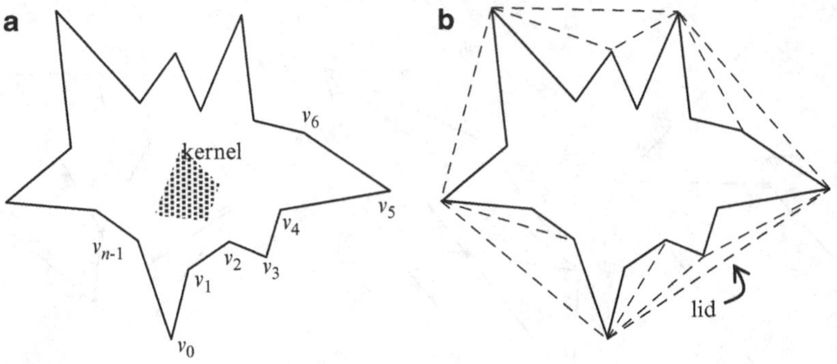

Fig. 8.41 (**a**) A star-shaped polygon with anticlockwise ordering of vertices. (**b**) The output of the Three Coins algorithm

are given in the counter-clockwise order, and that v_0 is a convex vertex (whose interior angle is less than 180°). We can always choose the vertex with minimum y-coordinate as v_0, since vertices with minimum or maximum coordinate values are guaranteed to be convex. The Three Coins algorithm uses the fact that on the convex hull, any three consecutive vertices must make a left turn when the hull is traversed in the anticlockwise direction. Starting with the first three points $A = v_0$, $B = v_1$, $C = v_2$, the algorithm checks if A, B, C form a left turn. If so, we move forward in the list of vertices by one step by replacing A with B, B with C, and C with the next vertex in the list. If the three vertices do not make a left turn, the middle point B is deleted from the list, and we move one step backward. This is done by replacing A with its predecessor, and B with A. For this particular case, before updating the values of A, B, C, we also add a new edge AC. The algorithm can be implemented using a stack S as given in the pseudo code below (Listing 8.12).

The edges added by the Three Coins algorithm are shown as dotted lines in Fig. 8.41b. As seen in the figure, the algorithm finds the convex hull of the star-shaped polygon, and also triangulates each of its pockets. A pocket is an exterior portion of the polygon that lies within its convex hull. Each pocket is a star-shaped polygon bounded by an edge of the convex hull. This bounding edge is called a lid. A pocket is always edge-visible with respect to its lid. It may also be noted that the Three Coins algorithm traverses each pocket in the clockwise direction while triangulating it. We can therefore apply the algorithm for triangulating a polygon that is edge-visible with respect to an edge E, by ordering its vertices in clockwise direction, and initiating the traversal from the second end point of E in the clockwise ordering of vertices (Fig. 8.42a). We denote this vertex as v_0. Initiating the algorithm from a different vertex can lead to an invalid triangulation (Fig. 8.42b).

We saw earlier in Sect. 8.7.1 that a star-shaped polygon can be triangulated from a vertex that lies within the kernel of the polygon. In the most general case, however, the kernel may not contain any of the vertices. Also, it may not be possible to directly apply the Three Coins algorithm, since a star-shaped polygon may not be edge-visible. Before applying the Three Coins algorithm, a star-shaped polygon is split

Listing 8.12 Procedure for the Three Coins algorithm

```
1.      Stack S;
2.      S.push(v₀);  S.push(v₁);      //v₁ on top of stack
3.      k = 1;
4.      while (k < n) do
5.      {
6.            C = vₖ;
7.            B = S.pop();
8.            A = S.peek();
9.            if (points A,B,C are collinear or
10.                make a left turn)
11.           {
12.                S.push(B);  S.push(C);
13.                k = k + 1;
14.           }
15.           else {
16.                Create the edge AC;
17.                if(A == v₀)
18.                {
19.                     S.push(C);
20.                     k = k + 1;
21.                }
22.           }
23.      }
```


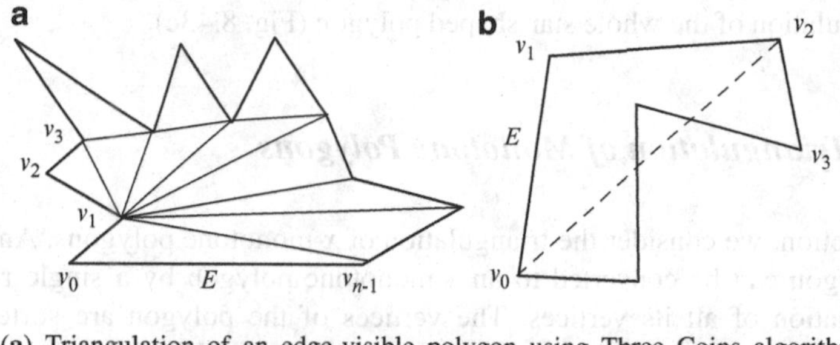

Fig. 8.42 (a) Triangulation of an edge-visible polygon using Three Coins algorithm. (b) An invalid triangulation resulting from an improper choice of the starting vertex.

into two by adding an edge from one of the vertices and passing through some point in the kernel. In Fig. 8.43a, this edge is shown as the line *VP*, where *V* is a vertex and *P* a point in the kernel. This edge intersects the polygon on the other side of the point where a temporary extra vertex *Q* is added. For the vertex decimation algorithm, the vertex selected for removal is connected to every vertex in its one-ring neighbourhood, and therefore belongs to its kernel (Fig. 8.18). Thus the point *P* is readily obtained. The extra point *Q* and the edge *PQ* are removed once both sides of the edge are triangulated.

Since the point *P* belongs to the kernel, the sub-polygons Γ_1, Γ_2 on either side of the edge *VQ* are edge-visible polygons (Fig. 8.43a). By ordering the vertices in the clockwise sense, the polygon Γ_1 can be triangulated using the Three Coin algorithm, starting from vertex *V*. Similarly Γ_2 can be triangulated starting from

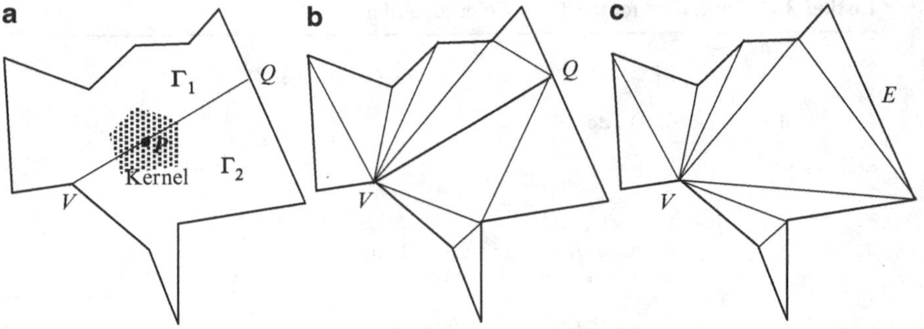

Fig. 8.43 (**a**) A star-shaped polygon is split into two by adding an edge though a vertex V and a point P in the kernel. (**b**) Each sub-polygon bounded by the new edge is triangulated. (**c**) The new edge is removed and the resulting hole is triangulated

vertex Q (Fig. 8.43b). The splitting edge VQ, the temporary vertex Q, and all edges incident at Q are now removed. The hole formed by this operation is actually an edge-visible polygon with respect to the edge to which Q belonged. This is because Q was previously connected to all vertices of the hole. We can therefore invoke the Three Coin algorithm again to triangulate the hole, and this process completes the triangulation of the whole star-shaped polygon (Fig. 8.43c).

8.7.4 *Triangulation of Monotone Polygons*

In this section, we consider the triangulation of x-monotone polygons. Any monotone polygon can be converted to an x-monotone polygon by a single rotational transformation of all its vertices. The vertices of the polygon are sorted in the ascending order of x coordinates. Let the sorted set be $V = \{v_0, v_1, \ldots, v_{n-1}\}$. The left-most vertex v_0 is a convex vertex where the upper and lower monotone chains meet (Fig. 8.44a). Similar to the Three Coins algorithm, the algorithm for triangulating a monotone polygon P also uses a stack S of vertices which is initialized with v_0 and v_1. Vertices are processed in the increasing order of x, and triangulation is done by adding edges from these vertices and splitting off triangles from the polygon wherever possible. The un-triangulated part of the polygon is labelled P'. The vertices stored in the stack at any stage of the algorithm are denoted by $s_0, s_1, \ldots, s_t$, where s_t is at the top of the stack. These are vertices that have been examined, but could not be fully processed, i.e., edges could not be generated from these vertices yet.

The vertices stored on the stack satisfy the following properties:

- s_0 is the left-most vertex of the polygon P' (Fig. 8.44b).
- $s_0, s_1, \ldots, s_t$ are consecutive vertices on either the lower chain (Fig. 8.44c) or the upper chain (Fig. 8.44d) of the polygon P'.
- $s_1, \ldots, s_{t-1}$ are reflex vertices in P'.

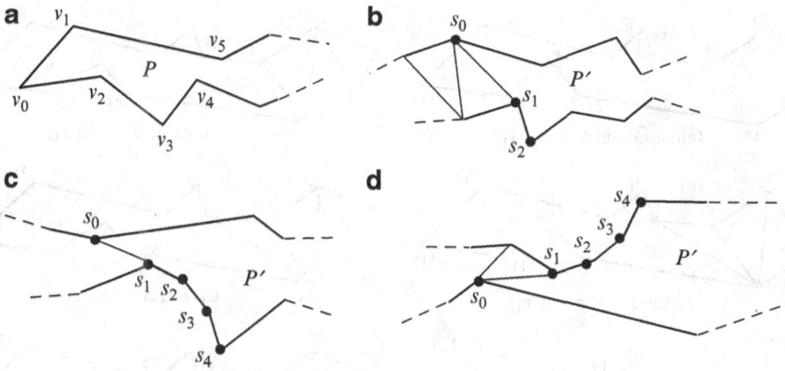

Fig. 8.44 (**a**) Ordering of vertices on an x-monotone polygon. (**b**) Stack vertices form a boundary of the untriangulated polygon P'. (**c**) A sequence of stack vertices on the lower chain. (**d**) A sequence of stack vertices on the upper chain

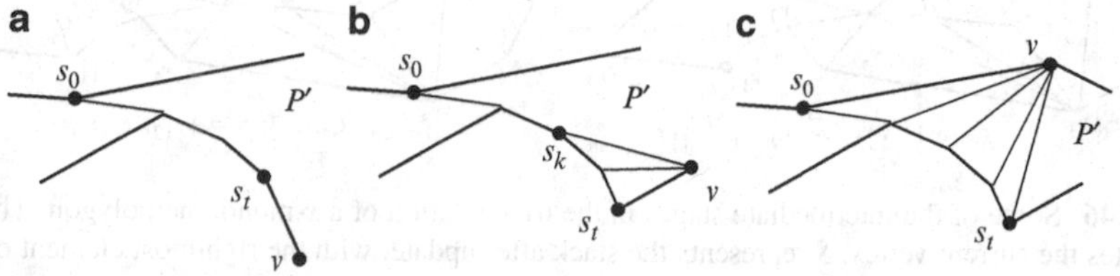

Fig. 8.45 (**a**) None of the stack vertices is removed and v is pushed onto the stack. (**b**) The updated stack contains elements $s_0 \ldots s_k, v$. (**c**) The updated stack contains only elements s_t and v

Since s_t is the last examined vertex, the next vertex $v \in V$ in the lexical ordering will always be on the right of s_t. Depending on the relative position of v with respect to the stack vertices, it will be either stored in the stack (becoming the next top of stack vertex), or used to create edges thereby removing some vertices from the stack. Three possible cases are shown in Fig. 8.45.

- Case 1: v is a adjacent to s_t, and s_t is a reflex vertex in P' (Fig. 8.45a). In this case, edges cannot be created from v, and therefore v is pushed onto the stack.
- Case 2: v is a adjacent to s_t, and s_t is a convex vertex in P' (Fig. 8.45b). At least one stack vertex can be connected to v by an edge. If the angle $s_{k-1}s_kv$ is less than 180° for some k such that $0 < k < t$, then vertices $s_k \ldots s_{t-1}$ can all be connected to v. The vertices $s_{k+1} \ldots s_t$ are removed from the stack, and v is pushed onto the stack.
- Case 3: v is adjacent to s_0 in P' (Fig. 8.45c). In this case, v lies on the opposite chain as the stack vertices and is therefore visible to every stack vertex. v is connected to vertices $s_1, .., s_t$, and all stack vertices are removed from the stack. s_t and v are then pushed onto the stack, with v now on the top of the stack.

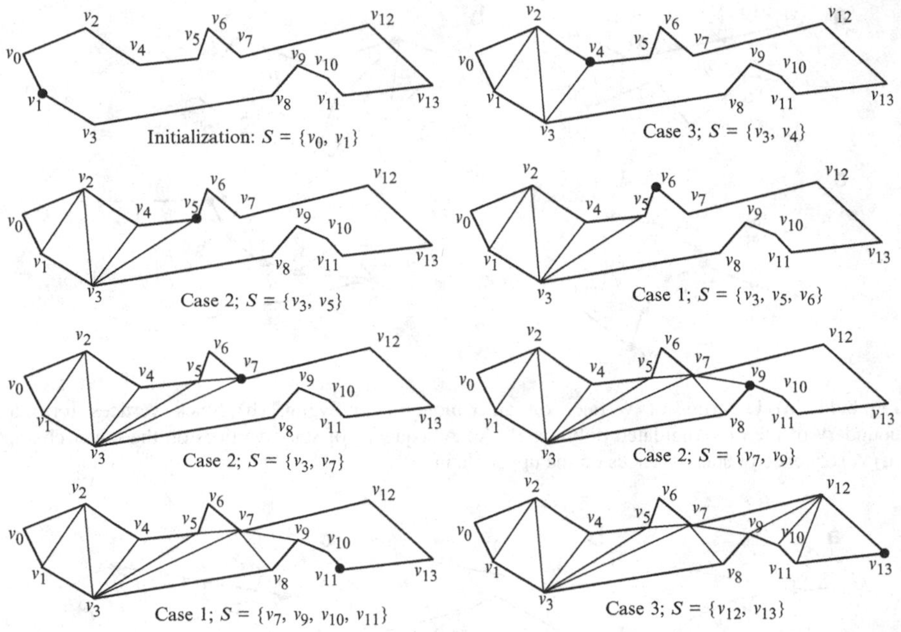

Fig. 8.46 Some of the intermediate stages in the triangulation of a x-monotone polygon. The *dot* indicates the current vertex. S represents the stack after update, with the rightmost element on top of stack

In all the three cases above, the current vertex v becomes the next top of stack element. The algorithm stops when the last vertex v_{n-1} is pushed onto the stack. The process of triangulation of an x-monotone polygon using the above algorithm is shown in Fig. 8.46.

The sorting of the vertices in the pre-processing stage of the algorithm requires $O(n \log n)$ time. After that, each vertex is examined only once and the algorithm performs n iterations. The total number edges added is $n-3$. Thus the triangulation algorithm alone (without considering the pre-processing stage) runs in $O(n)$ time. A pseudo-code of the algorithm is given in Listing 8.13.

8.8 Summary

This chapter outlined the fundamental properties of polynomial manifold meshes, important mesh operations and related algorithms. The chapter began with an outline of ASCII mesh file formats that are easy to create, read and modify. Such file formats are useful for developing and testing mesh processing algorithms with the help of simple polygonal models. Commonly used geometrical and topological properties of meshes were then introduced. The winged-edge and half-edge data

Listing 8.13 Pseudo-code for the triangulation algorithm

```
1.    Sort vertices of the polygon in ascending order of x
2.    Sorted set = {v₀, ... , v_{n-1}}
3.    Stack S;
4.    S.push(v₀);  S.push(v_);        //v₁ on top of stack
5.    k = 2;
6.    while (k < n-1) do
7.    {
8.         v = v_k;                   //Current vertex
9.         s_t = S.pop();             //Top of stack
10.        if(adj(v, s_t))            // v is adjacent to s_t
11.        {
12.             w = S.peek();         //Predecessor of s_t
13.             if(angle(w,s_t,v)>=180)
14.             {                     //Case 1
15.                  S.push(s_t);
16.             }
17.             else
18.             {    //Case 2
19.                  do {
20.                       addEdge(w, v);
21.                       u = S.pop();
22.                       if(S.isEmpty()) break;
23.                       w = S.peek();
24.                  } while(angle(w,u,v)<180);
25.                  S.push(u);
26.             }
27.        }
28.        else
29.        {         //Case 3
30.             u = s_t;
31.             while(not S.isEmpty()) {
32.                  addEdge(u, v);
33.                  u = S.pop();
34.             }
35.             S.push(s_t);
36.        }
37.        S.push(v);
38.        k = k+1;
39.   }
```

structures provide convenient representations of mesh neighbourhood information required for processing adjacency queries and localized geometry operations. The usefulness of both face based and edge based data structures has been demonstrated using examples.

Mesh simplification algorithms are heavily used in applications requiring multiple levels of detail for rendering objects. The vertex decimation and the edge collapse algorithms are iterative methods that progressively simplify a mesh based on a user-specified cost function. These algorithms could be used to reduce the number of vertices, edges and polygons in a mesh while preserving essential topological and shape characteristics. The quadric error metric is commonly used as the cost function for edge collapse operations. Mesh subdivision algorithms iteratively subdivide each triangle or quadrilateral of a mesh and re-adjust the positions of vertices using blending functions. They are used for modelling objects from a base mesh by applying a series of smoothing and approximation operations. The Loop subdivision algorithm is designed for triangular meshes, while the Catmull-Clark algorithm is particularly suitable for quadrilateral meshes. The $\sqrt{3}$ algorithm relies on an edge-flip operation for generating a smooth surface.

This chapter also gave an overview of the process of mesh parameterization using both planar and spherical embedding. Both methods use physics-based models and require iterative solutions of linear systems in the mesh vertex coordinates to obtain the embedding of a mesh in a different domain. The chapter concluded with an outline of polygon triangulation algorithms that could be applied to star-shaped and monotone polygons.

8.9 Supplementary Material for Chap. 8

The section `Chapter8/Code` on the companion website contains the following programs implementing and demonstrating the working of key algorithms discussed in this chapter.

1. **Mesh.cpp**

Additional files:
`Mesh.h`

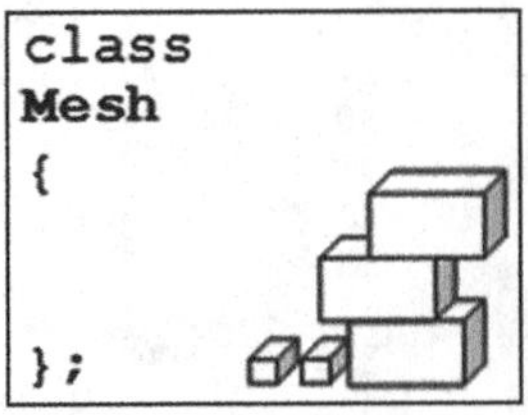

Here you will find the header and implementation files for a mesh class. Mesh data can be read from files stored in OFF and OBJ formats and internally represented using a vertex list and a polygon list. The class supports triangular and quadrilateral polygonal manifold meshes, and a half-edge data structure for storing the connectivity information.

2. **EdgeCollapse.cpp**

Additional files:
`Mesh.h`
`Mesh.cpp`
`mesh.off`

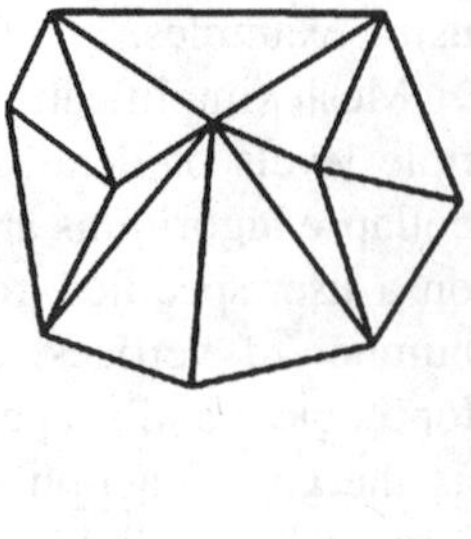

The program shows the working of the edge collapse algorithm described in Sect. 8.4.2. Mesh data is read from the file "mesh.off". The mesh is assumed to be a closed triangular mesh. The edge with the minimum error metric is highlighted in each step. Press space bar to advance to the next iteration.

3. **LoopSubdivision.cpp**

Additional files:
`Mesh.h`
`Mesh.cpp`
`mesh.off`

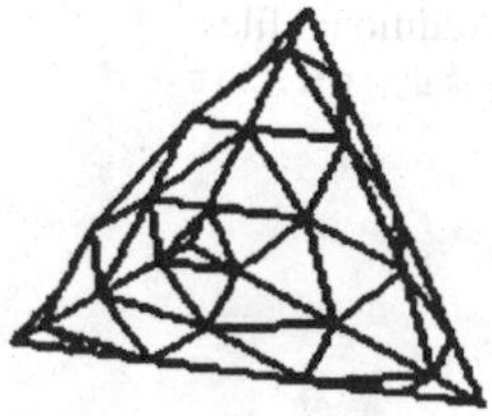

The program demonstrates the working of the Loop subdivision algorithm given in Sect. 8.5.2. Mesh data is read from the file "mesh.off". The mesh is assumed to be a closed triangular mesh. Press space bar to advance to the next iteration. The maximum number of iterations is set at 4. Pressing 'w' displays the wireframe model (default), and 's' displays the solid model.

4. **CatmullClark.cpp**

Additional files:
`Mesh.h`
`Mesh.cpp`
`mesh.off`

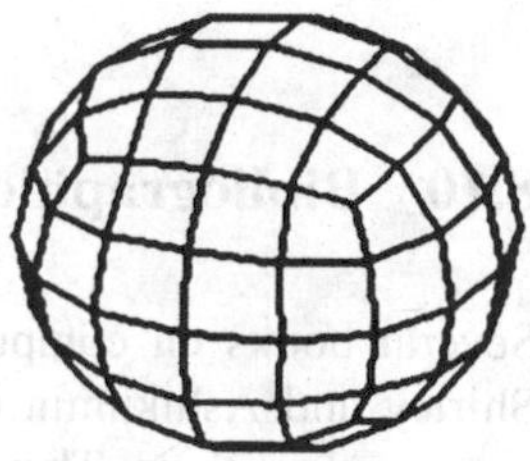

The program performs Catmull Clark subdivision on an input quadrilateral mesh, as described in Sect. 8.5.3. Mesh data is read from the file "mesh.off". The mesh is assumed to be a closed quadrilateral mesh. Press space bar to advance to the next iteration. The maximum number of iterations is set at 4. Pressing 'w' displays the wireframe model (default), and 's' displays the solid model.

5. **Delaunay.cpp**

Additional files:
`none`

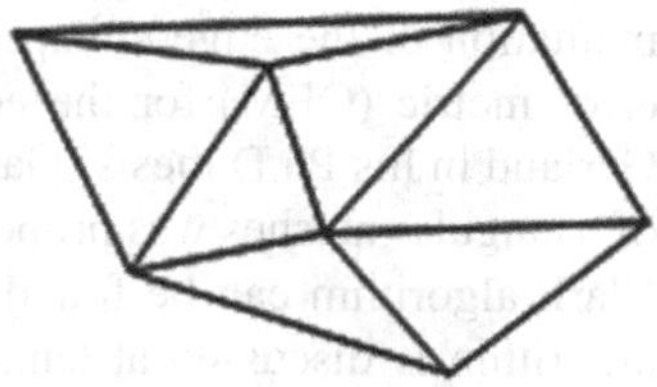

The program generates an incremental Delaunay triangulation of a set of user specified points using the edge flip operation (Sect. 8.7.2). The points are specified interactively using mouse input (left button). The maximum number of points is set at 20.

6. **ThreeCoins.cpp**

Additional files:
`polygon.dat`

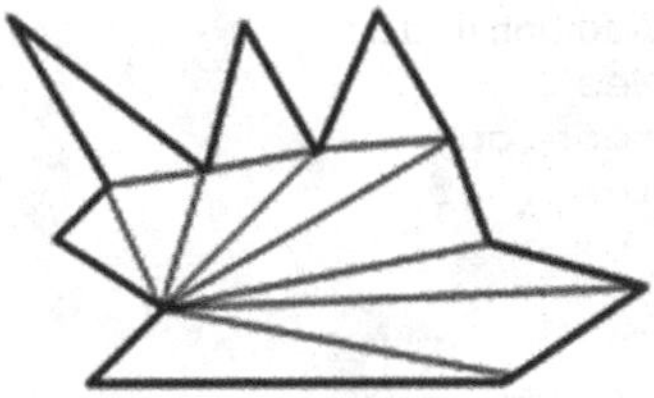

The program demonstrates the Three Coins algorithm by triangulating an edge visible polygon. The polygon definition is read into the program from the file "polygon.dat". The algorithm always starts from the first point in the input vertex list. The user should therefore ensure that the polygon is edge visible, and the first vertex is the correct initial vertex on the visible edge. The vertices are also assumed to be ordered in the clockwise sense. The algorithm may not generate a valid triangulation if any of these conditions is not satisfied.

8.10 Bibliographical Notes

Several books on computer graphics such as Foley (1996), Nielsen (2005) and Shirley and Ashikhmin (2007) give a good coverage of fundamental mesh processing algorithms. There have been a few recent publications (e.g., Botsch 2010; Edelsbrunner 2001; De Loera et al. 2010) that primarily deal with mesh algorithms and therefore serve as excellent references for development and research in this area.

The winged edge data structure was introduced by Baumgart (1972), and several enhancements have since been proposed by researchers for various types of mesh operations. Kettner (1998) gives a detailed description and comparison of edge-based representations of polyhedral meshes. Schroeder et al. (1992) presents the vertex decimation algorithm and its implementation aspects. A simple implementation of the edge collapse algorithm is given in Melax (1998). The quadric error metric (QEM) for the edge collapse operation was introduced by Michael Garland in his Ph.D thesis (Garland 1999). The Loop algorithm for the subdivision of triangular meshes was proposed by Charles Loop (1987). Details of the Catmull-Clark algorithm can be found in Catmull and Clark (1978). The $\sqrt{3}$ subdivision algorithm is discussed at length in Kobbelt (2000). A comprehensive analysis of subdivision algorithms can be found in Zorin (2006).

An introductory paper on mesh parameterization methods can be found in Bennis et al. (1991). Recent papers by Floater and Hormann (2005) and Saba et al. (2005) give an in-depth analysis of mesh parameterization algorithms.

References

Baumgart, B. (1972). *Winged edge polyhedron representation* (C. S. D. Stanford Artificial Intelligence Project, Trans.): Stanford University.

Bennis, C., Vezien, J.-M., & Inglesias, G. (1991). Piecewise surface flattening for non-distorted texture mapping. *SIGGRAPH Computer Graphics, 25*(4), 237–246.

Botsch, M. (2010). *Polygon mesh processing*. Natick: A K Peters.

Catmull, E., & Clark, J. (1978, September). Recursively generated B-spline surfaces on arbitrary topological meshes. *Computer Aided Design, 10*, 350–355.

De Loera, J. A., Rambau, J., & Santos, F. (2010). *Triangulations: Structures for algorithms and applications*. Heidelberg: Springer.

Edelsbrunner, H. (2001). *Geometry and topology for mesh generation*. Cambridge: Cambridge University Press.

Floater, M., & Hormann, K. (2005). Surface parameterization: A tutorial and survey. In *Advances in multiresolution for geometric modelling* (pp. 157–186). Heidelberg: Springer.

Foley, J. D. (1996). *Computer graphics: Principles and practice* (2nd ed. in C.). Reading/Wokingham: Addison-Wesley.

Garland, M. (1999). *Quadric-based polynomial surface simplification*. Ph.D., Carnegie Mellon, Pittsburgh (CMU-CS-99-105).

Kettner, L. (1998). *Designing a data structure for polyhedral surfaces*. In: Proceedings of the fourteenth annual symposium on Computational geometry, Minneapolis, Minnesota, United States.

Kobbelt, L. (2000). *Root3-subdivision*. In: Proceedings of the 27th annual conference on Computer graphics and interactive techniques, 25–27 July 2000, New Orleans, USA.

Loop, C. (1987). *Smooth subdivision surfaces based on triangles*. M.Sc., The University of Utah, Utah.

Melax, S. (1998, November). A simple, fast and effective polygon reduction algorithm. *Game Developer*, 44–49.

Nielsen, F. (2005). *Visual computing: Geometry, graphics, and vision*. Hingham/London: Charles River Media/Transatlantic, (distributor).

Saba, S., Yavneh, I., Gotsman, C., & Sheffer, A. (2005). *Practical spherical embedding of manifold triangle meshes*. In: Proceedings of the international conference on shape modeling and applications 2005, Boston, 15–17 June 2005, Cambridge, MA, USA.

Schroeder, W. J., Zarge, J. A., & Lorensen, W. E. (1992). Decimation of triangle meshes. *SIGGRAPH Computer Graphics, 26*(2), 65–70.

Sheffer, A., Praun, E., & Rose, K. (2006). Mesh parameterization methods and their applications. *Foundations and Trends in Computer Graphics and Vision, 2*(2), 105–171.

Shirley, P., & Ashikhmin, M. (2007). *Fundamentals of computer graphics* (2nd ed.). Wellesley/London: AK Peters.

Zorin, D. (2006). *Subdivision of arbitrary meshes: Algorithms and theory* (Institute of Mathematical Sciences lecture notes series). Singapore: World Scientific.

Chapter 9
Collision Detection

Overview

Collision detection is an integral component of game engines that are designed to provide realistic animations of object interactions with the player and the game environment. Physically realistic dynamic simulations such as flight simulators and mobile robot simulators also require efficient collision detection algorithms. Intersection tests form the backbone of collision detection algorithms. They are also used in ray tracing algorithms, acceleration algorithms such as view frustum culling and portal culling, and in real-time animations. This chapter gives an extensive coverage of methods used for testing if primitives and bounding volumes overlap.

Collision detection in a large scene consisting of several objects requires efficient methods to minimize the number of intersection tests. This chapter discusses the usefulness of bounding volume hierarchies and spatial partitioning trees such as octrees, *k*-d trees and bounding interval hierarchies, and includes a coverage of important algorithms in each category.

9.1 Bounding Volumes

Bounding volumes provide a convenient approximation of the space occupied by a mesh object or a collection of objects for the purpose of intersection testing and collision detection. A set of objects represented by a bounding volume must be contained entirely within the volume, so that if another object does not intersect this volume, it can be readily concluded that the object does not intersect anything within it. Commonly used bounding volumes are axis aligned bounding boxes (AABB), oriented bounding boxes (OBB), spheres, convex hulls and discrete oriented polytopes (*k*-DOP). All of these are closed volumes and have a convex shape. AABBs and spheres were introduced in Sect. 3.4 and their computation was given in Box 3.1 (Sect. 3.4). In this section, we will explore additional properties of these bounding volumes and also consider other relatively more

R. Mukundan, *Advanced Methods in Computer Graphics: With examples in OpenGL*,
DOI 10.1007/978-1-4471-2340-8_9, © Springer-Verlag London Limited 2012

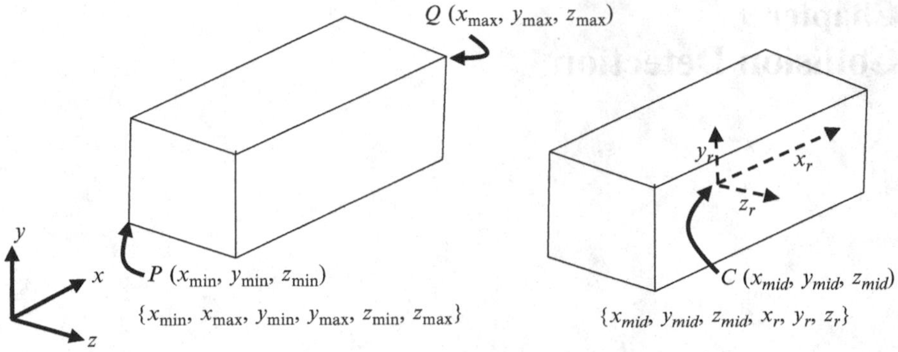

Fig. 9.1 Two different representations of an axis-aligned bounding box

complex geometries. It should be noted that mesh models of bounding volumes are not needed for collision detection algorithms, and therefore only mathematical representations of the regions they enclose are generally used. A mesh model is sometimes created only for the purpose of visualizing an algorithm.

9.1.1 Axis Aligned Bounding Box (AABB)

An axis aligned bounding box is given by six parameters ($x_{\min}, y_{\min}, z_{\min}$), ($x_{\max}, y_{\max}, z_{\max}$) representing the coordinates of two diagonally opposite vertices of the box. The bounding volume can also be defined by its mid point ($x_{\text{mid}}, y_{\text{mid}}, z_{\text{mid}}$) and the three half-width extents x_r, y_r, z_r along the principal axes directions (Fig. 9.1). The advantage of this representation over the former is that any translation of the box can be modelled by updating only the three coordinates of the midpoint, whereas in the former representation all six coordinates would need to be updated.

Given a set of mesh vertices with coordinates $\{x_i, y_i, z_i\}$, $i = 0 \ldots n-1$, we can compute the AABB parameters for the mesh object as follows:

$$
\begin{aligned}
x_{mid} &= \frac{1}{2}(x_{\max} + x_{\min}),\ y_{mid} = \frac{1}{2}(y_{\max} + y_{\min}),\ z_{mid} = \frac{1}{2}(z_{\max} + z_{\min}) \\
x_r &= \frac{1}{2}(x_{\max} - x_{\min}),\ y_r = \frac{1}{2}(y_{\max} - y_{\min}),\ z_r = \frac{1}{2}(z_{\max} - z_{\min})
\end{aligned}
\tag{9.1}
$$

where $x_{\min}$, $x_{\max}$ etc., are computed as given in Box 3.1 (Sect. 3.4).

9.1.2 Minimal Bounding Sphere

A sphere enclosing a set of vertices can be readily obtained by computing the centroid of the points and finding the maximum distance of the points from the

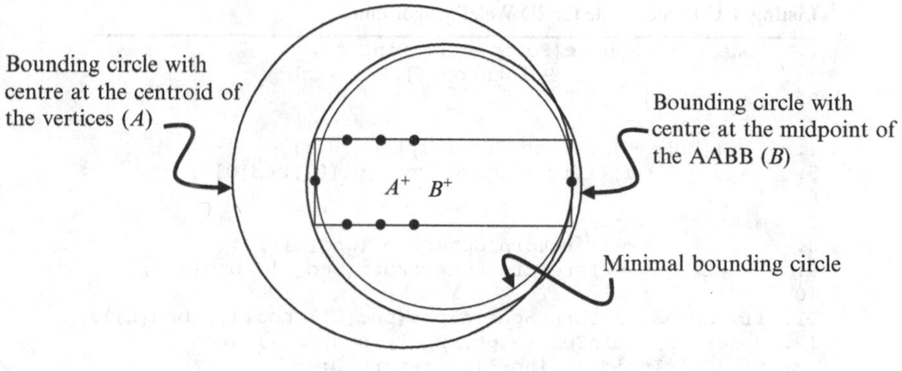

Fig. 9.2 A configuration of vertices for which neither the centroid of the points nor the centre of the AABB gives the minimal bounding circle

Fig. 9.3 The minimal bounding circle is updated to contain the new point on the boundary

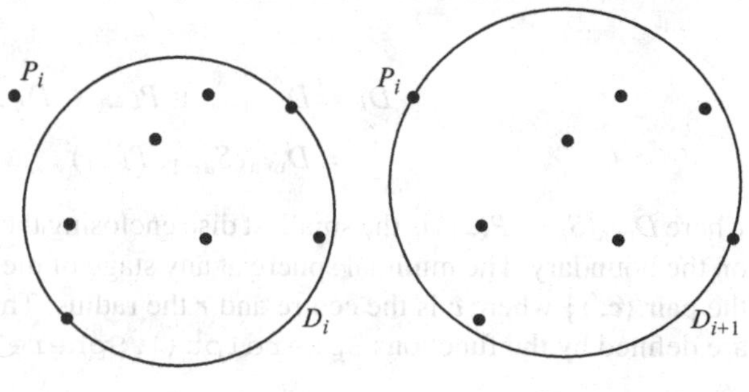

centre. Such a computation can lead to a larger than required bounding volume if the points are distributed unevenly or concentrated at one end of a mesh. Computation of the sphere from the AABB (see Box 3.1, Sect. 3.4) often gives a better approximation of the volume occupied by the mesh vertices. However, the method also does not give the optimal sphere that has the minimum volume. A two-dimensional version of this situation is illustrated in Fig. 9.2.

The Welzl's algorithm is an incremental method for the computation of the optimal bounding sphere of a given set of n points $S_n = \{P_0, P_1, \ldots, P_{n-1}\}$. The algorithm is based on the fact that if the smallest bounding sphere D_i for the points $S_i = \{P_0, P_1, \ldots, P_{i-1}\}$ is updated to include another point P_i that lies outside D_i, the new minimal bounding sphere D_{i+1} must have P_i on its surface. A two-dimensional example is given in Fig. 9.3.

The implementation of the Welzl's algorithm as a recursive function is given as a pseudo-code in Listing 9.1. The function is invoked as `minSphere(S, n, B, 0);` where the variable `S` represents the set S_n, and `B` is a set of boundary points which is initially empty. As shown below, the minimum sphere D_k is defined in terms of the minimum sphere D_{k-1} for $k-1$ points, with the point P_{k-1} removed. The initial value of k is n.

Listing 9.1 Pseudo code for 2D Welzl's algorithm

```
Sphere minSphere(Point pt[], int np,
                      Points bnd[],   int nb)
if (np==1)
{
   if (nb==0) return Sphere1pt(pt[0]);
   if (nb==1) return Sphere2pts(pt[0],bnd[0]);
}
else if(np==0)
     if (nb==1) return Sphere1pt(bnd[0]);
     if (nb==2) return Sphere2pts(bnd[0], bnd[1]);
}
if (nb==3) return Sphere3pts(bnd[0], bnd[1], bnd[2]);
Sphere D = minSphere(pt, np-1, bnd, nb);
if (D.isInside(pt[np-1])) return D;
bnd[nb] = pt[np-1];
nb++;
D = minSphere(pt, np-1, bnd, nb);
return D
```

$$\begin{aligned} D_k &= D_{k-1}, \quad \text{if } P_{k-1} \in D_{k-1} \\ &= D_{\min}(S_{k-1}, P_{k-1}) \end{aligned} \tag{9.2}$$

where $D_{\min}(S_{k-1}, P_{k-1})$ is the smallest disc enclosing the set of points S_{k-1} with P_{k-1} on the boundary. The minimal sphere at any stage of the algorithm is represented by the pair $\{\boldsymbol{c}, r\}$ where $\boldsymbol{c}$ is the centre and r the radius. The spheres for the base cases are defined by the functions `Sphere1pt()`, `Sphere2pts()` etc., as follows.

`Sphere1pt`(P): centre $\boldsymbol{c} = P$, radius $r = 0$
`Sphere2pts`(P, Q): centre $\boldsymbol{c} = (P+Q)/2$, radius $= |\boldsymbol{c}-P|$
`Sphere3pts`(P, Q, R): centre $\boldsymbol{c}$, radius r as given in Eqs. 9.4 and 9.6.
`Sphere4pts`(P, Q, R, T)): centre $\boldsymbol{c}$, radius r as given in Eq. 9.16.

As noted above, the minimal bounding sphere passing through two points is simply a sphere that has the two points at opposite ends of a diameter. The pair of points that are located diametrically opposite on a sphere are called antipodes. For three points P, Q, R, the sphere has the circle passing through the points as one of its great circles. In this case, the sphere's centre and radius are the same as that of the circle passing through the points. The interior angle at the vertex R of the triangle PQR is given by

$$\sin\theta = \frac{|\boldsymbol{a}\times\boldsymbol{b}|}{|\boldsymbol{a}|\,|\boldsymbol{b}|} \tag{9.3}$$

where $\boldsymbol{a} = P - R$, and $\boldsymbol{b} = Q - R$.

The radius of the circle (and therefore the sphere) through the three points can now be obtained as

$$r = \frac{|\boldsymbol{b}-\boldsymbol{a}|}{2\sin\theta} = \frac{|\boldsymbol{b}-\boldsymbol{a}|\,|\boldsymbol{a}|\,|\boldsymbol{b}|}{2\,|\boldsymbol{a}\times\boldsymbol{b}|} \tag{9.4}$$

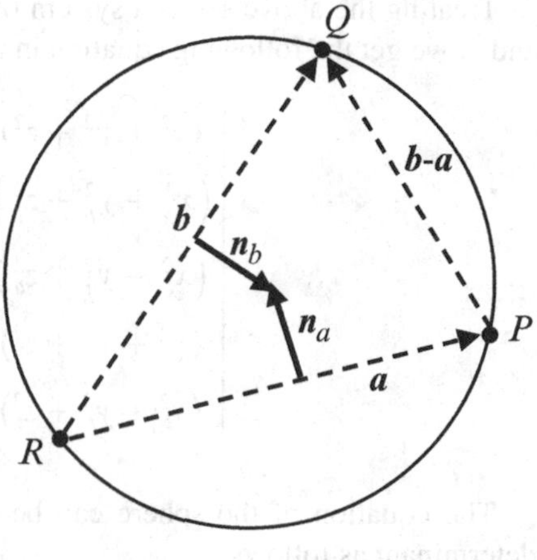

Fig. 9.4 Minimum sphere passing through three points

The directions along the perpendicular bisectors of the sides $\boldsymbol{a}$ and $\boldsymbol{b}$ towards the centre of the circle are given by (see Fig. 9.4)

$$\begin{aligned} \boldsymbol{n}_a &= (\boldsymbol{a} \times \boldsymbol{b}) \times \boldsymbol{a} \\ \boldsymbol{n}_b &= \boldsymbol{b} \times (\boldsymbol{a} \times \boldsymbol{b}) \end{aligned} \tag{9.5}$$

The position of the centre can be concisely expressed in terms of the above vectors as

$$\boldsymbol{c} = \frac{|\boldsymbol{b}|^2 \boldsymbol{n}_a + |\boldsymbol{a}|^2 \boldsymbol{n}_b}{2|\boldsymbol{a} \times \boldsymbol{b}|^2} + \boldsymbol{s} \tag{9.6}$$

where $\boldsymbol{s} = (x_s, y_s, z_s)$ denotes the position of the point R.

Four non-coplanar points P, Q, R, T uniquely determine a sphere in three dimensions. The parameters of the sphere are obtained from the most general form of a sphere given in terms of its centre $\boldsymbol{c} = (x_c, y_c, z_c)$ and radius r:

$$\begin{aligned} &(x - x_c)^2 + (y - y_c)^2 + (z - z_c)^2 = r^2, \quad \text{or equivalently,} \\ &(x^2 + y^2 + z^2) + ux + vy + wz + k = 0 \end{aligned} \tag{9.7}$$

where $u = -2x_c$, $v = -2y_c$, $w = -2z_c$, and $k = {x_c}^2 + {y_c}^2 + {z_c}^2 - r^2$. Since the four points P, Q, R, T are required to lie on the above sphere, we can substitute the coordinates of each point and obtain the following simultaneous equations:

$$\begin{aligned} \left({x_p}^2 + {y_p}^2 + {z_p}^2\right) + ux_p + vy_p + wz_p + k &= 0 \\ \left({x_q}^2 + {y_q}^2 + {z_q}^2\right) + ux_q + vy_q + wz_q + k &= 0 \\ \left({x_s}^2 + {y_s}^2 + {z_s}^2\right) + ux_s + vy_s + wz_s + k &= 0 \\ \left({x_t}^2 + {y_t}^2 + {z_t}^2\right) + ux_t + vy_t + wz_t + k &= 0 \end{aligned} \tag{9.8}$$

Treating the above set as a system of linear equations in the unknowns u, v, w, and k, we get the following equation in the coefficients:

$$\begin{vmatrix} (x^2+y^2+z^2) & x & y & z & 1 \\ \left(x_p^2+y_p^2+z_p^2\right) & x_p & y_p & z_p & 1 \\ \left(x_q^2+y_q^2+z_q^2\right) & x_q & y_q & z_q & 1 \\ \left(x_s^2+y_s^2+z_s^2\right) & x_s & y_s & z_s & 1 \\ \left(x_t^2+y_t^2+z_t^2\right) & x_t & y_t & z_t & 1 \end{vmatrix} = 0. \tag{9.9}$$

The equation of the sphere can be directly obtained by expanding the above determinant as follows:

$$\mathrm{M}_{11}(x^2+y^2+z^2) - \mathrm{M}_{12}x + \mathrm{M}_{13}y - \mathrm{M}_{14}z + \mathrm{M}_{15} = 0 \tag{9.10}$$

where M_{ij} are the minors given by

$$\mathrm{M}_{11} = \begin{vmatrix} x_p & y_p & z_p & 1 \\ x_q & y_q & z_q & 1 \\ x_s & y_s & z_s & 1 \\ x_t & y_t & z_t & 1 \end{vmatrix} \tag{9.11}$$

$$\mathrm{M}_{12} = \begin{vmatrix} \left(x_p^2+y_p^2+z_p^2\right) & y_p & z_p & 1 \\ \left(x_q^2+y_q^2+z_q^2\right) & y_q & z_q & 1 \\ \left(x_s^2+y_s^2+z_s^2\right) & y_s & z_s & 1 \\ \left(x_t^2+y_t^2+z_t^2\right) & y_t & z_t & 1 \end{vmatrix} \tag{9.12}$$

$$\mathrm{M}_{13} = \begin{vmatrix} \left(x_p^2+y_p^2+z_p^2\right) & x_p & z_p & 1 \\ \left(x_q^2+y_q^2+z_q^2\right) & x_q & z_q & 1 \\ \left(x_s^2+y_s^2+z_s^2\right) & x_s & z_s & 1 \\ \left(x_t^2+y_t^2+z_t^2\right) & x_t & z_t & 1 \end{vmatrix} \tag{9.13}$$

$$\mathrm{M}_{14} = \begin{vmatrix} \left(x_p^2+y_p^2+z_p^2\right) & x_p & y_p & 1 \\ \left(x_q^2+y_q^2+z_q^2\right) & x_q & y_q & 1 \\ \left(x_s^2+y_s^2+z_s^2\right) & x_s & y_s & 1 \\ \left(x_t^2+y_t^2+z_t^2\right) & x_t & y_t & 1 \end{vmatrix} \tag{9.14}$$

$$\mathbf{M}_{15} = \begin{vmatrix} \left(x_p^2 + y_p^2 + z_p^2\right) & x_p & y_p & z_p \\ \left(x_q^2 + y_q^2 + z_q^2\right) & x_q & y_q & z_q \\ \left(x_s^2 + y_s^2 + z_s^2\right) & x_s & y_s & z_s \\ \left(x_t^2 + y_t^2 + z_t^2\right) & x_t & y_t & z_t \end{vmatrix} \tag{9.15}$$

Since the four points are non-coplanar, from Eq. 9.11 we find that $\mathbf{M}_{11} \neq 0$. The centre and the radius of the minimal sphere are now readily obtained as follows:

$$c = \left(\frac{\mathbf{M}_{12}}{2\mathbf{M}_{11}}, \frac{-\mathbf{M}_{13}}{2\mathbf{M}_{11}}, \frac{\mathbf{M}_{14}}{2\mathbf{M}_{11}}\right)$$

$$r = \sqrt{x_c^2 + y_c^2 + z_c^2 - \left(\frac{\mathbf{M}_{15}}{\mathbf{M}_{11}}\right)} \tag{9.16}$$

9.1.3 Oriented Bounding Box (OBB)

The oriented bounding box (OBB) gives a closer approximation of the underlying mesh geometry compared to the AABB and the sphere. An OBB can be thought of as a rotated AABB, whose axes are aligned along mutually orthogonal principal directions of variance of the points with respect to the centroid. If the vertices of a mesh object are given by $\{x_i, y_i, z_i\}$, $i = 0 \ldots n-1$, we can compute their centroid $(\bar{x}, \bar{y}, \bar{z})$, and form the following matrix:

$$\mathbf{V} = \begin{bmatrix} x_0 - \bar{x} & x_1 - \bar{x} & \ldots & x_{n-1} - \bar{x} \\ y_0 - \bar{y} & y_1 - \bar{y} & \ldots & y_{n-1} - \bar{y} \\ z_0 - \bar{z} & z_1 - \bar{z} & \ldots & z_{n-1} - \bar{z} \end{bmatrix} \tag{9.17}$$

The scatter (or covariance) matrix $\mathbf{C}$ is a 3 × 3 symmetric matrix given by

$$\mathbf{C} = \frac{1}{n}\left(\mathbf{V}\mathbf{V}^T\right) = \frac{1}{n}\begin{bmatrix} \sum_{k=0}^{n-1}(x_k - \bar{x})^2 & \sum_{k=0}^{n-1}(x_k - \bar{x})(y_k - \bar{y}) & \sum_{k=0}^{n-1}(x_k - \bar{x})(z_k - \bar{z}) \\ \sum_{k=0}^{n-1}(x_k - \bar{x})(y_k - \bar{y}) & \sum_{k=0}^{n-1}(y_k - \bar{y})^2 & \sum_{k=0}^{n-1}(y_k - \bar{y})(z_k - \bar{z}) \\ \sum_{k=0}^{n-1}(x_k - \bar{x})(z_k - \bar{z}) & \sum_{k=0}^{n-1}(y_k - \bar{y})(z_k - \bar{z}) & \sum_{k=0}^{n-1}(z_k - \bar{z})^2 \end{bmatrix}$$

$$= \begin{bmatrix} \sigma_x^2 & \sigma_{xy} & \sigma_{xz} \\ \sigma_{xy} & \sigma_y^2 & \sigma_{yz} \\ \sigma_{xz} & \sigma_{yz} & \sigma_z^2 \end{bmatrix} \tag{9.18}$$

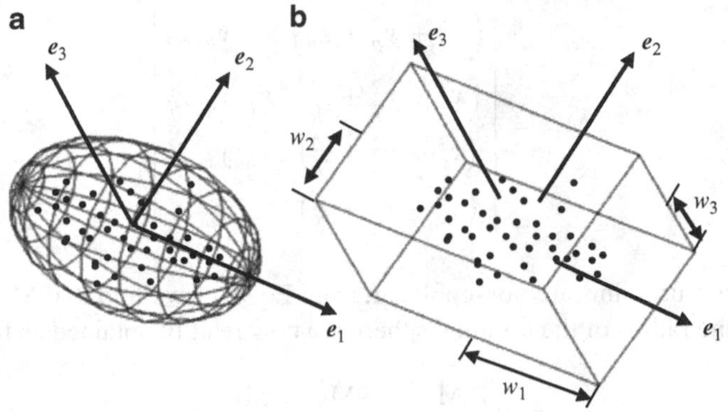

Fig. 9.5 (**a**) The eigenvalues and the eigenvectors of the covariance matrix can be used to compute an ellipse with axes along directions of maximum and minimum variance. (**b**) The oriented bounding box uses the ellipse's parameters

where ${\sigma_x}^2$ denotes the variance of the vector $\{x_i\}$, σ_{xy} the covariance between the vectors $\{x_i\}$, $\{y_i\}$, and so on. The above matrix therefore has real eigenvalues λ_1, λ_2, λ_3 and a mutually orthogonal set of eigenvectors $\boldsymbol{v}_1$, $\boldsymbol{v}_2$, $\boldsymbol{v}_3$. The normalization of each of these vectors yields an orthonormal basis $\boldsymbol{e}_1$, $\boldsymbol{e}_2$, $\boldsymbol{e}_3$. Treating the set of mesh vertices $\{x_i, y_i, z_i\}$, $i = 0 \ldots n-1$, as a point cloud, the unit vectors $\boldsymbol{e}_1$, $\boldsymbol{e}_2$, $\boldsymbol{e}_3$ define the principal axes directions of an ellipsoid with corresponding semi-axis lengths $\sqrt{\lambda_1}$, $\sqrt{\lambda_2}$ and $\sqrt{\lambda_3}$ (Fig. 9.5a). The OBB also has the same axis directions and half-width extents (Fig. 9.5b). The OBB can thus be completely specified by its centre $(\bar{x}, \bar{y}, \bar{z})$, its half-width extents w_1 $(=\sqrt{\lambda_1})$, w_2 $(=\sqrt{\lambda_2})$, w_3 $(=\sqrt{\lambda_3})$, and unit vectors $\boldsymbol{e}_1$, $\boldsymbol{e}_2$, $\boldsymbol{e}_3$ along its axes.

The matrix **M** with $\boldsymbol{e}_1$, $\boldsymbol{e}_2$, $\boldsymbol{e}_3$ as the column vectors gives the rotational transformation of the OBB with respect to the coordinate reference frame. The OBB does not always provide a tight fitting bounding box for the point cloud. This is because the covariance matrix depends on the distribution of the whole set of points, not just the points on the boundary that define the shape. Even changes in the locations of vertices that are inside the point cloud can affect the orientation of the OBB. One possible solution to this problem is to consider only the vertices on the convex hull of the mesh for the computation of the OBB. Another method that is used for the construction of the optimal OBB is to select the axis of the smallest eigenvalue, project all points on a plane perpendicular to this axis, and to compute the minimum area bounding rectangle of the projection. The chosen axis and the axes of the rectangle together define the orientation of the OBB. If we assume that $\lambda_1 \geq \lambda_2 \geq \lambda_3$, then $\boldsymbol{e}_3$ is the axis of projection. The points are then projected onto a plane orthogonal to $\boldsymbol{e}_3$, and the minimal rectangle of this set gives the other two axes $\boldsymbol{e}_1'$ and $\boldsymbol{e}_2'$ (Fig. 9.6a).

The minimal rectangle of a set of points on a plane can be obtained using the rotating calipers method. The method uses the convex hull of the points and two orthogonal pairs of support lines (Fig. 9.6b) such that one of the lines is always

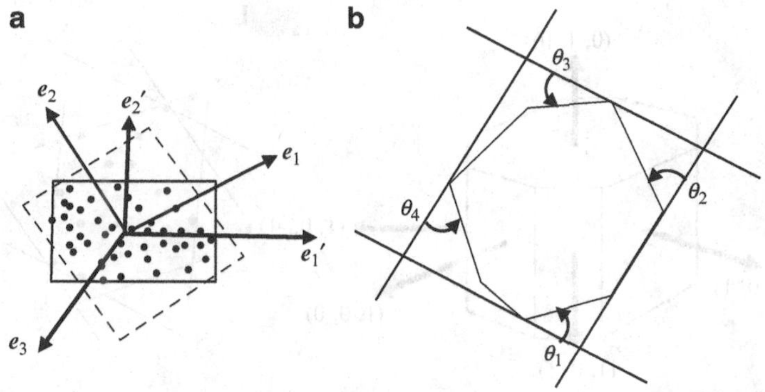

Fig. 9.6 (**a**) Computation of the optimal OBB using a projection of the vertices orthogonal to the axis of minimum eigenvalue. (**b**) The rotating calipers method

aligned with an edge of the convex hull. The remaining three lines pass through the vertices of the convex hull. The angles θ_i ($i = 1 \ldots 4$) made by each support line with the edge of the convex hull in anticlockwise order are computed and the minimum angle is found. All four support lines are rotated about the corresponding vertices of the hull by the minimum angle, and this step aligns one of the lines with another edge of the convex hull. The area of the newly formed rectangle is computed and the minimum area updated. The process is repeated until all edges of the convex hull have been processed. The computation of the convex hull using algorithms such as the Graham's Scan algorithm takes $O(n\log n)$ time. The rotating calipers method visits all edges of the hull in $O(n)$ time. The overall complexity of the optimal OBB computation algorithm is therefore $O(n\log n)$.

9.1.4 Discrete Oriented Polytope (k-DOP)

A polytope is a general term for a polyhedron in any arbitrary dimension. It is defined as a geometrical object with flat surfaces. Points, line segments, polygons and polyhedrons are respectively zero-, one-, two- and three-dimensional polytopes. In a three-dimensional space, a discrete oriented polytope is a closed convex polyhedron bounded by $k/2$ pairs of parallel planes, where k is an even integer and $k \geq 6$. Each pair of planes has a fixed orientation. Such a polyhedron is often referred to as a k-DOP. An AABB and an OBB are both bounded by three pairs of parallel planes, and are therefore 6-DOPs. A 10-DOP and the associated normal directions are shown in Fig. 9.7a. A k-DOP need not always have k sides. The example in Fig. 9.7b is a 8-DOP with only six sides, with two sides degenerating into points.

The components of the surface normal vectors of a k-DOP are usually chosen from the set $\{-1, 0, +1\}$. Each pair of parallel sides of a k-DOP has a fixed normal direction $\boldsymbol{n}_j$, $j = 0, \ldots (k/2)-1$. Their positions are determined such that the region

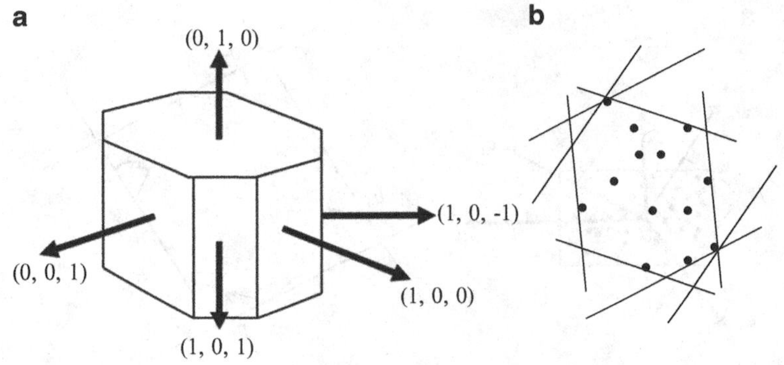

Fig. 9.7 **(a)** A 10-DOP and the normal directions of five of its sides. The remaining five sides are parallel to these and have opposite normal directions. **(b)** An 8-DOP with degenerate edges

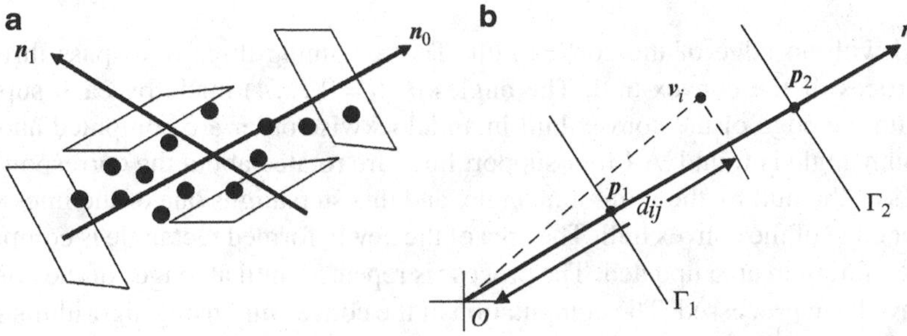

Fig. 9.8 **(a)** The positions of the planes are determined such that the vertices are tightly packed within each slab. **(b)** A slab formed by two parallel planes

between them tightly encloses the mesh vertices (Fig. 9.8a). Now consider two parallel planes Γ_1, Γ_2 having a normal direction $\boldsymbol{n}_j$ and passing through points $\boldsymbol{p}_1$, $\boldsymbol{p}_2$ respectively. The region between the parallel planes is called a slab. If a vertex $\boldsymbol{v}_i$ belongs to the slab formed by Γ_1, Γ_2, then $\boldsymbol{v}_i$ satisfies the equations

$$(\boldsymbol{v}_i - \boldsymbol{p}_1) \bullet \boldsymbol{n}_j \geq 0, \quad \text{and} \quad (\boldsymbol{v}_i - \boldsymbol{p}_2) \bullet \boldsymbol{n}_j \leq 0. \tag{9.19}$$

In a k-DOP, the values of $\boldsymbol{p}_1$, $\boldsymbol{p}_2$ are determined by the minimum and the maximum positions of the projections of mesh vertices $\boldsymbol{v}_i$, $i=0\ldots n-1$, on the vector $\boldsymbol{n}_i$ (Fig. 9.8b):

$$\begin{aligned} d_{ij} &= \boldsymbol{v}_i \bullet \boldsymbol{n}_j \\ dmin_j &= \min_i(d_{ij}) \\ dmax_j &= \max_i(d_{ij}) \\ \boldsymbol{p}_1 &= (dmin_j)\boldsymbol{n}_j; \quad \boldsymbol{p}_2 = (dmax_j)\boldsymbol{n}_j \end{aligned} \tag{9.20}$$

The k-DOP can be represented by the set $\{dmin_j,\ dmax_j,\ \boldsymbol{n}_j\}$, $j = 0 \ldots (k/2)-1$, that gives the $k/2$ intervals and direction vectors. The points $\boldsymbol{p}_1, \boldsymbol{p}_2$ were used only for the purpose of explaining the construction of the intervals, and are not stored. For fast overlap tests, it is desirable to have all k-DOPs in an application share surface normal directions from the same set. If the normal directions are pre-defined, then only the minimum and maximum values $\{dmin_j,\ dmax_j\}$, $j = 0 \ldots (k/2)-1$, need be stored. A point $\boldsymbol{p}$ belongs to a k-DOP if and only if the following conditions are simultaneously satisfied:

$$dmin_j \le (\boldsymbol{p} \bullet \boldsymbol{n}_j) \le dmax_j, \quad \text{for all } j. \tag{9.21}$$

9.1.5 Convex Hulls

The key properties of a convex polygon were outlined in Sect. 8.7.1. A convex hull of a set of points in two dimensions is defined as the unique convex polygon containing all the points and whose vertices are only points in the set. It is the minimal convex polygon formed by the intersection of all convex polygons containing the points. The convex hull therefore is the tightest fitting bounding volume. The convex hull can also be defined as the union of all triangles that can be formed using only points of the set. In this section, we will first outline the construction of two-dimensional convex hulls using an incremental hull update algorithm, and then extend the method to three-dimensional hulls.

The 2D incremental hull algorithm builds the hull starting with a triangle formed by joining the first three points in the set (provided they are non-collinear), and then iteratively adds one point at a time to the existing hull and updates it if necessary. If the vertices of the initial triangle are oriented in the anticlockwise sense, then the vertices of the convex hulls constructed in subsequent steps will also be oriented in the anticlockwise sense. Assume that the given set of points is $S_n = \{P_0, P_1, \ldots, P_{n-1}\}$, and the algorithm has constructed the convex hull of the first i points $S_i = \{P_0, P_1, \ldots, P_{i-1}\}$ $(3 \le i < n)$. We denote this convex hull by $C_i = \{Q_0, \ldots Q_{k-1}\} \subseteq S_i$. When the next point P_i is added, the convex hull C_i is traversed to check if the point is within the hull. This can be done by computing the signed area of the triangle $Q_j Q_{j+1} P_i$, $j = 0 \ldots k-1$, $(Q_k = Q_0)$ is positive (Eq. 2.9) for all j. If the point P_i is inside or on the hull, it is not updated, *i.e.*, $C_{i+1} = C_i$. If the point is outside the hull, the signed area changes sign from positive to negative at some vertex on the hull, and from negative back to positive at some other vertex. These vertices are called the split vertex and the merge vertex respectively (Fig. 9.9). Existing edges between these vertices are removed, and the point P_i are connected to these vertices to form the new convex hull C_{i+1}. The vertex set C_i is updated to C_{i+1} by removing the vertices between the split and the merge vertices and adding P_i.

At each step, the algorithm requires the traversal of the hull vertices to determine the locations of the split and merge vertices. The overall time complexity of the algorithm is therefore $O(n^2)$ for a naive implementation. $O(n\log n)$ implementations

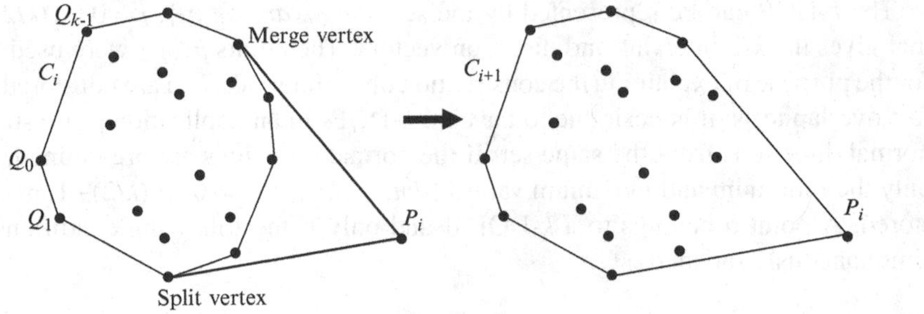

Fig. 9.9 Incremental construction of a two-dimensional convex hull

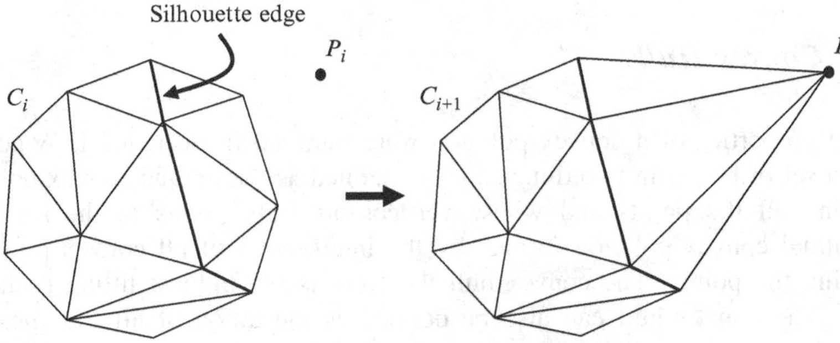

Fig. 9.10 Incremental construction of a three-dimensional convex hull

exist, but they cannot be directly extended to the three-dimensional convex hull algorithm. One of the popular algorithms in this class is the Graham Scan, which is the same as the Three-Coins algorithm (Sect. 8.7.3) with a pre-processing phase where the points P_i are initially sorted in the ascending order of the angles between the vectors $\boldsymbol{p}_i = P_i - P_0$ and the x-axis.

A natural extension of the incremental algorithm described above to a three-dimensional data set S_n consisting of n mesh vertices can be easily formulated. The algorithm begins with the construction of a tetrahedron from four non-coplanar points of the set S_n. The point inclusion test in the three-dimensional case uses signed distances (Eq. 2.24) instead of signed areas to determine if a new point P_i is within the existing convex hull. If the surface normal vectors of the triangles of the convex hull are all specified in the outward direction, then for any point inside the hull, the signed distance with respect to every triangle of the hull is negative. Otherwise, the point is outside the hull, and we can determine the edges between triangles where the transition from negative to positive takes place. These edges are called silhouette edges. Every triangle for which the signed distance is positive is visible with respect to the point P_i. These triangles are removed, and the point P_i is connected to the end points of every silhouette edge to form new triangles of the updated convex hull (Fig. 9.10).

At each step, the point inclusion step and the hull update step take $O(n)$ time. The total time complexity of the 3D incremental hull discussed above is thus $O(n^2)$.

9.2 Intersection Testing

The bounding volumes introduced in the previous section are often associated with methods that determine if two bounding volumes intersect. In this section, we will consider three different types of intersection tests using bounding volumes:

- Intersection between a bounding volume and a ray. Such intersection tests are used in advanced ray tracing algorithms where bounding volumes are employed to minimize the computation of ray intersections.
- Intersection between a bounding volume and a plane. Intersection testing of objects with planes is used in acceleration algorithms such as view frustum culling.
- Intersection between two bounding volumes of the same type. Collision detection algorithms often require the testing of intersections between bounding volumes.

A ray can be represented by the pair $\{\boldsymbol{p}, \boldsymbol{m}\}$, where $\boldsymbol{p} = (x_p, y_p, z_p)$ denotes the origin of the ray, and $\boldsymbol{m} = (x_m, y_m, z_m)$ a unit vector along the ray's direction. In parametric form (see also Eq. 2.13), the ray is given by the following equations:

$$
\begin{aligned}
x &= x_p + t x_m \\
y &= y_p + t y_m \\
z &= z_p + t z_m, \quad t \geq 0.
\end{aligned}
\tag{9.22}
$$

A plane always has a linear representation $ax + by + cz + d = 0$, where the vector $\boldsymbol{n} = (a, b, c)$ is along the direction of its normal vector. As shown in Eq. 2.22, the equivalent vector representation of a plane is $\boldsymbol{r} \bullet \boldsymbol{n} = -d$. If we assume that $\boldsymbol{n}$ is a unit normal vector, then the signed distance D of a point $\boldsymbol{v}$ to this plane is simply given by the expression $\boldsymbol{v} \bullet \boldsymbol{n} + d$ (see Eq. 2.24).

The following sections discuss methods of testing whether a bounding volume with a given representation intersects these primitive geometrical elements.

9.2.1 AABB Intersection

We first consider the intersection of an AABB given by the parameter set $\{x_{\min}, x_{\max}, y_{\min}, y_{\max}, z_{\min}, z_{\max}\}$ with a ray $\{\boldsymbol{p}, \boldsymbol{m}\}$ as in Eq. 9.22. A naïve approach is to check if the ray intersects any of the six sides of the AABB. For example, one of the sides parallel to the *xy*-plane is given by the equation $z = z_{\min}$. We first compute the value of t from Eq. 9.22 by substituting $z = z_{\min}$, and then use this value to find x and y. The value of t is denoted as $t^{(z)}_{\min}$. The ray intersects this plane if and only if the following three conditions are simultaneously satisfied:

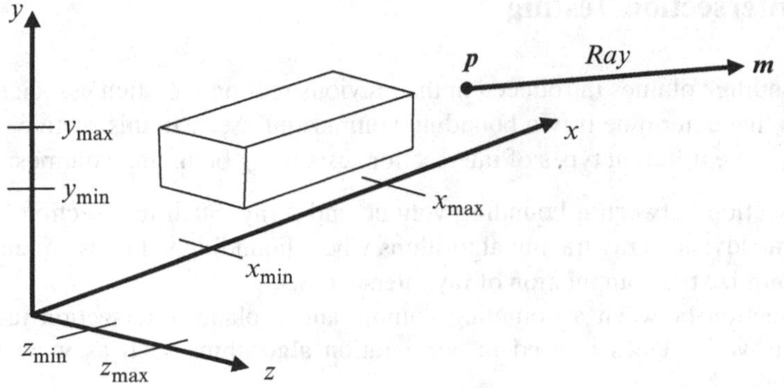

Fig. 9.11 AABB intervals along the principal axes, and a non-intersecting ray

$$t^{(z)}_{\text{min}} = \frac{z_{\text{min}} - z_p}{z_m} \geq 0,$$

$$x_{\text{min}} \leq \left(x_p + t^{(z)}_{\text{min}} x_m\right) \leq x_{\text{max}},$$

$$y_{\text{min}} \leq \left(y_p + t^{(z)}_{\text{min}} y_m\right) \leq y_{\text{max}} \tag{9.23}$$

Similarly, the ray can be tested against the other planes of the AABB. A moment's thought will reveal that it is not always necessary to test all six planes for intersection with the ray. At most three sides of the AABB will be visible to the point $\boldsymbol{p}$ if the point is outside the box (which is usually the case). We can also make use of the axis-aligned nature of the sides to determine if the ray is directed away from the AABB and therefore would not intersect the volume (Fig. 9.11). If a ray satisfies *any* of the following six conditions, it will not intersect the AABB.

$$(x_p < x_{\text{min}}) \text{ and } (x_m \leq 0)$$
$$(y_p < y_{\text{min}}) \text{ and } (y_m \leq 0)$$
$$(z_p < z_{\text{min}}) \text{ and } (z_m \leq 0)$$
$$(x_p > x_{\text{max}}) \text{ and } (x_m \geq 0)$$
$$(y_p > y_{\text{max}}) \text{ and } (y_m \geq 0)$$
$$(z_p > z_{\text{max}}) \text{ and } (z_m \geq 0) \tag{9.24}$$

If none of the above conditions is true, then we can identify the three faces visible to $\boldsymbol{p}$ by comparing its coordinates against the corresponding intervals of the AABB. As an example, if $(x_p > x_{\text{max}})$ and $(y_p < y_{\text{min}})$ and $(z_p > z_{\text{max}})$, then the ray need be compared only with the planes $x = x_{\text{max}}$, $y = y_{\text{min}}$, and $z = z_{\text{max}}$.

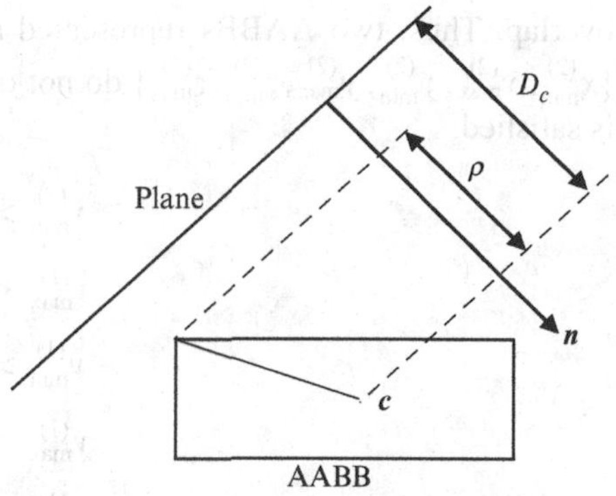

Fig. 9.12 AABB-Plane intersection test using the projected distances along the normal vector

The testing of intersection of an AABB with a plane $\boldsymbol{r}{\bullet}\boldsymbol{n} = -d$, $|\boldsymbol{n}| = 1$, can be done by computing the signed distances of the vertices $\boldsymbol{v}_i$, $i = 1..8$, of the AABB with respect to the plane. If some vertices are on or above the plane, and some below the plane, then the plane intersects the AABB. In other words, if $D_i = \boldsymbol{v}_i{\bullet}\boldsymbol{n} + d$ is non-zero and has a positive value for all i, then the AABB is entirely above the plane; if D_i is non-zero and has a negative value for all i, then the AABB is below the plane; otherwise the plane intersects the AABB. The amount of computation can be reduced by first determining the diagonal of the AABB that is closely aligned with the normal vector $\boldsymbol{n}$, and then using only the two opposite endpoints of this diagonal to check if they are on either sides of the plane. Note that an AABB has only four principal diagonals, and the selection of the diagonal closest to $\boldsymbol{n}$ is done by using the dot-product between $\boldsymbol{n}$ and the unit vectors along the four diagonals.

Another AABB-plane intersection test (which will be extended to OBBs in the next section) uses the projection of diagonal vectors (vectors from the centre of the AABB to the vertices) on the normal vector $\boldsymbol{n}$ of the plane (Fig. 9.12). For this method, we use the representation of the AABB given by the centre $\boldsymbol{c} = (x_{\text{mid}}, y_{\text{mid}}, z_{\text{mid}})$ and the three half-width extents x_r, y_r, z_r. The largest projected distance by any vertex of the AABB on the unit normal vector $\boldsymbol{n} = (x_n, y_n, z_n)$ is given by

$$\rho = |x_r x_n| + |y_r y_n| + |z_r z_n| \tag{9.25}$$

The shortest distance of the centre from the plane is $D_c = \boldsymbol{c}{\bullet}\boldsymbol{n} + d$. The plane intersects the AABB if and only if

$$D_c \leq \rho \tag{9.26}$$

The overlap test using two AABBs can be easily performed taking advantage of their axis-aligned property. Since the respective axes are always parallel, two AABBs overlap only if their projected intervals (see Fig. 9.11) along each axis overlap. Thus, two AABBs represented as $\{x^{(1)}_{\min}, x^{(1)}_{\max}, y^{(1)}_{\min}, y^{(1)}_{\max}, z^{(1)}_{\min}, z^{(1)}_{\max}\}$, and $\{x^{(2)}_{\min}, x^{(2)}_{\max}, y^{(2)}_{\min}, y^{(2)}_{\max}, z^{(2)}_{\min}, z^{(2)}_{\max}\}$ do not overlap if *any* of the following conditions is satisfied:

$$\begin{aligned}
x^{(1)}_{\min} &> x^{(2)}_{\max} \\
x^{(1)}_{\max} &< x^{(2)}_{\min} \\
y^{(1)}_{\min} &> y^{(2)}_{\max} \\
y^{(1)}_{\max} &< y^{(2)}_{\min} \\
z^{(1)}_{\min} &> z^{(2)}_{\max} \\
z^{(1)}_{\max} &< z^{(2)}_{\min}
\end{aligned} \tag{9.27}$$

If the AABBs are represented using their midpoint and half-width extents as $\{x^{(1)}_{mid}, y^{(1)}_{mid}, z^{(1)}_{mid}, x^{(1)}_r, y^{(1)}_r, z^{(1)}_r\}$ and $\{x^{(2)}_{mid}, y^{(2)}_{mid}, z^{(2)}_{mid}, x^{(2)}_r, y^{(2)}_r, z^{(2)}_r\}$, then the overlap test can be suitably modified as follows. In this case, the requirement for bounding volume overlap is that the projected distance between the centres must be less than or equal to the sum of the corresponding half-width extents along each axis. Conversely, if *any* of the following conditions is satisfied, the two AABBs do not overlap.

$$\begin{aligned}
\left|x^{(1)}_{mid} - x^{(2)}_{mid}\right| &> \left(x^{(1)}_r + x^{(2)}_r\right) \\
\left|y^{(1)}_{mid} - y^{(2)}_{mid}\right| &> \left(y^{(1)}_r + y^{(2)}_r\right) \\
\left|z^{(1)}_{mid} - z^{(2)}_{mid}\right| &> \left(z^{(1)}_r + z^{(2)}_r\right)
\end{aligned} \tag{9.28}$$

Since an AABB is also an OBB, the intersection tests given in the next section can also be applied to an AABB.

9.2.2 OBB Intersection

If an OBB is given by the parameters $\{\bar{x}, \bar{y}, \bar{z}, w_1, w_2, w_3, \boldsymbol{e}_1, \boldsymbol{e}_2, \boldsymbol{e}_3\}$, the eight vertices of the bounding volume are given by

$$v = \boldsymbol{c} \pm w_1\boldsymbol{e}_1 \pm w_2\boldsymbol{e}_2 \pm w_3\boldsymbol{e}_3 \tag{9.29}$$

where $\boldsymbol{c} = (\bar{x}, \bar{y}, \bar{z})$. The six faces of the OBB have the following equations:

$$
\begin{aligned}
(\boldsymbol{r} - \boldsymbol{c}) \bullet \boldsymbol{e}_1 &= \pm w_1 \\
(\boldsymbol{r} - \boldsymbol{c}) \bullet \boldsymbol{e}_2 &= \pm w_2 \\
(\boldsymbol{r} - \boldsymbol{c}) \bullet \boldsymbol{e}_3 &= \pm w_3
\end{aligned} \tag{9.30}
$$

To test the intersection of a ray $\{\boldsymbol{p}, \boldsymbol{m}\}$ (see Eq. 9.22) with the above OBB, a brute force algorithm would first identify the faces visible to the point $\boldsymbol{p}$ by taking the dot-product of $\boldsymbol{m}$ with the unit vectors $\boldsymbol{e}_1$, $\boldsymbol{e}_2$, $\boldsymbol{e}_3$. For example, the positive side of $\boldsymbol{e}_1$ is not in the direction of (and therefore will not intersect) the ray if *any* of the following two conditions is satisfied.

$$
\begin{aligned}
(\boldsymbol{p} - \boldsymbol{c}) \bullet \boldsymbol{e}_1 &< w_1 \\
\boldsymbol{m} \bullet \boldsymbol{e}_1 &> 0
\end{aligned} \tag{9.31}
$$

The point of intersection is obtained by the value of the ray parameter t by substituting the ray equation $\boldsymbol{r} = \boldsymbol{p} + t\boldsymbol{m}$ in the equations of the planes that are visible to the ray. The point of intersection is further checked if it is within the corresponding faces, with the help of their vertex coordinates.

A faster ray intersection test was introduced by Kay and Kajiya (1986) based on the representation of the OBB using three slabs, where each slab is bounded by a pair of planes given in Eq. 9.30. The parameter values $t_{\min}^{(i)}, t_{\max}^{(i)}$ for each slab $(i = 1..3)$ are computed as shown in the example for $i = 1$ below:

$$
\begin{aligned}
&\text{If} \quad \boldsymbol{m} \bullet \boldsymbol{e}_1 > 0, \quad t_{\min}^{(1)} = \frac{-w_1 - (\boldsymbol{p} \cdot \boldsymbol{e}_1)}{(\boldsymbol{m} \cdot \boldsymbol{e}_1)}, \quad t_{\max}^{(1)} = \frac{w_1 - (\boldsymbol{p} \cdot \boldsymbol{e}_1)}{(\boldsymbol{m} \cdot \boldsymbol{e}_1)} \\
&\text{If} \quad \boldsymbol{m} \bullet \boldsymbol{e}_1 < 0, \quad t_{\min}^{(1)} = \frac{w_1 - (\boldsymbol{p} \cdot \boldsymbol{e}_1)}{(\boldsymbol{m} \cdot \boldsymbol{e}_1)}, \quad t_{\max}^{(1)} = \frac{-w_1 - (\boldsymbol{p} \cdot \boldsymbol{e}_1)}{(\boldsymbol{m} \cdot \boldsymbol{e}_1)}
\end{aligned} \tag{9.32}
$$

After computing the minimum and maximum values for all three slabs, the following values are obtained:

$$
\begin{aligned}
u_{\min} &= \max \left\{ t_{\min}^{(1)}, t_{\min}^{(2)}, t_{\min}^{(3)} \right\} \\
u_{\max} &= \min \left\{ t_{\max}^{(1)}, t_{\max}^{(2)}, t_{\max}^{(3)} \right\}
\end{aligned} \tag{9.33}
$$

The ray intersects the OBB if $u_{\min} \le u_{\max}$. This condition means that the intersection of the three $[t_{\min}, t_{\max}]$ intervals on the ray is non-zero. The two-dimensional version of the above method is depicted using an intersecting and a non-intersecting ray in Fig. 9.13.

The testing of intersection of an OBB with a plane $\boldsymbol{r} \bullet \boldsymbol{n} = -d$, $|\boldsymbol{n}| = 1$, can be done exactly like the methods outlined for a AABB in the previous section. The

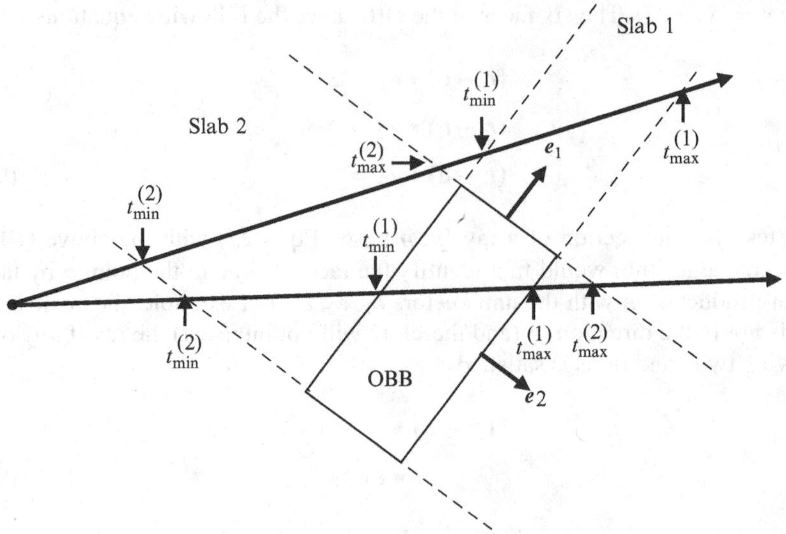

Fig. 9.13 The intersection of rays with the slabs of an OBB

first method computes the signed distances of the vertices v_i, $i = 1..8$, of the OBB with respect to the plane, and if some vertices are found to be on or above the plane, while others below the plane, then it is concluded that the plane intersects the OBB. This method could be further simplified using only the two end-vertices of the principal diagonal that is closely aligned to $\boldsymbol{n}$. We can also extend the method based on projected distances (Fig. 9.12) to OBBs. The longest projected distance on $\boldsymbol{n}$ generated by vectors from the centre of the OBB to its vertices is given by

$$\rho = w_1|\boldsymbol{e}_1 \bullet \boldsymbol{n}| + w_2|\boldsymbol{e}_2 \bullet \boldsymbol{n}| + w_3|\boldsymbol{e}_3 \bullet \boldsymbol{n}| \tag{9.34}$$

The above quantity is then compared with the shortest distance of the centre $\boldsymbol{c}$ of the OBB from the plane given by $D_c = \boldsymbol{c} \bullet \boldsymbol{n} + d$. As previously shown in the case of an AABB, the plane intersects the OBB if $D_c \leq \rho$.

A naïve algorithm for overlap test between two OBBs would compare every edge of one OBB with every face of the other OBB. In total, such a method would require $12 \times 6 \times 2 = 144$ edge-face intersection tests. The number of intersection tests can be considerably reduced if we use the separating axis theorem. The theorem states that if two OBBs do not overlap, then there exists a separating plane between them, and equivalently, the vertices of the OBBs project into disjoint intervals on any axis perpendicular to the separating plane. The direction perpendicular to the separating plane is called the separating axis direction. The theorem further states that the separating plane, if it exists, is parallel to either a face of one of the OBBs, or a plane formed by two edges, one from each OBB. The 15 possible directions for the separating axis are: ${\boldsymbol{e}_1}^{(1)}$, ${\boldsymbol{e}_2}^{(1)}$, ${\boldsymbol{e}_3}^{(1)}$, ${\boldsymbol{e}_1}^{(2)}$, ${\boldsymbol{e}_2}^{(2)}$, ${\boldsymbol{e}_3}^{(2)}$, ${\boldsymbol{e}_1}^{(1)} \times {\boldsymbol{e}_1}^{(2)}$, ${\boldsymbol{e}_1}^{(1)} \times {\boldsymbol{e}_2}^{(2)}$, ${\boldsymbol{e}_1}^{(1)} \times {\boldsymbol{e}_3}^{(2)}$, ${\boldsymbol{e}_2}^{(1)} \times {\boldsymbol{e}_1}^{(2)}$, ${\boldsymbol{e}_2}^{(1)} \times {\boldsymbol{e}_2}^{(2)}$, ${\boldsymbol{e}_2}^{(1)} \times {\boldsymbol{e}_3}^{(2)}$, ${\boldsymbol{e}_3}^{(1)} \times {\boldsymbol{e}_1}^{(2)}$, ${\boldsymbol{e}_3}^{(1)} \times {\boldsymbol{e}_2}^{(2)}$, ${\boldsymbol{e}_3}^{(1)}$

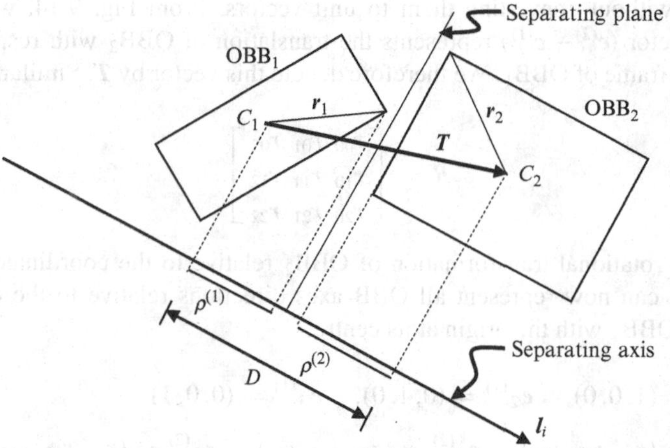

Fig. 9.14 Computation of projected distances on a separating axis

$\times\, e_3^{(2)}$. We denote these directions by l_i ($i = 1..15$). Note that some of these vectors are not unit vectors.

In Fig. 9.14, r_1 denotes a vector from the centre of the first OBB to one of its vertices that give the largest projection on the separating axis l_i. Let us momentarily assume that l_i is a unit vector. Then, the projected distance is given by $\rho_i^{(1)} = |r_1 \bullet l_i|$. From Eq. 9.29, the eight possible values for r_1 are $\pm\, w_1 e_1 \pm w_2 e_2 \pm w_3 e_3$. The maximum projected distance is obtained by taking the positive values for each projected component. Noting that w_1, w_2 and w_3 are always positive, we can define

$$\rho_i^{(1)} = w_1 |e_1 \bullet l_i| + w_2 |e_2 \bullet l_i| + w_3 |e_3 \bullet l_i| \tag{9.35}$$

Similarly, for the second OBB we obtain $\rho_i^{(2)} = |r_2 \bullet l_i|$. In the following, we use superscripts in the summation to distinguish between parameters associated with the first and the second OBBs.

$$\rho_i^{(1)} = \sum_{k=1}^{3} w_k^{(1)} \left| e_k^{(1)} \bullet l_i \right|$$

$$\rho_i^{(2)} = \sum_{k=1}^{3} w_k^{(2)} \left| e_k^{(2)} \bullet l_i \right| \tag{9.36}$$

The projected distance of the line of centres on l_i is $D_i = |(c^{(2)} - c^{(1)}) \bullet l_i|$. The two OBBs are separated if, for some i,

$$D_i > \rho_i^{(1)} + \rho_i^{(2)}, \quad i = 1..15. \tag{9.37}$$

The above inequality remains unchanged if we multiply both sides by a constant $|l_i|$. This means that the separating axis directions l_i can be used in the above equations without converting them to unit vectors. From Fig. 9.14, we observe that the vector $(\boldsymbol{c}^{(2)} - \boldsymbol{c}^{(1)})$ represents the translation of OBB_2 with respect to the coordinate frame of OBB_1. We therefore denote this vector by $\boldsymbol{T}$. Similarly, let

$$\boldsymbol{R} = \begin{bmatrix} r_{00} & r_{01} & r_{02} \\ r_{10} & r_{11} & r_{12} \\ r_{20} & r_{21} & r_{22} \end{bmatrix} \tag{9.38}$$

denote the rotational transformation of OBB_2 relative to the coordinate frame of OBB_1. We can now represent all OBB axes directions relative to the coordinate system of OBB_1 with the origin at its centre:

$$\begin{aligned} &\boldsymbol{e}_1{}^{(1)} = (1,0,0), \quad \boldsymbol{e}_2{}^{(1)} = (0,1,0), \quad \boldsymbol{e}_3{}^{(1)} = (0,0,1) \\ &\boldsymbol{e}_1{}^{(2)} = (r_{00}, r_{10}, r_{20}), \quad \boldsymbol{e}_2{}^{(2)} = (r_{01}, r_{11}, r_{21}), \quad \boldsymbol{e}_3{}^{(2)} = (r_{02}, r_{12}, r_{22}) \end{aligned} \tag{9.39}$$

In this reference system, we can also write $\boldsymbol{T} = t_1\boldsymbol{e}_1{}^{(1)} + t_2\boldsymbol{e}_2{}^{(1)} + t_3\boldsymbol{e}_3{}^{(1)}$ where

$$t_1 = (\boldsymbol{c}^{(2)} - \boldsymbol{c}^{(1)}) \bullet \boldsymbol{e}_1{}^{(1)}, \quad t_2 = (\boldsymbol{c}^{(2)} - \boldsymbol{c}^{(1)}) \bullet \boldsymbol{e}_2{}^{(1)}, \quad t_3 = (\boldsymbol{c}^{(2)} - \boldsymbol{c}^{(1)}) \bullet \boldsymbol{e}_3{}^{(1)} \tag{9.40}$$

It can be seen that with the above selection of the reference frame, the expressions for D_i, $\rho^{(1)}$, $\rho^{(2)}$ get highly simplified, reducing the number of operations needed to evaluate the inequality in Eq. 9.37. For example, when $\boldsymbol{l}_i = \boldsymbol{e}_1{}^{(1)} \times \boldsymbol{e}_1{}^{(2)}$, we get the following expressions for the projected distances:

$$\begin{aligned} D_i &= |\boldsymbol{T} \bullet \boldsymbol{l}_i| = \left|t_2\boldsymbol{e}_2{}^{(1)} \bullet (\boldsymbol{e}_1{}^{(1)} \times \boldsymbol{e}_1{}^{(2)}) + t_3\boldsymbol{e}_3{}^{(1)} \bullet (\boldsymbol{e}_1{}^{(1)} \times \boldsymbol{e}_1{}^{(2)})\right| \\ &= |-t_2r_{20} + t_3r_{10}| \\ \rho_i{}^{(1)} &= w_2{}^{(1)}\left|\boldsymbol{e}_2{}^{(1)} \bullet (\boldsymbol{e}_1{}^{(1)} \times \boldsymbol{e}_1{}^{(2)})\right| + w_3{}^{(1)}\left|\boldsymbol{e}_3{}^{(1)} \bullet (\boldsymbol{e}_1{}^{(1)} \times \boldsymbol{e}_1{}^{(2)})\right| \\ &= w_2{}^{(1)}|r_{20}| + w_3{}^{(1)}|r_{10}| \end{aligned}$$

$$\begin{aligned} \rho_i{}^{(2)} &= w_2{}^{(2)}\left|\boldsymbol{e}_2{}^{(2)} \bullet (\boldsymbol{e}_1{}^{(1)} \times \boldsymbol{e}_1{}^{(2)})\right| + w_3{}^{(2)}\left|\boldsymbol{e}_3{}^{(2)} \bullet (\boldsymbol{e}_1{}^{(1)} \times \boldsymbol{e}_1{}^{(2)})\right| \\ &= w_2{}^{(2)}|-r_{11}r_{20} + r_{21}r_{10}| + w_3{}^{(2)}|-r_{12}r_{20} + r_{22}r_{10}| \\ &= w_2{}^{(2)}|r_{02}| + w_3{}^{(2)}|r_{01}| \end{aligned} \tag{9.41}$$

The last expression given above is derived based on the fact that $\boldsymbol{e}_1{}^{(2)} \times \boldsymbol{e}_2{}^{(2)} = \boldsymbol{e}_3{}^{(2)}$ and $\boldsymbol{e}_1{}^{(2)} \times \boldsymbol{e}_3{}^{(2)} = -\boldsymbol{e}_2{}^{(2)}$. The complete set of expressions for the above quantities for the 15 possible choices of $\boldsymbol{l}_i$ is given in Table 9.1.

Table 9.1 Formulae for computing projected distances of OBB radii and the line of centres for 15 separating axis directions

l_i	D_i	$\rho_i^{(1)}$	$\rho_i^{(2)}$
$e_1^{(1)}$	$\lvert t_1\rvert$	$w_1^{(1)}$	$w_1^{(2)}\lvert r_{00}\rvert + w_2^{(2)}\lvert r_{01}\rvert + w_3^{(2)}\lvert r_{02}\rvert$
$e_2^{(1)}$	$\lvert t_2\rvert$	$w_2^{(1)}$	$w_1^{(2)}\lvert r_{10}\rvert + w_2^{(2)}\lvert r_{11}\rvert + w_3^{(2)}\lvert r_{12}\rvert$
$e_3^{(1)}$	$\lvert t_3\rvert$	$w_3^{(1)}$	$w_1^{(2)}\lvert r_{20}\rvert + w_2^{(2)}\lvert r_{21}\rvert + w_3^{(2)}\lvert r_{22}\rvert$
$e_1^{(2)}$	$\lvert t_1 r_{00} + t_2 r_{10} + t_3 r_{20}\rvert$	$w_1^{(1)}\lvert r_{00}\rvert + w_2^{(1)}\lvert r_{10}\rvert + w_3^{(1)}\lvert r_{20}\rvert$	$w_1^{(2)}$
$e_2^{(2)}$	$\lvert t_1 r_{01} + t_2 r_{11} + t_3 r_{21}\rvert$	$w_1^{(1)}\lvert r_{01}\rvert + w_2^{(1)}\lvert r_{11}\rvert + w_3^{(1)}\lvert r_{21}\rvert$	$w_2^{(2)}$
$e_3^{(2)}$	$\lvert t_1 r_{02} + t_2 r_{12} + t_3 r_{22}\rvert$	$w_1^{(1)}\lvert r_{02}\rvert + w_2^{(1)}\lvert r_{12}\rvert + w_3^{(1)}\lvert r_{22}\rvert$	$w_3^{(2)}$
$e_1^{(1)} \times e_1^{(2)}$	$\lvert -t_2 r_{20} + t_3 r_{10}\rvert$	$w_2^{(1)}\lvert r_{20}\rvert + w_3^{(1)}\lvert r_{10}\rvert$	$w_2^{(2)}\lvert r_{02}\rvert + w_3^{(2)}\lvert r_{01}\rvert$
$e_1^{(1)} \times e_2^{(2)}$	$\lvert -t_2 r_{21} + t_3 r_{11}\rvert$	$w_2^{(1)}\lvert r_{21}\rvert + w_3^{(1)}\lvert r_{11}\rvert$	$w_1^{(2)}\lvert r_{02}\rvert + w_3^{(2)}\lvert r_{00}\rvert$
$e_1^{(1)} \times e_3^{(2)}$	$\lvert -t_2 r_{22} + t_3 r_{12}\rvert$	$w_2^{(1)}\lvert r_{22}\rvert + w_3^{(1)}\lvert r_{12}\rvert$	$w_1^{(2)}\lvert r_{01}\rvert + w_2^{(2)}\lvert r_{00}\rvert$
$e_2^{(1)} \times e_1^{(2)}$	$\lvert t_1 r_{20} - t_3 r_{00}\rvert$	$w_1^{(1)}\lvert r_{20}\rvert + w_3^{(1)}\lvert r_{00}\rvert$	$w_2^{(2)}\lvert r_{12}\rvert + w_3^{(2)}\lvert r_{11}\rvert$
$e_2^{(1)} \times e_2^{(2)}$	$\lvert t_1 r_{21} - t_3 r_{01}\rvert$	$w_1^{(1)}\lvert r_{21}\rvert + w_3^{(1)}\lvert r_{01}\rvert$	$w_1^{(2)}\lvert r_{12}\rvert + w_3^{(2)}\lvert r_{10}\rvert$
$e_2^{(1)} \times e_3^{(2)}$	$\lvert t_1 r_{22} - t_3 r_{02}\rvert$	$w_1^{(1)}\lvert r_{22}\rvert + w_3^{(1)}\lvert r_{02}\rvert$	$w_1^{(2)}\lvert r_{11}\rvert + w_2^{(2)}\lvert r_{10}\rvert$
$e_3^{(1)} \times e_1^{(2)}$	$\lvert -t_1 r_{10} + t_2 r_{00}\rvert$	$w_1^{(1)}\lvert r_{10}\rvert + w_2^{(1)}\lvert r_{00}\rvert$	$w_2^{(2)}\lvert r_{22}\rvert + w_3^{(2)}\lvert r_{21}\rvert$
$e_3^{(1)} \times e_2^{(2)}$	$\lvert -t_1 r_{11} + t_2 r_{01}\rvert$	$w_1^{(1)}\lvert r_{11}\rvert + w_2^{(1)}\lvert r_{01}\rvert$	$w_1^{(2)}\lvert r_{22}\rvert + w_3^{(2)}\lvert r_{20}\rvert$
$e_3^{(1)} \times e_3^{(2)}$	$\lvert -t_1 r_{12} + t_2 r_{02}\rvert$	$w_1^{(1)}\lvert r_{12}\rvert + w_2^{(1)}\lvert r_{02}\rvert$	$w_1^{(2)}\lvert r_{21}\rvert + w_2^{(2)}\lvert r_{20}\rvert$

9.2.3 Sphere Intersection

Sphere intersection tests are relatively simpler than the tests required for other types of bounding volumes. Collision detection algorithms often use spheres as the first level of bounding volumes so that intersection tests could be quickly carried out. In such situations, more accurate computations using tighter bounding volumes are performed only if necessary. The condition for the intersection of a ray $\{\boldsymbol{p}, \boldsymbol{m}\}$ with a sphere $\{\boldsymbol{c}, r\}$ can be easily obtained by substituting the ray's parametric representation (see Eq. 9.22) into the sphere's equation:

$$(\boldsymbol{p} + t\,\boldsymbol{m} - \boldsymbol{c}) \bullet (\boldsymbol{p} + t\,\boldsymbol{m} - \boldsymbol{c}) = r^2 \tag{9.42}$$

Since $\boldsymbol{m}$ is a unit vector, the above equation can be re-written as follows:

$$t^2 + 2t\,\boldsymbol{m} \bullet (\boldsymbol{p} - \boldsymbol{c}) + (\boldsymbol{p} - \boldsymbol{c}) \bullet (\boldsymbol{p} - \boldsymbol{c}) - r^2 = 0. \tag{9.43}$$

The above quadratic in t will have real roots only if

$$\{\boldsymbol{m} \bullet (\boldsymbol{p} - \boldsymbol{c})\}^2 - (\boldsymbol{p} - \boldsymbol{c}) \bullet (\boldsymbol{p} - \boldsymbol{c}) + r^2 \geq 0. \tag{9.44}$$

The above inequality gives the necessary condition for the intersection of the ray. Depending on the signs of the real roots of the equation (if the above condition is satisfied), we can classify the solution into four different categories:

- Roots are equal and positive. The ray is tangential to the sphere.
- Roots are unequal and positive. The ray intersects the sphere at two distinct points. The minimum value of t gives the point closest to the origin of the ray.
- One root is positive and the other negative. The origin of the ray is inside the sphere.
- Both roots are negative. The ray is directed away from the sphere and the points of intersection are behind the origin of the ray.

The last condition mentioned above can also be checked using a simple test. If $\boldsymbol{m}\bullet(\boldsymbol{c} - \boldsymbol{p}) < 0$, then the sphere is behind the ray.

A plane given by $\boldsymbol{r}\bullet\boldsymbol{n} = -d$ intersects the sphere $\{\boldsymbol{c}, r\}$ if the distance of the centre of the sphere from the plane is less than the sphere's radius r. Assuming that $|\boldsymbol{n}| = 1$, the necessary condition for intersection is (see also Eq. 2.24)

$$(\boldsymbol{c} \bullet \boldsymbol{n}) + d \leq r \tag{9.45}$$

Two spheres $\{\boldsymbol{c}_1, r_1\}$ and $\{\boldsymbol{c}_2, r_2\}$ intersect if and only if the distance between their centres is less than the sum of their radii:

$$|\boldsymbol{c}_1 - \boldsymbol{c}_2| \leq r_1 + r_2. \tag{9.46}$$

9.2.4 k-DOP Intersection

We saw in Sect. 9.1.4 that a k-DOP can be represented by $k/2$ slabs $\{dmin_j, dmax_j, \boldsymbol{n}_j\}, j = 0 \ldots (k/2)-1$, where $\boldsymbol{n}_j$s are unit normal directions associated with the slabs. The slab-based intersection test outlined in Sect. 9.2.2 can be directly extended for a k-DOP as shown below. For a given ray $\{\boldsymbol{p}, \boldsymbol{m}\}$, the interval of intersection on each slab can be obtained using the following equations (see Eq. 9.32):

$$\begin{aligned}
&\text{If} \quad \boldsymbol{m} \bullet \boldsymbol{n}_j > 0, \quad t_{\min}^{(j)} = \frac{-w_j - (\boldsymbol{p} \bullet \boldsymbol{n}_j)}{(\boldsymbol{m} \bullet \boldsymbol{n}_j)}, \quad t_{\max}^{(j)} = \frac{w_j - (\boldsymbol{p} \bullet \boldsymbol{n}_j)}{(\boldsymbol{m} \bullet \boldsymbol{n}_j)} \\
&\text{If} \quad \boldsymbol{m} \bullet \boldsymbol{n}_j < 0, \quad t_{\min}^{(j)} = \frac{w_j - (\boldsymbol{p} \bullet \boldsymbol{n}_j)}{(\boldsymbol{m} \bullet \boldsymbol{n}_j)}, \quad t_{\max}^{(j)} = \frac{-w_j - (\boldsymbol{p} \bullet \boldsymbol{n}_j)}{(\boldsymbol{m} \bullet \boldsymbol{n}_j)}
\end{aligned} \tag{9.47}$$

where $w_j = (dmax_j - dmin_j)/2$. After computing the minimum and maximum values for all the slabs, the following values are obtained:

$$\begin{aligned}
u_{\min} &= \max_j \left\{ t_{\min}^{(j)} \right\} \\
u_{\max} &= \min_j \left\{ t_{\max}^{(j)} \right\}
\end{aligned} \tag{9.48}$$

The ray intersects the k-DOP if and only if the intersection of the slab intervals is non-empty. The necessary and sufficient condition for intersection is $u_{\min} \le u_{\max}$.

An overlap test involving a k-DOP and a plane can be implemented by first computing the vertices of the k-DOP and comparing them with the plane to determine if some of them are located either on the plane or on either sides of the plane. The vertex positions are obtained by taking three planes of the k-DOP at a time and computing their point of intersection using the method described in Sect. 2.4.

The complexity of intersection tests using only k-DOPs can be significantly reduced if they are all constructed using the same set of normal directions. Two such k-DOPs $\{dmin_j^{(1)}, dmax_j^{(1)}, \boldsymbol{n}_j\}$, $\{dmin_j^{(2)}, dmax_j^{(2)}, \boldsymbol{n}_j\}$, $j = 0 \ldots (k/2)-1$, overlap if and only if *all* corresponding pairs of intervals $[dmin_j^{(1)}, dmax_j^{(1)}]$, $[dmin_j^{(2)}, dmax_j^{(2)}]$ overlap. Thus, if the following condition is satisfied for *any* j, then the two k-DOPs do not overlap.

$$\left(dmin_j^{(1)} > dmax_j^{(2)}\right) \text{ or } \left(dmax_j^{(1)} < dmin_j^{(2)}\right) \tag{9.49}$$

9.2.5 *Triangle Intersection*

Bounding volume hierarchies (detailed in the next section) have to facilitate overlap tests using not only bounding volumes but also primitives at the lowermost levels of the tree. Since triangles are the most widely used mesh primitives, we discuss below the intersection tests using triangles. A triangle T will be represented by its three vertices as $\{\boldsymbol{p}_1, \boldsymbol{p}_2, \boldsymbol{p}_3\}$. The unit normal vector of the plane of the triangle will be denoted by $\boldsymbol{n}$. In the following, we assume that the triangle and the primitive it is tested against are both defined in a common reference frame.

The intersection of a ray $\{\boldsymbol{q}, \boldsymbol{m}\}$ with the triangle T is computed by first checking if the ray intersects the plane of the triangle, and then determining if the point of intersection lies within the triangle. If the ray is not parallel to the plane of the triangle ($\boldsymbol{m}\bullet\boldsymbol{n} \neq 0$), the intersection point is given by the value of the parameter t in Eq. 2.23. If $t \ge 0$, the ray intersects the plane of the triangle, and the point of intersection given by $\boldsymbol{s} = \boldsymbol{q} + t\boldsymbol{m}$. If the three vector scalar triple products $((\boldsymbol{p}_2 - \boldsymbol{p}_1) \times (\boldsymbol{s} - \boldsymbol{p}_1))\bullet\boldsymbol{m}$, $((\boldsymbol{p}_3 - \boldsymbol{p}_2) \times (\boldsymbol{s} - \boldsymbol{p}_2))\bullet\boldsymbol{m}$ and $((\boldsymbol{p}_1 - \boldsymbol{p}_3) \times (\boldsymbol{s} - \boldsymbol{p}_3))\bullet\boldsymbol{m}$ all have the same sign (see Eq. 2.10), then the point of intersection lies inside the triangle. If any of the cross product is zero, the intersection point lies on the boundary of the triangle. If it is not necessary to compute the actual point of intersection with the triangle, then the above test can be simplified into the condition that the values of $((\boldsymbol{p}_1 - \boldsymbol{q}) \times (\boldsymbol{p}_2 - \boldsymbol{q}))\bullet\boldsymbol{m}$, $((\boldsymbol{p}_2 - \boldsymbol{q}) \times (\boldsymbol{p}_3 - \boldsymbol{q}))\bullet\boldsymbol{m}$, $((\boldsymbol{p}_3 - \boldsymbol{q}) \times (\boldsymbol{p}_1 - \boldsymbol{q}))\bullet\boldsymbol{m}$ have the same sign for a valid intersection. We now deal with the case $\boldsymbol{m}\bullet\boldsymbol{n} = 0$ separately. In this case, the ray must also lie on the plane of the triangle in order to possibly intersect it. The necessary condition for this is $(\boldsymbol{q} - \boldsymbol{p}_1)\bullet\boldsymbol{n} = 0$. If the condition is satisfied, then we compare the ray with the edges of the triangle to determine the

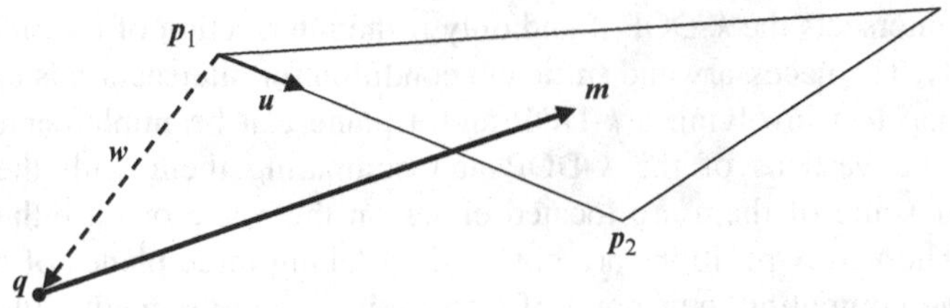

Fig. 9.15 Intersection of a ray with an edge of a triangle given by the line segment p_1p_2

intersection points. As an example, we consider the intersection of the ray $\{\boldsymbol{q}, \boldsymbol{m}\}$ with the line segment $\boldsymbol{p}_1\boldsymbol{p}_2$ (Fig. 9.15), assuming that both lines are coplanar. Let $\boldsymbol{u} = \boldsymbol{p}_2 - \boldsymbol{p}_1$, and $\boldsymbol{w} = \boldsymbol{q} - \boldsymbol{p}_1$.

If the ray intersects the line segment, then their projections on to any of the principal planes must also intersect. The intersection test can thus be reduced to a two-dimensional problem, by selecting only two coordinates for which both $\boldsymbol{u}$ and $\boldsymbol{m}$ are non-zero and non-coincident vectors. In this two-dimensional space, let $\boldsymbol{u} = (u_1, u_2)$, $\boldsymbol{m} = (m_1, m_2)$, and $\boldsymbol{w} = (w_1, w_2)$. Any point on the line segment $\boldsymbol{p}_1\boldsymbol{p}_2$ is given in parametric form as $\boldsymbol{p}_1 + s\boldsymbol{u}$ $(0 \le s \le 1)$, and any point on the ray as $\boldsymbol{q} + t\boldsymbol{m}$. At a valid intersection point, we must have $\boldsymbol{p}_1 + s\boldsymbol{u} = \boldsymbol{q} + t\boldsymbol{m}$. This equation leads to the following two simultaneous linear equations in s and t:

$$\begin{aligned} s\,u_1 - tm_1 &= w_1 \\ s\,u_2 - tm_2 &= w_2 \end{aligned} \tag{9.50}$$

from which we get

$$s = \frac{w_1m_2 - w_2m_1}{u_1m_2 - u_2m_1}$$

$$t = \frac{w_1u_2 - w_2u_1}{u_1m_2 - u_2m_1} \tag{9.51}$$

If the above values for s and t satisfy the conditions $0 \le s \le 1$, $t \ge 0$, then the ray intersects the edge $\boldsymbol{p}_1\boldsymbol{p}_2$ of the triangle. The denominators in the above expressions become zero when the vectors $\boldsymbol{u}$ and $\boldsymbol{m}$ become parallel, in which case, the ray does not intersect the triangle.

Intersection tests with a triangle and a plane $\boldsymbol{r}\bullet\boldsymbol{n} = -d$ can be performed as previously discussed in the context of AABB intersections, by computing the signed distances D_i of the vertices of the triangle from the plane as $D_i = \boldsymbol{p}_i\bullet\boldsymbol{n} + d$, $i = 1,2,3$. If any of the signed distances is zero, or if any two distances have opposite signs, then the plane intersects the triangle.

We now consider the problem of computing the intersection of one triangle with another. Here, we assume that the triangles are on two different planes, and as previously done for the ray intersection test, we will deal with the intersection of two coplanar triangles separately. Let the two triangles be $T_1 = \{\boldsymbol{p}_1, \boldsymbol{p}_2, \boldsymbol{p}_3\}$,

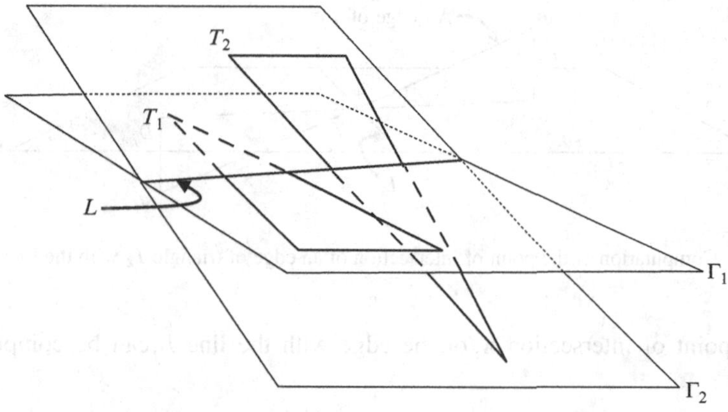

Fig. 9.16 An example showing the configuration of two triangles where the plane containing one intersects the other

and $T_2 = \{q_1, q_2, q_3\}$. The plane Γ_1 containing the first triangle is given by $\boldsymbol{r}\bullet\boldsymbol{n}_1 = -d_1$, where $\boldsymbol{n}_1$ is obtained by normalizing the vector $(\boldsymbol{p}_2 - \boldsymbol{p}_1) \times (\boldsymbol{p}_3 - \boldsymbol{p}_1)$, and $d_1 = -\boldsymbol{p}_1\bullet\boldsymbol{n}_1$. Similarly the plane Γ_2 containing the second triangle is also obtained as $\boldsymbol{r}\bullet\boldsymbol{n}_2 = -d_2$. We then use the procedure outlined in the previous paragraph to determine if the first triangle T_1 is intersected by the plane Γ_2, and if the second triangle T_2 is intersected by the plane Γ_1. If any of these tests fails, then the triangles do not intersect. Otherwise, the plane of each triangle intersects the other triangle as shown in Fig. 9.16. The line of intersection L of the planes also intersects both triangles.

The two triangles overlap if the intervals of the triangles on the line L overlap. The equation of the line L is given by

$$\boldsymbol{r} = \boldsymbol{v} + t(\boldsymbol{n}_1 \times \boldsymbol{n}_2) \tag{9.52}$$

where, $\boldsymbol{v}$ is a point on the line. To determine this point, we first select a component of $\boldsymbol{n}_1 \times \boldsymbol{n}_2$ which is non-zero. If the x component of $\boldsymbol{n}_1 \times \boldsymbol{n}_2$ is non-zero, we will be able to find a point $\boldsymbol{v} = (0, y, z)$ on L by solving the following two equations obtained from the fact that this point lies on both the planes.

$$\begin{aligned} yn_{1y} + zn_{1z} + d_1 &= 0 \\ yn_{2y} + zn_{2z} + d_2 &= 0 \end{aligned} \tag{9.53}$$

Having obtained the parameters defining the equation of the line L, the next step is to find the points of intersection of the line with the triangles. Consider an edge of the triangle T_2 that intersects the line L as shown in Fig. 9.17. Such an edge can be identified as having vertices that give opposite signs for signed distances with respect to the plane Γ_1. Let the vertices be $\boldsymbol{q}_i$, $\boldsymbol{q}_j$, with $|D_i|$, $|D_j|$ denoting the magnitudes of the respective signed distances.

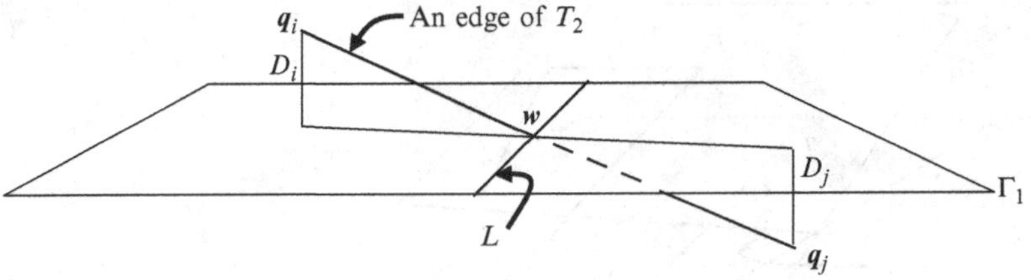

Fig. 9.17 Computation of the point of intersection of an edge of triangle T_2 with the line L

The point of intersection $\boldsymbol{w}$ of the edge with the line L can be computed as follows:

$$\begin{aligned} \boldsymbol{w} &= \boldsymbol{q}_i + \frac{|\boldsymbol{w} - \boldsymbol{q}_i|}{|\boldsymbol{q}_j - \boldsymbol{q}_i|}(\boldsymbol{q}_j - \boldsymbol{q}_i) \\ &= \boldsymbol{q}_i + \frac{|D_i|}{(|D_i| + |D_j|)}(\boldsymbol{q}_j - \boldsymbol{q}_i) \end{aligned} \tag{9.54}$$

The position of $\boldsymbol{w}$ corresponds to a value of the parameter t on the line L. This value can be obtained from Eq. 9.52, by substituting $\boldsymbol{w}$ for $\boldsymbol{r}$, and choosing any component that has a non-zero value for $\boldsymbol{n}_1 \times \boldsymbol{n}_2$. Similarly, we can obtain another value of the parameter t for the other edge of T_2 that intersects L. Thus we have the interval $[t_1, t_2]$ of the line segment on L obtained by its intersection with T_2. Repeating the whole process for the triangle T_1, and computing the signed distances of its vertices with respect to Γ_2, we can find the interval $[s_1, s_2]$ intersected by the triangle on L. If both intervals overlap, then the two triangles intersect.

Another approach to determining if the triangles overlap in three dimensions was recently proposed by Raabe et al. (2009). It uses the separating axis theorem (see Sect. 9.2.2), considering triangles as degenerate polytopes. If $\boldsymbol{u}_1, \boldsymbol{u}_2, \boldsymbol{u}_3$ and $\boldsymbol{v}_1, \boldsymbol{v}_2, \boldsymbol{v}_3$ denote the vectors along the sides of the two triangles (e.g., $\boldsymbol{u}_1 = \boldsymbol{p}_2 - \boldsymbol{p}_1$) then 9 separating axes directions can be formed as $\boldsymbol{l} = \boldsymbol{u}_i \times \boldsymbol{v}_j$ $(i, j = 1, 2, 3)$. The vertices $\boldsymbol{p}_i$ and $\boldsymbol{q}_i$ are projected on to each separating axis $\boldsymbol{l}$, and intervals $[t_1, t_2]$, $[s_1, s_2]$ computed as follows:

$$\begin{aligned} t_1 &= \min_i\{\boldsymbol{p}_i \bullet \boldsymbol{l}\}, \quad t_2 = \max_i\{\boldsymbol{p}_i \bullet \boldsymbol{l}\} \\ s_1 &= \min_i\{\boldsymbol{q}_i \bullet \boldsymbol{l}\}, \quad s_2 = \max_i\{\boldsymbol{q}_i \bullet \boldsymbol{l}\} \end{aligned} \tag{9.55}$$

If the intervals do not overlap for any of the separating axes directions, then the triangles do not overlap. We now consider the problem of determining if two triangles on the same plane intersect. Here we can use a simplified version of the separating axis theorem. Two non-overlapping triangles lying on a common plane can be separated by a line parallel to one of the six sides. This means that if the triangles do not overlap, their vertices can be projected on to disjoint intervals on a line orthogonal to one of the sides (Fig. 9.18).

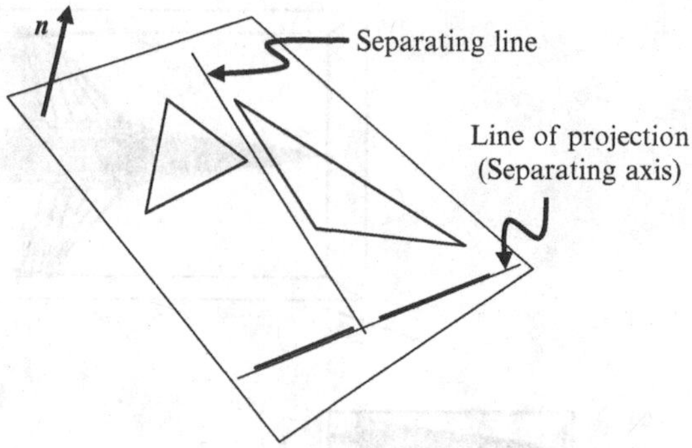

Fig. 9.18 The separating axis theorem applied to a pair of co-planar triangles

We need to consider only six separating axis directions given by $\boldsymbol{u}_i \times \boldsymbol{n}$ and $\boldsymbol{v}_i \times \boldsymbol{n}$ $(i = 1,2,3)$. The vertices of each triangle are projected on to the separating axis vector, and the projected intervals for the triangles computed as outlined above (Eq. 9.55). If any of the interval pairs are disjoint, then the triangles do not overlap.

9.3 Bounding Volume Hierarchies

Bounding volume hierarchies (BVH) were briefly introduced in Sect. 3.4 in the context of scene graphs. Using a BVH, the space enclosed by a collection of objects that are located close to each other in a scene can be hierarchically represented in terms of bounding volumes of subgroups within the collection, with the leaf nodes containing sufficiently small object parts and optionally their bounding volumes. In this representation, a parent node stores the combined bounding volume of a set of objects in the child nodes. A bounding volume for a single complex mesh object may also be subdivided into groups of bounding volumes of smaller components or parts of the mesh. A bounding volume hierarchy can therefore be viewed as a multi-scale representation of an object using bounding volumes. The hierarchical tree structure of bounding volumes is useful in significantly reducing the amount of pair-wise overlap tests. Bounding volume overlap tests are performed from the root of the tree to determine if the overall bounding volume intersects another primitive or another bounding volume. If the intersection test fails at this point, further tests using smaller sub-volumes stored in child nodes are not carried out. The complexity of intersection tests can thus be reduced using a well designed hierarchy. Some of the design considerations are

- the efficiency and speed of computing the bounding volume parameters
- the optimality of the computed bounding volumes
- the amount of overlap between bounding volumes of sibling nodes
- the frequency of updates

The following two sections describe commonly used strategies for the construction and traversal of bounding volume hierarchies.

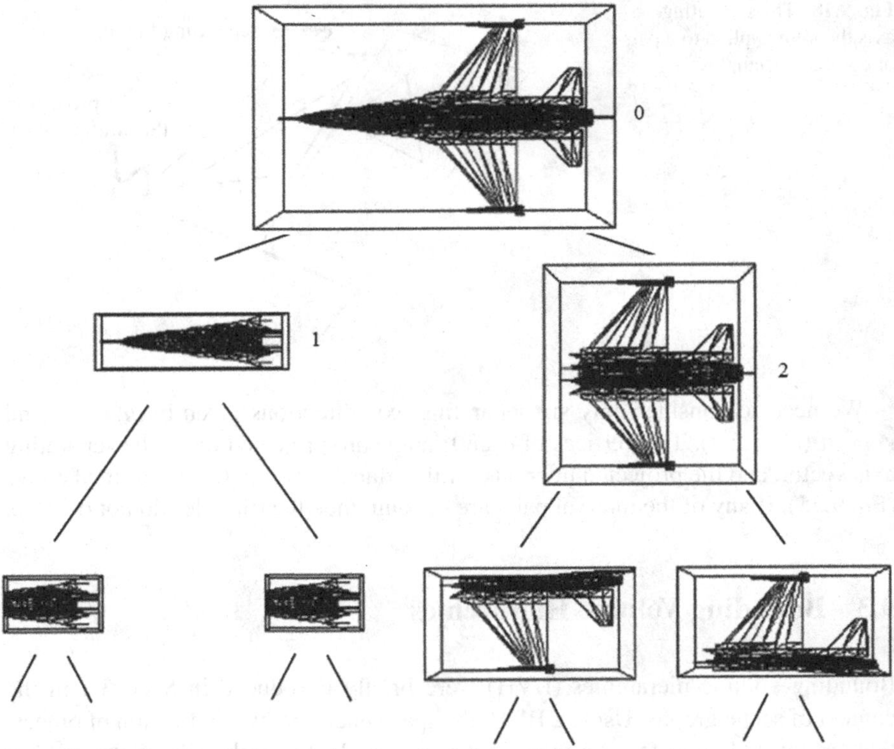

Fig. 9.19 A bounding volume hierarchy using AABBs formed using top-down construction

9.3.1 Top-Down Design

The top-down construction of a bounding volume hierarchy starts with the formation of the bounding volume of an object, then recursively subdivides the mesh object into two nearly equal parts and stores their bounding volumes in the child nodes. The partitioning of the mesh is usually done by axis aligned splitting planes. Mesh primitives are assigned to either the left or the right child node based on the location of their centroids with respect to the splitting plane of the current node. The bounding volumes of the mesh sections stored in the child nodes are then computed. This process is repeated until a maximum level for the binary tree is reached, or until a node contains only a sufficiently small number of primitives.

A bounding volume hierarchy constructed using AABB in the top-down fashion is shown in Fig. 9.19. At each node, the longest axis of the AABB is chosen, and the plane perpendicular to this axis passing through the centre of the AABB is selected as the splitting plane. For example, if the AABB is given by its mid point (x_{mid}, y_{mid}, z_{mid}) and the three half-width extents x_r, y_r, z_r, and if $x_r > y_r$, and $x_r > z_r$, then the plane parallel to the yz-plane through the midpoint is chosen as the splitting plane.

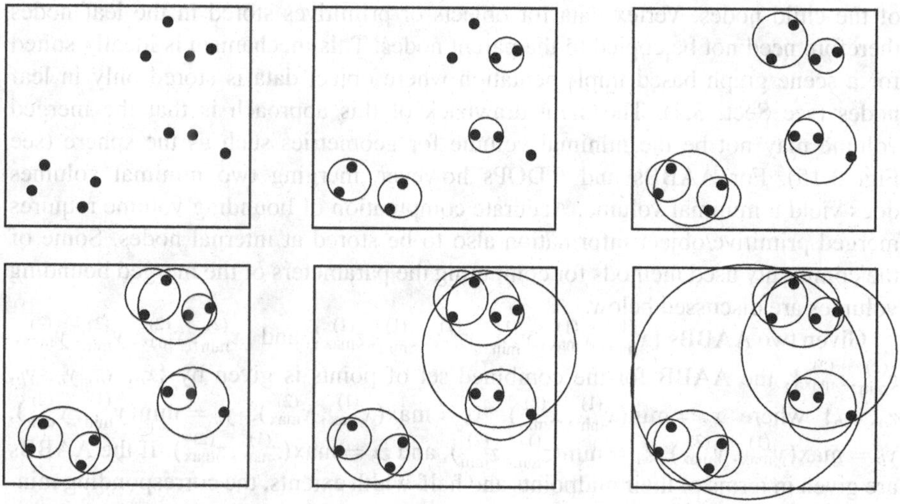

Fig. 9.20 An agglomerative clustering algorithm forms small cluster groups and merges them recursively based on pair-wise distances between existing clusters

The triangles of the mesh whose centres have the x-coordinate less than x_{mid} are assigned to the left child, and the remaining triangles to the right child. In Fig. 9.19, the yz-plane was chosen as the splitting plane at nodes 0 and 1, and the xz-plane at node 2.

The top-down approach is particularly suitable for run-time construction of bounding volume hierarchies of large mesh objects using simple mesh partitioning strategies as outlined above. Therefore, most of the BVH algorithms use this method.

9.3.2 Bottom-Up Design

The bottom-up design approach is suitable for creating bounding volume hierarchies of a group of small objects that are located near each other. The construction of the tree starts with the bounding volumes of each object in the group which are then combined pair-wise, based on a distance measure. The bounding volume of the combined object is recomputed. This process is repeated until the bounding volume of the entire group is constructed at the root node. It is easy to see that methods like this run in parallel with agglomerative (bottom-up) hierarchical clustering algorithms that use pair-wise distances to form larger and larger groups of objects (Fig. 9.20).

The bottom-up construction has the advantage that the bounding volume updates at a parent node can be done by simply merging together the bounding volumes of the child nodes. Vertex data for objects or primitives stored in the leaf nodes therefore need not be copied to the parent nodes. This mechanism is ideally suited for a scene graph based implementation where object data is stored only in leaf nodes (see Sect. 3.4). The main drawback of this approach is that the merged volume may not be the minimal volume for geometries such as the sphere (see Fig. 3.15). For AABBs and *k*-DOPs however, merging two minimal volumes does yield a minimal volume. Accurate computation of bounding volume requires merged primitive/object information also to be stored at internal nodes. Some of the commonly used methods for computing the parameters of the merged bounding volumes are discussed below.

Given two AABBs $\{x^{(1)}_{\min}, x^{(1)}_{\max}, y^{(1)}_{\min}, y^{(1)}_{\max}, z^{(1)}_{\min}, z^{(1)}_{\max}\}$, and $\{x^{(2)}_{\min}, x^{(2)}_{\max}, y^{(2)}_{\min}, y^{(2)}_{\max}, z^{(2)}_{\min}, z^{(2)}_{\max}\}$, the AABB for the combined set of points is given by $\{x_a, x_b, y_a, y_b, z_a, z_b\}$ where $x_a = \min(x^{(1)}_{\min}, x^{(2)}_{\min})$, $x_b = \max(x^{(1)}_{\max}, x^{(2)}_{\max})$, $y_a = \min(y^{(1)}_{\min}, y^{(2)}_{\min})$, $y_b = \max(y^{(1)}_{\max}, y^{(2)}_{\max})$, $z_a = \min(z^{(1)}_{\min}, z^{(2)}_{\min})$, and $z_b = \max(z^{(1)}_{\max}, z^{(2)}_{\max})$. If the AABBs are given in terms of their midpoints and half-width extents, the corresponding min-max values are computed and the merged volume parameters obtained as above. These parameters could then be converted back to the midpoint coordinates and half-width extents.

The equations for computing the parameters of a sphere formed by merging together two spheres were given in Eq. 3.3. Merging two OBBs is done by collecting the vertices (Eq. 9.29) of both OBBs and computing a new OBB for these 16 points using the methods outlined in Sect. 9.1.3.

Two *k*-DOPs can be easily merged if they share the same set of normal vectors. The method is exactly the same as that used for AABBs. If the *k*-DOPs are given by $\{dmin_j^{(1)}, dmax_j^{(1)}, \mathbf{n}_j\}$, $\{dmin_j^{(2)}, dmax_j^{(2)}, \mathbf{n}_j\}$, $j = 0 \ldots (k/2)-1$, then the combined volume is $\{dmn_j, dmx_j, \mathbf{n}_j\}$, where $dmn_j = \min(dmin_j^{(1)}, dmin_j^{(2)})$ and $dmx_j = \max(dmax_j^{(1)}, dmax_j^{(2)})$, for all j.

9.3.3 Collision Testing Using Hierarchy Traversal

Collision between a primitive (e.g., a ray) and an object (or a group of objects) can be detected by traversing the bounding volume hierarchy of the object(s) from the root node in a recursive manner. At each step, an overlap test is performed by comparing the bounding volume stored at a node of the tree with the primitive. Such a method is useful in reducing the number of ray-object intersection tests in ray tracing algorithms and also in games, where for instance, a ray represents the direction of flight of a bullet. A recursive ray intersection algorithm is given as a pseudo code in Listing 9.2. In this code, `node.volume` represents a structure that stores bounding volume parameters at a node, and `overlap()` is a method that tests if the given ray intersects the volume. At a leaf node, the ray is tested with the object primitive stored at that node.

Listing 9.2 Ray-object intersection testing using a BVH

```
findIntersection(Ray ray, Node node) {
if(node==null) return false;
if(!isLeaf(node)) {
   if (!overlap(ray, node.volume)) return false;
   findIntersection(ray, node.left);
   findIntersection(ray, node.right);
} else {
   if(!overlap(ray, node.object)) return false;
   else return true;
}
```

Listing 9.3 Collision testing using two BVHs (Simultaneous descent)

```
findIntersection(Node a, Node b) {
if((a==null)||(b==null)) return false;
if(!isLeaf(a)) {
   if (!overlap(a.volume, b.volume)) return false;
   if(!isLeaf(b)) {
         findIntersection(a.left, b.left);
         findIntersection(a.left, b.right);
         findIntersection(a.right, b.left);
         findIntersection(a.right, b.right);
   } else {
         findIntersection(a.left, b);
         findIntersection(a.right, b);
   }
 } else {
    if(!isLeaf(b)) {
         if(!overlap(a.volume, b.volume)) return false;
         findIntersection(a, b.left);
         findIntersection(a, b.right);
    } else {    //both a and b are leaf nodes
         if(!overlap(a.object, b.object)) return false;
         else return true;
    }
}
```

Object-object intersection tests can be done using their respective bounding volume hierarchies. This process will require a systematic procedure that specifies how the trees must be traversed. A commonly used technique is to descend both hierarchies simultaneously using a depth-first approach. If the objects represented by the hierarchies intersect, the recursion will terminate at the leaf nodes of both trees. A pseudo-code for the method is given in Listing 9.3. In this code, node 'a' belongs to the first tree, and 'b' belongs to the second tree. The procedure is called by passing the root nodes of the trees as parameters. It is assumed that the leaf nodes contain both primitive data (e.g., vertices of a triangle) as well as the bounding volume.

An example showing two binary trees and the sequence of node comparisons used by the above method is given in Fig. 9.21. In this example, the primitives at nodes a_3 and b_8 intersect.

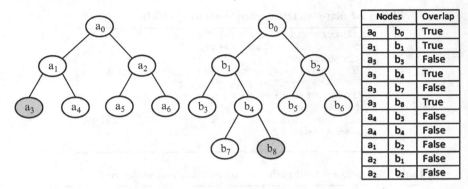

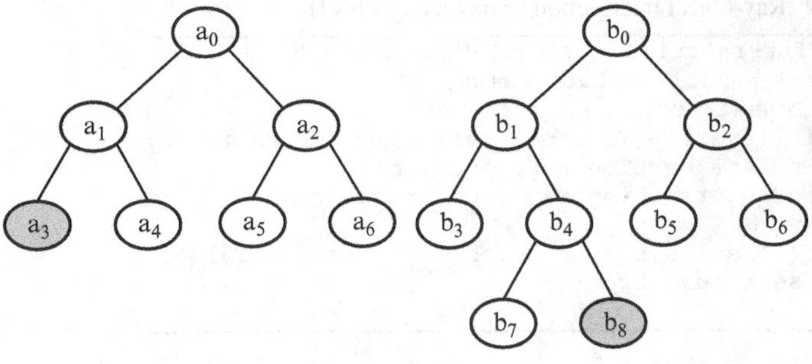

Nodes		Overlap
a_0	b_0	True
a_1	b_1	True
a_3	b_3	False
a_3	b_4	True
a_3	b_7	False
a_3	b_8	True
a_4	b_3	False
a_4	b_4	False
a_1	b_2	False
a_2	b_1	False
a_2	b_2	False

Fig. 9.21 An example showing the simultaneous descend of two bounding volume hierarchies

9.3.4 Cost Function

The evaluation of the performance of a BVH-based method for collision detection is usually done with the help of a cost function. There are primarily three types of important operations performed:

- Bounding volume updates are often required when the object undergoes translational and rotational transformations.
- Bounding volume overlap tests are performed when an internal node of a BVH is compared with an internal node of another BVH.
- Primitive intersection tests are performed at the leaf nodes of a bounding volume hierarchy.

The cost function is the aggregate of the costs for each of the above operations, and is defined as

$$F = n_u C_u + n_v C_v + n_p C_p \tag{9.56}$$

where C_u is the average cost of updating a bounding volume, n_u the number of bounding volumes updated, C_v the average cost of testing if a pair of bounding volumes overlap, n_v the number of bounding volume overlap tests performed, C_p is average cost of testing if a pair of primitives intersect, and n_p the number of primitive intersection tests performed. The value of n_v will be large if several bounding volume overlap tests are done at internal nodes even when the primitives at the leaves do not intersect. Therefore, selecting a tight fitting bounding volume for the construction of the BVH helps in bringing down the value of n_v. However, tight fitting bounding volumes such as convex hulls generally have a higher value of C_v compared to AABBs and spheres. Reducing the number of internal nodes results in a reduction in n_u. The cost functions C_u, C_v, and C_p may be defined based on the number of geometrical computations such as vector products involved in each operation.

9.4 Spatial Partitioning

In this section, we will look at some of the important spatial partitioning tree structures useful for collision detection. If a scene consists of n objects that can move and potentially collide with each other, the number of pair-wise tests required is $n(n-1)/2$. Spatial partitioning techniques help to subdivide the entire three-dimensional space occupied by the objects into a set of regions. Using such techniques we can quickly determine if objects in a group are *not* likely to intersect objects in another group (because they belong to disjoint regions), and thus eliminate the need for performing pair-wise tests between members of the two groups. A region based grouping of objects such that a member within any group is guaranteed not to intersect any member belonging to any of the other groups is called broad-phase collision detection. The grouping also suggests that objects within the same group may potentially collide. Pair-wise intersection tests using methods discussed in the previous section are used only to detect collision between objects within each group. Pair-wise tests using both bounding volumes and primitives are collectively called the narrow phase collision detection methods. Figure 9.22 provides an example showing the reduction in pair-wise tests achieved by a grid-based partitioning of the space into disjoint regions.

9.4.1 *Octrees*

An octree defines a regular partitioning of an axis-aligned cube into eight equally sized sub-cubes (octants) by dividing the cube by half along each of the axis. Each sub-cube is again divided into eight sub-cubes in a similar manner. The process of recursively subdividing the cube continues until a pre-specified maximum for the depth of the tree has been reached, or the cube size has become smaller than a

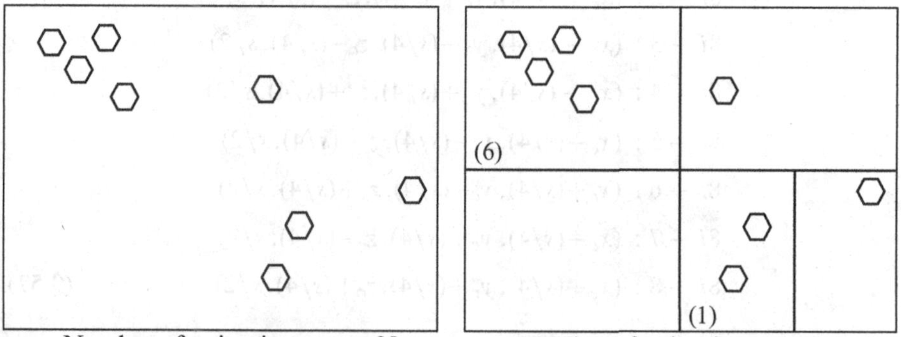

Fig. 9.22 An example showing the reduction in the number of pair-wise tests using spatial partitioning

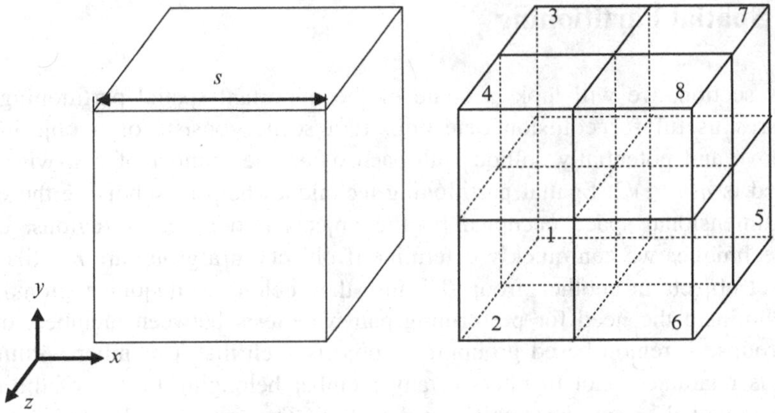

Fig. 9.23 A subdivision of a cube into octants. Cube indices are assigned based on the positions of the sub-cubes relative to the midpoint of the parent

pre-specified minimum value. If the number of primitives within a cube is less than a threshold value, and in particular, if a cube is empty, it is not subdivided further. The initial cube encloses the whole three-dimensional space occupied by the objects, and forms the root node of the octree. Each internal node of an octree has exactly eight children corresponding to the sub-cubes of the parent node. A node is subdivided only when necessary.

The geometrical information about a cube is stored in terms of the position of its midpoint and size. Each cube is also assigned a unique index (Fig. 9.23). The root node has index 0, and its children have indices 1–8. We use the notation $i{:}(x_c, y_c, z_c, s)$ to denote the cube with index i, centre (x_c, y_c, z_c) and side length s. When the cube is subdivided into eight octants, its children are stored as follows:

$$\begin{aligned}
8i+1 &: (x_c-(s/4), y_c-(s/4), z_c-(s/4), s/2)\\
8i+2 &: (x_c-(s/4), y_c-(s/4), z_c+(s/4), s/2)\\
8i+3 &: (x_c-(s/4), y_c+(s/4), z_c-(s/4), s/2)\\
8i+4 &: (x_c-(s/4), y_c+(s/4), z_c+(s/4), s/2)\\
8i+5 &: (x_c+(s/4), y_c-(s/4), z_c-(s/4), s/2)\\
8i+6 &: (x_c+(s/4), y_c-(s/4), z_c+(s/4), s/2)\\
8i+7 &: (x_c+(s/4), y_c+(s/4), z_c-(s/4), s/2)\\
8i+8 &: (x_c+(s/4), y_c+(s/4), z_c+(s/4), s/2)
\end{aligned} \tag{9.57}$$

Using the above index representation, a node among a group of child nodes has an index $k = 8i + j$, $j = 1..8$. The parent's index i can be obtained from k using the integer division $(k-1)/8$. Applying the transformation $b = (k-1) \bmod 8$, we get

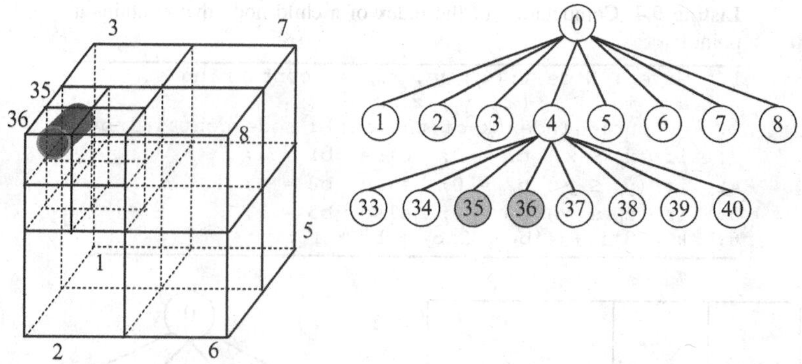

Fig. 9.24 Space partitioning using octrees

a value between 0 and 7 which can be represented using 3 bits. If the lowermost bit of b is 1, it indicates that the node is located towards the positive z direction from its parent. A bit value 0 indicates that the node is in negative z direction. The middle bit similarly gives the node's relative location along y direction (1: positive, 0: negative). The highest bit gives the x-direction. As an example, if a node's index is 30, its parent has the index 3, and $b=5$ (=101 binary). The x and z coordinates of the node's centre are greater than that of its parent, while the y-coordinate is less. We can also use the index information to compute the bounding planes of a cube. Every cube except the root is bounded on three sides by axis-aligned splitting planes through the centre of its parent. These planes are $x=x_c$, $y=y_c$, $z=z_c$, where (x_c, y_c, z_c) is the midpoint of the parent cube. The remaining three bounding planes are given by the bit values of b. For the example given above, where b has a binary value 101, the three remaining bounding planes are $x=x_c+(s/2)$, $y=y_c-(s/2)$ and $z=z_c+(s/2)$. Note that s is the size of the parent, not the sub-cube under consideration. A cube's six bounding planes can also be directly obtained from its own centre and size, but the former method uses three common planes for every child of a given parent node, and requires only three additional planes for each child.

Figure 9.24 shows the subdivision of a three-dimensional volume containing a cylindrical object. The indexing of this volume using an octree is also shown in the figure. The initial volume is divided into eight octants as the volume is non-empty. In the next step, the non-empty volume with index 4 is further subdivided into eight octants. The indices of the children of node 4 have values from 33 to 40 ($8*4+j$, $j=1..8$). The object intersects the sub-cubes 35 and 36, and is therefore included in both these nodes. Further subdivision of these nodes is likely to produce intersection of the object with all sub-cubes, and therefore may not be carried out.

A top-down traversal of the octree from the root node is often performed to locate the smallest cube of the tree that contains a given point $P=(x_p, y_p, z_p)$. If the current node is i:(x_c, y_c, z_c, s), we can identify the next node containing P using its index k computed as given in Listing 9.4.

Listing 9.4 Computation of the index of a child node that contains a point P

```
Given: Node i:(x_c, y_c, z_c, s) containing
a point P = (x_p, y_p, z_p).
Output:  Index k of the child node containing P
if (x_p ≤ x_c) b1 = 0;  else  b1 = 1;
if (y_p ≤ y_c) b2 = 0;  else  b2 = 1;
if (z_p ≤ z_c) b3 = 0;  else  b3 = 1;
k = 8*i + 4*b_1 + 2*b_2 + b_3 + 1 ;
```

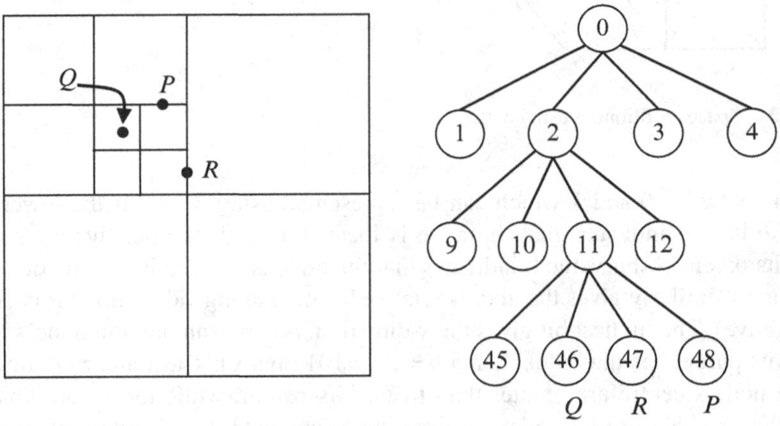

Fig. 9.25 An example showing quadtree subdivision and traversal

The two-dimensional equivalent of an octree is called a quadtree. A quadtree represents subdivisions of a square using four child nodes. For a quadtree, the computation of the index k in Listing 9.4 will use only the x and y coordinates. The corresponding formula for the index of the child node is $k = 4*i + 2*b_1 + b_2 + 1$. A group of four child nodes will thus have indices of the form $4i + j$ ($j = 1..4$). The position of a square relative to its parent is south-west if $j = 1$, north-west if $j = 2$, south-east if $j = 3$, and north-east if $j = 4$. This subdivision scheme establishes the method for quadtree descent, illustrated in Fig. 9.25. Note that a point on a vertical splitting line gets assigned to the square on its left, and a point on a horizontal splitting line gets assigned to the square below it. Note also that empty squares are not subdivided further. A similar traversal algorithm can be formulated for an octree.

We now use the octree traversal algorithm for finding the leaf nodes where a three-dimensional object is stored (as in Fig. 9.24). The object is stored in every leaf node it overlaps. To simplify the problem, we use the AABB of the object given in terms of the parameters $\{x_{min}, x_{max}, y_{min}, y_{max}, z_{min}, z_{max}\}$. We descend the octree using the points $P = (x_{min}, y_{min}, z_{min})$ and $Q = (x_{max}, y_{max}, z_{max})$ as discussed in the previous paragraph, and find the lowest node containing both P and Q. This internal node represents the minimum volume of the subdivision that contains the entire AABB, and hence the entire object. The children of this node are recursively examined to check if any of the sub-cubes overlap the given AABB. Since a cube itself is an AABB, we can use the AABB intersection test in Sect. 9.2.1 for this purpose. If a node does not overlap the given AABB, its children need not be tested. This process is repeated until we reach the leaf nodes and return the indices of those leaf nodes that overlap the AABB. This information is vital for the broad-phase collision detection of the object. The object can potentially intersect only other objects or primitives stored at these leaf nodes.

A bounding sphere enclosing an object can also be stored in an octree using a procedure similar to that described above. An octree node $i{:}(x_c, y_c, z_c, s)$ overlaps a bounding sphere with centre at position $\boldsymbol{p} = (x_p, y_p, z_p)$ and radius r if and only if the distance between the centre of the sphere and the centre of node (cube) is less than or equal to the radius of the sphere. To avoid the square-root computation, this condition is usually expressed as follows:

$$(x_c - x_p)^2 + (y_c - y_p)^2 + (z_c - z_p)^2 \le r^2 \tag{9.58}$$

In the next section, we will look at a recursive binary partitioning tree that is comparatively easier to traverse than an octree.

9.4.2 *k*-d Trees

A *k*-dimensional tree, also known as a *k*-d tree, represents a subdivision hierarchy that is generated by splitting a volume along one axis at a time, and changing the axis in a cyclic fashion at each subdivision step. A three-dimensional volume is commonly split first along the *x*-axis using a plane parallel to the *yz*-plane, then along the *y*-axis using a splitting plane parallel to the *xz*-plane, and then along the *z*-axis. The process continues in the next step by again splitting along the *x*-axis. In our discussion we will assume that the splitting planes are chosen in the *x*-*y*-*z* order. A *k*-d tree is a special case of a binary space partitioning (BSP) tree where splitting planes can have arbitrary normal directions.

At the root level, every point that has the *x*-coordinate less than or equal to a chosen value x_{00} is put into the left child node, and points with *x*-coordinate greater than x_{00} goes to the right child. The points in the child nodes are split using *y*-coordinate values y_{01} and y_{11}. Choosing the splitting values x_{00}, y_{01}, y_{11}, etc., as the median values of the points within the node gives nearly equal number of points in both child nodes, and results in a well balanced tree. An example showing the binary space partitioning of a planar region using a 2-d tree is shown in Fig. 9.26. The splitting values are shown inside the nodes. The first subscript gives the node's position within the same level, starting from 0 for the leftmost node. The second subscript indicates the level the node is in.

A three-dimensional *k*-d tree stores the minimum and maximum extents of the volume it represents at the root using the six coordinate values $\{x_{mn}, x_{mx}, y_{mn}, y_{mx}, z_{mn}, z_{mx}\}$. The root node also stores the value x_{00} of the splitting plane used at

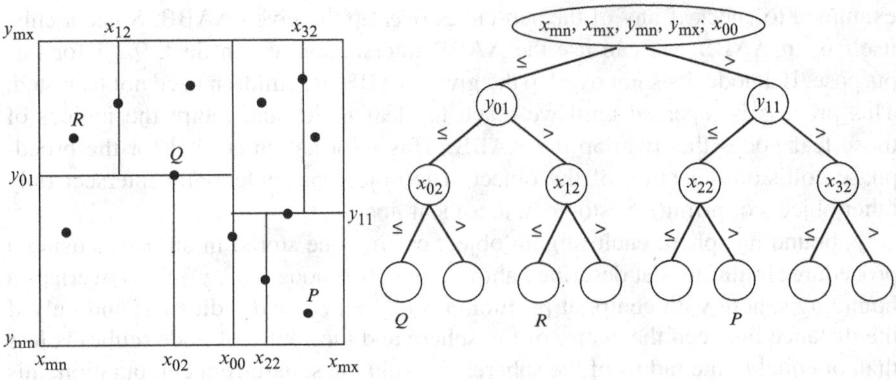

Fig. 9.26 A binary partition of a two-dimensional region using a 2-d tree

Listing 9.5 Sequential traversal of a *k*-d tree for locating a point P

```
Given: A point (px, py, pz).
Output:  Leaf node containing P
node = root
axis = 1     //x-axis
If P is outside the AABB {xmn, xmx, ymn, ymx, zmn, zmx}
     return null                  // P outside the volume
while (!node.isLeaf())          //not a leaf node
{
     if (axis == 1) {        //split along x
          if(px ≤ node.value) node = node.left
          else  node = node.right
     }
     else if (axis == 2) {         //split along y
          if(py ≤ node.value) node = node.left
          else  node = node.right
     }
     else if (axis == 3) {         //split along z
          if(pz ≤ node.value) node = node.left
          else  node = node.right
     }
     axis = axis + 1
     if (axis > 3) axis = 1
  }
  return node
```

that level. The AABB of the left child is given by $\{x_{mn}, x_{00}, y_{mn}, y_{mx}, z_{mn}, z_{mx}\}$ and that of the right child by $\{x_{00}, x_{mx}, y_{mn}, y_{mx}, z_{mn}, z_{mx}\}$. Child nodes generally store only splitting plane values, but algorithms such as the ray intersection test discussed below require AABB parameters of leaf nodes. Both the construction and the traversal of a *k*-d tree are done in a top-down fashion, starting from the root node that either represents a three-dimensional scene or the axis-aligned bounding box of a group of objects. The traversal of a *k*-d tree to leaf node where a point P can be either inserted or located, follows the pattern of the well-known sequential binary tree search algorithm. The pseudo-code for the method is given in Listing 9.5.

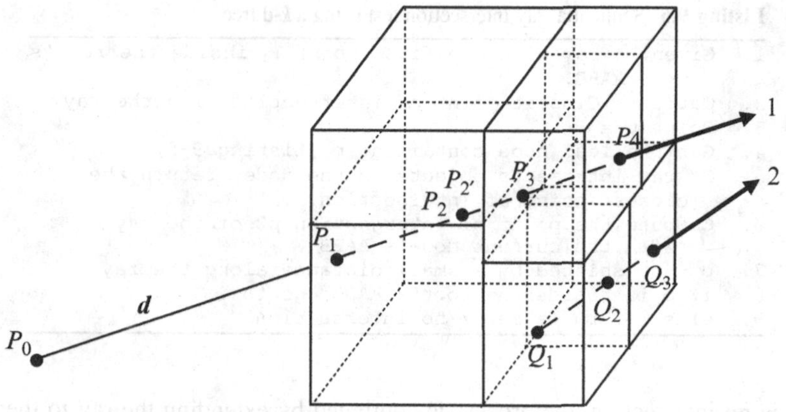

Fig. 9.27 Ray intersections with a volume represented by a *k*-d tree

The broad-phase collision detection of objects is done by first identifying the leaf nodes of the *k*-d tree where an object's bounding volume is stored. Every node of a *k*-d tree represents an axis-aligned box, and therefore the methods given in the previous section can be directly used locate the positions of an AABB or a bounding sphere (see Eq. 9.58) within a *k*-d tree.

A *k*-d tree is also used for ray tracing acceleration, as it can effectively restrict the computation of ray intersection tests along the direction of the ray. The root of the *k*-d tree represents the AABB of the scene of objects to be ray traced. The primary ray typically originates from a view point outside the scene. A secondary ray, on the other hand may originate from a point inside the scene. In Fig. 9.27, ray-1 originates at P_0, enters the AABB of the root node of the *k*-d tree at P_1 and exits the scene at P_4. Ray-2 originates at a point Q_1 within the scene and exits the volume at Q_3. In the case of ray-1, we can compute the position of P_1 as well as the entry and exit distances P_0P_1, P_0P_4 using the parametric equation of the ray and the equations of the bounding planes of the AABB (see Sect. 9.2.1). Using the method in Listing 9.5, we can identify the leaf node of the *k*-d tree where P_1 (or Q_1 for ray-2) is located. The ray is tested for intersection with the objects stored at this leaf node. If an intersection occurs, the point of intersection closest to the origin of the ray is returned. Otherwise, the ray is compared with the AABB of the leaf node and the next intersection point P_2 with the current node is computed. This point is extended further by a small amount ε along the direction of the ray to get a point $P_2{}'$ that lies well within another node of the *k*-d tree:

$$P_2{}' = P_2 + \varepsilon \boldsymbol{d} \tag{9.59}$$

where $\boldsymbol{d}$ is the unit vector along the ray direction. The *k*-d tree is traversed again from the root to identify the leaf node to which $P_2{}'$ belongs. The objects in this node are then compared with the ray to determine if there is an intersection, and if

Listing 9.6 Sequential ray intersection test using a *k*-d tree

```
1.  Given: A ray with the first point P1 inside the root's
         AABB.
2.  Output:  Closest point of intersection with the ray
3.  Point p = P1
4.  Get the leaf node containing p (Listing 9-5)
5.  If ray intersects objects in the node, return the
      closest point of intersection.
6.  Compute the point of intersection p2 of the ray
       with the current node's AABB
7.  p = p2 shifted by a small distance along the ray
8.  if p is inside the root's AABB, go to 4
9.  else return false   //no intersection
```

there is no intersection, the process is continued by extending the ray to the next cell, and so on until the ray exits the AABB of the root node. The algorithm visits all leaf nodes intersected by the ray in a near to far order. Objects and primitives in the remaining leaf nodes are not compared with the ray. The pseudo-code for this method of sequential ray intersection test is given in Listing 9.6.

A *k*-d tree based spatial partitioning is useful in finding the point closest to a given point P within a three-dimensional volume. The location of the closest point gives information about the object which could most likely collide with the object or the bounding volume containing P.

As shown in the two-dimensional example in Fig. 9.28, the algorithm for finding the nearest neighbour of P begins with the traversal of the *k*-d tree to the leaf node containing P and finding the closest point to P within that leaf node. The squared value of the distance between the two points is stored as the current minimum value of r^2. The position of P and the value of r^2 together are used to compare the sphere centred at P with the AABBs of other leaf nodes of the *k*-d tree using Eq. 9.58 for possible overlap. If a leaf node overlaps the sphere, the squared distances of points in that node from P are computed and if a value lower than the current minimum is found, then the value of r^2 is updated with the lowest found in that node. The process continues as shown in Fig. 9.28, until all nodes that overlap the sphere have been examined. The point that generated the minimum value for r^2 is selected as the nearest neighbour of P. The sphere-AABB overlap test excludes a large number of points that are separated from P by a distance greater than r from being compared.

We saw earlier that both an octree and a *k*-d tree may store the same object in several leaf nodes if the object overlaps the volume of those nodes. For an octree, the splitting planes are fixed, but in a *k*-d tree, we can select the position of the splitting plane. Several heuristics, such as the surface area heuristics have been proposed in the literature to minimize the amount of object overlap at leaf nodes. The next section introduces a subdivision structure that combines the desirable attributes of a *k*-d tree and a bounding volume hierarchy.

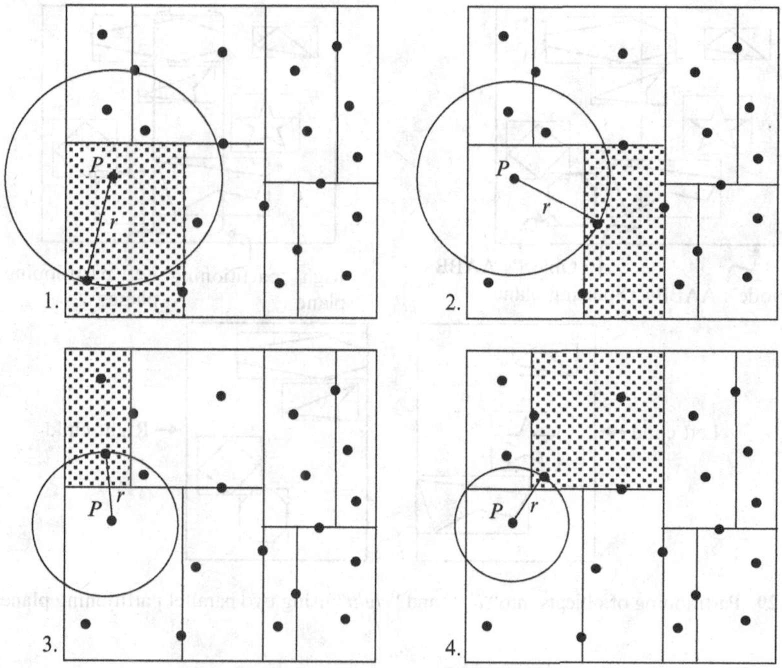

Fig. 9.28 A sequence of computations performed on a *k*-d tree to find the nearest neighbour of a point *P*

9.4.3 Boundary Interval Hierarchy

A bounding interval hierarchy is a structure similar to a *k*-d tree, but uses two parallel partitioning planes for each node. For a given node, the plane perpendicular to and passing through the midpoint of the longest axis of the node's AABB is first chosen as the splitting plane. Assume that this axis is in the *x*-direction, and the position of the splitting plane is x_0. The AABBs of the objects within the node's volume are then sorted along this axis. The objects whose AABBs have all *x*-coordinates less than or equal to x_0 are assigned to the left child. AABBs that are entirely on the right of the splitting plane are assigned to the right child. Objects whose AABBs intersect the splitting plane are classified as belonging to the left or right child depending on which side of the splitting plane the AABBs have maximum overlap. The left partitioning plane is then defined using the maximum value of the *x*-coordinates of the AABBs belonging to the left child, and the right plane is defined using the minimum value of the *x*-coordinates of the AABBs belonging to the right (Fig. 9.29). The process continues by splitting each child node along the longest axis and defining two partitioning planes along that axis. A node containing only a single object is not subdivided further.

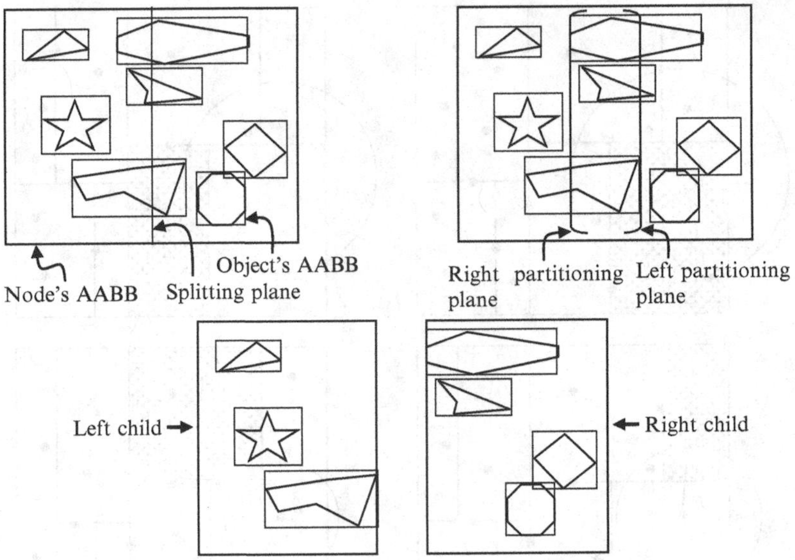

Fig. 9.29 Partitioning of objects into "*left*" and "*right*" using two parallel partitioning planes

The primary differences between a *k*-d tree and a bounding interval hierarchy are listed below.

- A *k*-d tree selects axes cyclically and defines a perpendicular splitting plane at the median point along the current axis direction, or alternatively uses a heuristic to position the splitting plane. A bounding interval hierarchy uses the longest axis of the current AABB, and the splitting plane is always positioned at the midpoint.
- In a *k*-d tree, the AABBs of the objects in a node are not sorted. A bounding interval hierarchy sorts AABBs along each axis. This speeds up the process of repeated classification of objects as left or right of splitting planes along the same axis.
- A *k*-d tree stores only the splitting plane position and optionally the parameters of the node AABB. A bounding interval hierarchy requires the positions of two partitioning planes and the axis information to be stored.

By using two partitioning planes, a bounding interval hierarchy is able to classify each object in a node volume uniquely as either "left" or "right", without the need for placing an object that overlaps the splitting plane in both child nodes. A clear separation of objects is thus achieved, and the AABBs of the child nodes are closely aligned with the object AABBs within the nodes. The interval hierarchy thus provides a hierarchy of axis aligned bounding volumes and also a spatial ordering similar to that of the *k*-d tree. Bounding interval hierarchies have been found particularly useful for real-time ray tracing.

9.5 Summary

This chapter has covered the main aspects of collision detection algorithms including the representation of objects using bounding volumes, intersection tests between primitives and bounding volumes (BV) and hierarchical structures that are useful for minimizing the amount of pair-wise object/primitive comparisons required in overlap tests.

The important methods discussed in the context of bounding volume construction are the Welzl's algorithm for computing the minimum bounding sphere, the computation of oriented bounding boxes, and the incremental construction of three-dimensional convex hulls. Algorithms for primitive-BV intersection tests and BV-BV intersection tests have been presented in detail. The separating axis theorem and the slab-based method are extremely useful for intersection tests involving oriented bounding boxes.

The chapter also presented methods for the construction and traversal of bounding volume hierarchies. Spatial partitioning structures such as the octree and the *k*-d tree are useful for broad-phase collision detection as well as ray tracing algorithms. Both structures use axis aligned splitting planes to facilitate efficient computation of ray intersection tests. The bounding interval hierarchy is a structure that combines the features of a bounding volume hierarchy and a *k*-d tree.

9.6 Supplementary Material for Chap. 9

The section `Chapter9/Code` on the companion website contains the following programs implementing and demonstrating the working of key algorithms discussed in this chapter.

1. **BoundingCircle.cpp**

Additional files:
`none`

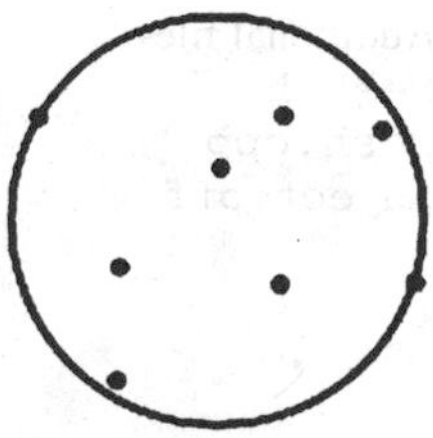

The program demonstrates the working of Welzl's algorithm for computing the minimum bounding circle for a set of points on the plane of display. Points are inserted by the user interactively using left mouse clicks. As each point is added, the minimum bounding circle is updated as discussed in Sect. 9.1.2. Press 'c' to refresh the screen.

2. **InsertionHull.cpp**

Additional files:
`none`

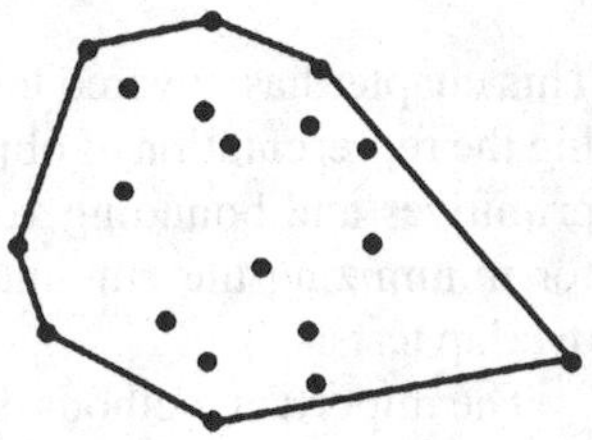

The program demonstrates the insertion hull algorithm for incrementally constructing the convex hull of a set of points. Points are added interactively using left mouse clicks. As each point is added, the convex hull is updated using the algorithm discussed in Sect. 9.1.5. Press 'c' to refresh the screen and to start over again.

3. **BVH_AABB.cpp**

Additional files:
`Mesh.h`
`Mesh.cpp`
`object.off`

The program loads a mesh file "object.off" and displays the bounding volume hierarchy constructed using AABBs (Sect. 9.3.1). It also shows the position of a ray (whose parameters are defined in the program) relative to the AABB, and the intersection points if the ray intersects the AABB. Press the 'z' key to go to left child of the current node and 'x' to the right child. Use left and right arrow keys to change the view direction.

4. **BVH_Sphere.cpp**

Additional files:
`Mesh.h`
`Mesh.cpp`
`object.off`

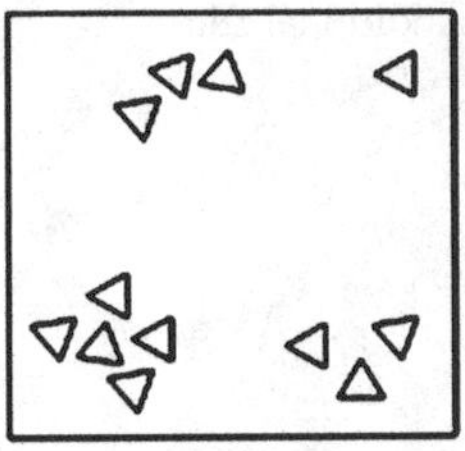

The program uses a cluster of triangles to demonstrate the bottom-up construction of a bounding volume hierarchy of spheres (Sect. 9.3.2). Clicking the left mouse button anywhere within the window causes the intersected bounding circles to be highlighted. Triangles that are excluded from intersection tests are also highlighted in grey color.

5. **KdTree.cpp**

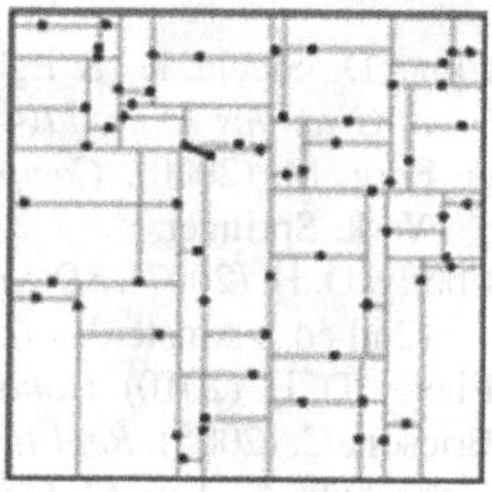

Additional files:
```
Mesh.h
Mesh.cpp
object.off
```

The program generates a set of randomly distributed points and displays the *k*-d tree partitioning of the two-dimensional space. The program also demonstrates the nearest neighbour algorithm using the traversal of the *k*-d tree. The user inputs a point using left mouse click, and presses space bar to initiate the *k*-d tree search for the closest point. All points visited by the traversal algorithm are highlighted. The point found closest to the input point is also marked by a red coloured line segment connecting the two points.

9.7 Bibliographical Notes

Two important reference books for learning and developing collision detection algorithms are Ericson (2005) and van den Bergen (2003). These books deal with all aspects of collision detection including primitive tests, bounding volumes and acceleration algorithms. Books on real-time rendering (Moller et al. 2008) and game engine design (Eberly 2007; Eberly 2010) also give an extensive coverage of collision detection techniques. Collision detection is an area where a large number of computational geometry algorithms are used. Methods for pair-wise intersection tests, point inclusion tests, proximity tests and the construction of convex hulls are discussed in detail in de Berg (2000), O'Rourke (1998) and similar books on computational geometry.

Early development in collision detection methods were based mainly on primitive intersection tests and spatial partitioning. Samet's books (1990a, b) provided a comprehensive guide to spatial data structures. Toussaint (1983) introduced the rotating calipers algorithm, and Welzl (1991) the method for computing the smallest bounding disc. In the late 1990s some fundamental papers on bounding volume hierarchies using AABBs (van den Bergen 1997), OBBs (Gottschalk et al. 1996), triangle intersection tests (Moller 1997), and *k*-DOPs (Klosowski et al. 1998) appeared.

Three recent publications on the use of hierarchical structures for ray tracing are Wald and Havran (2006), Cline et al. (2006), and Hapala and Havran (2011). Bounding interval hierarchies are introduced and their applications to real-time ray tracing discussed in Wachter and Keller (2006).

References

Cline, D., Steele, K., & Egbert, P. (2006). Lightweight bounding volumes for ray tracing. *Journal of Graphics Tools, 11*(4), 61–71.

de Berg, M. (2000). *Computational geometry: Algorithms and applications* (2nd rev. ed.). New York: Springer.

Eberly, D. H. (2007). *3D game engine design: A practical approach to real-time computer graphics* (2nd ed.). Amsterdam/London: Morgan Kaufmann.

Eberly, D. H. (2010). *Game physics* (2nd ed.). Burlington: Morgan Kaufmann/Elsevier.

Ericson, C. (2005). *Real-time collision detection*. Amsterdam/Boston: Elsevier.

Gottschalk, S., Lin, M. C., & Manocha, D. (1996). *OBB-Tree: A hierarchical structure for rapid interference detection.* In: Computer graphics (SIGGRAPH), New Orleans (pp. 171–180).

Hapala, M., & Havran, V. (2011). Kd-tree traversal algorithms for ray tracing. *Computer Graphics Forum, 30*(1), 199–213.

Kay, T. L., & Kajiya, J. T. (1986). *Ray tracing complex scenes.* In: Proceedings of computer graphics SIGGRAPH-86, Dallas (pp. 269–278).

Klosowski, J. T., Held, M., et al. (1998). Efficient collision detection using bounding volume hierarchies of k-DOPs. *IEEE Transactions on Visualization and Computer Graphics, 4*(1), 21–36.

Moller, T. (1997). A fast triangle-triangle intersection test. *Journal of Graphics, GPU and Game Tools, 2*(2), 25–30.

Moller, T., Haines, E., & Hoffman, N. (2008). *Real-time rendering* (3rd ed.). Wellesley: A.K. Peters.

O'Rourke, J. (1998). *Computational geometry in C* (2nd ed.). Cambridge: Cambridge University Press.

Raabe, A., Tietjen, T., & Anlauf J. K. (2009). *An exact and efficient triangle intersection test hardware.* International conference on computer graphics theory (GRAPP-09), Lisbon, Portugal (pp. 355–360).

Samet, H. (1990a). *Applications of spatial data structures: Computer graphics, image processing, and GIS*. Reading: Addison-Wesley.

Samet, H. (1990b). *The design and analysis of spatial data structures*. Reading: Addison-Wesley.

Toussaint, G. (1983). *Solving geometric problems with the rotating calipers.* In: 2nd IEEE Mediterranean Electrotechnical Conference (MELECON '83), Athens.

van den Bergen, G. (1997). Efficient collision detection of complex deformable models using AABB trees. *Journal of Graphics Tools, 2*(4), 1–14.

van den Bergen, G. (2003). *Collision detection in interactive 3D environments*. San Francisco: Morgan Kaufmann.

Wachter, C., & Keller, A. (2006). *Instant ray tracing: The bounding interval hierarchy*. In: Eurographics symposium on rendering, 26–28 June 2006, Cyprus (pp. 139–149).

Wald, I., & Havran, V. (2006). *On building fast kd-trees for ray tracking and on doing that in O(NlogN).* In: IEEE symposium on interactive ray tracing, 18–20 Sep 2006, Salt Lake City, Utah (pp. 61–69).

Welzl, E., et al. (1991). Smallest enclosing disks. In H. Maurer (Ed.), *New results and new trends in computer science* (Lecture notes in computer science, Vol. 555, pp. 359–370). New York: Springer.

Appendices

Appendix A: Geometry Classes

This section gives a description of the methods in `Point3`, `Vec3`, `Triangle` and `Matrix` classes. The static relationships between the classes are shown in Fig. A.1.

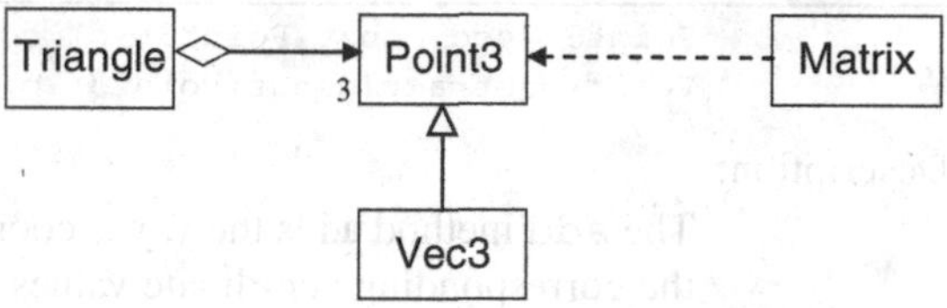

Fig. A.1 Relationships between geometry classes

A.1 Point3 Class

Fields

```
protected:
      static float EPS;
public:
      float _x, _y, _z, _h;
```

Description:

The data members of the class store the coordinates of a point. For programming convenience, the coordinates are declared as `public`, so that they can be directly accessed without the need for getter methods. The fourth component _h is initialized to 1 for points and 0 for vectors. This component is not used for computing the norm, scalar product, and other operations such as addition, subtraction and negation.

The static field `EPS` is a threshold used for checking if a floating point value is close enough to zero. Its value is set to 1.E-6.

R. Mukundan, *Advanced Methods in Computer Graphics: With examples in OpenGL*, DOI 10.1007/978-1-4471-2340-8, © Springer-Verlag London Limited 2012

Constructors

```
public:
      Point3(float x, float y, float z = 0)
             : _x(x), _y(y), _z(z), _h(1.0)   {}
      Point3()
             : _x(0.0), _y(0.0), _z(0.0), _h(1.0)   {}
```

Description:

The first constructor sets the values of *x*, *y*, *z* coordinates using its arguments. The *h* value is initialized separately to a default value 1.0. The second no-argument constructor initializes a point to the origin.

Distance computation

```
float norm() const;
```

Description:

This method computes the distance to a point from the origin or the length of a vector.

Addition and subtraction

```
Point3* add(const Point3* p) const;
Vec3* subtract(const Point3* p) const;
```

Description:

The `add` method adds the *x*, *y*, *z* coordinates of the current point with the corresponding coordinate values of `p`, and produces a new point. The *h* coordinate values are not added. The resulting point is assigned an *h* value 1.0. This method is overridden in the subclass `Vec3` which sets the *h* value to 0. The `subtract` method similarly subtracts the coordinates of `p` from that of the current point and produces a vector originating at `p`.

Negation

```
Point3* negate() const;
```

Description:

This method negates the *x*, *y*, *z* coordinates of the current point. The *h* coordinate value is not negated.

Scalar multiplication

```
Point3* scalarMult(float c) const;
```

Description:

This method scales the *x*, *y*, *z* coordinates of the current point by the constant factor `c`, and produces a new point. The resulting point is assigned an *h* value 1.0.

Conversion to standard form

```
Point3* standard();
```

Description:

This method converts the current point to standard form by applying the transformation: $(x, y, z, h) \Rightarrow (x/h, y/h, z/h, 1)$, provided $h \neq 0$.

Output

```
void print() const;
```

Description:

This method prints the x, y, z, h coordinates of the current point or vector.

A.2 Vec3 Class

The `Vec3` class is a subclass of `Point3`.

Fields

```
private:
      static float RADTODEG;
public:
      static const Vec3* X_AXIS;
      static const Vec3* Y_AXIS;
      static const Vec3* Z_AXIS;
```

Description:

The static field `RADTODEG` stores the multiplication factor ($= \pi/180$) for conversion from radians to degrees.

The static fields `X_AXIS`, `Y_AXIS`, `Z_AXIS` store respectively the orthogonal basis vectors (1, 0, 0), (0, 1, 0) and (0, 0, 1).

Constructors

```
public:
      Vec3(float x, float y, float z = 0)
          : Point3(x, y, z){_h = 0;}
      Vec3() {_h = 0;}
```

Description:

The constructors invoke the base class constructors and additionally set the value of `_h` to 0.

Dot and cross products

```
float dot(const Vec3* v) const;
Vec3* cross(const Vec3* v) const;
```

Description:

The `dot` method returns the dot product of the current vector and `v`. The `cross` method returns a vector as the result of the cross product between the current vector and `v`.

Vector normalization

```
void normalize();
```

Description:

The method converts the current vector to a unit vector by dividing its components by the length of the vector.

Reflection of a vector

```
Vec3* reflect(const Vec3* n) const;
```

Description:

The method computes the reflection of the current vector with respect to $\boldsymbol{n}$ using the formula in Eq. 2.5.

Computation of angles

```
float angle(const Vec3* v) const;
float angle2(const Vec3* v) const;
float signedAngle(const Vec3* v, const Vec3* w) const;
```

Description:

The method `angle` first converts the current vector and the input vector `v` to unit vectors, and then computes the angle between them using the inverse cosine of the dot product of the two vectors. The value is returned in degrees in the range [0, 180]. The method `angle2` uses both dot and cross products to compute the angle using the formula $\theta = \tan^{-1}(|\boldsymbol{u} \times \boldsymbol{v}|, \boldsymbol{u} \bullet \boldsymbol{v})$. The `singedAngle` method uses Eq. 2.6. to compute the signed angle between the current vector and `v` with respect to a given view direction `w`.

A.3 Triangle Class

Fields

```
private:
    const Point3 *_a, *_b, *_c;
```

Description:

The data members of the class store references to the three vertices of a triangle.

Constructors

```
public:
    Triangle(const Point3* a, const Point3* b, const Point3* c)
        : _a(a), _b(b), _c(c)  {}
```

Description:

The non-default constructor requires three references to objects of the `Point3` class. Methods of the class use these points as vertices of the triangle.

Computation of area

```
float area() const;
float signedArea2D() const;
float signedArea3D(const Vec3* w) const;
```

Description:

The method `area` computes the area of the current triangle using the cross product of vectors along two edges as given in Eq. 2.3. The method `signedArea2D` returns the area of the triangle which has a negative sign if the angle between the normal direction and the z-axis is greater than 90°. The function `signedArea3D` uses a similar approach by using a user specified vector $\boldsymbol{w}$ instead of the z-axis (Eq. 2.8).

Computation of barycentric coordinates

```
Point3* barycentricCoords(const Point3* p) const;
```

Description:

This method computes the barycentric coordinates of the point `p` with respect to the current triangle using area ratios as given in Eq. 2.48.

Barycentric mapping

```
Point3* barycentricMap
 (const Point3* p, const Triangle* t) const;
```

Description:

A point `p` and a triangle `t` containing `p` are given. This method computes the image of `p` in the current triangle as shown in Fig. 2.12.

Point inclusion test

```
bool isInside(const Point3* p) const
```

Description:

This function uses barycentric coordinates to determine if a point `p` lies within and on the plane of the current triangle.

Bilinear interpolation

```
Point3* bilinear(int k1, int k2) const
```

Description:

This method returns a point computed using the bilinear interpolation formula in Eq. 2.45. The arguments k_1 and k_2 must satisfy the condition that k_1, k_2, and $k_1 + k_2$, all have values in the range [0, 1].

OpenGL drawing

```
void draw() const;
```

Description:

This method draws the current triangle using OpenGL functions.

A.4 Matrix Class

Fields

```
private:
      float _v[4][4];
```

Description:

The `Matrix` class represents the data structure for a 4×4 matrix, with its values stored in the two-dimensional array `_v`.

Constructors

```
public:
      Matrix()
      Matrix(float values[][4])
      Matrix(const Vec3* u, const Vec3* v, const Vec3* w)
```

Description:

The default constructor initializes the matrix with the identity matrix. The second constructor initializes the matrix using a two-dimensional array of values. The values are stored in row-major order. The third constructor forms the matrix using three vectors ***u***, ***v***, ***w*** as the first three columns of the matrix. The last column has values 0, 0, 0, 1.

Identity matrix

```
      void identity();
```

Description:

This method resets the current matrix to the identity matrix.

Accessing matrix elements

```
      float valueAt(int i, int j) const;
```

Description:

This is a getter method that returns the value of `_v[i][j]`.

Setting matrix elements

```
      void setValue(int i, int j, int value);
```

Description:

This is a setter method that replaces the value of `_v[i][j]` with `value`.

Transpose and inverse

```
      void transpose();
      void inverse();
```

Description:

The method `transpose` modifies the current matrix by replacing it with its transpose. Similarly `inverse` replaces the current matrix with its inverse, provided the matrix is invertible. If the determinant of the current matrix is 0, it is not changed.

Point transformation

```
Point3* transform(const Point3* p);
```

Description:

This method returns a new point computed by pre-multiplying the point p by the current matrix.

Matrix copy

```
Matrix* copy();
```

Description:

Often it is required to keep a copy of the current matrix before computing its transpose or inverse. This method returns a reference to a new matrix object that contains the same values as the current matrix.

Output

```
void print();
```

Description:

This method prints the values of the current matrix in 4×4 format.

Appendix B: Scene Graph Classes

This section gives an outline of the methods in the scene graph classes. A description of these classes can be found in Sect. 3.5. The static relationships between the classes are shown in Fig. B.1.

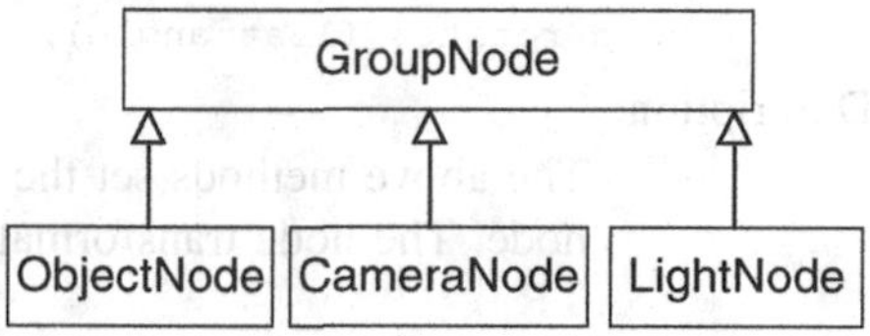

Fig. B.1 Relationships between scene graph classes

B.1 GroupNode Class

Fields

```
private:
      list<GroupNode*> _children;
protected:
      GroupNode* _parent;
      float _tx, _ty, _tz, _angleX, _angleY, _angleZ;
```

Description:

The list variable `_children` stores references to the children of the current group node, in an STL list structure. The access level for this variable is declared as `private` since all subclasses are leaf nodes that do not have children. Each group node also stores a reference to its parent node in the variable `_parent`. It has a value `NULL` for the root node. Every group node also stores the translation parameters `_tx`, `_ty`, `_tz` and rotation angles `_angleX`, `_angleY`, `_angleZ` which define the transformation of the current node to the coordinate frame of the parent node.

R. Mukundan, *Advanced Methods in Computer Graphics: With examples in OpenGL*, DOI 10.1007/978-1-4471-2340-8, © Springer-Verlag London Limited 2012

Constructors

```
GroupNode()
```

Description:

The class contains only one no-argument constructor that initializes the parent node to `NULL` and the transformation parameters to zeros.

Add/remove child

```
void addChild(GroupNode* node);
void removeChild(GroupNode* node);
```

Description:

The method `addChild` includes the specified `node` as a child node of the current node. The method `removeChild` removes the specified `node`, if it exists, from the list of children of the current node.

Node transformation

```
void translate(float tx, float ty, float tz);
void rotateX(float angle);
void rotateY(float angle);
void rotateZ(float angle);
```

Description:

The above methods set the transformation parameters of the current node. The node transformation is always assumed to be of the form **TR**.

Inverse transformation

```
void inverseTransform() const;
```

Description:

This method uses OpenGL functions to push the matrices for the inverse transformation $(\mathbf{TR})^{-1} = \mathbf{R}^{-1}\mathbf{T}^{-1}$ of the current node to the transformation stack. Note that this function does not explicitly generate the inverse transformation matrix.

Scene rendering

```
void render();
virtual void draw();
```

Description:

This method gets the singleton object of the `CameraNode`, sets up the view transformation matrix and calls the method `draw`. A scene is rendered by invoking this method on the root node.The `draw` method is not directly invoked by the application. It is indirectly invoked on a group node via the method `render`. The `draw` method uses OpenGL functions to push the current node's transformation matrix to the transformation stack, and recursively calls itself on all child nodes. This polymorphic method causes objects to be drawn when invoked on leaf nodes.

Parent node

```
GroupNode* getParent() const;
```

Description:

This getter method returns the reference to the parent of the current node.

B.2 ObjectNode Class

The `ObjectNode` class is a subclass of `GroupNode`.

Fields

```
public:
    enum ObjType
        { CUBE, SPHERE, TORUS, TEAPOT, CONE, TETRAHEDRON};
private:
        ObjType _object;
        float _scaleX, _scaleY, _scaleZ;
        float _colorR, _colorG, _colorB;
```

Description:

The enumerated type `ObjType` defines a collection of GLUT objects which users can specify in the constructor to display an object. At the time of construction, the user can specify its scale factors `_scaleX`, `_scaleY`, `_scaleZ`, and also its material colour using the normalized values in the range [0, 1] for `_colorR`, `colorG`, `colorB`.

Constructors

```
public:
    ObjectNode()        : GroupNode(),  _object(CUBE),
            _scaleX(1.0f), _scaleY(1.0f), _scaleZ(1.0f),
            _colorR(1.0f), _colorG(1.0f), _colorB(1.0f)  {}
```

Description:

The constructor initializes the object type to CUBE, the scale factors to 1, and the object material colour to white.

Setter methods

```
    void setObject(ObjType object,
        float scaleX, float scaleY, float scaleZ);
    void setColor(float colorR, float colorG, float colorB);
```

Description:

The method `setObject` is used to change the parameters of the current object, including its type and scale factors. The `setColor` method modifies the material colour of the current object.

B.3 CameraNode Class

The `CameraNode` class is a subclass of `GroupNode`.

Fields

```
private:
    float _fov, _aspect, _near, _far;
    static bool flag;
```

Description:

The data members `_fov`, `_aspect`, `_near`, `_far` define the perspective view frustum of the camera in terms of the field of view, aspect ratio, near plane distance and the far plane distance. The Boolean variable `flag` ensures that at most one instance of the class is created.

Constructors

```
private:
    CameraNode(): GroupNode(), _fov(60.0f), _aspect(1.0f),
                  _near(1.0f), _far(1000.0f) {}
```

Description:

The `CameraNode` class is a singleton class with a `private` constructor. The only instance of the class is available through the static method `getInstance()`. By default, the camera view frustum has 60° field of view, aspect ratio 1, near plane distance 1, and far plane distance 1,000.

Setter method

```
void perspective
    (float fov, float aspect, float near, float far);
```

Description:

This setter method allows you to change the default frustum parameters of the camera object.

View transformation and projection

```
void viewTransform() const;
void projection() const;
```

Description:

The `viewTransform` method traverses the scene graph from the camera node towards the root node, and pushes the inverse transformation matrices of each node onto the transformation stack using OpenGL functions. The method calls the `inverseTransform` method of the `GroupNode` class for this operation.
The method `projection` sets up the projection matrix using OpenGL functions. Both the above methods are not usually invoked directly by the user. The `render` method of the `GroupNode` class invokes both the methods to set up the view and projective transformations for the rendering pipeline.

B.4 LightNode Class

The `LightNode` class is a subclass of `GroupNode`.

Fields

```
private:
      int glLight;
```

Description:

This integer field can be assigned a value between 0 and 7. A value *i* corresponds to the named light source GL_LIGHT*i* defined in OpenGL.

Constructors

```
public:
      LightNode(int glLight): GroupNode(),_glLight(glLight) {}
```

Description:

The constructor specifies the index of the OpenGL light source to be used for the current object of the `LightNode` class. The default position of the light node is (0, 0, 0). The position can be changed by specifying transformation parameters for the node using the `translate` method. Note that all other light source parameters will have to be defined separately by the user with the help of OpenGL functions.

Setter Method

```
      void setLight(int glLight);
```

Description:

This setter method allows the user to change the current light source used by the object.

Appendix C: Vertex Skinning Classes

This section gives an outline of the methods in the `SkinnedMesh`, `Skeleton` and `SkeletonNode` classes used for vertex skinning. A description of these classes can be found in Sect. 4.8. A class diagram showing the relationships between the classes is given in Fig. C.1.

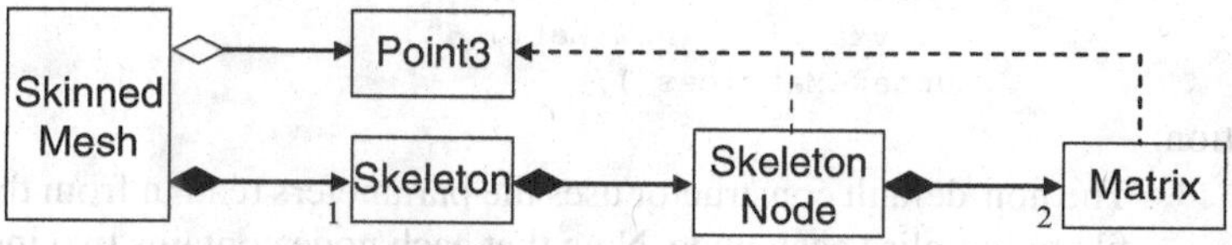

Fig. C.1 Relationships between the classes used for vertex skinning

C.1 SkeletonNode Class

The structure of the `SkeletonNode` class is similar to that of the `GroupNode` class.

Fields

```
private:
        list<SkeletonNode*> _children;
        int _firstIndex, _lastIndex, _parentIndex;
        SkeletonNode* _parent;
        float _tx, _ty, _tz, _angleX, _angleY, _angleZ;
        Matrix *_matrix, *_invMatrix;
```

Description:

Every skeleton node is implicitly a group node, and can store references to a number of children in the list `_children`. A skeleton node represents a bone. It also stores a pair of indices `_firstIndex` and

R. Mukundan, *Advanced Methods in Computer Graphics: With examples in OpenGL*,
DOI 10.1007/978-1-4471-2340-8, © Springer-Verlag London Limited 2012

_lastIndex defining a range of mesh vertices that are attached to the bone. The translation parameters are stored in variables _tx, _ty, _tz, and the Euler angles in _angleX, _angleY, _angleZ. The overall transformation matrix and its inverse are updated whenever any of the joint angles is changed. Each node is assigned a unique index starting form 1. The index 0 is reserved for the root node which represents the origin of the world coordinate system. The parent index _parentIndex establishes the link between the current node and its parent node.

Constructors

```
public:
    SkeletonNode(int parentIndx,
        float tx, float ty, float tz,
        int firstIndx, int lastIndx)
          : _parent(NULL),
            _tx(tx), _ty(ty), _tz(tz),
            _angleX(0.0), _angleY(0.0), _angleZ(0.0),
            _firstIndex(firstIndx), _lastIndex(lastIndx),
            _parentIndex(parentIndx)
          {     _matrix = new Matrix();
                _invMatrix = new Matrix();
                updateMatrices();    }
```

Description:

The non-default constructor uses the parameters read in from the input file to initialise each node. Note that each node contains two instances of the matrix class. Both the transformation matrix and its inverse are updated using the input parameters. There is also a default constructor that initializes all transformation parameters to 0.

Add/remove child:

```
void addChild(SkeletonNode* node);
void removeChild(SkeletonNode* node);
```

Description:

These methods are exactly the same as the corresponding methods in the GroupNode class (Appendix B).

Bone transformations: translation

```
void translate(float tx, float ty, float tz);
```

Description:

The translation parameters of the bones are set at the time of construction, and do not change afterwards. Only the translation of the base node (with respect to the world coordinate frame) is defined in the animation phase. This method is therefore usually invoked by the translateBase method of the Skeleton class.

Bone transformations: rotation

```
void rotateX(float angle);
void rotateY(float angle);
void rotateZ(float angle);
```

Description:

These methods are used to set the rotation angle(s) of a bone during the animation phase. The methods are normally invoked by the `rotate` method of the `Skeleton` class.

Setter methods

```
void attachVertices(int firstIndx, int lastIndx);
void setParentIndex(int parentIndx);
```

Description:

These methods alter the vertex indices and the parent index of the current bone.

Getter methods

```
int getParentIndex() const;
int getFirstIndex() const;
int getLastIndex() const;
Matrix* getMatrix() const;
Matrix* getInverseMatrix() const;
SkeletonNode* getParent() const;
int getChildCount() const;
```

Description:

These methods allow you to examine the transformation matrices, vertex indices, the parent index and the number of children of the current node.

Transformation update

```
void updateMatrices();
```

Description:

This method updates the transformation matrix and its inverse, and is invoked whenever any of the transformation parameters is changed.

Pre-processing phase

```
vector<Point3*> preprocessPhase(vector<Point3*> vertices);
void transform1
 (vector<Point3*> vertices, float tx, float ty, float tz);
```

Description:

The pre-processing phase builds the product matrix given in Eq. 4.9 and transforms the mesh vertex list to create a new list of vertices V'. The method `preprocessPhase` returns this new vertex list. The method in turn invokes `transform1` which traverses the skeleton tree from the root, visits every node, combines the inverse translation components, and applies the transformation on the node's vertex list.

Animation phase

```
vector<Point3*> animationPhase(vector<Point3*> vertices);
void transform2(vector<Point3*> vertices, Matrix matrix);
```

Description:

In the animation phase, the updated matrices incorporating joint angle rotations are gathered in the form of a product matrix given in Eq. 4.10. The vertex list obtained from the pre-processing phase is transformed using the matrix. The transformed vertex coordinates returned by `animationPhase` are used for rendering the mesh for that particular frame. This method invokes `transform2` which traverses the skeleton tree from the root, post-multiplies the product matrix with the matrix at the current node, and transforms the node's vertices obtained from the pre-processing phase.

C.2 Skeleton Class

Fields

```
private:
        SkeletonNode* _root;
        SkeletonNode* _base;
        vector<SkeletonNode*> _bones;
```

Description:

Each skeleton tree is referenced by its root node, stored in the variable `_root`. This node is created by the constructor. The base node (`_base`) is a special node in the skeleton tree that has the root node as its parent. The transformations of the base node define the position and the orientation of the entire mesh in the world coordinate frame. The class also maintains a list of references to the skeleton nodes as they are created by the `loadSkeleton` method.

Constructors

```
public:
    Skeleton()
      : _root( new SkeletonNode() )  {}
```

Description:

The constructor creates the root node of the skeleton and initializes it with the default transformation parameters.

Getter method

```
SkeletonNode* getRoot() const;
```

Description:

The getter method returns the reference to the root node.

Loading skeleton data

```
void loadSkeleton(const string& filename);
```

Description:

This method loads skeleton data from a file formatted as shown in Fig. 4.18, and creates an instance of the `SkeletonNode` class for each bone. The method also calls `attachBones` that creates the hierarchical relationships between nodes (bones).

Bone transformations

```
void rotate(int i,
      float angleX, float angleY, float angleZ);
void translateBase(float tx, float ty, float tz);
```

Description:

The translation parameters specifying the spatial offsets of each bone relative to its parent are assigned to the nodes through the constructor. These parameters are used for transforming vertices in the pre-processing phase. In the animation phase, only the joint angle rotations and the translation of the base node can change. The `rotate` method specifies the joint angles of the *i*th bone. The `translateBase` method changes the translation parameters of the base node. These two methods are usually called within the display loop of the application.

C.3 SkinnedMesh Class

Fields

```
private:
      vector<Point3*> _verticesV;
      vector<Point3*> _verticesVT;
      vector<Point3*> _verticesW;
      vector<Polygon*> _polygons;
      PolyType _polytype;
      float _colorR, _colorG, _colorB;
      Skeleton* _skeleton;
public:
   enum PolyType {TRIANGLE, QUAD};
```

Description: The vertex lists `verticesV`, `_verticesVT`, `_verticesW` represent the lists V, V', W shown in Fig. 4.11. The lists contain the mesh coordinates in the bind pose, after the pre-processing phase, and after the animation phase respectively. The polygon list `_polygons` store the vertex indices of the mesh polygons. For the sake of simplicity, each mesh is assigned a single material colour given by `_colorR`, `_colorG`, `_colorB`. A mesh can be either a triangular or a quad mesh. The variable `_skeleton` stores the reference to the skeleton associated with the mesh.

Constructors

```
public:
    SkinnedMesh(PolyType polytype)
        : _polytype(polytype), _skeleton(NULL)  {}
```

Description:

The constructor specifies only the polygon type of the mesh using the enumerated types `TRIANGLE`, and `QUAD`. Mesh data is loaded using `loadMesh` method. The application must also load skeleton data using an instance of the `Skeleton` class, and attach the skeleton object using the `attachSkeleton` method.

Loading a mesh

```
void loadMesh(const string& filename);
```

Description:

This method loads mesh data from a file formatted as shown in Fig. 4.19. The number of vertices per polygon in the file should match the polygon type provided to the constructor. The method also populates the vertex lists `_verticesV` and `_verticesW` with the initial vertex coordinates obtained from the file. The polygon list `_polygons` is also populated with polygon data.

Getter method

```
Skeleton* getSkeleton() const;
```

Description:

The getter method returns the reference to the skeleton object attached to the current `SkinnedMesh` object.

Setting mesh colour

```
void setColor(float colorR, float colorG, float colorB);
```

Description:

The method sets a material colour for the entire mesh.

Attaching a skeleton

```
void attachSkeleton(Skeleton* skeleton);
```

Description:

This method associates a skeleton object with the current mesh. The pre-processing of mesh vertices V to obtain an intermediate set of vertices V' (Eq. 4.9) is also initiated at this stage.

Rendering a mesh

```
void render();
```

Description:

This method is usually called inside the display loop of the application for redrawing the mesh with the updated joint angle configuration. Typically, this method is called after specifying the bone transformations using the `rotate` method of the `Skeleton` class.

Appendix D: Quaternion Classes

This section gives an outline of methods in the classes that represent quaternion and dual quaternion numbers. Figure D.1 shows the static relationships between the classes and the geometry classes.

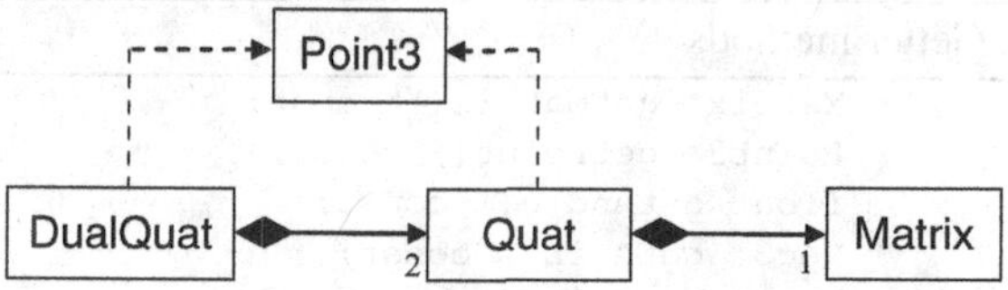

Fig. D.1 Relationships between the quaternion classes and the geometry classes

D.1 Quaternion Class

Fields

```
private:
      Matrix* _mat;
      static float RADTODEG;
      static float DEGTORAD;
      static float EPS;
public:
      float _q0, _q1, _q2, _q3;
```

Description:

Every quaternion object has an associated 4×4 transformation matrix `_mat`. The matrix elements are not automatically updated. The user needs to call `updateMatrix` to compute the values of the matrix elements. The constants `RADTODEG` and `DEGTORAD` store the conversion factors from radians to degrees and degrees to radians

DOI 10.1007/978-1-4471-2340-8,

respectively. The quaternion components `_q0`, `_q1`, `_q2`, `_q3` are declared as public as they are frequently accessed. `EPS` stores the constant value 1.E-6 used as a threshold for checking if a value is close to zero.

Constructors

```
public:
        Quat(float q0, float q1, float q2, float q3);
        Quat(const Point3* p);
        Quat(float angle, const Vec3* axis);
        Quat()
```

Description:

The first constructor initializes an object with four quaternion components. The second constructor takes a point $P = (x, y, z)$ as the argument, and forms the pure quaternion $(0, x, y, z)$. The third constructor forms a unit quaternion using the angle and axis of a three-dimensional rotation as parameters. The quaternion is constructed as per Eq. 5.44. The fourth no-argument constructor initializes the quaternion components to (1, 0, 0, 0).

Getter methods

```
        Matrix* getMatrix() const;
        Point3* getPoint() const;
        float getAngle() const;
        Vec3* getAxis() const;
        Vec3* getEuler() const;
```

Description:

The first getter method given above returns the current matrix `_mat`. The second getter method returns the last three components `_q1`, `_q2`, `_q3` of the current quaternion as a point. The third and fourth getter methods return respectively the angle and axis of the equivalent rotation given by Eqs. 5.45 and 5.46. The method `getEuler` extracts the Euler angles from the quaternion components using Eq. 5.56.

Quaternion operations

```
        Quat* add(const Quat* q) const;
        Quat* subtract(const Quat* q) const;
        Quat* mult(const Quat* q) const;
        Quat* scalarMult(float term) const;
        Quat* conjugate() const;
        Quat* negate() const;
```

Description:

The methods listed above perform algebraic operations of addition, subtraction, multiplication, scalar multiplication, conjugation and negation, and return the resulting quaternion.

Quaternion norm

```
float norm() const;
```

Description:

The above method returns the magnitude of the current quaternion (Eq. 5.17).

Quaternion matrix

```
void updateMatrix();
```

Description:

Each quaternion object has an associated transformation matrix as given in Eq. 5.23. The above method must be called whenever a quaternion component has changed, in order to update this matrix.

Quaternion transformation

```
Point3* transform(const Point3* point);
```

Description:

The above method transforms a point using the current quaternion according to the formula $P' = QPQ*$.

Conversion to unit quaternion

```
void normalize();
```

Description:

The method `normalize` converts the current quaternion to a unit quaternion.

Quaternion interpolation

```
Quat* lerp(float t, Quat* q);
Quat* slerp(float t, Quat* q);
```

Description:

The above methods perform linear (`lerp`) and spherical linear (`slerp`) interpolations between the current quaternion and the supplied quaternion `q`, and return an intermediate quaternion for the parameter value given by `t`.

Output

```
void print();
```

Description:

The above method prints the component values of the current quaternion.

D.2 Dual Quaternion Class

Fields

```
private:
Quaternion *_quat1, *_quat2;
```

Description:

Each dual quaternion is composed using two quaternions _quat1, _quat2 as described in Sect. 5.9.2.

Constructors

```
DualQuat(const Quat* quat1, const Quat* quat2);
DualQuat(float angle, const Vec3* axis, const Vec3* trans);
DualQuat(const Point3* p);
```

Description:

The first constructor shown above forms a dual quaternion using two quaternion components. The second constructor using the rigid-body transformation parameters (angle and axis of rotation, and translation vector) to construct the equivalent dual quaternion. The third constructor creates the dual quaternion $(1, 0, 0, 0, 0, x, y, z)$ using the coordinates (x, y, z) of the specified point.

Getter methods

```
Quat* getQuat1() const;
Quat* getQuat2() const;
Point3* getPoint() const;
```

Description:

The first two methods shown above return respectively the first and the second quaternion components of the current dual quaternion. The third method returns the last three elements (of the second quaternion component) as the coordinates of a point.

Product of two dual quaternions

```
DualQuat* mult(const DualQuat* q) const;
```

Description:

The above method returns the product of the current dual quaternion and the specified dual quaternion (q). The product is computed using the formula in Eq. 5.85.

Product of a dual quaternion and a quaternion

```
DualQuat* multQuat(const Quat* q) const;
```

Description:

The above method returns the product of the current dual quaternion and the specified quaternion (q). The product is computed using the formula in Eq. 5.86.

Dual quaternion transformation

```
Point3* transform(const Point3* point);
```

Description:

The above method transforms a point using the current quaternion according to the formula in Eq. 5.97.

Output

```
void print();
```

Description:

The above method prints the component values of the current dual quaternion.

Index

R. Mukundan, *Advanced Methods in Computer Graphics: With examples in OpenGL*,
DOI 10.1007/978-1-4471-2340-8, © Springer-Verlag London Limited 2012